WASPS

A

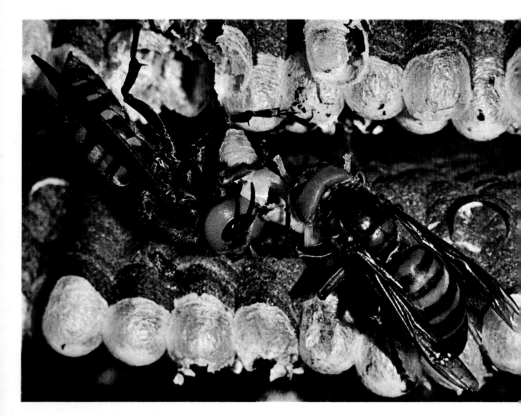

FRONTISPIECE. 'After entering the nest and slaughtering the occupants, workers of the giant Japanese hornet, *Vespa mandarinia*, tearing apart a pupa of another hornet species, *Vespa tropica*.'

WASPS

An account of
the biology and natural history of
solitary and social wasps

by

J. PHILIP SPRADBERY

Senior Research Scientist
Division of Entomology, Commonwealth Scientific and
Industrial Research Organisation, Canberra,
Australia

With a foreword by
PROFESSOR O. W. RICHARDS, F.R.S.

UNIVERSITY OF WASHINGTON PRESS
SEATTLE

First published in Great Britain in 1973
Published in the United States of America by the
University of Washington Press in 1973
Copyright © 1973 by J. Philip Spradbery

Printed in Great Britain

Library of Congress Cataloging in Publication Data.

Spradbery, J. Philip.
  Wasps; an account of the biology and natural history of solitary and social wasps.

  (Biology series)
  Bibliography: p.
  1. Wasps. I. Title.
QL568.V5S65   595.7'98   73-7872
ISBN 0-295-95287-3

FOREWORD

Of all the main groups of social insects (ants, bees, wasps, and termites) the social wasps are the smallest in terms of number of species and although some species are familiar to the non-specialist public, our knowledge of their behaviour is still very incomplete. There has been no recent account of British wasps and never one with the scope of the present work. The British wasp fauna is small even by European standards and Dr Spradbery has rightly provided a survey of the behaviour of the social wasps of other countries, since one understands the British species better by seeing them in perspective and some facets of behaviour are more easily observed in smaller colonies building exposed combs. This is particularly important if one wishes to suggest the possible way in which the large and highly organized colonies of British species may have been evolved.

It will be found that Dr Spradbery gives a very complete account of our wasp colonies, their initiation, growth and reproduction, their enemies and commensals, and their interactions with man which are far from being purely obnoxious since they destroy many insect pests. There is an appendix which shows how the species of our social and also related solitary wasps can be identified. Wherever possible he tells us what is known of the behaviour of the individuals which when integrated in the whole colony, leads to the construction of large, complicated nests, to the rearing of some thousands of young and later, in temperate climates, to a rapid disintegration in the autumn. The direct observation of these processes is often difficult and may require special cages, cinematography and prolonged, often continuous observation. The clear, consecutive account which Dr Spradbery is able to give us has been built up from the work of many observers over many years and, as he says, more workers are now studying wasps and the subject is rapidly growing. Dr Spradbery's work will serve not only as an introduction to our present knowledge but also as a guide for those who wish to make useful additions to the subject.

O. W. RICHARDS

'It is only those who have learned to love wasps as some naturalists love bees who will be at the pains to understand them.'

EDWARD LATHAM ORMEROD
British Social Wasps, published 1868

CONTENTS

APPENDICES

PREFACE

This monograph aims to provide a detailed account of the ways of wasps such that specialist and naturalist alike can better appreciate the wasps' diverse and remarkable habits. Although professional students of wasp biology are few, it is hoped that this volume will appeal to a wide range of entomologists, ethologists, teachers, and research workers, and act as a source of reference and possibly inspiration to those who appreciate wasps as an under-studied group of enormous interest and research potential.

Although the wasps of Europe predominate in the text, due to my familiarity with them and the bias of previously published work, I have included, where appropriate, much that concerns wasps from other parts of the world. Although less well understood, the more primitive wasps of South-east Asia and South America offer much that helps our understanding of the diversity of social organization and its evolution.

'W A S P S' is not a popular narrative in the journalistic sense but is intended to be a comprehensive account of the subject and the casual reader may well pass over some of the more detailed sections. For example, Chapter 2, which describes the morphology and anatomy of wasps, is primarily for reference to which the reader may turn for details or names of structures or in conjunction with the Keys to British species of wasps.

I hope the reader will share my interest in if not affection for wasps and that some may be stimulated to indulge in their study.

This book could not have been written without the help and support of colleagues and friends and the patience of my family. It is a pleasure to thank the many people who have, by words and actions, encouraged me throughout the past two years. For obtaining the raw materials, the books and references, I am indebted to a number of librarians, notably

Frances Barnes of C.S.I.R.O. and Mary Blagden of The Royal Entomological Society of London and also the services of the Australian
Scientific Liaison Office, London. For access to unpublished inform-
ation, 'in press' manuscripts and permission to quote from unpublished
theses, I am grateful to M. E. Archer, T. S. Arnold, H. V. Danks,
R. Edwards, F. Ennik, Dr J. B. Free, J. C. Felton, K. M. Guichard,
H. G. Hurrell, J. Ishay, J. L. Madden, M. Matsuura, N. B. Potter,
Professor O. W. Richards, E. Rivnay, S. Yamane, and P. F. Yeo. For
their help with translations I thank Angelica and M. Kunz, and E. O.
Miezitis (German), K. Abrahamsson and J. Forster (Swedish), and F. D.
Cumbrae-Stewart (Greek). Several people have kindly made nests and
insect material available to me including W. D. Hamilton, G. E. J.
Nixon, Professor S. Sakagami, Professor G. C. Varley, R. C. Watkins,
and I. H. H. Yarrow.
    The distribution maps which appear in Appendix IV are due in large
measure to the co-operation of several specialists and museum authori-
ties and I would like to thank A. F. Amsden (National Museum of
Wales), J. Berreen (Birmingham Museum), P. F. Bird (City Museum,
Bristol), A. Brindle (Manchester Museum), J. Douglas, G. Else, W. M.
Guichard, C. O'Riordan (National Museum of Ireland), Professor
G. C. Varley (University Museum, Oxford), and P. F. Yeo for their help.
I am indebted to Dr J. Heath and his staff at the Biological Records
Centre for preparing the maps. There is much unpublished work of
mine in this book and I wish to thank P. F. L. Boreham, J. Gower, June
Olley, and D. A. Ratkowsky who helped me with statistical problems
and research facilities.
    I wish to thank Blackwell Scientific Publications for permission to
use the original blocks for Figures 58, 60, 64, and 65. All other figures
are printed for the first time and where I have drawn on previously
published work, this is acknowledged in the legends. The manuscript
was typed by Jan Gillie, Margaret Reid, and Rosanne Waller and I am
grateful to them for carrying out their onerous task so efficiently. For
their help with the checking of proofs and the preparation of indices I
am indebted to my wife and Mariam Nor.
    I am indebted to colleagues who have criticized parts of the draft manu-
script and it is a pleasure to thank R. A. Bedding (11), C. G. Butler (10),
J. B. Free (4, 5), A. W. Frankland (12), W. D. Hamilton (14), Professor
T. R. E. Southwood (9), L. R. Taylor (9), and I. H. H. Yarrow (Appendix I) for their comments, although errors which remain are entirely my
own. I am also grateful to the Director and Staff of the Commonwealth
Institute of Entomology for checking the nomenclature of mite and
insect names.
    For providing the original photographic material, it is a pleasure to
acknowledge T. S. Arnold (Plate Xb), B. K. Filshie (Plates Ib, IV,

XXVII, and XXVIII), M. Matsuura (Frontispiece), and A. D. Johnston (jacket and all other Plates except Plate XXV).

I am grateful to the Executive of the Commonwealth Scientific and Industrial Research Organization, Australia, for granting me their approval to undertake the writing of this book, and for the support of the Chief of the Division of Entomology, Dr D. F. Waterhouse, F.R.S.

I am particularly indebted to a number of people who, in various ways, made the preparation and writing of this book a more rewarding and less tedious task than it would otherwise have been. Throughout the gestation period I have been helped by my colleague, Alan D. Johnston, whose sustaining enthusiasm is gratefully acknowledged. Thanks are due to Dr Ian H. H. Yarrow of the British Museum (Natural History) for his constant advice and encouragement and the forbearance with which he answered my many queries. It is difficult to envisage writing about wasps without the influence of Professor O. W. Richards, F.R.S., who has been an inspiration for many years and whose generosity in allowing me access to his collection of references, unpublished notes, and papers made this work feasible. Finally, I thank my wife, Monica, whose support throughout the project has been complete.

J. PHILIP SPRADBERY

Hobart, Tasmania
April 1973.

CHAPTER 1

AN INTRODUCTION

More than four and a half thousand years ago King Menes, Pharaoh of Egypt, was fatally stung by a wasp. The Children of Israel were told: 'I will send hornets before thee which shall drive out the Hivite, the Canaanite and the Hittite before thee' (Exodus xxiii:28). An old German proverb says 'God made the bee but the Devil made the wasp', while Aristophanes in his play *The Wasps*, ridiculed the Athenian jury under the guise of wasps, describing them as the most irascible and peevish of creatures. Yet, such a bad reputation is not altogether deserved for we now know that the wasp's role is often beneficial and their predatory activities help suppress numerous pests. The social wasps which build carton nests from wood fibres inspired man to copy their ways and produce paper from wood pulp, while many believe that the first earthenware vessels made by the tribal Indians of America were inspired by the clay nests of Potter Wasps. Above all, wasps are fascinating creatures to study for they display an enormous range of social behaviour, much of it little understood, in spite of their frequent incursions into our lives. Man's contact with wasps has probably led to more calumny than for any other insect for, traditionally, they have been creatures to be feared. I believe this reputation to be ill-founded and due primarily to a history of ignorance of their role in nature.

During the third century B.C., Aristotle's observations on wasps, which were recorded by his students at Lyceum, were remarkably perceptive for their time. His descriptions of the life cycle and colony development in social wasps ('sphex') and hornets ('anthrenes') in Book IX of the *Historia Animalia* were to be without parallel for more than two thousand years. Caste differences were appreciated, while the solitary phase of nest initiation by the queen and the fact that only queens survive the winter by hibernating, were all noted. His description

1

of mating behaviour ('covering') is remarkably precise and the suggestion that the frequency of the queen's wing-beat might attract males is very much a present-day idea. A recent translation of Aristotle's account of wasp and hornet biology will be found at the end of this chapter.

During the classical period, other writers such as Ovid (*circa* 50 B.C.) in his *Metamorphoses*, Pliny the Elder (A.D. 60) in *Historia Naturalis*, and Virgil (30 B.C.) in the *Georgics* were far from scientific in their interpretations of wasp biology (König 1896). The prevailing concept of spontaneous generation led them to believe that wasps were created from the decomposing carcasses of horses – the warhorse producing hornets. During the Middle Ages, Aldovrandi (1638) wrote briefly about wasps in his *De Animalibus Insectis* while a wasp was pictured in Mourret's *Theatorum Insectorum* published in 1550. Remarkably little scientific progress was made until the last century – even as late as 1807, Hollingshed the English naturalist gave considerable credence to Pliny's writings.

With the scientific renaissance in the mid- to late-eighteenth century, the majority of the European social wasps and many of the solitary species were scientifically named during the era of Linnaeus, Fabricius, Gmelin, and Panzer. In 1719 de Réaumur published the first article of his *Histoire des Guêpes* in the memoires of the Royal Academy of Science in Paris. The great French naturalist described the biology of various social wasps, and included figures of them and their nests. Réaumur also included a drawing of a *Chartergus* nest from South America. The local Indians still sell these nests as curios to travellers. A series of monographs on solitary and social wasps was published by Henri de Saussure between 1852 and 1858. Important contributions were also made by Paul Marchal (1896) and Robert du Buysson (1903, 1905) although the observations of Charles Janet (1895-1903) surpassed all contemporary accounts with their details of nesting activities and colony development.

Continental naturalists dominated the study of wasps during the last century, although in 1858 Frederick Smith published the *Catalogue of British Fossorial Hymenoptera, Formicidae and Vespidae in the British Museum* which included descriptions of the British wasps. In 1896 Edward Saunders drew up the first key to separate them in his book, *The Hymenoptera Aculeata of the British Islands*. More than a century ago, Edward L. Ormerod, a physician by profession, published the first monograph on the biology of the British social wasps, the 'Natural History of Wasps' (1868). Extensive observations and experiments on social wasps were made by Sir John Lubbock, a notable politician and naturalist, during the latter part of the nineteenth century. Lubbock (1876) even maintained a *Polistes* colony at his home on one occasion, his fondness for wasps eliciting the following epitaph when the queen eventually died: 'she could but wag her tail, a last token of gratitude and affection.'

At the beginning of the present century, foundations for the study of South American wasps were laid down by Adolfo Ducke and the father and son von Iherings (see Richards and Richards 1951), while the travels of Francis X. Williams (1919, 1928), in the Pacific islands and South America added considerably to an appreciation of the diversity of the tropical wasp fauna. In 1922, William Mortimer Wheeler published his series of classic lectures on social organization in insects, *Social Life Among the Insects*, which formed the basis of a comprehensive review in *The Social Insects* which appeared in 1928.

The greatest strides in our understanding of wasp biology have been undertaken during the past thirty years, beginning in Italy where Leo Pardi's intensive observations on *Polistes* colonies led to an appreciation of the interactions between the members of a colony with his discovery of a pecking order or dominance hierarchy among the adults. These studies were followed up and extended by Édouard-Philippe Deleurance and his school in Paris during more than a decade of behavioural and physiological studies on *Polistes*. The traditional interest in wasps by French entomologists has been continued with distinction by Hubert Montagner whose experimental studies on behaviour and physiology have been directed at the social Vespinae, a notoriously difficult group of wasps to manipulate because of their large and often aggressive populations and enclosed nests.

The Oriental region has always been of great interest to entomologists and many of Japan's leading hymenopterists, notably Kunio Iwata, Kimio Yoshikawa, and Shiochi Sakagami, have made intensive studies of the solitary and social wasps of Japan and other parts of south-east Asia. In Israel, Jacob Ishay and his collaborators have now worked for a decade on the biology of the Oriental Hornet, *Vespa orientalis* F., solving many of the mysteries of colony life, notably the means of communication in colonies. In 1969, colleagues of Ishay, headed by R. Ikan, isolated and identified the 'queen substance' pheromone from the hornet.

There has been an intensification of interest in tropical wasps since the publication in 1951 of O. W. and M. J. Richards's observations on the social wasps of South America. The spate of recent expeditions to the Mato Grosso in Brazil, which were made feasible by the opening up of land routes since the creation of the new capital city, has given added impetus to such studies.

Many of the more recent developments in wasp research have been reviewed in scientific journals (Spradbery 1965, Richards 1971a and) in the books, *The Wasps* (1970) by Howard E. Evans and Mary Jane

Eberhard, and *The Insect Societies* (1971) by Edward O. Wilson. The former book provides an excellent introduction, interpreting the word wasp in its widest entomological sense, while the latter, with its encyclo-paedic coverage, will surely be the standard reference book on social insects for a very long time to come.

The modern English word 'wasp' was derived from the Anglo Saxon words *waefs, waeps, waesp* which presumably originated from the root *webh* – to weave, with reference to the paper nests of the social wasps. There is considerable similarity in the colloquial term for a wasp throughout the Indo-European languages and dialects with, for example, the Lithuanian 'vaspa', Latvian 'lapsene', old Prussian 'wobse', Russian 'ovsa', Bulgarian 'vosa', Spanish 'avispa', Portuguese 'abispa', Italian 'vespa', and German 'wespe'. It is of interest that in the contemporary language of Japan, there is no colloquial word which distinguishes wasps from bees, the word 'kebachi' sufficing for both. The word 'wasp' has a wide layman's usage, embracing virtually all members of the Hymenoptera – the insect order to which the bees, wasps, ants, and allied insects belong. Even among entomologists, opinions vary with regard to its use. In its broadest sense it includes all Hymenoptera except bees, ants, and the suborder Symphyta. With respect to this mono-graph, the word is used in its more restricted sense to comprise those members of the superfamily Vespoidea – the True Wasps (see Fig. 1).

The Hymenoptera are a highly organized and abundant order with a range of behaviour and specialization without parallel in the insect world. Although estimates of their numbers vary, it is generally accepted that there are about a quarter of a million species within the suborders Symphyta and Apocrita. The parasite Apocrita, the Terebrantia or Parasitica, outnumber the aculeate species. The Symphyta, so called because the abdomen is broadly attached to the thorax, are wholly plant or wood feeders during larval life and the adult females have ovipositors adapted for sawing or boring into plant tissue in order to lay their eggs. The Symphyta include the sawflies and woodwasps. The Aprocrita are characterized by having the abdomen deeply constricted behind the first abdominal segment which is fused to the thorax to form the propodeum. This Suborder is divided into the Terebrantia (from the latin *terebra*, borer) a predominantly parasitic group in which the ovipositor is adapted for piercing and ovipositing in host material, and the Aculeata (from the latin *aculeus*, prickle or sting) which includes all the social Hymenoptera and the fossorial or digger wasps. The ovipositor of aculeates is used for paralysing prey or defending the nest and not for egg laying. However, the characters whereby the Terebrantia and Aculeata may be separated are not entirely consistent and many

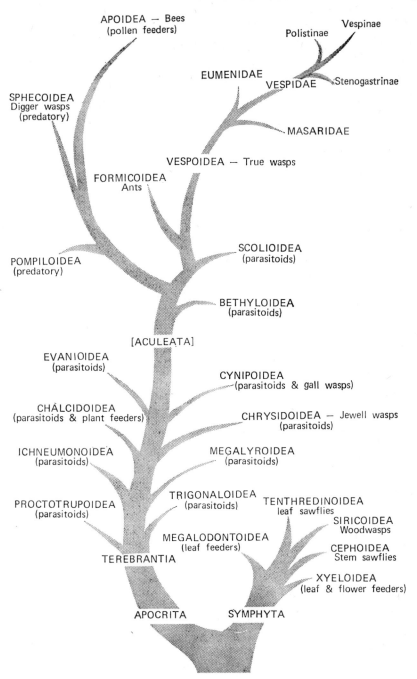

Figure 1. Dendogram showing the probable affinities of the major groups of Hymenoptera.

entomologists prefer to abandon the terms and consider the Apocrita simply as a series of superfamilies. Nevertheless, the distinction is sometimes useful and is indicated on the dendogram in Figure 1.

The Hymenoptera probably originated 300 million years ago during the late Palaeozoic which marked the end of the Carboniferous era. During the Mesozoic era which followed and lasted for 230 million years, the order diversified until, by the Eocene some 60 million years ago, vespoid wasps related to our contemporary social wasp fauna had evolved.

The number of aculeate species is in the order of 50,000, the majority represented by 10,000 to 15,000 ants and 20,000 bees, of which the majority are solitary. The most primitive aculeates are represented today by the Scolioidea, digger wasps, which are parasitic on the larvae of ground-dwelling scarab beetles as well as sphecoid and vespoid wasps. Ancestral scolioids probably gave rise to the three major lines of aculeate evolution which culminated in the bees, wasps, and ants.

The evolutionary branch giving rise to the True Wasps split off early to produce the ants – a wholly social group (including some parasitic species). In Figure 1 I have indicated the likely branching within the Vespoidea which comprises three families, the Eumenidae, Masaridae, and Vespidae. The Masaridae are the only vespoid group which provision cells with nectar and pollen, all others being carnivorous during the larval stages. Although no masarid wasps occur in the British Isles, several species are found in continental Europe. The Masaridae and Eumenidae are wholly solitary in their behaviour.

The Vespidae comprise three subfamilies, the primitive Stenogastrinae of south-east Asia, the widely distributed and diverse Polistinae, and the Vespinae which include British social wasps. Although there are thousands of species of vespoid wasps, only 800 or so are social or sub-social.

Definitions of social organization are largely determined by the interests of the specialist. For example, ornithologists would consider the nesting behaviour of birds and the rearing of young by the parents to be a full expression of sociality. However, among insects there is a greater range of social behaviour with species that have explored to varying degrees almost every conceivable avenue of sociality. It is this often bewildering array of social phenomena among wasps that has made their study a particularly absorbing and satisfying one for ethologists and students of evolutionary processes.

Most entomologists would agree that to be truly social an insect must qualify on three counts. The first criterion is that members of the same species co-operate in the care of the young; secondly, that a reproductive division of labour be apparent with reproducing individuals being aided by more or less sterile members; and finally, that generations overlap so that the offspring assist the parent or parents (Wilson 1971). To distinguish true social life ('eusocial') from intermediate forms of social organization, Michener (1969) has defined various levels of sociality among insects. A fully solitary species is one in which there is no co-operation in brood rearing and no reproductive division of labour or overlap of generations – the converse of eusocial organization. Examples in which adults care for their immature stages such as occurs in many earwigs, beetles, bugs, and crickets is defined as sub-social. In these cases, the parent guards the larval or nymphal food source from competition by other members of the species or parasites of various kinds. They may also protect the young from fungal disease and environmental extremes. Cases in which individuals of the same generation are aggregated within a composite nest structure or shelter are defined as communal and examples include many species of sawfly, tent caterpillars, and groups of hibernating beetles. The advantages of communal organization include protection from natural enemies and the vagaries of climate, and often a more efficient exploitation of available food sources. Instances in which the members of a communal group co-operate in the care of the brood such as occurs in many euglossine bees and most Stenogastrinae are called quasisocial. The final category in pre-social organization is the somewhat theoretical situation in which a reproductive division of labour occurs in a quasi-social group and is termed semi-social. This situation occurs temporarily in some *Polistes* wasps and halictine bees when colonies are established by two or more females. In these cases, one female, through a ritualized dominance struggle, becomes the sole egg layer, the remaining females behaving as non-reproductives or workers. However, with the emergence of offspring which remain on the nest and assist in the rearing of larvae, the organization eventually becomes eusocial.

Distinctions between the solitary and social members of the Vespoidea are primarily on a behavioural and physiological level, there being a conspicuous lack of structural specialization. The facility with which both solitary and social wasps integrate their physical activities during flight or when capturing prey and manipulating building materials is another family characteristic. Feeding habits are also comparable for the adults feed mainly on carbohydrates while the larvae are largely insectiverous.

Ecologically, the two families are quite different for the solitary wasps make small nests with a few cells, generally using mud or clay in their construction, while the social wasps usually construct large paper-like nests fabricated from vegetable materials. Eumenid wasps tend to disperse their nests within a small area, the extent determined by the availability of suitable nest sites and building materials while the social wasps concentrate their domestic activities within the confines of a single nest unit in which hundreds or thousands of brood are reared. The large and distinctive nests of the social wasps create a further and perhaps more imposing difference between the families, for the sheer number of individuals in a large colony frequently leads to their intrusion into our human lifes. It is very probable that most people have had wasps dispute the ownership of a sandwich, seen a nest or two and perhaps been stung, while personal experience of the solitary wasps is likely to be meagre.

In the British Isles, the wasp fauna is notable for the paucity of species, only Eumenidae and Vespidae being represented while none of the wide-ranging Polistinae are found, although the ubiquitous *Polistes* is occasionally introduced from continental Europe. Of the fifty or sixty species of Vespinae which occur in the world, only seven are found in Britain, while twelve are distributed throughout Europe and sixteen occur in North America.

The British species include the numerically dominant ground-dwelling wasps, *Paravespula vulgaris* (Linnaeus) and *P. germanica* (Fabricius), the unobtrusive *Vespula rufa* (L.) with its associated social parasite *Vespula austriaca* (Panzer), and the two bush or tree nesting species, *Dolichovespula norwegica* (F.) and *D. sylvestris* (Scopoli) (see 'Check list of British Vespoidea p. 339). The hornet, *Vespa crabro* L., also occurs in Britain (though not in Ireland) and has become established in North America. The eumenid fauna is very poorly represented, for only 22 of the 100 species on the European list are found in the British Isles (see Check list p. 320). Many of these solitary wasps are extremely local in their distribution and the majority are restricted to southern England where the climate is more equable.

At this point I should perhaps offer some justification for the use of several generic names for the social wasps of Britain. During the eighteenth century when Linnaeus, Fabricius, and others began the scientific naming of insects, the all-embracing generic name *Vespa* (from the Latin word for a wasp) was used for virtually all wasps, both social and solitary. Some major renaming was obviously necessary and several new genera of solitary wasps were established by the late nineteenth century. *Vespa* was retained for the social species until 1869 when C. G. Thomson erected a new genus, *Vespula* (the diminutive of *Vespa*) for all social wasps, reserving *Vespa* exclusively for hornets. In 1916, Rohwer proposed the genus *Dolichovespula* (from the Greek *dolichos*, long) for the tree or bush nesting species which are charac-terized by their long 'cheeks' or malar space, and in 1938 Blüthgen placed the subterranean nesting species, *vulgaris germanica* and *rufa* into a new genus, *Paravespula*. More recently, Blüthgen (1943) subdivided *Dolichovespula* and *Paravespula*, creating a number of sub-genera: *Dolichovespula* was split into *Boreovespula* (to include *norwegica*), *Metavespula* (to include *sylvestris*) and *Dolichovespula* (no British representative); and *Paravespula* into *Allovespula* (to include *rufa*) and *Paravespula* (to include *vulgaris* and *germanica*). If Blüthgen's nomenclature is accepted, there are five generic and subgeneric names available for the six species of social wasps in Britain. I hardly think such a separation is justified, yet retention of the original *Vespula* grouping*, while being useful as a collective name, obscures the considerable differences among the Vespinae. On morphological and biological grounds there is reasonable justification for treating *Dolichovespula*, *Paravespula*, and *Vespula* as distinct genera. Many differences will become apparent from succeeding chapters, namely the siting and size of nests, details of nest architecture, the duration of colony life, and complexity of social organization.

Paravespula species (*vulgaris* and *germanica*) are undoubtedly the most highly developed group with the largest colonies, while *Dolichovespula* species (*norwegica* and *sylvestris*) form a distinct genus which construct small, predominantly aerial nests. *Vespula rufa* is somewhat intermediate with small subterranean nests and a social organization and colony size similar to *Dolichovespula*. There is no reason why the social parasite, *austriaca* should be placed in a different genus for it is morphologically very close to its host *V. rufa*, the major differences being associated with its parasitic habit. A further justification for the nomenclature that has been adopted in this book is its almost universal use by Continental entomologists and most British taxonomists.

Of all the social insects, the wasps are the poor relations when measured in terms of scientific papers and books. I estimate that there are fewer than 3,000 publications on wasps compared to 12,000 on termites (W. A. Sands, personal communication), 35,000 on ants (Sudd 1967), and a prodigious 50,000 on bees (J. B. Free, personal communication). Economic considerations have undoubtedly contributed to these disparities. Yet the wasps provide, in their range of behaviour and levels of sociality, the clearest examples of the stages which led from solitary to social life and are deserving of considerably more study. Their abundance has prompted Professor Jean Leclercq of Belgium to suggest that the common social wasps be used as standard entomological material for schools and universities because they are ideal subjects for introducing basic concepts of taxonomy, structure, behaviour, and social organization.

*Where *Vespula* appears in the text without species names, it is being used as the collective word in the original Thomson sense.

Since the publication more than a century ago of Ormerod's *Natural History of Wasps*, there has been no book devoted to the biology and natural history of the True Wasps. Until recently, published information has been meagre and widely scattered in the literature, although the last decade has seen a resurgence of interest which has led to a much greater understanding of their biology. This is especially true of population studies, evolutionary genetics and the physiological and biochemical aspects of communication. A stage has now been reached when a review and synthesis of current ideas and lines of research is appropriate.

ARISTOTELIS HISTORIA ANIMALIVM[1]

Book 9, ch. 41

The [lore] about the bees, then, is of that fashion, but of the wasps[2] there are two kinds. Of these the wild ones are rare, they live in the mountains, and bring forth not underground but in trees. In shape they are bigger and more elongated and black skinned more than the others, but they are variegated and all with stings and stronger[3] and their wound is more painful than of those[4]. Indeed, their sting is proportionately bigger than theirs. These, then, live the whole year through, and are seen even in winter flying out of cut trees, but they live lurking in holes during the winter. Yet their haunt is in pieces of wood. Of these are the *metrae*[5] and the workers, as also of the tamer [wasps].

Now what is the nature of the worker and of the *metra* in the tamer is clear. For there are of the tamer wasps two kinds, the leaders,[6] whom they[7] call *metrae*, and the workers. The leaders are much bigger and gentler. The workers do not live the whole year through, but they all die when winter sets in (now this is manifest: for at the beginning of winter their workers become sluggish and by the solstice they quite disappear), but the leaders, which are called *metrae*, are seen through the whole winter and lurk in holes in the ground. For many ploughing and digging in the winter have seen *metrae*, but no-one workers.

The birth of wasps is in this wise. The leaders when they take a place with a good view make themselves nests and[8] put together what they call combs[9] which are small, with as it were four doors or thereabouts, in which wasps are born and not *metrae*. When those have grown, again after those they put together other bigger ones, and again when those have grown others, so that when autumn comes wasps' nests[10] are very many and big, in which the leader, which is called *metra*, no longer begets wasps but *metrae*. These are

---

1. Aristotle: Researches on Living Things (c. 330 B.C.). 2. Σφῆκες, *spheces*. 3. *or* braver. 4. i.e. bees. 5. Μῆτραι, *metrae*, wombs. Latin, *matrices*. The word might be of foreign or aboriginal origin in its application to wasps. 6. Ηγεμόνες, *hegemones*. 7. i.e. men. 8. Σφηκωνεῖς, *sphecones*. 9. Κηρία, *ceria*. 10. Σφηκία, *sphecia*.

big grubs[11] up on the top of the nest in contiguous cells[12] four or a little more, almost as those of the leaders in the combs.

When the worker wasps are born in the combs, the leaders no longer work but the workers bring them in their food, and this is clear from the [fact] that the leaders no longer fly out from the workers but staying within take their rest. Whether the leaders of the year before, when they have made new leaders, are put to death by the new wasps, and this fits equally, or they can live a longer time does not yet appear. Nor has anyone who has looked seen old age neither of a *metra* nor of the wild wasps nor any other suffering of that sort. The *metra* is broad and heavy, and thicker and bigger than the [ordinary] wasps and because of its weight not strong enough for flying, nor can they fly much. So they always sit in the nest, fashioning and governing their internal [arrangements]. In most nests there are those that are called *metrae*.

There is a dispute whether they have stings or are stingless, but they are likely, like the leaders of the bees, to have [them] but not to put [them] forth or cast [them]. But of the wasps, some are stingless, like drones[13] and others have a sting. The stingless are smaller and feebler, and do not defend themselves. They that have stings are bigger and strong. Some call these males and the stingless females. Towards winter many of those having stings seem to cast [them]. But we have not yet happened on [a case] with our own eyes.

Wasps are born more in droughts and in rugged places. They are born underground and fashion their combs of rubbish and earth, each from one beginning as from a root. They use for food [what they take] from certain flowers and from fruits, but [take] most [of it] from animal food. As yet some have been observed covering[14] others, but whether both stingless or having stings or one with and one without has not yet been observed. And of the wild [variety some have been] seen covering, one of them having a sting, but of the other it has not been observed. The offspring does not seem to come from birth but straightway to be bigger than a wasp's birth. If one takes a wasp by the feet and lets its wings buzz, the stingless will fly towards [it] but they that have stings will not fly towards [it], which some use as evidence that the ones are male and the others female. In winter there are found in holes some having stings and some not having [stings]. The former build small and few nests, the latter many and large. They that are called *metrae* are found at the turn of the season, many around elm trees. They choose the sticky and gummy [ones]. A multitude of *metrae* was somewhere born when in the year before there were many wasps and much rain. They are caught around overhanging banks and straight cracks in the ground and all appear to have stings.

Ch. 42

The [lore] about the wasps, then, is of that fashion, but the hornets[15] live not gathering flowers like the bees but eating many different

---

11. Σκώληκες, *scholeces*. 12. Θυριδες, *thyrides*. 13. Κηφῆνες, *cephenes*.
14. As a stallion covers a mare. 15. Ἀνθρῆναι, *anthrenae*.

form of flesh (wherefore also they stay round dung. For they hunt the big flies and when they have caught [one], having taken off the head, they fly off bearing the rest of the body), and they attack sweet fruit. They use then the food that has been mentioned and they have leaders like the bees and the wasps. And these leaders are bigger in size proportionately to the hornets than the wasps' to the wasps or the bees' to the bees. This one also spends his time within, like the leader of the wasps. The hornets make their hive[16] underground, carrying out earth like the ants.

There is no swarm, as of the bees, neither of these nor of the wasps, but always the newer ones that come into being stay there and they make the hive bigger carrying out the earth. The hives become great. So far from a flourishing hive three or four baskets of combs have been taken out. Nor do they store food like the bees, but they lurk in holes for the winter but most of them die. But if even all is not yet clear. The leaders are not more than one in the hives, as in those of the bees, and they destroy the hives of the bees. When any of the hornets have wandered away from the hive, turning to certain wood they make combs of a kind often seen on the surface, and in this they make one leader. This when he is come out and is grown, goes away taking [them] and settles [them] with himself into a hive. Of the covering of hornets nothing has yet been observed nor whence the offspring is born.

In the bees, then, the drones and the kings are stingless and of the wasps some are stingless, as has been said earlier, but all the hornets appear to have stings. Yet it is rather [a question] to be looked at about the leader, if he has a sting or not.

Book 5, ch. 23

The hornets and the wasps make combs for the offspring, when they have not a leader but have strayed away and not found [the hive], the hornets in a place high above the ground and the wasps in holes, but when they have a leader, underground. All their combs are six-sided, as also those of the bees, and the comb is put together not of wax, but of rubbish and cobwebby stuff. The comb of the hornets is much hollower than that of the wasps. They put in offspring, like the bees, as big as a drop sideways in the cell[17] and it sticks to the wall. The offspring is not at the same time in all the cells, but in some they are already big so as even to fly, in some nymphs[18] in others still grubs. There is dung only round the grubs, as also with the bees. And when they are nymphs they are motionless and the cell is smeared over. Vertically in the cell of the offspring there is as big as a drop of honey in the combs of the hornet. The larvae[19] of these are born not in the spring but in the autumn. They clearly take their growth most in the seasons of full moon. Both the offspring and the grubs are held not from the bottom of the cell but across it.

Translated from the Royal Prussian Academy's edition of Aristotle's Works, 2nd ed., Berlin, 1960, by F. D. Cumbrae-Stewart, Esq., Barrister-at-Law, Hobart, Tasmania.

---

16. Σμῆνος, *smenos.*   17. Κύτταρος, *cyttarus.*   18. Νύμφαι, *nymphae.*
19. Σχάδονες, *schadones.*

CHAPTER 2

FORM AND FUNCTION

Wasps have received scant attention by morphologists and physiologists. The anatomy and morphology of Eumenidae and Vespidae are very similar and, except where indicated in the text, the following description is intended to cover both families. The studies of Duncan (1939) on American Vespinae give a more detailed account of adult structure.

ADULT MORPHOLOGY

The adult wasp (Plate I – top) has a jointed exoskeleton or cuticle consisting of a series of hard plates, the sclerites, which are either joined by membranes for flexibility, closely articulated for precise movements, or fused to form protective areas and rigid attachments for the locomotor systems. The membranes are restricted to the neck, the petiole, wing and leg joints, and the intersegmental membranes of the abdomen, where they permit the necessary movement of the head and locomotor organs, and manipulation of the genitalia. The segmental plan on which the insect is based consists of a dorsal sclerite (tergite) and ventral sclerite (sternite) joined by lateral membraneous areas (pleura). These segments are grouped into three main regions, the head, thorax, and abdomen, in which the basic segmental plan is modified or even lost. From the sterno-pleural region arise the jointed appendages characteristic of the Arthropoda, with three pairs of walking legs on the thorax, and a series of head appendages which are modified for feeding and other activities. The terminal abdominal appendages are incorporated into the external genitalia.

Much of the cuticle is covered with hairs, the setae, which are predominantly sensory in function, especially those found on the antennae, mouthparts, and genital palps. Single hairs, or tufts of hairs, at the junctions of sclerites act as proprioreceptors, sense organs which continually monitor the position of the various parts of the body and

help the insect to maintain its stability. In *Dolichovespula saxonica*,
(F), the hair-tufts or hair-plates are found at the antennal, cervical,
petiole, and coxal joints (Markl, 1962). Setae may sometimes be of
considerable value in taxonomic studies.

The black and yellow coloration of the Vespoidea is a striking
characteristic of the superfamily in Britain, although red, orange, and
metallic colours are not uncommon in wasps from other parts of the
world. Different colours are produced by the differential absorption
and reflection of light. Black is produced if all visible wavelengths are
absorbed, white if all are reflected, the absorption of light being due
to pigments and reflection to structural features of the surfaces. The
black coloration of wasps is produced by the pigment melanin which
occurs in granular form within the cuticle, while the yellow colours are
created by the pterin pigment, xanthopterin, which is metabolically
important in growth and differentiation. Apart from the metabolic
functions of these pigments, the coloration of wasps is important in
their defence.

A predator which attacks a wasp and is subsequently stung, would
establish a painful association between being stung and the yellow
and black banded insect. In this way very few encounters would be
experienced before the predator learnt to avoid wasp-like prey. This
is possibly one reason why the different wasp species look so alike, for
predators would only have to learn the basic colour pattern of one wasp
species to avoid the others, rather than the more wasteful process of
learning to avoid several dissimilar patterns. The eumenid wasps, which
use their sting only to paralyse prey and not for defence, presumably
gain considerable advantage by having colour patterns which mimic
those of the vespid wasps.

The shape and position of colour patterns in wasps are of considerable
importance in their taxonomy.

The Head

The head consists of a strongly sclerotized capsule composed of
fused sclerites, joined to the thorax by a flexible membraneous neck
(Figs. 2, 4). The lines or grooves on the surface of the capsule
indicate either the fusion of formally distinct sclerites, or ridges on the
inside of the cuticle which form an endoskeleton (the tentorium) for
the protection of delicate organs and for the attachment of muscles.
Those lines which indicate the fusion of sclerites are called sutures,
and the remainder are called sulci. The head of wasps is typically
hypognathous – the mouthparts directed downwards, with the long
axis of the head being vertical. The head is the main receptor area of
the wasp, bearing the compound eyes and ocelli, the antennae, and the
sense organs associated with the mouthparts. In many eumenid wasps,

small hair-filled depressions on the head, the fovea, possibly have a
sensory function.

The grooves on the head capsule are the post-occipital suture which
forms a ring round the occipital foramen through which the neck passes,
the occipital sulcus which often forms a well-defined ridge or carina

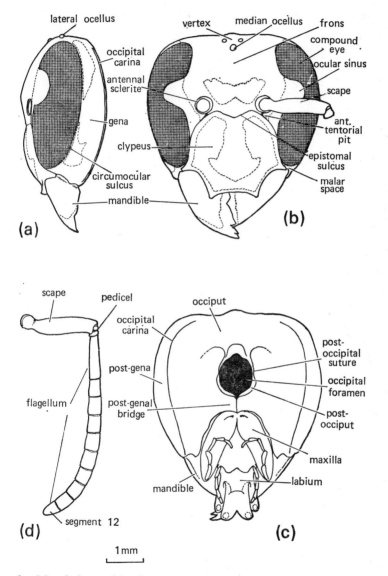

Figure 2. Morphology of head structures, *Paravespula vulgaris* queen: (a) lateral
view of head; (b) frontal view of head; (c) posterior view of head; (d) antenna
(original).

marking off the posterior part of the head capsule, the epistomal sulcus between the ventral margin of the antennal sockets and enclosing the anterior tentorial pits, the antennal sulcus which forms a circle around the antennal socket, and the circumocular sulcus surrounding the compound eyes. The tentorial pits indicate where arms of the tentorium are invaginated.

The sclerites which form the head capsule are the vertex (dorsal part of head continuous with frons and genae, bearing the ocelli and fovea), the frons (area between compound eyes), the clypeus (fused dorsally to frons along the epistomal sulcus), antennal sclerite (circular sclerite articulating with scape of antenna), the occiput (dorsal part of head between occipital sulcus and post-occipital suture), post-gena (ventral part of head between occipital sulcus and post-occipital suture forming a post-genal bridge posteriorly and providing support for the

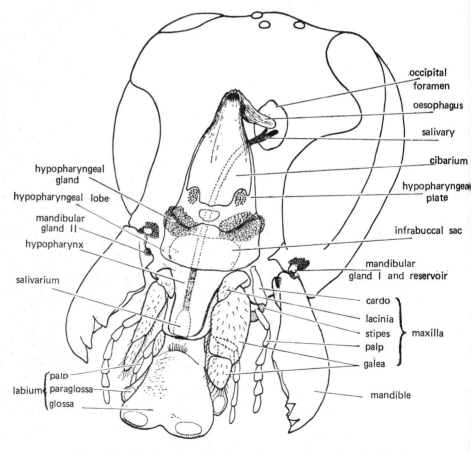

Figure 3. Mouthparts of *Paravespula germanica* worker (original).

I (top). Lateral view of *Paravespula germanica* queen to show appendages and major parts of the body; (below) scanning electron micrographs of sting tip (lancet) showing the series of small barbs.

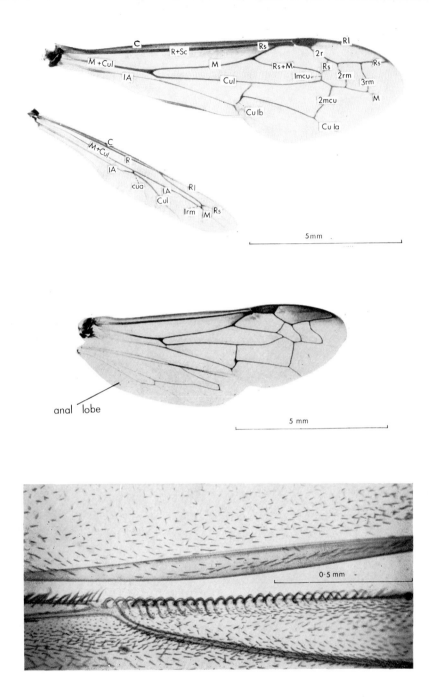

II (top). Fore and hind wings of *Paravespula vulgaris* worker, longitudinal veins are named in capital letters, cross-veins in lower-case; (middle) fore and hind wings of *Ancistrocerus parietum* female; (bottom) frenal fold, above, and hamuli or wing hooks, below, of P. germanica worker.

a

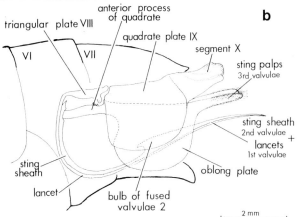

anterior process
of quadrate

triangular plate VIII

quadrate plate IX

segment X

VI

VII

b

sting palps
3rd valvulae

sting sheath
2nd valvulae +

lancets
1st valvulae

oblong plate

sting
sheath

lancet

bulb of fused
valvulae 2

2 mm

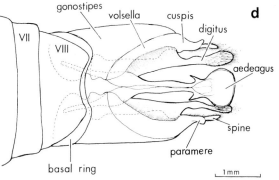

c

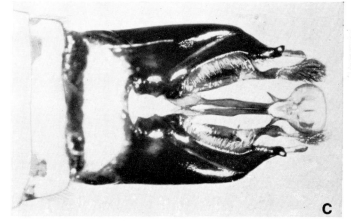

gonostipes

volsella

cuspis

d

digitus

VII

VIII

aedeagus

spine

paramere

basal ring

1 mm

III (*a*) and (*b*). Terminal part of
abdomen of *Paravespula germanica*
queen to illustrate structure of
sting; (*c*) and (*d*) terminal part of
abdomen of *Paravespula vulgaris*
male to illustrate the intromittent
organ, ventral view.

musculature of the mouthparts), and the post-occiput (defined by the post-occipital suture anteriorly, forming a sclerite around the cervical foramen and bearing condyles for the articulation of the thorax).

The Eyes. The compound eyes are dominant structures of the head, occupying a greater part of the capsule, and giving the wasps the acuteness of vision which is characteristic of the group. The compound eye in Vespoidea is excised along its inner margin to form a kidney-shaped sinus. The large number of facets or retinal elements which comprise the compound eye would account for the high degree of visual acuity in wasps. There has been little research into colour vision of wasps, although Mazokhin-Porshnyakov (1960) suggests that *P. vulgaris*, *D. sylvestris*, and *V. rufa* can distinguish green, yellow, and orange, but there is no evidence yet that wasps can perceive ultra-violet light in the same way as the honeybee.

The ocelli, which are well developed in wasps, consist of a group of visual cells (rhabdoms) beneath a common lens. They are undoubtedly light-sensitive organs, but their exact function is not fully understood. They possibly accentuate the response to light stimuli perceived by the compound eyes (Müller 1931) and may have some relevance in the regulation of diel (circadian) rhythms. In the nocturnal polybiine wasps, *Apoica* spp, the ocelli are enlarged (Richards and Richards 1951).

The Antennae. The antenna is composed of a basal segment, the scape, which articulates with the head via the antennal sclerite, a one-segmented pedicel, and a flagellum composed of 12 segments in females and 13 segments in males. This sexual dimorphism is further emphasized in some eumenid males which have the terminal segments modified to form a hook – probably used to retain the female's antennae during courtship. Together with the eyes, the antennae are the principal sense organs and they are covered in a wide variety of sense cells, including sensory hairs or sensillae, and various peg and plate organs (Plate IV). These sense cells, derived from epidermal cells and incorporating cuticullar structures, are principally concerned with the reception of tactile and olfactory stimuli but possibly function as temperature and humidity receptors also. Scanning electron microscope pictures of the seventh antennal segment of *V. rufa* specimens show that the female castes and males have similar sense organs. The dominant structures are the trichoid sensillae, hair-like processes jutting out from the surface. There are three styles, a long thin one, a long but broader type, and a shorter conical-styled seta. The first two types are probably mechano-receptors and the cone-shaped sensillae are likely to be olfactory

C*

receptors. The 'plate organs', placoid sensillae, are abundant on the antennae where they function as olfactory receptors. In the honeybee, they are known to be sensitive to 'queen substance' and the odour produced by the Nassonov gland (Kaissling and Renner 1968). Peg-like organs, sensillae basiconica, are scattered infrequently over the surface of antennal segment seven, appearing in the females as recessed structures although in males, they protrude considerably (compare c and d, Plate IV). The functions of sensillae basiconica are imperfectly understood, suggestions ranging from mechanoreceptors due to stretching of surrounding cuticle or compression of the peg, to receptors sensitive to temperature, humidity, and carbon dioxide concentration. No other surface sense organs were detected but they may well occur on segments other than those I have studied. A similar range of sensillae have been demonstrated in *Polistes'* antennae, although many of the trichoid and basiconicoid sensillae are corrugated or with helical striations (Callahan 1970).

Boistel and others (1956) in antennogram studies on *Vespula* species, noted that deformation of the antenna by bending produced marked electrical activity, and a variety of odours also produced electrical responses in the antenna. A sense organ common to all insects with annulated antennae is Johnston's organ which is found in the pedicel. This organ detects movements of the flagellum and probably behaves as a flight-speed indicator when the flagellum is bent back on the pedicel due to wind speed.

The males of some species of wasp (e.g. *V. crabro*) have longitudinal keels on the flagellar segments which probably have a sensory function, and can be useful characters in taxonomic studies (Plate IV e, f). Further functions of antennae in vespine wasps include their role in trophallaxis, for it is with these appendages that food exchange is initiated and maintained (Montagner 1964), and cell construction (Eberhard 1969).

The Mouthparts. The appendages which comprise the mouthparts of wasps are designed primarily for biting, licking, and mastication, and are comparatively unmodified when compared to a primitive hymenopteran such as the sawfly. The principal components are the labrum in front of, and median hypopharynx behind the mouth, paired mandibles and maxillae laterally, with an unpaired labium forming a lower lip (Fig. 3).

The labrum, which is hidden to a greater or lesser extent by the elongated clypeus, bears numerous sensory setae and an epipharynx which extends from its ventral surface to form a dorsal lip to the mouth. The labium is composed of a large prementum which is deeply pouch-like in form, and a ligula which is made up of elongated para-

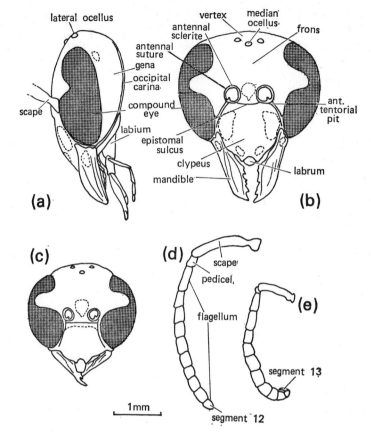

Figure 4. Morphology of head structures, *Ancistrocerus parietum* (after Felton 1954): (a) lateral view of female; (b) frontal view of female; (c) frontal view of male; (d) antenna of female; (e) antenna of male.

glossae and a bilobed, spatulate glossa with four-segmented labial palps. In Vespidae, the paraglossae are part of the functional licking apparatus, but in Eumenidae they are elongate and more palpate in form and are possibly more sensory in function.

The maxillae are relatively unmodified and very similar throughout the Vespoidea, being composed of a cardo, stipes, a reduced lacinia, and broad galea, with six-segmented palpi. The cardo articulates with the head capsule via the sub-gena while the galeae sheath the labium dorsally.

Functionally, the mandibles are used for biting, tearing, shearing, and carrying prey; picking up stones and debris while excavating or practising nest hygiene; scraping woody fibres from plant material or soil from the ground during nest construction; and in the young adult they are the structural passport for chewing their way through the cocoon cap or earthen plugs of the rearing cell. Consequently, the mandibles are stout and heavily sclerotized, with a toothed cutting edge along the inner, distal margin. Imms (1957) succinctly describes the mandibles of wasps as structures of 'industrial rather than trophic function'.

Adult wasps feed on a liquid or semi-liquid diet for large particles of food cannot travel down the narrow oesophagus where it passes through the cervical region. The labium and maxillae have a well-developed musculature (Duncan 1939) and may be extruded up to 4 mm from their resting position behind the mandibles. With its finger-like paraglossae and lobed glossa, the labium in action is best described as a 'hand' with fingers extended, taking fluid with a scooping and grabbing movement. Fluid is retained through capillary action by the rows of small spatulate setae covering the surface of the labium, and is transferred to the maxillae and thence to the hypopharynx in a 'wiping-off' action. Food passes over the floor of the hypopharynx and into the cibarium, the latter acting as a sucking pump due to the rapid expansion and contraction of its associated musculature. The feeding motions described here may be readily observed down the microscope, using a lightly anaesthetized wasp.

An unusual structure found in the head of wasps is the infrabuccal pouch or gnathal sac, situated below the hypopharyngeal lobe. Its function appears to be that of a receptacle for the dust and detritus wiped off the mouthparts during grooming. It opens through a slit-like mouth and microscopic particles of dust are found inside. There is no apparent means of emptying the pouch.

Most of the surface area of the mouthparts are well endowed with sensory hairs of various lengths which are used for testing food, although the lobes of the lacinia and galea probably serve a secondary function as cleaning organs (of the brush or broom variety) for the antennae, maxillary and labial palps, and the forelegs.

The mouthparts of vespine wasps are slightly modified according to the sex or caste of the individual (Green 1931). For example, males have proportionally smaller mandibles for their head size, and the labium in workers is somewhat reduced, although their paraglossae are conspicuously larger. These differences are of obvious functional importance in the wasp colony, for males do not forage and an increase in the 'licking up' capacity of workers would be an advantage when collecting fluids.

Food finding among the Vespoidea is a result of responses to distant and proximal stimuli, perceived as an amalgam of olfactory, visual, tactile, and gustatory messages. As will be seen in the chapters concerning Eumenidae and foraging in Vespidae, the range of food is wide.

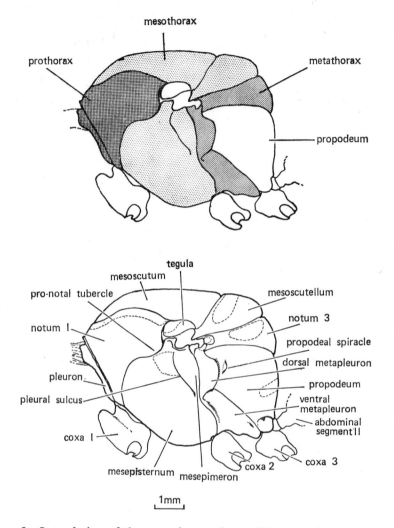

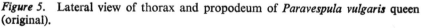

Figure 5. Lateral view of thorax and propodeum of *Paravespula vulgaris* queen (original).

The Thorax and Appendages

The thorax consists of three segments, the prothorax anteriorly, mesothorax centrally, and metathorax posteriorly, with legs attached to each segment, and wings attached to the meso- and metathoracic segments. Thus, the thorax is the major locomotor centre of the adult. In common with all Aprocrita, the first abdominal segment, the propodeum, is closely joined to the thorax, the fusion taking place during pupation.

The Thorax (Figs. 5 and 6). The prothorax, which is the smallest thoracic segment, is divided into a dorsal notum I (pronotum) which is attached to the second segment along the anterior margin of the mesothorax, and a pleuron (or propectus) which is formed by the fusion of the propleuron, prosternum, and cervical sclerite, and can move on the pronotum. The pronotum is sharply angled between its anterior and posterior margins to form a pronotal collar on its anterior face which is produced laterally to form the pronotal angles, which are of systematic importance in Eumenidae. Posteriorly, the pronotum is produced backwards to form the swollen, pronotal tubercles which cover the prothoracic spiracles. The prosternum is contiguous with

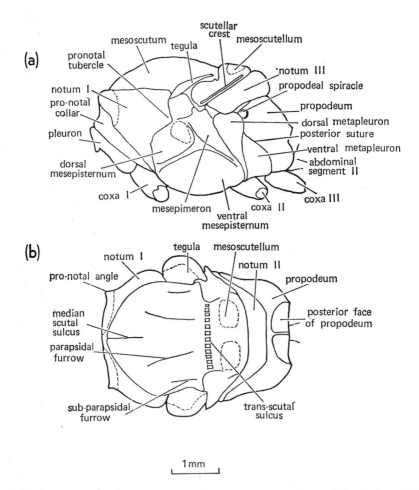

Figure 6. Thorax and propodeum of *Ancistrocerus parietum* (after Felton 1954): (a) lateral view of female; (b) dorsal view of female.

the other sclerites of the propleura and is generally only visible by dissection. The coxae of the forelegs occur below the propleuron.

The mesothorax is the largest thoracic segment, underlining the importance of this region which houses much of the flight muscles and to which the large forewings are attached. This segment is divided into a dorsal mesonotum, composed of the mesoscutum and mesocutellum, and a ventro-lateral mesopleuron (or mesopectus) composed of an anterior mesepisternum and posterior mesepimeron divided by the pleural sulcus. The sculpturing of the mesopleuron is important in the separation of *Symmorphus* species.

The metathorax, which bears the relatively smaller hindwings, is divided into a metanotum (notum III) a narrow sclerite which, in the Vespidae, is extended angularly into the propodeum, and the metapleuron (metapectus). The metapleuron is composed of the original sternite and pleuron, and is secondarily divided into a dorsal and ventral part by an oblique sulcus in the Vespidae. The second thoracic spiracle is situated at the junction of the mesepimeron, metanotum, and dorsal metapleuron. The thoracic spiracles of aculeates are of taxonomic significance (Richards 1971 b).

Propodeum (Fig. 7). Although the propodeum is, by origin, the first abdominal segment, its fusion with the thorax makes it more convenient to discuss its structure here.

The propodeum is represented by a single sclerite which bears the first abdominal, or propodeal, spiracle. The original sternite is lost, the sternum being membraneous. The posterior face in Eumenidae is relatively specialized, marked off from the rest of the propodeum by a dorso-lateral carina and a ventral shelf. The various processes produced from the carina, and the microsculpture of the posterior face are important features in eumenid taxonomy. The second abdominal segment articulates with the propodeum by a double ball-and-socket joint.

The Wings (Plate II). The Vespoidea have a strongly developed pair of forewings with smaller hindwings held together by a row of hooks or hamuli along the front edge of the hindwing, engaging a narrow fold, the frenal fold, on the hind margin of the forewing (Plate IIc). The number of hamuli is possibly related to flying ability (Richards 1949), and the consistently higher density of hamuli per unit length of wing in worker wasps compared to queens and males (Blackith 1958b) supports this hypothesis. When held at rest, the wings are pleated or folded longitudinally along the abdomen, a characteristic of all British and most other Vespoidea which gave the group its old name of Diploptera ('doubled wings'). The nomenclature of the veins

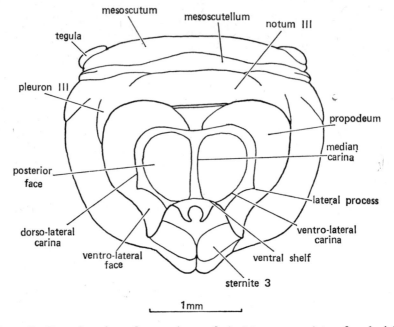

Figure 7. Posterior view of propodeum of *Ancistrocerus parietum* female (after Felton 1954).

and the cells they enclose has been subject to much confusion and there is no universal system of labelling them. The system adopted here is based on Richards (1956), the name of the cell being derived from the vein along its anterior margin or, in the case of composite anterior veins, the name is derived from the posterior one (Plate II a). The wings articulate with the thorax by means of the axillary sclerites, the tegula being part of the wing rather than a thoracic structure. The wings of Vespoidae are very similar, but the Eumenidae may be distinguished by the possession of a marked anal lobe (or alula) on the hindwing (Plate IIb).

There has been little research on the physiology of flight in Vespoidea. Sotavalta (1947) has determined that the vibration of wings in wasps varies between 117 and 247 beats per second. The Eumenidae have been recorded at 117 to 175 strokes per second while in Vespidae, maximum rates were recorded when the temperature was maintained at 23-24°C. The function of the wings apart from their use in flight, includes ventilation of the nest and distribution of heat by fanning, and possibly a communication function as an alarm signal (Nixon 1934d).

The Legs (Fig. 8). The legs of wasps are relatively unmodified

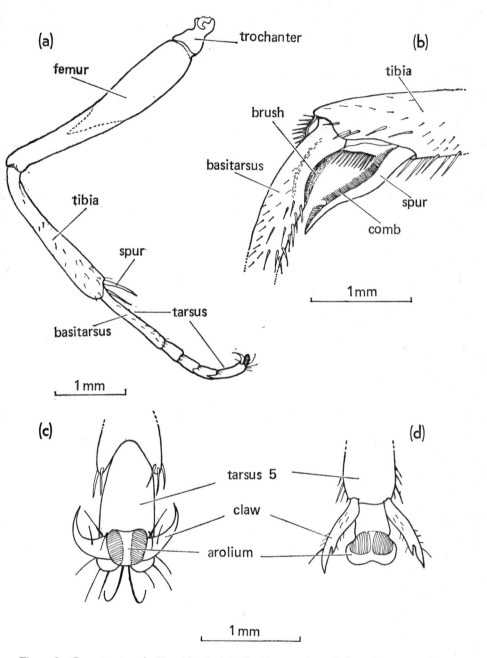

Figure 8. Leg structure in Vespidae (original): (a) mesothoracic leg of *Paravespula vulgaris*; (b) grooming organ on prothoracic leg of *Paravespula vulgaris*; (c) pretarsus of *P. vulgaris*; (d) pre-tarsus of *Ancistrocerus parietum*.

structures, each consisting of the coxa, which articulates with the thorax, the trochanter, the femur, tibia, and a five-segmented tarsus. On the foreleg (prothoracic leg) the tibial spur is modified and, together with a hairy invagination of the basitarsus, forms an antennal grooming organ. The antennae are pulled through the apparatus repeatedly to remove detritus. There is a similar organ on the middle leg (mesothoracic leg) which is used to brush the wings during grooming behaviour.

There are two differences in leg structure between the Vespidae and Eumenidae, the latter possessing only one unmodified spur on the mid-leg tibia compared to two in Vespidae, while the tarsal claws of Eumenidae have an inner tooth, but are simple in Vespidae. Apart from the obvious function of walking, the legs are used in many other ways – for grasping prey or mates, excavating soil and as accessory building tools, and also for transporting prey.

The Abdomen

The first segment of the abdomen is the propodeum which is fused to the thorax, the remaining abdominal segments being termed the gaster. The gaster is attached to the propodeum by a narrow stalk, the anterior part of the second abdominal tergite, called the petiole. In female wasps (Fig. 9a) there are six visible segments making up the gaster, and seven in males (Fig. 9b, c), the remaining segments being modified to form the sting mechanism or male genitalia. The basic components of each segment are a dorsal tergite and ventral sternite, with a spiracle on the antero-lateral margin of the tergite. Although generally visible on abdominal segments two and three, the remaining five spiracles are hidden in the Vespinae, although more may be visible in old queens due to the extension of the abdomen (physogastry) which accompanies their ovariole development.

An interesting structural feature of the terminal abdominal sternite in social Vespidae has been recently described by Van der Vecht (1968) (Fig. 10a). This sclerite has a 'specialized area' at its base which, with associated tufts of hairs, could be implicated in the dispersal of pheromones – chemical substances produced by insects which release certain specific behaviour patterns, or determine physiological development (Karlson and Butenandt 1959). Further details are given in the section concerning glands.

The Sting (Plate III). The sting is derived from the modified sclerites and appendages of abdominal segments eight, nine, and ten, and lies hidden in a pouch between segments seven and eight when retracted. The large lateral sclerites of segment nine make up the major part of the sting, the tergites and sternites connected by a mem-

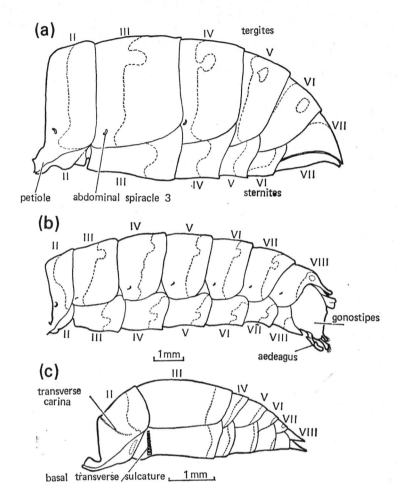

Figure 9. Lateral view of abdomen: (a) queen of *Paravespula vulgaris*; (b) male of *P. vulgaris;* (c) (after Felton 1954) male of *Ancistrocerus parietum.*

brane with, posteriorly, a hair-fringed lobe derived from the tenth segment. This lobe is considerably smaller in Eumenidae.

The active part of the sting consists of smooth lancets derived from the first valvulae which are attached to the first valvifers of the eighth segment. The lancets, which in Vespidae are slightly barbed (but not nearly as much as in the honeybee), are protected by a sting sheath, the fused second valvulae. The two pairs of valvulae are collectively termed the terebra and it is this which is thrust into the victim. The third valvulae are developed from the posterior part of the second valvifer and form prominent, hair-covered sting palps.

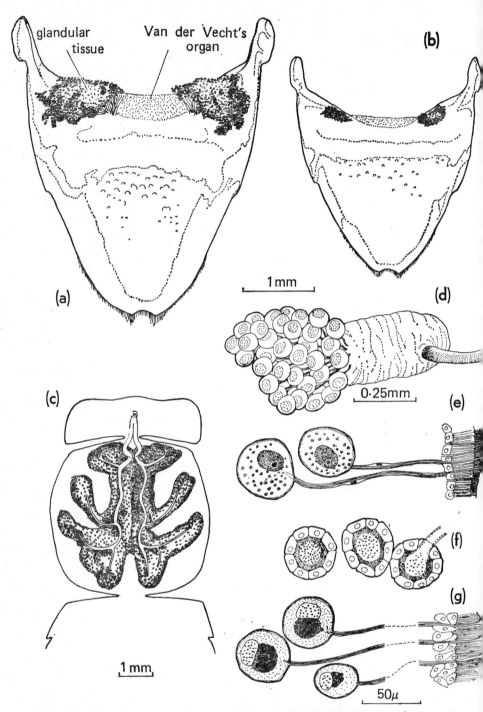

Figure 10. Wasp Glands (original): (a) VI – sternite of gaster, *Paravespula germanica* queen; (b) VI – sternite of gaster, *P. germanica* worker; (c) thoracic gland of *P. germanica* worker; (d) mandibular gland I of *P. germanica* worker; (e) hypopharyngeal gland cells, *P. germanica* queen; (f) thoracic gland cells, old *P. germanica* worker; (g) VI – sternite gland cells, *P. germanica* queen.

The sting is used as a weapon and not for egg-laying in aculeate Hymenoptera, oviposition being effected via a genital opening anterior to the first valvifers. The action and some details of the pharmacology and pathology of stings will be discussed in more detail in Chapter 12.

Male Genitalia (Plate III). There is much controversy concerning the possible derivation of the external parts of the male genitalia, and in the nomenclature of the structures concerned. The dominant conflict concerns the original abdominal appendages and whether or not they are incorporated in the genitalia of the contemporary wasp. For descriptive purposes I will use the terminology of Richards (1956).

The genitalia, which are probably derived from the ninth sternite, are normally retracted into a pouch lying between abdominal segments eight and nine. There are five groups of parts, an unpaired basal ring or gonocardo anteriorly, which encloses a pair of plates, the gonostipes (basiparameres), which in turn enclose the elongate aedeagus (penis). From the postero-ventral surface of each gonostipes are lobes, the volsellae, attached anteriorly but free posteriorly, where each divides to form the digitus and the cuspis.

In Eumenidae, each gonostipes has long spines projecting posteriorly which often give the impression of a double sting (the 'pseudosting' of Evans and Eberhard 1970), but they are less obvious in Vespidae. By mimicking the female sting the pseudosting possibly confers some protective advantage to the males.

ADULT ANATOMY

Alimentary System

The alimentary canal of the adult is divided into three main regions, the foregut or stomodaeum, the midgut, and the hindgut or proctodaeum (Fig. 11). The foregut and hindgut are ectodermal in origin and have a cuticular lining.

The foregut consists of a mouth, pharynx, oesophagus, crop and proventriculus. The pharynx has well-developed musculature and appears to have a pump-like action to enable sucking and swallowing of liquid food. The simple tube-like oesophagus traverses the thoracic region and where it enters the abdomen via the petiole, is expanded to form the crop. The crop, which in Vespidae is small in queens and largest in workers (Green 1931), is a fluid-storage organ used principally by foraging wasps when collecting carbohydrates or water and is equivalent to the 'honey-stomach' of the honeybee. The proventriculus is well developed, acting as a pump in conjunction with the pharynx (Green 1931). Compared to the honeybee, the proventriculus of wasps is a considerably inferior organ for filtering particles from the crop,

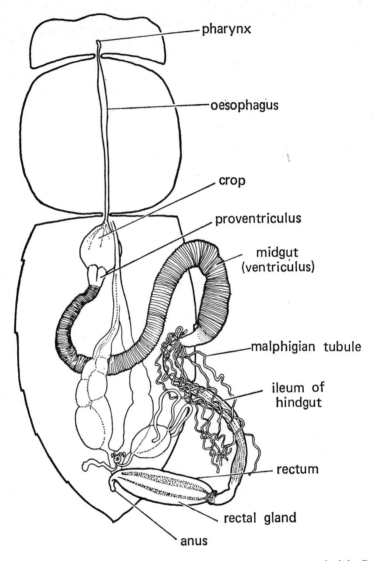

Figure 11. Alimentary system of *Paravespula germanica* queen (original).

and is correlated with the adult wasp's essentially liquid diet (Bailey 1954).

The midgut is a relatively long tube, with pronounced circular muscle bands which give it an annulated appearance. This region of the gut is the principal absorptive area where enzymes are produced and digestion takes place. Many insects have a protective lining to the midgut, the peritrophic membrane, which contains chitin and is secreted by the midgut epithelium. This membrane is highly developed in wasp larvae, several distinct layers being secreted daily, and protects the delicate gut lining from the coarse pieces of indigestible prey cuticle.

The hindgut, which conveys undigested food along the small intestine or ileum to the exterior via the rectum, bears the malphigian tubules which are of small diameter, but long and very numerous. Their main

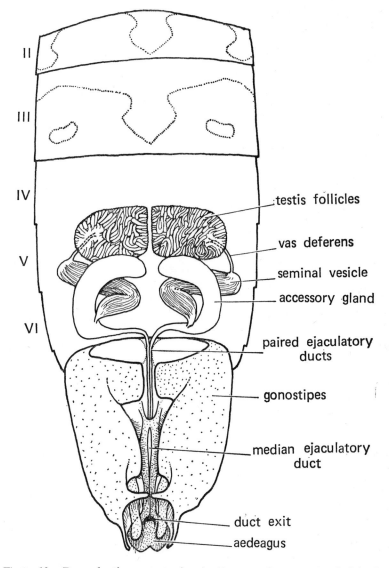

Figure 12. Reproductive system of male, *Paravespula germanica* (original).

function is that of nitrogenous excretion in the form of insoluble uric acid. The ileum which has folded walls to increase its surface area, is used primarily for water absorption. The rectum is a prominent enlargement of the hindgut, with six pairs of rectal glands which probably facilitate the resorption of water and possibly salts and amino acids. The development and histology of the rectal glands of wasps has been studied by Evenius (1933).

Reproductive System

The male and female reproductive organs consist of paired gonads connected by paired ducts to a common, median duct which opens to the exterior via the external genitalia. A description based on the genitalia of males and juvenile queens *Paravespula* is given here, but details of ovariole development, and anatomical differences associated with caste will be discussed more fully elsewhere. Post-embryonic development of the genitalia is described by Takamatsu (1949).

Male Reproductive Anatomy (Fig. 12).   The paired testes consist of tightly packed follicles or testis tubes, close together in the mid-line but not in contact, and enclosed by a peritoneal membrane, the scrotum. The testes have a liberal supply of tracheae, indicative of a region with a high metabolic rate, presumably due to the processes associated with spermatogenesis. Relatively short sperm ducts, the vas deferens, lead into large seminal vesicles which are yellowish in colour and in which the sperm is stored. The seminal vesicles open into the base of a large, opaque white gland, the function of which is unknown, but is probably associated with sperm maintenance or spermatophore production. The paired ejaculatory ducts pass postero-ventrally through a gap in the musculature at the base of the phallus, becoming a single median duct on entering the aedeagus. This duct continues inside the sclerotized aedeagus and opens dorsally on to its spoon-like distal end.

Female Reproductive Anatomy (Fig. 13). Wasps have paired ovaries, consisting of six pairs of ovarioles in Vespinae and three pairs in Eumenidae and Polistinae (Bordas 1931). The ovarioles are typically polytrophic, each developing egg or oocyte alternating with groups of nutritive or nurse cells. The numbers of oocytes in each ovariole varies according to the state of sexual development and has been calculated as high as 250 to 300 in *P. germanica* (with a total of 3,000 to 3,600 oocytes in both ovaries) and 12 to 15 in *Eumenes pomiformis* (F.) (72 to 90 in both ovaries) (Bordas 1931).

The ovarioles open into paired oviducts which meet medially to form a common oviduct, posteriorly, the vagina. The sperm-storage organ, the spermatheca, opens into the vagina dorsally. The spermatheca

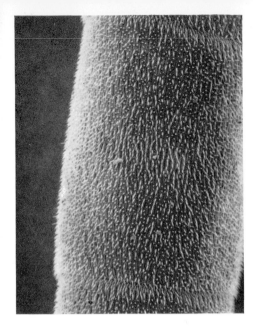

IV (a–f). Scanning electron micrographs of wasp antennae

(a) antennal segment of *Vespula rufa* (×100)

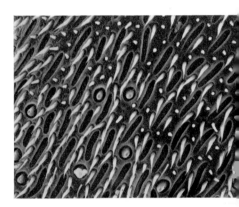

(b) detail of same segment (×300)

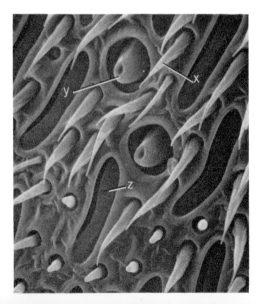

(c) detail of same segment to show tricoid sensilla, x = campaniform sensilla, y = placode sensilla, z = ×1000.

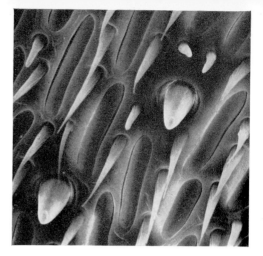

(*d*) detail of antennal segment of *V. rufa* male (×1000)

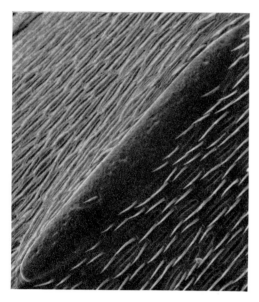

(*e*) tyloid on antennal segment of *Vespa crabro* male (×250).

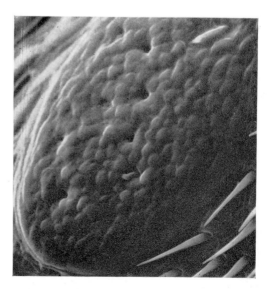

(*f*) detail of tyloid (×1000).

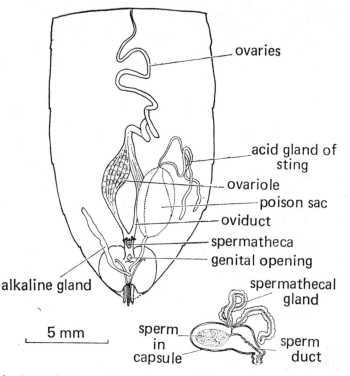

Figure 13. Reproduction system of queen, *Paravespula germanica*: details of spermotheca, inset (original).

is relatively small in Vespinae although larger than in Eumenidae, consisting of a semi-transparent and pliable sperm capsule, a convoluted sperm duct opening into the vagina, and a bifurcate spermathecal gland (Fig. 13, inset). The capsule is lined with striated, columnar epithelium and, according to Marchal (1894), has a cuticular membrane. The sperm, with their long tails moving inside the capsule, are readily seen in freshly killed material.

Exocrine Glands

Many glands occur in adult wasps which are important to feeding and some which may have a communications function. This account is based on personal studies of *Paravespula* species, although Heselhaus (1922) has described and figured the major glands and compared them with the honeybee, bumble bee, and solitary bees. The considerable volume of work on the histology and functions of glands in the honeybee (e.g. Snodgrass 1925, 1956) invites comparison with homologous glands in the wasp, although I doubt whether identical functions will be demonstrated in many of the glands under discussion.

D

The glands concerned with feeding are found in the head and thoracic regions and comprise the mandibular, hypopharyngeal, and thoracic glands. The thoracic gland is also referred to as the labial or salivary gland. The principal mandibular gland (mandibular gland I) has a thin-walled reservoir in which the secretions from about 50 to 70 monocellular gland cells are stored and from which a sclerotized duct (Fig. 10d) leads to the proximal edge of the mandibles (Fig. 3). The morphological and histological details of this gland are similar in both female castes and also in males, which suggests that its function may be lubricatory or that it helps to maintain the mandibular region in a suitable condition for feeding activities. Its small size compared to the mandibular gland in the honeybee suggest that it does not function in the capacity of a brood-food producing gland as in worker bees, or a source of pheromones as in the queen bee.

The smaller mandibular gland (mandibular gland II) lies inside the hollow base of the mandible, opposite mandibular gland I. This gland, which apparently has not been previously described, is possibly homologous with the post-genal gland of the honeybee although in social wasps it is clearly associated with the mandible. Mandibular gland II is composed of a group of monocellular gland cells with individual ducts leading to the inner edge of the mandible where they discharge their secretions through the membrane connecting the mandible to the maxilla.

The hypopharyngeal gland is the dominant head gland with respect to size, the glandular tissue lying beneath the hypopharyngeal plate and communicating with the bucco-pharyngeal cavity through long narrow ducts which pass through fine pores in the sclerotized plate (Fig. 10e). The gross features of this gland are similar in males and females in contrast to the honeybee in which the comparable gland is absent in males and queens. Its function in the honeybee worker is the production of the protein component of brood food and the enzymes involved in honey production such as invertase and a glucose oxidase. The hypopharyngeal gland of wasps could be implicated in feeding larvae although its functions have yet to be confirmed.

Close to the hypopharyngeal gland there is a pair of concavities in the hypopharyngeal plate with large pores opening onto the floor of the pharynx. Within the concavities are columnar cells which are probably sensory in function for they are served by a network of nerve fibres which arise from a prominent nerve passing directly from the brain. Snodgrass (1956) refers to homologous cells in the worker bee as sense organs. Individual cells or small patches of gland cells are scattered throughout much of the bucco-pharyngeal region (Heselhaus 1922). They are sub-epithelial in origin and probably function by maintaining the areas they serve in optimum condition for feeding or testing food.

The thoracic gland (Fig. 10c) extends throughout much of the thorax, with its various branches passing between the major flight muscles. Each lobule is composed of numerous cells to form an acinus (Fig. 10f). In newly emerged wasps, the lining cells of the acinus are narrow but they increase in size as the wasp ages. Secretory products accumulate in the central lumen of the acinus from which fine tubules lead to the densely branched system of ducts which pass through the wasp's neck as paired tubes, joining to form a common salivary duct in the head, and ending in a dilated chamber, the salivarium, at the distal end of the hypopharynx (Fig. 3). In the honeybee, thoracic gland secretion is almost pure water and is used for softening, diluting, and lubricating anything that a bee licks, chews, washes or ingests (Simpson 1960). Similar functions can be attributed to the thoracic gland of wasps, and its secretion is probably of importance to emerging adults which soften the pupal capping with fluid. Thoracic gland secretion may also be important during carton-making, possibly producing a 'size' which helps to glue the wood pulp.

Within the abdomen of females, two major glands occur, the 1·5 to 2·5 cm long sting or acid gland which produces venom (Fig. 13), and the paired glands on the sixth gastral sternite (Fig. 10a and b). The glandular tissue on sternite VI is found on either side of the unsclerotized basal area, Van der Vecht's organ, and in view of its intimate relationship with this region the gland will be called Van der Vecht's gland. Considerably more developed in queens than workers, each monocellular gland cell communicates with the outer surface of the sternite through long, fine ducts. Where it reaches the surface of the cuticle the duct expands to form a trumpet-shaped opening (Fig. 10g). By using the scanning electron microscope, these holes or pores are readily seen on the surface of the cuticle on either side of Van der Vecht's organ.

It is tempting to speculate on the possible function of this gland, for the combination of a large gland with an associated dispersal zone (the hair-lined basal area) suggest that a volatile substance is produced by the gland and evaporated from this region. As other evidence suggests (see Chapter 8) the 'queen substance' pheromone in large wasp colonies is most likely to be diffused through the colony in a gaseous phase rather than obtained from the queen by licking her body, as in honeybees. Furthermore, with distension of the gaster due to ovariole development, Van der Vecht's organ is generally exposed in old queens although in workers and young queens it is normally completely hidden by the overlapping sternite V. In workers the glandular area is considerably smaller than in queens and the gland cells are also smaller (20–35 μ, compared to 40–50 μ in queens).

Other monocellular glands are found in the gaster, those associated

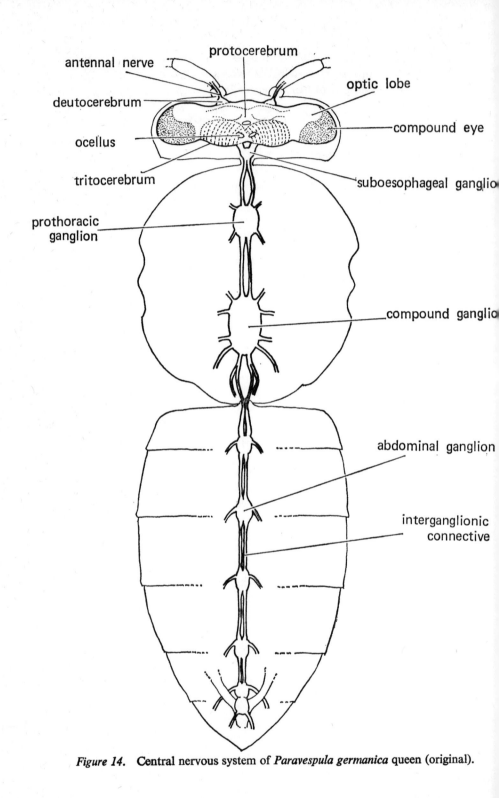

Figure 14. Central nervous system of *Paravespula germanica* queen (original).

with sternite V opening onto the cuticle in the same way as Van der Vecht's gland. They are, however, few in number and not conglomerated to form well-defined glandular tissues.

Nervous System

The central nervous system is composed of the brain and a series of ventral segmental ganglia from which nerve fibres pass to the various parts of the body (Fig. 14). The central nervous system of wasps enables integration of body's activities and permits a high degree of learning.

The brain (Fig. 15) is the dominant feature of the central nervous system, both in size and in its capacity as principal co-ordinating centre for complex behaviour patterns. The brain is composed of four major regions, the protocerebrum which includes the corpora pedunculata or 'mushroom bodies' and central body; the optic lobes; deutocerebrum with its antennal lobes; and tritocerebrum from which the ventral nerve cord extends posteriorly. The functioning of these various parts of the brain is not well understood and analogies with vertebrate brain function do not appear too helpful. A ten ´1910) has compared the brains of various Hymenoptera and found that the mushroom bodies increased in relative size from the primitive sawflies to the social insects, and that the female castes possessed larger mushroom bodies than the males. The increase in size of the mushroom bodies is paralleled by an increase in the surface area of the cups or calyces which probably enables a greater complexity of neural architecture.

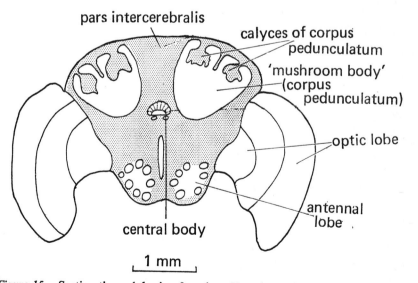
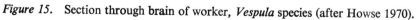

Figure 15.   Section through brain of worker, *Vespula* species (after Howse 1970).

By comparing the ratio of volume of calyx/volume of central body (which indicates head width), Howse and Williams (1969) found an increase in the ratio, similar to von Alten's results, which placed *Vespula* and *Bombus* (Bumble bee) at the top of the hymenopteran ladder. It appears that the increase in the calyx/central body ratio is correlated with increasingly sophisticated foraging activity which demands high levels of complex behaviour, including visual learning of foraging routes and orientation to and from the nest. The primary functions of the mushroom bodies appear to be concerned with memory storage and the co-ordination of sequential patterns of activity (Howse 1972).

Between the tritocerebrum of the brain and the first ventral nerve ganglion, two nerves pass around the oesophagus. This first ganglion, the sub-oesophageal ganglion, is formed by the fusion of mandibular, maxillary, and labial ganglia and controls the effector systems associated with feeding and seizing prey. In the primitive condition there are three thoracic ganglia but in *Vespula* (Fig. 14) the meso and metathoracic ganglia are fused to form a compound ganglion. The thoracic ganglia have nerves which extend to the legs and wings and innervate these appendages. The abdominal ganglia are six in number with the two distal ones partly fused where they pass over the paired oviduct in females. The ganglia are linked by paired connectives, and from each ganglion a pair of peripheral nerves extends to each abdominal segment.

CHAPTER 3

SOLITARY WASPS – THE EUMENIDAE

Solitary wasps are of generally local distribution, unobtrusive, and not often associated with man's urban world. Although harmless to us, reserving their sting for paralysing insect prey and unable to use it for defending themselves or their nests, their taxonomic name – Eumenidae, the Gracious Ones – is a euphemism coined by the Greeks to describe the Furies.

In common with the great majority of wasps, immature eumenid wasps are entomophagous, the insect prey being provided in the form of bulk supplies in individual cells constructed by the female. Except in rare instances, there is no contact between parent and offspring and their biology is thus typically solitary. The male's sole contribution to the future of the progeny is the insemination of females, for they take no part in the search for nest sites, nest construction or provisioning.

Typically, the solitary wasps prepare simple nests composed of one or more cells in excavated soil, hollowed-out plant material, or by the construction of aerial clay flasks. The cell or cells which comprise a nest become the focal point of the wasp's activities to which she will return time and again with building materials and prey. When a cell has been prepared, the egg is deposited – often attached to the cell by a thin filament – and then the cell is filled with a variable number of paralysed insect larvae. The most common are larvae of Lepidoptera although larvae of other insect orders have been recorded as prey. The sealed cell containing the prey and developing wasp larva has been described by Cooper (1957) as a 'developmental microcosm'.

In localities where nesting is particularly favourable, large congregations of the same species may occupy a relatively small nesting area, but there is no evidence of co-operation among founding females or between parents and emerging offspring, although some collective protection from predators may accrue from these associations.

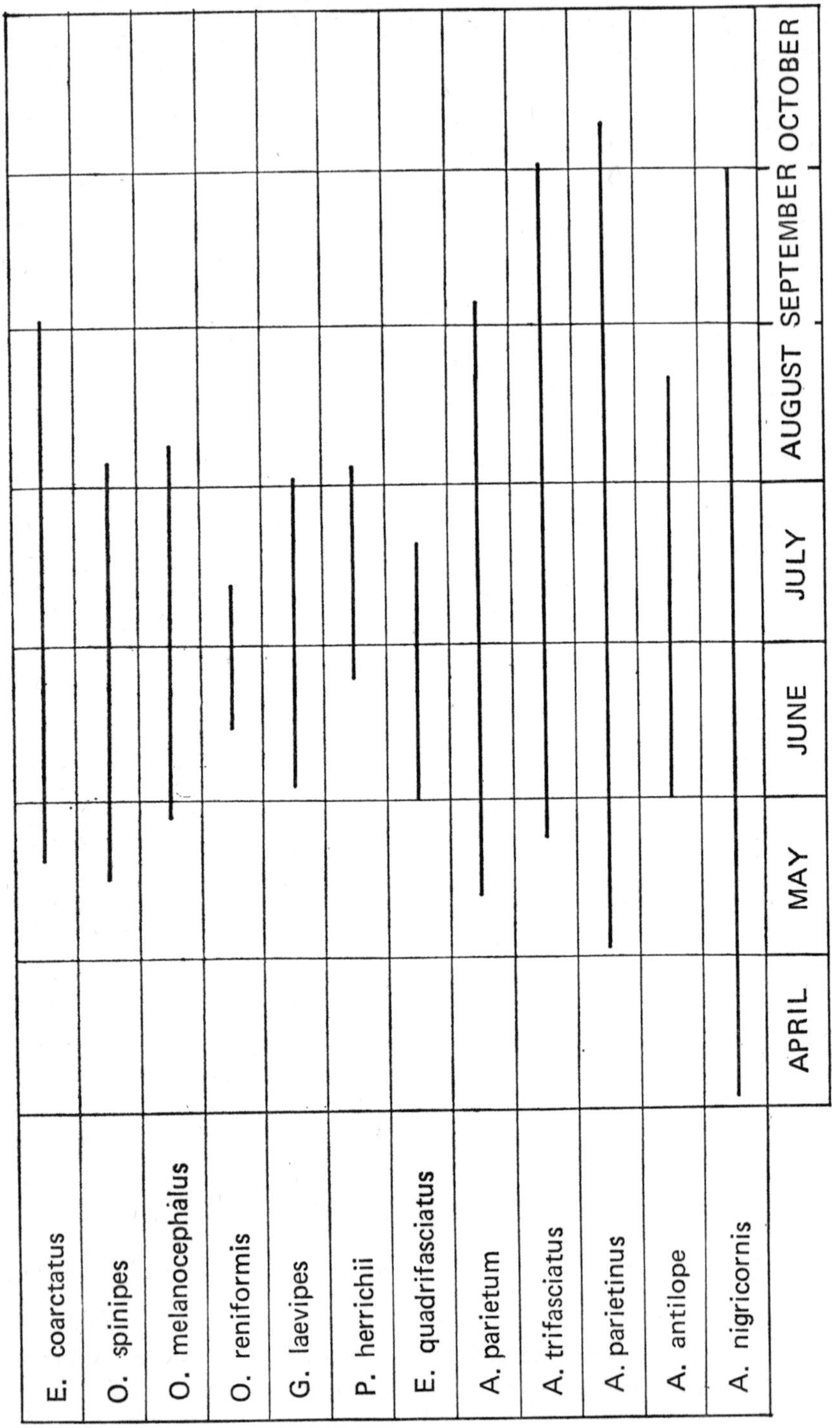

E. coarctatus

O. spinipes

O. melanocephalus

O. reniformis

G. laevipes

P. herrichii

E. quadrifasciatus

A. parietum

A. trifasciatus

A. parietinus

A. antilope

A. nigricornis

APRIL MAY JUNE JULY AUGUST SEPTEMBER OCTOBER

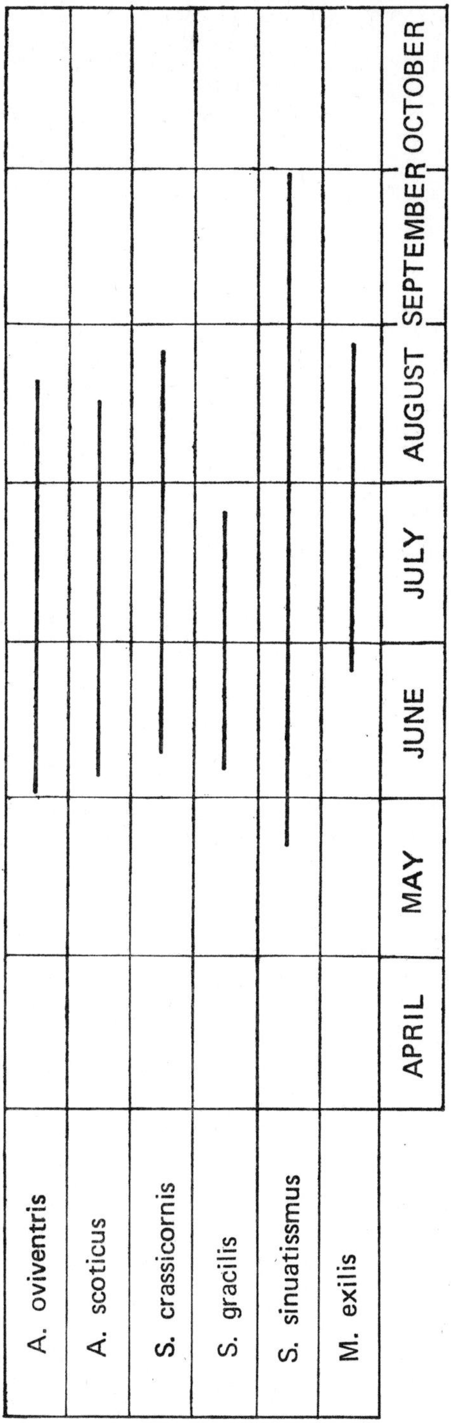

Figure 16. Flight period of British Eumenidae (original).

ADULT BEHAVIOUR AFTER EMERGENCE

The emergence of adult wasps from the cells in which they were reared varies in time depending on the species and climatic conditions, but the majority of species are engaged in adult activities during the mid- to late summer period (Fig. 16). Mating takes place shortly after the emergence of adults, followed by the search for nest sites and the preparation and mass provisioning of rearing cells by the females.

Mating Behaviour

Adult males emerge from their cells one to several days before the females a phenomenom which is probably universal among the Eumenidae, favouring outbreeding within the population. This could be further reinforced if males undergo a post-emergence maturation period during which emigration takes place. The females which emerge later are most receptive to the advances of the males immediately or shortly after their emergence from the cells, although Cooper (1955) found newly emerged virgin *Ancistrocerus antilope* (Panzer) females to be coy, showing hostility towards males whose task was to seduce the recalcitrant female. While awaiting the emergence of females, males often perform characteristic nuptial flights, moving back and forth in a defined area, often in the same locality where they emerged. These flights have been called 'sun dances' (Rau 1935) and groups of twelve or more males will participate – the daily dance continuing for up to a month in the North American species studied. Congregations of male wasps on a bank containing nest tunnels have been recorded by Isely (1913) who observed males inspecting the entrances of open burrows. At two burrows, the males tried to enter and in these Isely found females ready to emerge, the males presumably responding to some sex attractant or aphrodisiac emitted by the young adult females.

The following account of mating behaviour in eumenid wasps is based on the detailed observations of Cooper (1955) on the tube-dwelling species, *Ancistrocerus antilope*, in America.

When a male wasp finds a receptive female or his initial advances meet with success, he mounts the female from above and establishes a firm grip with his legs around the female's thorax and petiole, gripping on to the anterior margin of the pronotum with his mandibles so that their abdomens are close together and parallel. Chapman (1870) considers that the tridentate femur of male *Odynerus spinipes* L. (Fig. 95b) is used to hold the wing of the female during copulation, for the teeth of the femur fit between the wing veins. Once mounted the male strokes and rapidly taps the female's antennae with his own and curls his abdomen forward and under the female, then the phallus is extended and, with the parameres spread, the intromittent organ is pushed out along the female's sternites. When the tips of the abdomens are together the parameres and associated structures seize the tip of the female's abdomen and her genital chamber is prised open. The twisting movements of the male, if successful, cause the sting to be pushed out as the phallus is inserted. An attempt at intromission may last from 20 to 60 seconds.

Duration of copulation varied from 10 to 30 minutes, although pairing may occupy from 4 minutes to 5 hours depending on the receptiveness of the female and the determination of the male. For example, intromission may be attempted from 4 to 16 times, followed by up to one hour's rest between attempts. During intromission the male occasionally strokes or taps the female's antennae while she remains passive, walks about or even flies with the male dangling free beneath her. Similar behaviour has been described for Japanese species of *Eumenes* (Iwata 1953).

Grooming

After mating, indeed following many other activities such as emergence from the cell or foraging, wasps in common with most other insects spend a considerable amount of time grooming. The insect flight machine requires constant attention to be maintained at peak efficiency, and grooming is certainly one of the more important contributions to this end. Dust, dirt, or liquids are acquired on the often hairy body of the wasp and their presence is the likely stimulus for grooming. The legs and mouthparts are used to brush, comb, or wash the body free of foreign matter. Grooming may also occur as a displacement activity if the wasp is frustrated in some of its activities or exposed to conflicting situations and drives (Evans 1966).

Adult Feeding

Most adult wasps feed exclusively on carbohydrates derived mainly from the nectaries of flowers and the honey-dew of aphids. The short tongues of the Vespoidea restrict the range of available flowers to those with shallow corollas or plants with extrafloral nectaries, although cases where wasps 'rob' flowers with inaccessible nectaries by chewing through the corolla probably occur.

The species of flowers visited by eumenid wasps vary according to the flowering period of the plant and the flight period of the wasp – the range of plant species visited by wasps depending on the season. *Ancistrocerus antilope* has been recorded on Blackberry, Raspberry, Parsnip, Meadowsweet, Goldenrods and *Aster* (Cooper 1953), and, with *Ancistrocerus parietum* and *A. oviventris*, on (Wesmael) on Danewort, Privet, Ergngium, snd Thistles (Fahringer 1922). *Eumenes* has been observed foraging for nectar on Danewort (Fahringer 1922), and *Symmorphus gracilis* (Brullé) recorded at flowers of Meadowsweet (Morley 1898). Some species of *Symmorphus* are attracted to Figwort, Wild Parsnip, and Spurge (K. M. Guichard, personal communication). The Umbelliferae, Euphorbiaceae and Rosaceae provide the principal sources of available nectar and are constant rendezvous for many aculeate wasps – a habit often taken advantage of by the entomologist armed with collecting tube, camera, or notebook.

Although carbohydrates are the basic food for adult wasps, there are several instances of females malaxating their prey and ingesting the oozing body fluids. Malaxation of the prey is probably concerned primarily with the pre-treatment of prey prior to their storage in the cells, but the blood of the prey could be an important component in the diet of the female which requires protein for the development of eggs. For example, Isely (1913) has recorded prey malaxation in American Eumenidae, while Rau (1945) saw an adult of *Odynerus* consume the entire body contents of a caterpillar. In Japan, Iwata (1953) saw *Eumenes* females regularly bite their prey and suck in the haemolymph, and on one occasion a female used the green haemolymph of a caterpillar to prepare mud pellets for nest building.

Nesting Behaviour

When the inseminated female reaches maturity certain nesting drives become apparent, namely the search for a suitable nest site which is often accompanied by appetitive digging or excavating during which time the nesting instinct increases in intensity (Evans 1966). Eumenid wasps tend to be locally distributed, nesting sites often remaining constant for successive years, probably because of the quality and availability of the nesting situation. This frequently results in quite large aggregations in a closely defined area. For example, *Pseudepipona herrichii* (Saussure) in Britain is only found in two or three localities in the Studland area of Dorset where relatively large numbers of females nest in very small patches of ground (Spooner 1934).

Once a site has been selected, the female begins nesting by excavating soil to produce a burrow, clearing out pith from the broken stem of a plant or begins collecting moistened clay for building. The manner in which the wasps prepare sites and build their nests shows great diversity, from simple excavated pockets in the soil, to series of cells in hollowed-out plant stems and the delicate ceramic flasks of the true potter wasps (Table 1).

The Burrowers

Many eumenid wasps burrow in earth to prepare cells for their

TABLE 1
Summary of nesting habits of British Eumenidae

NEST TYPE	SPECIES
1. BURROWERS	
(a) Simple cells, no clay used	*Pseudepipona herrichii*
(b) Subterranean clay cells, no chimney	*Ancistrocerus scoticus*
(c) Excavated cells, clay chimney present	*Odynerus spinipes*
	Odynerus melanocephalus
	Odynerus reniformis
	? *Odynerus simillimus*
2. TUBE DWELLERS	
(a) Simple clay partitions	*Ancistrocerus parietum*
	Ancistrocerus gazella
	Ancistrocerus trifasciatus
	Ancistrocerus parietinus
	Ancistrocerus antilope
	Ancistrocerus nigricornis
	Ancistrocerus quadratus
	Symmorphus gracilis
	? *Symmorphus crassicornis*
	Symmorphus sinuatissimus
	Symmorphus connexus
	Euodynerus quadrifasciatus
	Microdynerus exilis
(b) Clay, thimble-shaped cells	*Gymnomerus laevipes*
(c) Occupation of miscellaneous sites (e.g. insect galls, angles of walls)	*Ancistrocerus parietum*
	Ancistrocerus trifasciatus
	Symmorphus sinuatissimus
3. MUD-DAUBER	*Ancistrocerus oviventris*
4. AERIAL FLASKS	*Eumenes coarctatus*

progeny, and a variety of architectural styles has been recorded among the British species. The least specialized nests are those of *Pseudepipona herrichii* in the coarse, sandy soils of south-east Dorset which have been described in some detail by Spooner (1934). This species burrows into the hard but friable ground where bare patches occur in the sparse, heathland vegetation. The female removes sand particles with her mandibles and deposits them at one at a time some 2 to 5 cm from the burrow until she has excavated a short tunnel with a round cell some 1 to 4 cm below the surface (Fig. 17a). When the cell has been fully excavated, the wasp strengthens it by wetting the walls with saliva and polishing them, but there is no use of clay or mortar in cell construction or in sealing them and the main entrance to the burrow. After the cell is provisioned, the wasp simply fills the neck of the cell with sand particles and then proceeds to excavate a further cell or two off the main burrow. In a similar American species the female fills the nest entrance by vigourously scraping a heap of loose sand to the entrance and pushing it in with her forelegs. When several heaps have been pushed down, the wasp tamps down the loose grains with her legs, the filling-up of a burrow taking about five minutes (Isely 1913).

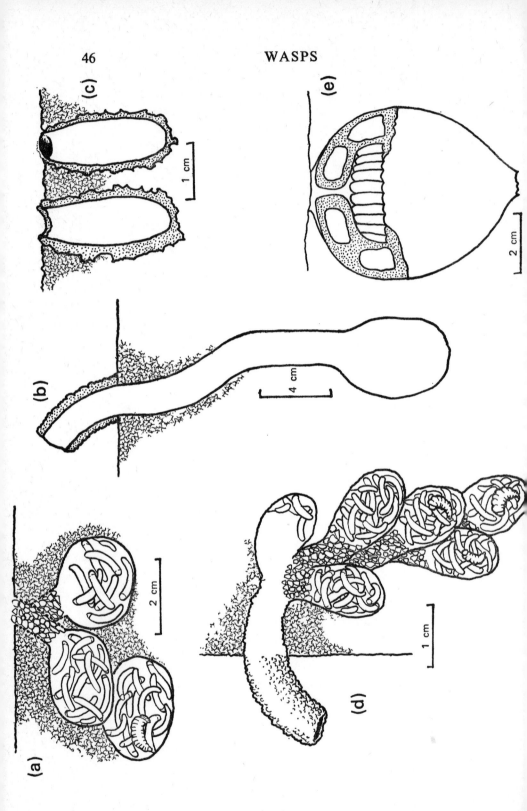

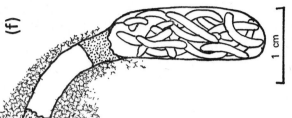

(f)

(g)

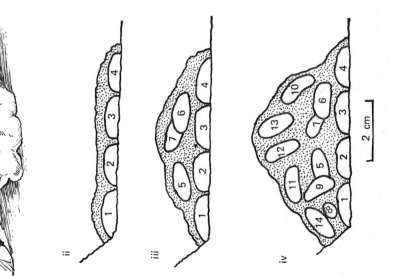

(h)

Figure 17. Nest structures in some British Eumenidae: (a) *Pseudepipona herrichii* (after Spooner 1934); (b) *Odynerus melanocephalus* (after Nielsen 1932); (c) *Ancistrocerus scoticus* (after Julliard 1950); (d) *Odynerus spinipes* (after Bristowe 1948); (e) *Ancistrocerus parietum* in abandoned embryo nest of *Vespula* (after Maneval 1925); (f) *Ancistrocerus parietum* in beetle exit hole (after Nielsen 1932); (g) *Gymnomerus laevipes* (after Bristowe 1948); (h) *Ancistrocerus oviventris*, ii-iv stages in building where numbers refer to the order in which cells were constructed (after Nielsen 1932).

A further stage in the design and structure of underground nests is the construction of simple clay flasks by *Ancistrocerus scoticus* (Curtis) in bare, flat ground (Julliard 1950). The cells are like elongated olives in shape and composed of a hard, clay cement containing tiny grains of sand with larger stones encrusting the exterior (Fig. 17c). The inner surface is smooth and the orifice, which is flush with the ground, is sealed with a concave cap which fits neatly on the rim of the opening. Apparently there is no chimney or turret extending beyond the surface of the ground. Single cells are often clumped together in large numbers to form 'colonies' which become very evident if surrounding soil is blown or washed away to reveal the tops of the cells.

Many British Eumenidae construct cells in the hard earth of flat ground or vertical banks, using the excavated soil to build temporary chimneys of variable design and length. The chimney probably protects the nest from rain and may inhibit parasites and predators from entering the cells. Those which build in vertical banks include *Odynerus spinipes* while *Odynerus melanocephalus* (Gmelin) (Nielsen 1932) and *Odynerus reniformis* (Gmelin) (Yarrow 1943) burrow in both horizontal and

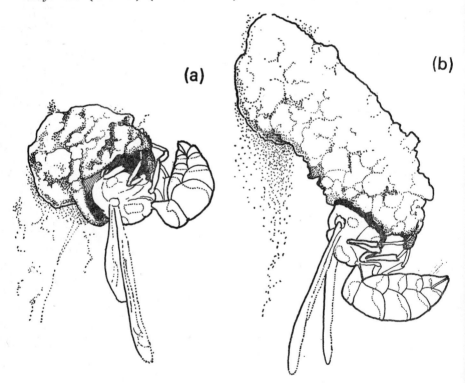

(a)

(b)

Figure 18.   *Odynerus reniformis* female building chimney (drawn from photographs by Olberg 1959).

vertical surfaces. Probably the earliest description of the biology of a eumenid wasp is Réaumur's classic account in 1742 of the nesting habits of *Odynerus spinipes*. One of the most detailed accounts of the nesting behaviour of a chimney-maker is that of Isely (1913) on the American species, *Odynerus papagorum* Viereck, which excavates its nests in the vertical walls of clay banks. Isely observed that the female walks rapidly to and fro across a few square cm of a bank when searching for a suitable nest site. Occasionally she stops and tests the surface with her mandibles, then after a few minutes, flies around the area, alights on the bank and repeats the performance. Finally, after a brief zig-zagging orientation flight, she flies off for water and then returns to the place she had previously surveyed, wets a spot and begins digging. The wasp digs rapidly, using her mandibles and forelegs to drag the moistened clay to the edge of the burrow and prepare a solid foundation for the chimney wall. The excavated earth is put in place with the mandibles then, with mandibles and forelegs, it is worked from within while the tip of the abdomen is pressed against the outer wall to support it. As she excavates, the wasp moves round relative to the burrow axis so that a ring of foundation is soon established (Fig. 18). When the chimney becomes too long for the wasp to pull clay to the edge, she begins to make pellets which are carried out in her mandibles and added to the rim of the chimney. While pressing the pellet to the inside of the chimney with her mandibles and forelegs, the outer part of the tube is supported by the curled-over abdomen. After a few minutes excavating, the wasp flies off to replenish the water which is used to soften the clay, and within about a quarter of an hour, the digging wasp is virtually hidden by the chimney.

One wasp took less than an hour to build a chimney of 3 cm length. The end of the chimney is normally curved over so that the entrance faces downwards which may well help to keep the burrow and cells from getting wet should it rain. When the chimney is complete (the length is variable even in the same species of wasp), the excavated pellets of soil are discarded, either by the female backing out of the tube to drop the pellet from her mandibles while clinging to the mouth of the chimney or during a very brief flight. After provisioning the first cell, the second cell is excavated off the main burrow. Isely noted that sometimes a wasp will collect clay from the bank at some distance from the nest in order to extend the chimney, even after the wasp had begun discarding pellets of earth earlier.

Although the water collected by the wasp is undoubtedly used to soften the earth and assist its further excavation, it is possible that salivary secretions may play a part in rendering the substrate suitable for digging. As expressed by Kirby and Spence (in Step 1932), *Odynerus spinipes* is 'provided with a slightly glutinous liquor which it pours out

E

of its mouth that, like the vinegar with which Hannibal softened the Alps, acts upon the cement of the sand (in the mortar of walls), and renders the separation of the grains easy to the double pickaxe with which the wasp is furnished'.

The completed nests of *Odynerus spinipes* contain 5 or 6 cells and the chimney, which is made of pellets of mud with spaces between them, is rarely more than 3 cm long (Fig. 17d) (Bristowe 1948). The nest of *Odynerus reniformis* which is made up of 1 to 3 cells (Nielsen 1932), is somewhat different for the chimney is invariably longer and without spaces between the pellets. When the nest is complete, the chimney is wholly or, in the case of *Odynerus reniformis*, partially demolished and the clay is used to seal the entrance to the burrow. *Odynerus melano-cephalus* excavates its nest in bare patches of soil and constructs rather short curved chimneys (Fig. 17b) made up of a great number of small pellets well cemented together (Nielsen 1932), which may be as high as 4 cm from the ground (Billups 1884). According to Drogoszewski (in Blüthgen 1961), *Odynerus simillimus* F. Morawitz constructs nests similar to *Odynerus spinipes* and *reniformis* with very short (0·5 cm long) chimneys.

The Tube-Dwellers

The utilization of hollow cavities in plant material for nests is practised by a wide variety of bees and wasps. Typically, a nest consists of a series of linearly arranged cells along the length of a hollowed-out stem, the cells being separated by mud partitions. The diameter of the tube used, the numbers of cells to a nest, and the architectural details of the partitions vary according to the species of inhabitant. The variety of tubes used by wasps is considerable, although plants with large pith centres such as Blackberry (*Rubus*) and Elder (*Sambucus*) are most commonly used, and also the straw of thatched roofs, reed stems, holes in walls or masonry, and the disused burrows of wood-boring insects. Among some of the more bizarre nesting sites of these wasps are the central hole of a cotton reel used by *Ancistrocerus parietinus* (L.) (Richardson 1920), beetle flight-holes in wooden posts by *Microdynerus exilis* (Herrich-Schaeffer) (Jones 1937), *Ancistrocerus parietum* (Alfken 1915), and *Symmorphus sinuatissimus* Richards (Morley 1898), and the utilization of disused plant galls of *Cynips kollari* by *Ancistro-cerus trifasciatus* (Müller) (Fitch 1879) and *Symmorphus sinuatissimus* (Bischoff 1927). The exploitation of fortuitous holes and cavities has been frequently recorded. For example, the use of holes in the old mortar between brickwork by *Ancistrocerus parietum* (George 1906), *A. nigricornis* (Curtis) (Spooner 1935), and *A. antilope* (Westwood 1834), the construction of a 14-celled nest in an old razor-case by *Ancistrocerus quadratus* (Panzer) (Smith 1867), and the use of folds in a piece of paper, and the bore of a flute by the same species. *Ancistro-cerus parietinus* built its cells in the gap between books and the back of a bookcase on one occasion (Hobby 1938). Perhaps *Ancistrocerus parietum* is the leader in exploiting odd situations, nests being found in a disused embryo nest of *Paravespula vulgaris* (Fig. 17e), in the angle formed between a bookcase and window ledge (Latter 1935), and in disused nests of *Odynerus* species (Nielsen 1932). One of the most curious instances of nesting by an eumenid wasp is the case of an *Ancistrocerus antilope* female which built and provisioned a nest in the cavity of a window frame of a commuter train in France (Pierre 1922). Despite the train making several trips each day, the wasp suc-ceeded in completing its nest.

When a suitable tube or hole has been found, the wasp first clears out any remaining pith and debris and begins the collection of building materials. Most wasps use damp pellets of mud or clay, often collected from areas of bare ground where water, stored in the crop, is used to soften the soil. Many species construct a preliminary plug, probably stimulated by the roughness of protruding fibres at the end of the tube, but the habit is certainly not universal, even in the same species. The preliminary plug may be built flush with the end of the tube or as a partition some distance from the inner end (Fig. 19d). After provision-ing the first cell, a partition is built close to or several millimetres from the stored prey. The thickness of these cell partitions varies. In *Ancistrocerus antilope* for example, they are 0·5 to 4·0 mm thick, average 1·5 mm (Krombein 1967), and in *Microdynerus exilis* they are 0·5 to 2·5 mm thick (Danks 1971). Variations in the material used to make partitions are many, for example *Gymnomerus laevipes* (Shuckard) uses a fine mude cement while *Microdynerus exilis* sometimes utilizes the remains of excavated pith and incorporates fairly coarse grains of sand (Danks 1971).

The cell partitions exhibit two constant features in their structure, namely, the surface facing the inner end of the tube is generally convex and roughened in texture, while the outward facing surface is concave and smooth (Fig. 19c) – two factors that have considerable importance in the orientation of the wasp larva and its subsequent emergence as an adult. The partitions also serve the more immediate functions of protecting the food store and wasp larva from the elements, inhibiting the entry of parasitic and predatory insects, and providing adequate living space for the wasp while preventing cannibalism between adjacent larvae.

The length of provisioned cells varies between and among species, and also between consecutive cells made by the same female. Taylor (1922), Rau (1932, 1945), Cooper (1953), and Krombein (1967) amongst others have amassed data on the relationship between the size of cells

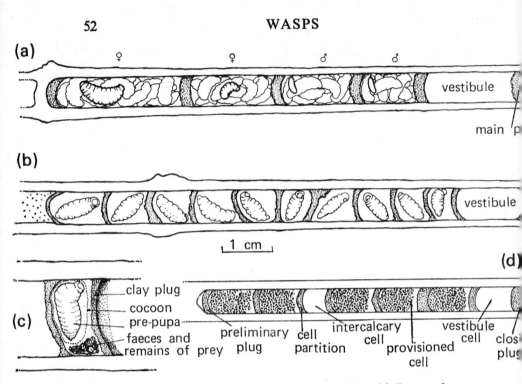

Figure 19. Nest structures in tube-dwelling Eumenidae: (a) *Symmorphus connexus* (after Jørgensen 1942); (b) *Symmorphus parietinus*; (c) detail of one cell of *S. parietinus*; (d) terminology (after Krombein 1967).

and the sex of wasp inhabitant in a variety of stem-nesting Eumenidae. In the American species *Odynerus foraminatus* Saussure for example, females were found in cells of 19 to 25 mm length and males in cells 10 to 13 mm (Rau 1932), and in *Ancistrocerus antilope*, the mean length of female cells was 21·6 mm and 17·2 mm in male cells, although this pattern was not always adhered to rigidly (Krombein 1967). The longer, female cells are normally the first to be constructed at the inner end of the tube.

A slight variation on the theme of partitioned cells in tubes is the nest constructed by *Gymnomerus laevipes* which makes thimble-shaped cells seated one on top of the other (Fig. 17g), or side by side if built in a horizontal stem (Bristowe 1948, Danks 1971).

The vestibular cell (Fig. 19d) is found in most stem-boring aculeates (Krombein 1967), being variable in length but with a thicker terminal plug at the open end of the tube. In *Ancistrocerus antilope* the plug is 1 to 10 mm thick (mean, 4·5 mm) (Krombein 1967). Occasionally, the vestibular cell is divided into two or more lengths by the construction of thin partitions, their function possibly originating as a protection against unfriendly callers.

Intercalary cells (Fig. 18d) – empty cells interspersed between pro-visioned cells – are sometimes found in nests and, because they are sealed with partitions similar to vestibular plugs, Krombein (1967) has suggested that they may be a relic from the evolutionary past when wasps made single cells with a protective vestibular cell in the outer part of the tube. With increasing specialization, the wasps have placed several of these single cells together to produce a series of cells, inter-spersed with the empty, intercalary cells. However, other stimuli to build intercalary cells could have arisen as a result of parasitism, inter-ference with the preceding cell, or contamination of its contents.

The Mud-Dauber

Although the name 'mud-dauber' is generally used to describe species of the sphecoid, *Sceliphron*, which construct groups of mud cells on walls and provision them with spiders, this descriptive name certainly applies to one of our British wasps, *Ancistrocerus oviventris*. This species is a crude builder in clay, its nests consisting of several cells covered by a layer of protective, camouflaging mud. The nests are certainly less aesthetically pleasing than those of *Sceliphron*, so much so that Bignell (1881) described them as looking like lumps of mud which had been carelessly thrown against a wall. The wasp often utilizes crevices in rocks (Fig. 17h), but also indentations in stone columns or the carved lettering of monuments and gravestones (Bignell 1881). There is one record of the wasp building its nest inside a lock, the hard clay not surprisingly putting it out of action (Sheppard 1926).

The nest is generally composed of 3 to 5 cells, although a 14-cell nest has been recorded (Nielsen 1932). Though little has been published on the nesting behaviour of *Ancistrocerus oviventris*, the collection of building materials and their manipulation in cell construction are probably similar to other wasps which fashion mud nests. The individual cells have smooth interior surfaces but are rough externally and, as seen in Figure 17 ii-iv, a row of cells is built initially on the substrate, with additional cells placed on top of them. When the last cell has been provisioned, several loads of clay are collected and used to mask the individual cell shapes with a protective layer (Nielson 1932). The Australasian potter wasp, *Eumenes latreilli petiolaris* Schulz, similarly camouflages its cells by plastering mud over groups of them (Laird 1949).

The Potter Wasp

The only British representative of the true potter wasps is *Eumenes coarctatus* (L.), a heathland species found locally in southern England. The delicate, spherical clay cells are fixed to stones and walls, or the

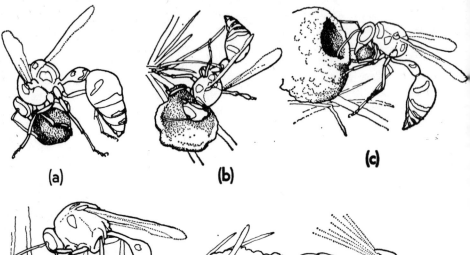

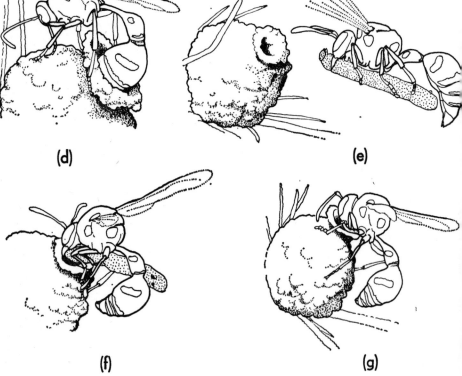

Figure 20. *Eumenes coarctatus,* sequence of nesting behaviour (drawn from photographs by Olberg 1959): (a) collecting soil; (b) building base of cell on pine shoot; (c) returning with mud pellet; (d) ovipositing; (e) returning with prey; (f) provisioning cell; (g) sealing cell opening with mud pellet.

stems of heather (*Calluna*) and gorse (*Ulex*). Although several may be placed side by side, they never form a mass or clump as in *Ancistrocerus oviventris*. Observations on the British species are meagre, and this account of *Eumenes'* biology is based largely on the classic work of Iwata (1953) on the Japanese species, supplemented by the excellent photographic records of Olberg (1959).

In common with other eumenid wasps which use mud in cell construction, *Eumenes* collects raw materials from dry earth, using water to soften the ground and make the soil malleable (Fig. 20a). The water is obtained from streams, ponds, puddles, and even the dew on plants, one intake of water into the wasp's crop being sufficient to prepare 2 to 4 pellets of clay. The pellet is carried back to the nest site in the mandibles, supported by the forelegs which help to knead the bolus of moist clay. The weight of moist pellets was 33 to 68 mg depending on the size and species of females. By measuring the weight of individual pellets comprising the nest and the total weight of completed, multi-celled nests, Iwata was able to estimate that in one species, a female carried 740 loads of clay, involving travel of approximately 158 km between nest and soil source, while another female travelled 335 km during nest construction.

The initiation of a cell involves the preparation of a clay disc or plate (Fig. 20b) which anchors the cell to the substrate. The technique employed by *Eumenes* in building a cell involves the construction of clay rings, first to the basal disc and later on top of each other, the wasp working the clay with the mandibles and forelegs, with her head directed towards the centre of the pot. The pellets of mud are drawn sideways and upwards, the female thinning the pellets economically as the walls take shape (Fig. 20c). The inside wall of the cell is smoothed by the wasp's mouthparts while the tarsi of the forelegs support the outside of the cell which is left somewhat rougher in texture. When the pot is complete, the female turns the wall of the neck inside out to form a collar, so that the cell assumes its typical flask shape.

The time required to build one pot is remarkably brief, 1 to 2 hours in the Japanese species while in the Afro-Asiatic species, *Eumenes maxillosus* de Geer, 5 cells were built in two days, the rate of cell construction being dependent on the level of rainfall (Roubaud 1916). The number of pellets used to build one cell varied from 10 to 30 in the Japanese *Eumenes* species. Closure of the pot is generally effected with a single pellet of mud (Fig. 20g) after which the collar is smoothed down.

It is of interest that the mud nests of some eumenid wasps are camouflaged with vegetable materials after their completion. For example, some species incorporate lichens into the outer layer of the cell, the European *Symmorphus bifasciatus* (L.) covers the terminal plug of its tube nest with chips of wood (Malyshev 1911), and the Japanese *Eumenes architectus* Smith collects wood pulp like the social wasps and plasters the surface of its cell with paper (Iwata 1939).

FORAGING ACTIVITIES

With the completion of the cell, the female lays an egg inside it and then begins the search for suitable prey with which to provision it. Most eumenid wasps store larvae of Lepidoptera, principally tortricids and geometrids, although some wasps prey on beetle larvae such as *Phytonomus* species and curculionids. The range of species preyed upon by the wasp depends to some extent on genetic factors and also upon the relative availability of prey within the hunting area of the wasp. In *Eumenes pedunculatus* (Panzer), for example, more than thirty different species of larval Lepidoptera have been recorded as prey (Chevalier 1922, and others) although the dominant prey species were *Cochylis hybridella* (Huebner) and *Plutella xylostella* (L.). *Odynerus spinipes* and *Odynerus reniformis* prey on *Phytonomus* species (Micheli 1930 and Adlerz 1907), *Symmorphus crassicornis* (Panzer) preys on *Chrysomela populi* (L.) (Smith 1858), and *Odynerus laevipes* stores the curculionid, *Hyperba* (Bristowe 1948). A list of prey found in cells of eumenid wasps is given in Table 2.

TABLE 2

The number of provisioned larvae per cell in some eumenid wasps

WASP SPECIES	PREY	NUMBER OF LARVAE PER CELL	SOURCE
Eumenes spp. (Japan)	Geometridae	5 (3–8)	
"	Tortricidae	9 (4–16)	
"	Noctuidae	5 (3–8)	Iwata 1953
"		9 (7–11)	
"		12 (3–35)	
P. herrichii	Tortricidae	11 (8–13)	Spooner 1934
O. spinipes	*Phytonomus* sp. (Chrysomelidae)	— (7–33)	Nielsen 1932
O. spinipes	*Hyperba* sp. (Curculionidae)	30 —	Bristowe 1948
A. oviventris	Microlepidoptera	— (4–8)	Mjoberg 1909
G. laevipes	*Hyperba* sp.	— (21–22)	Bristowe 1948
A. antilope	Gelechioidea, Pyralidae	9 (4–15)	Cooper 1953
A. antilope	Gelechioidea, Pyralidae	7 (3–13)	Medler & Fye 1956
S. sinuatissimus		— (10–17)	Jørgensen 1942

ranges are given in parentheses

Hunting Behaviour

Females searching for prey fly from plant to plant, spending much time running over the vegetation until a host larva is found. Several prey species inhabit silk webs or a combination of web and rolled leaves, their extraction by the wasp being of particular interest. Isely (1913) has described how the American species, *Odynerus dorsalis F.*, extracts caterpillars of the Spotted Skipper from the Poppy Mallow. When the female comes across the crumpled leaf which indicates the host's location, it tears at the silken nest, first one end and then the other, working furiously to dislodge the caterpillar. After one to several minutes of frenzied activity, the wasp jerks the prey from its protective cover, seizes it by the neck and stabs it two or three times beneath the thorax with its sting. After malaxating the prey briefly, it is carried back to the nest. Spooner (1934) has seen similar behaviour in *Pseudepipona herrichii* which collects tortricid caterpillars from their webbed cocoons in the heather. The wasp first bites a hole through the web and then thrusts its sting into it until the caterpillar wriggles out through a hole and falls to the ground. To locate the prey, the wasp drops from the web to the ground beneath it and proceeds to search in the immediate vicinity for signs of the caterpillar. If the prey is able to crawl into the undergrowth quickly enough it may escape detection while the wasp repeats the free-fall from the web two or three times.

Almost identical behaviour has been recorded in *Ancistrocerus antilope* by Mauvezin (1886), although Buckle (1929) maintained that the wasp abandoned caterpillars which had dropped on to the ground, and Cooper (1953) never saw this species cause caterpillars to drop to the ground when hunting prey.

Stinging

As soon as the prey is captured it is immobilized by the wasp, mainly by stinging and, to a greater or lesser extent, by chewing it. It was believed by early workers that the paralysis of prey was obtained by the wasp injecting venom directly into one or more of the thoracic nerve ganglia, but the studies of Rathmayer (1962) on the bee-hunting wasp, *Philanthus triangulum F.*, has shown that the effect on the prey is probably brought about by peripheral blockage in the main neuromuscular region (the thorax) and not through the central nervous system.

The prey is either seized by the anterior end or, after capture, manipulated so that it is held at this end by the mandibles and forelegs. The abdomen is then curved forward and the sting thrust into the thoracic and proximal segments of the gaster. Iwata (1953) has shown that the thoracic and first few segments of the abdomen are paralysed, the distal abdominal segments rarely so (Table 3), and that pupation of the unparalysed portion of the caterpillar may take place in the cell.

TABLE 3

The degree of paralysis of geometrid caterpillars following stinging by *Eumenes*
(from Iwata 1953)

PREY	SEGMENTS OF CATERPILLAR BODY												
	Head	Thorax							Abdomen					
		I	II	III	I	II	III	IV	V	VI	VII	VIII	IX	X
1	2	0	0	0	0	1	2	2	2	2	2	2	2	2
2	2	1	0	1	0	0	1	1	1	2	2	2	2	2
3	2	1	1	0	0	0	0	0	2	2	2	2	2	2
4	2	1	0	0	0	1	2	2	2	2	0	2	2	2

0 = complete paralysis; 1 = feeble movements; 2 = active when stimulated by a pin prick

The *Eumenes* studied by Iwata sting their prey 3 to 5 times, and in *Ancistrocerus antilope* Cooper (1953) found an average of 2·9 sting 'blood clots' on the gelechiid caterpillar hosts.

Prey Carriage

Generally, the prey is held by the mandibles which grip the neck region so that the ventral side is uppermost, with the forelegs helping to hold the prey close to the ventral surface of the wasp's body. There are certain variations in prey carriage techniques, depending on the species of wasp and also the size of prey (see Fig. 20e). For example, *Symmorphus connexus* does not apparently use her legs to transport prey but simply lets it dangle from her mandibles while in flight, although if the prey is heavy, the middle pair of legs is used to support it (Jørgensen 1942).

Provisioning

When the female returns to her nest with a prey larva, she pushes it down into the burrow, pot (Fig. 20f), or chimney with her head, then backs out of the nest. If the larva is incompletely paralysed it may prove difficult to push into the burrow and Isely (1913) has observed an *Odynerus* female malaxate a prey larva into submission after several unsuccessful attempts to get it into the burrow. Latter (1913) reports that *Ancistrocerus parietum* pushes its prey into the cell by butting them with her head.

The numbers of prey per cell vary considerably, depending on the species of wasp, size of cell and sex of prospective occupant, size and instar of prey, and the species of prey. Some data illustrating the numbers of prey larvae per cell is given in Table 2, which give some idea of the extremes to be found. Meddler and Fye (1956) found a significant correlation between the length of cell and the number of stored prey in *Ancistrocerus antilope*, while Krombein (1967) noted that cells in which females would be produced contained an average of 7·4 larvae (range 6-10), with 6·1 larvae (range 4-8) in male cells. Spooner (1934) observed in *Pseudepipona herrichii* that the variations in number of prey per cell were due principally to differences in the size of the prey.

Although the prey in a cell is generally of one species, there are records of more than one species in a cell; for example, pyralid and gelechiid caterpillars in a cell of *Ancistrocerus antilope* (Cooper 1953). Provisioning with different prey species, which occurs most frequently in the autumn, is possibly a reflection of dwindling caterpillar populations which would force the wasp to consider a wider host list.

The prey are generally packed quite tightly into the cells, frequently in a tangled mass with few vacant spaces, although in long cells of *Ancistrocerus antilope*, the caterpillars may be placed neatly in the cell, head to tail (Malyshev 1911).

The time required to provision a cell may vary considerably, weather conditions, and prey availability being major controlling factors. One *Ancistrocerus antilope* female made and provisioned one cell a day for twelve consecutive days, and another female completed five cells in two days, although in cool weather, one wasp took more than a week to provision three cells (Cooper 1953). The *Eumenes* species studied by Iwata in Japan spent between half an hour and nine hours to secure a caterpillar prey, the average for different species varying from 1·25 to 3·7 hours per victim. Isely noted that one wasp collected eighteen caterpillars, one every 1·5 to 8 minutes. An *Odynerus spinipes* female collected 7 larvae in 54 minutes (an average of one larva every 7·7 minutes), the daily average being 22 larvae (Bristowe 1948).

DEVELOPMENT

Oviposition

In all eumenid wasps the female lays an egg in the completed cell before foraging for prey, although Isely (1913) suggests that in some American species, a few prey may be placed in the cell before oviposition. To lay an egg, the wasp normally backs into the cell or inserts the abdomen into the completed cell (Fig. 20d), oviposition taking from one to several minutes. Hartman (1944) has observed an *Odynerus* female oviposit in a glass tube in which she had constructed her nest. Once she has backed into the cell, the female's abdomen contracts slowly and rhythmically, the tip of the abdomen being retracted and extended, each extension causing the tip to touch the wall of the cell. Soon, a whitish secretion appears which is applied to the wall where it sticks in place and, as the abdomen is withdrawn, a thread is drawn out which hardens instantly to form a flexible but strong suspensory filament. As the abdomen continues to be moved, the egg body slides out attached to the filament.

The position of the egg in the cell may be of some significance for, in tube dwellers it is normally attached to the ceiling of the cell near its inner end (Cooper 1953), and in flask cells, it is suspended from the upper surface of the cell, which would facilitate subsequent provisioning without damaging the egg when prey was pushed into the cell (Iwata 1953).

The Egg

The eggs of all British Eumenidae, except *Gymnomerus laevipes* (Bristowe 1948), have a thin filament of variable length, attached to the cell wall, with the egg body suspended from it (Fig. 21a). The egg body is white, distinctly glistening shortly after being laid, with an elongate-kidney shape, the egg having a slight curve in the dorso-lateral plane. In *Ancistrocerus antilope*, the egg is about 2·8 mm long and 0·9 mm wide, with a filament of about 0·7 mm (Krombein 1967) which, at its distal end, is expanded to form a small attachment disc. The filament is

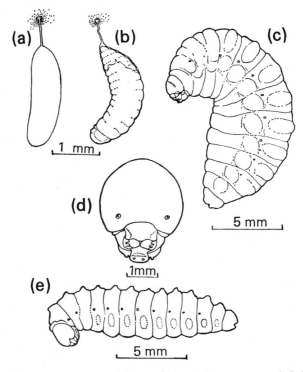

Figure 21. Immature stages of Eumenidae: (a) egg suspended by filament; (b) first-instar larva of *Symmorphus sinuatissimus* (after Jørgensen 1942); (c) mature larva of *Eumenes* (after Grandi 1934); (d) head of mature larva of *S. sinuatissimus* (after Enslin 1921); (e) pre-pupa of *S. sinuatissimus* (after Enslin 1921).

apparently longer in tube dwellers than in other types of nesters (Jørgensen 1942).

The egg hatches in 2 to 4 days (mean, 2·5 days) in *Ancistrocerus antilope* (Cooper 1953), and 2 to 3 days in *Symmorphus connexus* (Curtis) (Jørgensen 1942), although the egg period may be shorter if high temperatures prevail (e.g. 45 hours in a Japanese *Eumenes*, Iwata 1953).

The Larva

At the time of hatching, the chorion of the egg becomes wrinkled at its caudal end and splits along about one third of the way from the cephalic end so that the head of the larva comes out. The first-instar larva may either slip out of the shell immediately (as in *Eumenes*, Iwata 1953) or remain suspended within it for a day or so while feeding on the nearest prey (Fig. 21b) (Jørgensen 1942).

The young larva sucks the body juices after lacerating the body and puncturing the cuticle of the prey with its mandibles. As the larva grows, the mouthparts become more heavily sclerotized with suceeding instars, and it is able to eat the residues of sucked-out prey, finally consuming much of their exuviae, but declining the hard head capsules. One larva of *Symmorphus connexus* was seen to consume 26 prey in six days and when offered further hosts under experimental conditions continued to feed, finally eating 42 out of the total of 50 prey offered to it (Jørgensen 1942).

The duration of the larval stages was 6 days (range, 5 to 7) in *Ancistrocerus antilope* (Cooper 1953), about 15 days in *Ancistrocerus oviventris* (Bignell 1881), and 7 days (range, 5 to 12) in the Japanese *Eumenes* (Iwata 1953). There are probably five larval instars (3 to 5, according to Cooper 1953) in common with the social Vespidae (Potter 1965). The eumenid larvae accumulate undigested food in the midgut lumen during the feeding stage in the same way as the larvae of social wasps.

Pupation

When feeding is completed, the larva rests for a day or so (Medler and Fye 1956) or immediately begins (Jørgensen 1942) to spin the cocoon. Many eumenid wasps spin a brown plate ('spin-plate') at the base of the cell (e.g. *Symmorphus connexus*, *S. sinuatissimus*, and *Ancistrocerus trifasciatus*, Jørgensen 1942) from which the cocoon is initially anchored. The cocoon is generally thin, whitish yellow or brown, and rather tough and, depending on the species, may be firmly attached to the cell walls (e.g. *Microdynerus exilis*, Danks 1971; *Symmorphus connexus*, Jørgensen 1942) or lie relatively freely within the cell.

In *Ancistrocerus parietinus*, the remains of prey larvae lie outside the cocoon (Fig. 18c), but in *Eumenes* species, the cocoon is in two layers with prey remnants between them. Towards the end, or shortly after spinning, the waste products stored in the gut are voided in the form of moist but compact pellets which are invariably placed at the posterior end of the cell in the tube-dwelling species and possibly serve as a cue for orientation within the cell.

If development proceeds without an intervening winter diapause, the pre-pupal period may occupy 5 to 6 days (Jørgensen 1942), pupation taking place in a further 3·5 to 4·5 days and emergence of adults 15 days (range, 11-17 days) after pupation occurred (Cooper 1953). Thus, development from the time of oviposition to emergence of the adult was 29 to 35 days in non-diapausing *Ancistrocerus antilope*. If development takes place in late summer in multivoltine (two or more generations per year) species, or if the wasp is univoltine (one generation per year), the pre-pupal stage may last as long as six to eight months.

During pupation, the compound eyes become pigmented first, the black pigmentation of the body beginning in the thoracic region and spreading throughout the rest of the body. Future yellow areas of cuticle appear greyish white initially, until the black pigmentation of the integument is completed, and they then gradually become bright yellow. Once the yellow coloration is complete, the pupal skin wrinkles and in a day or two, the skin is cast. The teneral adults remain within the cocoon for some days as the cuticle hardens and the wings become strong. As the adult begins to emerge from the cell, it moistens the hard clay plugs (where they exist), using quantities of a clear fluid stored in the body, thereby softening the clay and facilitating its exit. A summary of the durations of the immature stages is given in Table 4.

TABLE 4

The durations of the immature stages of *Ancistrocerus antilope* (in days)
(after Cooper 1953)

STAGE	DURATION		DAY OF OCCURRENCE
	Mean	range	
Hatching of egg	2·5	2–4	2·5
Feeding completed	6	5–7	8·5
Spinning started	1	1	9·5
Cocoon finished	3	2–4	12·5
Meconium shed	1·5	1–2	14·0
Pupal stage	4	3·5–4·5	18·0
Pigmentation complete	13	11–17	31·0
Pupal exuvium shed	—	1–2·5	33·0
Emergence of adult	—	2–3	35–36

Adult Emergence

Wasps which have matured in a series of cells in narrow tubes where turning round is often impossible, must be orientated towards the nest exit and not perish in vain attempts to emerge through the blind end of the tube or burrow.

The factors which determine successful orientation in stem-dwelling eumenid wasps have been studied by Cooper (1957) in America. When the larva finishes feeding and begins to spin its cocoon, it moves around the cell from one end to the other and finally faces towards the end of the cell which leads to the exit. Experimental manipulation of the cell walls showed that this non-random orientation is due to their shape and texture. At its inner end, the wall is concave and smooth while the outer end is rough in texture and slightly convex or at least irregular in shape. Any of these features alone acts as a signal to the larva, and a comparison of textures or shapes is unnecessary. The concavity of the inner wall is apparently the strongest stimulus and the rough outer wall probably reinforces the 'message'. This delayed message to offspring by the parent female was described by Cooper as 'a beautiful instance of communication, in a digital code and with stored information, between two dissimilar organisms (the adult and larva) whose interrelated activities are widely disparate in time'.

Because the eggs in the inner cells of tube-dwellers are laid several days before the completion of the outer cells, it may be thought that the inner-cell occupants should mature first and find their exit blocked by wasps still undergoing their development. However, there are several factors which prevent this sequence of events, the most important being the sex of the occupant. As seen earlier in this chapter, females generally occur in the first-built cells with males in the outer cells. Female cells are generally longer and contain more prey which would promote a subsequent increase in the duration of the larval stage of the wasp. Pupation of males following the completion of larval feeding, tends to occur one or two days before females and Krombein (1967) has noted that the male's pupal period may be 2 to 4 days shorter than that of the female. These cumulative factors tend to favour the more rapid development of the males. A further point ensuring successful emergence is the fact that adult wasps spend some days in the cells while wings and cuticle harden so that, when emergence begins, they should be ready to leave the nest, generally in groups of males followed later by females. Krombein (1967) suggests that the vibrations caused by adults chewing through the clay partitions may act as a signal to wasps in adjacent cells to begin their exodus. If the occupant of a cell near the exit dies during development, the succeeding wasps must chew through an extra clay wall and possibly a dead adult, a feat not always accomplished successfully, with the subsequent death of all wasps in the series behind it (Krombein 1967).

PARASITES, PREDATORS AND ASSOCIATES

The characteristic nest of the eumenid wasp provides a protected environment of relatively high constant humidity, rich in prey, and with a sluggish wasp inhabitant. It is therefore of little wonder that this ecological niche has been exploited by a variety of entomophagous and associated organisms. To take advantage of the situation, the major problem besetting the intruder is that of access to a cell – a problem which has been solved in often ingenious ways. A further consideration is that of exit from the cell if the associated organism has no means of its own to get through a clay wall. These organisms rely on the adult wasp, and a delicate balance must be maintained with the host and its food supply to ensure an eventual departure.

Acarina – The Mites

Many associations between mites and eumenid wasps have been recorded, from the casual to the highly integrated, the most familiar being the saproglyphid mite, *Kennethiella* (=*Ensliniella*) *trisetosa* (Cooreman), associated with *Ancistrocerus antilope*. The biology of this mite has been principally studied by Cooper (1955) and Krombein (1967).

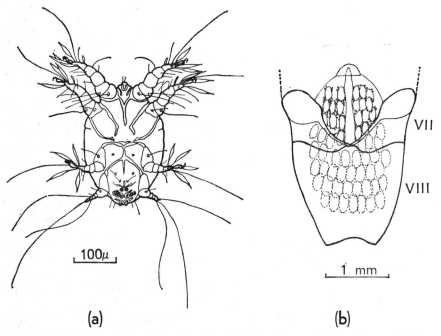

(a)   (b)

Figure 22. The saproglyphid mite, *Kennethiella trisetosa* (after Cooper 1955): (a) ventral view of deutonymph; (b) mites in acarinarium within ventral genital chamber of *Ancistrocerus antilope* male.

V. Winter and spring queens
(top left) Hibernating queen with wings tucked under the abdomen.
(bottom left) *P. vulgaris* queen adding pulp to the envelope of an embryo nest.
(below) Same embryo nest with envelope partially removed to show queen tending larvae in their cells.

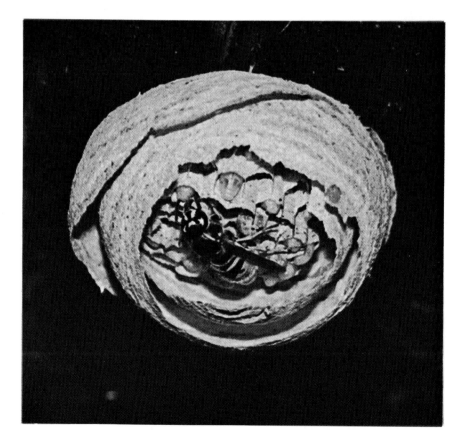

K. trisetosa is a perfectly adapted parasite, feeding on the pupal stage of the wasp but never causing its death. Emerging male wasps bear large numbers of hypopi (the immature, resting stage or deuto-nymph, Fig. 22a) on various parts of the propodeum, notably on the ventro-lateral and posterior faces, while the females have none or very few of them when they emerge from the cell. In a sample of 155 males and 122 females, only 12 per cent of the females and 83 per cent of the males harboured mites, while the maximum load of deutonymphs was 407 (mean, 134) on the male and 19 (mean, 4·3) on the female. These differences are due to the habit of the female wasp larvae which clean out their cells before pupation, thereby destroying any mites which may occur, probably by devouring them for mite remains have been found in larval faeces.

On the male propodeum, the mites are arranged regularly rather like shingles or tiles on a roof facing posteriorly or, if the load is particularly dense, perpendicularly to the surface of the cuticle. In about half of the infested male wasps, Cooper found large numbers of mites (180 or more) in the genital chamber. This is a broad but shallow space between the combined eighth and ninth sternites and the ventral surface of the phallus, with the mites visible through the transparent cuticle of the eighth sternite. Here, they form rows, facing outwards towards the junction of the eighth tergite and ninth sternite (Fig. 22b). In male wasps there is a negative correlation between the numbers of mites on the propodeum and those in the genital acarinarium (place on host occupied by mites) which is caused by the migration of mites from the propodeum to the genital acarinarium during copulation by the wasp. For example, large loads of mites are found on the propodeum in young male wasps, medium loads in both acarinaria of older ones,

TABLE 5

Pattern of mite movements between a male and female *Ancistrocerus antilope*
(after Cooper 1955)

LOCATION OF MITES	NUMBERS OF MITES					
	newly emerged wasps before copulation*		before the observed copulation†		after the observed copulation	
	♂	♀	♂	♀	♂	♀
Propodeum	238+	0	11	0	21	14
Genital chamber	0	0	227	0	67	121
Total	238+	0	238	0	88	135

* the number of mites on the male would be greatly in excess of 238.
† by this stage, the male had mated one or more times, with the resulting migration of mites from propodeum to genitalia, and the presumed loss of some of them to the female(s).

F*

and small numbers in the genital acarinarium of the oldest wasps. During repeated matings, the mites migrate from the propodeum to the genitalia of the male and from there to the female until the genital acarinarium is exhausted of mites or nearly so (see Table 5).

During intromission when the male phallus is extended and thrust into the genital opening of the female, the mites on the propodeal acarinaria are, to quote Cooper, 'suddenly galvanized to activity and they break ranks'. A few mites climb straight on to the female wasp, but the majority stream down the male's abdomen and reach the wasps' genital openings where a constant movement of mites to and fro may be seen. After copulation, the female scrapes off any mites on her abdomen, but the male grooms less vigorously and mites which failed to get to the genital opening move back to their original positions on the propodeum.

The stimulus to move from propodeum to genitalia is evoked only during actual intromission, mechanical and other disturbing factors failing to stimulate any movement of the mites.

It is probable that the mites which find their way into the genital opening of the female wasp are transferred to a cell when the abdomen is introduced during oviposition. The numbers of deutonymphs making their way to the cell are few, Krombein (1966) finding from one to four per cell, and it is likely that they change into the next stage, the tritonymph, soon after arrival, becoming adu't while the wasp larva is developing. The non-gravid adult mites are about 700 μ long, and they feed on the pre-pupal stage of the wasp by sucking in the host's haemolymph after piercing its cuticle. Shortly after the pupation of the wasp, the gravid mite – now 1,080 μ long and 830 μ wide – lays its eggs on the host's body or the cocoon walls. These eggs hatch after 2 to 5 days into six-legged larvae 200 μ long and after a further day or so, moult into eight-legged protonymphs. As the adult colour patterns of the wasp develop, the mites moult again to form the deutonymphs – the hypopial stage – and begin to cluster on the propodeum of the teneral male adult.

Such cases of venereal transmission of mites have been recorded in other species of *Ancistrocerus* (Cooper 1955) but it is certainly not universal in all mite/eumenid wasp associations. Some mites of the genus *Vespacarus*, for example, live as hypopi on the abdomens of both male and female wasps, often in acarinaria formed by a depression at the base of the second abdominal tergite, and are neither transferred during mating nor found in the genital openings. Still other species have no specific acarinaria but cluster beneath the margins of abdominal tergites.

Certain acarine mites are predatory on wasps, destroying their eggs and developing on the food stores, relying on wasps from adjacent mite-free cells to provide egress from the cell and transfer during the hypopial stage. Others are scavengers within nests, using the adult wasp for transport but not feeding on it at any stage (Krombein 1967).

Pyemotid mites, including the ubiquitous grain-itch mite, *Pyemotes*, are commonly found in nests which they probably enter during the provisioning stage. Attaching itself to the wasp larva or its prey, the female mite feeds on the haemolymph until its abdomen swells into a large sac in which the eggs develop into adults. The male mites emerge first, inseminating the females as they emerge from the genital pore of the parent (Krombein 1967). The pyemotid mites kill the wasp larvae by virtually sucking them dry, and can be a serious pest of the wasp, especially in laboratory cultures.

Stylopization by Strepsiptera

The Strepsiptera are an unusual group of parasitic insects, sometimes placed by taxonomists in the order Coleoptera with which they have some similarities, particularly with the parasitic beetles of the family Rhipiphoridae, but the superficial resemblance is probably due to the convergent evolution of the two groups. The presence of a strepsipteran in an adult insect causes certain internal disturbances due to displacement of the viscera, and can cause curious alterations in external structure and effect the secondary sexual characters so that one sex may assume certain morphological attributes of the other (Salt 1928).

Typically, the adult female (Fig. 23d) retains much of its larval form with a sac-like body enclosed in the final larval skin, and a chitinized cephalothorax. The cephalothorax is extruded between the abdominal sclerites of the host, the rest of the body being hidden in its abdominal cavity (Fig. 23a, b). The females are structurally degraded for they lack an alimentary system, food being absorbed from the haemolymph of the host through the body wall. A brood canal runs anteriorly, opening by a slit in the cephalothorax through which the first-instar, hexapod larvae — the triungulin larvae (Fig. 23e) — leave the female after developing viviparously in her body. Several thousand triungulin larvae, which are about 0·5 mm long, are produced by a single female. Linsley and MacSwain (1957) found 9-10,000 triungulin larvae per female in *Stylops pacifica*. These small larvae scatter over the body of the host and thence to flowers visited by the wasp. Once it has gripped on to another (female) wasp visiting the flower, it is transported to a nest where it eventually enters the host larva.

Eggs and pupae are unsuitable host material and Krombein (1967) has found five dead stylopid larvae in the dead embryo of a wasp. Entry through the host cuticle is apparently brought about through enzymatic action and once inside the host, the parasite moults into a

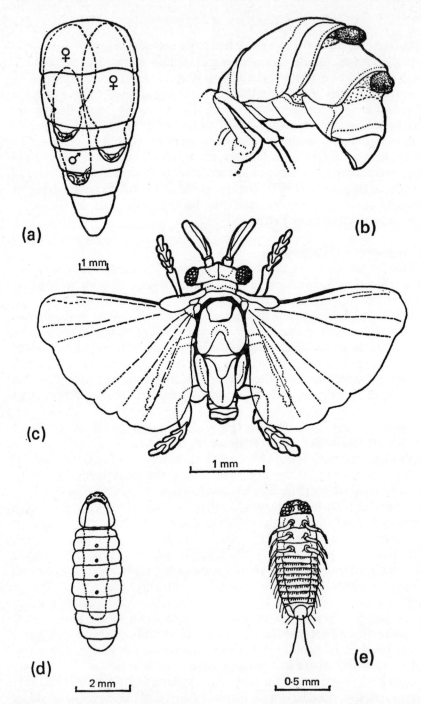

Figure 23. Strepsiptera: (a) abdomen of parasitized male (after Maeta 1963);
(b) abdomen of female wasp with two male strepsiptera (from a photograph by
Maeta 1963); (c) male *Stylops* (after Pierce, from Imms 1957); (d) adult female;
(e) triungulin larva (after Bohart 1941).

white, legless larva, growing rapidly within the haemocoele. Pupation and adult development take place within the last larval skin or skins of the parasite.

Strepsiptera protrude through the intersegmental membranes of the adult host after the wasp pupates but before it emerges from the cell (Krombein 1967). Extrusion is brought about by the pupal parasite working its way through the membranes between the abdominal sclerites. The males, which Salt (1928) describes as 'grotesque little creatures', are about 4 mm long (Fig. 23c). A remarkable feature of the male is the reduction of the forewings, which look like the halteres of Diptera, and the enlargement of the hindwings. They are strong fliers, seeking out female Strepsiptera that remain partly extruded from the wasp, during their brief adult existence of a few hours (Gauss 1959). To facilitate insemination, the male has a long, hooked aedeagus with which it is able to reach the partially concealed female.

The parasitization of a wasp by a strepsipteran is called stylopization, the effect on the host ranging from significant morphological and even anatomical changes (particularly in the andrenid bees, Salt 1928, 1931) to minor changes in the secondary sexual characters such as colour, shape of clypeus, puncturation of the cuticle, and distribution of setae. The effects are probably greater when the parasite invades a very immature host larva, but strepsiptera do not penetrate the host's organs although organs may be displaced as the parasites grow. Stylopized *Odynerus* females have been seen to copulate satisfactorily (Salt 1931). The distortion of viscera and some reduction in the reproductive organs may result from heavy parasitization, these internal changes being caused by inadequate nutrition following depletion of the host's fat body and haemolymph. Salt (1928) concludes that stylopization causes a disturbance in the nutritive balance of the host which may in turn affect the sex hormones, thereby producing intersex forms.

Data relating to rates of parasitism by strepsiptera are meagre, Linsley and MacSwain (1957) finding 9 to 16 per cent parasitism and Krombein (1967) 5 to 10 per cent. Maeta (1963a) found 27 per cent of a Japanese eumenid species parasitized by *Pseudoxenos iwatai* Eksai. It is likely, however, that unsuccessful attempts to parasitize eggs, or excessive numbers entering larval wasps contribute to heavy mortality in the juvenile stages and Krombein has calculated that strepsiptera may parasitize up to 47 per cent of available hosts.

Diptera – The Flies

Krombein (1967) has recorded bombylid flies of the genus *Anthrax* as parasitoids of eumenid wasps in America. The female hovers in front of the nest ovipositing into the cells by retracting its abdomen towards the entrance and flipping eggs into or near the cell. The fly larva upon hatching makes its way into a cell where it waits for the wasp to spin its cocoon before devouring the pre-pupa or pupa. The fly pupates within the host cocoon and later leaves the cell by using its crown of teeth to bore through the wall, its abdominal setae aiding its movement to the nest entrance where it later moults into an adult.

Scavenging flies, Phoridae, are also found in solitary wasp nests, but details of the group will be dealt with elsewhere for they are better known as associates of social wasps.

Miltogrammini flies (family Sarcophagidae) are predatory in cells of several eumenid species, the females laying eggs in cells which are being provisioned, the fly larvae killing the wasp eggs before feeding on the stored prey. Several cells may be invaded by one fly before it migrates to the nest entrance prior to pupation (Krombein 1967).

Hymenopterous parasitoids

Several families of Hymenoptera include species which are parasitoids on eumenid wasps, notably the Ichneumonidae, Eulophidae, and Chrysidae (Table 6).

TABLE 6
Hymenopterous parasitoids of eumenid wasps

SPECIES	PARASITOID	SOURCE
E. coarctatus	Acroricnus (= Mesotenes) stylator Thunb.	Ratzeburg 1852
	Chrysis ignita (L.)	Ratzeburg 1852
	Cryptus spinosus Gravenhorst	Ratzeburg 1852
	Cryptus viduatorius Fabricius	Ratzeburg 1852
O. spinipes	Chrysis viridula L.	Bristowe 1948
	Chrysis cyanea (L.)	Yarrow 1945
	Chrysis fulgida L.	Housiaux 1922
	Chrysis ignita (L.)	Housiaux 1922
	Spintharis neglecta (Shuckard)	Yarrow 1945
	Omalus auratus (L.)	Fahringer 1922
	Melittobia acasta (Walker)	Balfour Browne 1922
O. reniformis	Chrysis viridula L.	Housiaux 1922
G. laevipes	Melittobia acasta (Walker)	Giraud 1869
A. parietum	Chrysis ignita (L.)	Chapman 1869
	Hedychrum nobile (Scopoli)	Housiaux 1922
	Chrysis fulgida L.	Housiaux 1922
	Chrysis viridula L.	Housiaux 1922
A. parietinus	Chrysis ignita (L.)	Hobby 1938
A. antilope	Chrysis ignita (L.)	Housiaux 1922
	Chrysis ruddii Shuckard	Yarrow 1945
A. nigricornis	Pachyophthalmus signatus (Meigen)	Chevalier 1924
A. oviventris	Chrysis ignita (L.)	Bignell 1882
S. sinuatissimus	Melittobia acasta (Walker)	Jørgensen 1942
	Chrysis ignita (L.)	Jørgensen 1942
	Chrysis viridula L.	Jørgensen 1942
S. connexus	Chrysis ignita (L.)	Alfken 1915

N.B. Although based partly on Continental records, all parasitoids are recorded in the British Isles.

Ichneumonidae.—Two ichneumonid parasitoids of American eumenid wasps have been noted by Krombein (1967), while in Europe 14 ichneumonid species have been described as parasitoids of *Gymnomerus laevipes* alone (Danks 1968). The females penetrate the woody walls or clay cells of their hosts with their ovipositors and lay eggs on the wasp larvae within the cell. The parasitoid larva consumes the wasp after first puncturing its cuticle and sucking out the haemolymph.

Eulophidae.—The well-known eulophid, *Melittobia acasta* Walker, a chalcid parasitoid of several insects including solitary and social Vespoidea and Diptera, is familiar because of the account of its biology by Balfour Browne (1922). The chalcid was discovered as a parasitoid of *Odynerus spinipes* in Cambridge, although Giraud (1869) had earlier described its association with *Gymnomerus laevipes* in France. The adults are found from May to September, there being 2 to 5 generations a year. In the spring, after mating within the cell of the host, the females (Fig. 24b) break through the wall, but the males (Fig. 24a), which are comparatively short-lived and do not feed, never leave the cell. On entering the cell of the host, the female feeds upon the oozing haemolymph of host larvae and occasionally the eggs, after puncturing the cuticle with its ovipositor (Fig. 24c). No apparent short-term effects are sustained by the host as a result of repeated feeding activity by the chalcid adults.

Oviposition on the host may be delayed if mating has not taken place, or if the host is not a mature larva or a pupa. If suitable material is available, the chalcid stings the host once or several times by inserting its ovipositor into its body in much the same way as it does when feeding, but no attempt is made to feed at the wounds. Stinging probably anaesthetizes the host and may help to preserve it. The eggs (Fig. 24d) are laid singly or in groups on the surface of the cuticle, with, as Balfour Browne expressed it, 'the abdomen slowly expanding and contracting until, after a few such movements, a slight bulge appears at the base of the ovipositor on its anterior side and this bulge rapidly passes downwards and the egg suddenly shoots out near the apex. It is a most extraordinary sight and looks like a conjuring trick to see the comparatively enormous egg appear from the exceedingly fine tube'. Maximum fecundity is in excess of a thousand eggs during the three months of adult life. The egg, which adheres lightly to the host, hatches in 2 to 9 days, the young larva feeding on the haemolymph after piercing the cuticle with its fine, sclerotized mandibles which also help anchor it to the host. Under optimum conditions, the larva matures in 8 to 9 days and pupation takes about seven days. Overwintering of the parasitoid takes place in the larval stage.

Emerging male offspring may mate with the parent female within the cell, especially if she was not successfully mated prior to entering the new cell, in which case her first crop of offspring are all males.

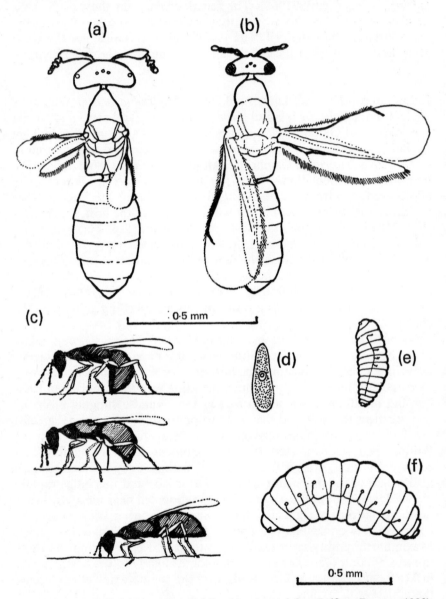

Figure 24. The chalcid parasite, *Melittobia acasta* (after Balfour Browne 1922): (a) adult male; (b) adult female; (c) female feeding on host after puncturing the host's cuticle with the ovipositor; (d) egg; (e) first-instar larva; (f) second-instar larva.

Despite the high fecundity of *Melittobia acasta*, the percentage of nests successfully invaded is low, although in a similar species, Krombein (1967) found up to 12·4 per cent (of 872 trap nests) parasitized in one locality of Washington D.C. One factor contributing to low levels of parasitism is the limited power of dispersal of the female, for the insect is capable of only very limited flight of a few inches at a time, its movement to other 'colonies' or cells of wasps being thereby severely curtailed.

Chrysididae.—The chrysid wasps, commonly called cuckoo, jewel, or ruby-tailed wasps, are the dominant parasitoids of solitary aculeate wasps and bees. The form of parasitism adopted by the chrysid is often typically cuckoo-like, the food store of the wasp providing sustenance for the chrysid after it has destroyed the egg or young larva of the rightful owner, but some chrysids behave like ichneumonids, feeding on the mature larva of the wasp.

Chrysid females (Fig. 25a) have often been observed keeping surveillance in the close proximity of wasp nests, watching the activities of the eumenid females as they return with prey and the mud to build the cell partitions. Krombein (1967) found several tube-nests in which chrysids had parasitized several cells in sequence, indicating that once a nest is located, the chrysid remains near it, ovipositing in successive cells as they are completed by the eumenid. If two chrysids take up stations near the same nest, one invariably chases the other away (O. W. Richards, personal communication), or they may even engage in a brief conflict (Jørgensen 1942) so it appears that chrysids have territorial areas which they zealously protect. Watching from 5 cm (Chevalier 1931) to 20 cm (O. W. Richards, personal communication) away from the nest, the chrysid will occasionally enter the nest while the eumenid is foraging and make a quick inspection. If conditions are suitable for oviposition, she wheels round and puts her abdomen into the cell and oviposits (Chapman 1869). Should the eumenid return while the chrysid is in or on the nest, the eumenid will chase it away. Isely (1913) observed a eumenid female pick up a chrysid which had rolled itself into a protective ball in the burrow, carry it out and drop it like a mud pellet.

Although oviposition takes place in provisioned, unsealed cells, chrysids will also tear down newly made partitions in an endeavour to gain access to the cell (Isely 1913, Chevalier 1931). The egg of the chrysid is either laid on the paralysed prey larvae (Chevalier 1931) or some distance from them (Jørgensen 1942) in the case of *Chrysis ignita* (L.) and *Chrysis neglecta* Schuckard, but *Chrysis bidentata* L. oviposits on full-grown larvae of its host, *Odynerus spinipes*, during or shortly after it spins the cocoon (Chapman 1869). *Chrysis bidentata* breaks

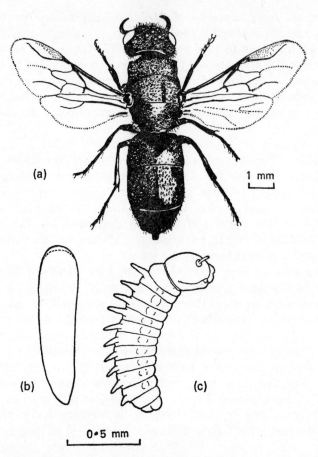

Figure 25. (a) *Chrysis viridula* female; (b) egg of *Chrysis cyanea*; (c) first-instar larva of *C. cyanea* (b and c after Danks 1971a).

open the partitions, Chapman (1869) having recorded one female burrowing through 1 cm of mud wall to gain access to the cell. This species lays 6 to 10 eggs on a host, pushing its ovipositor through the cocoon wall to reach the mature wasp larva. Normally only one egg hatches and, in common with all chrysids, only one parasite is reared per wasp host. The apparent waste of eggs in those species which lay two or more eggs per cell may be a means of overcoming egg mortality caused by movements of the prey or wasp larva.

The eggs of *Chrysis ignita* hatch within 24 hours, those of *Chrysis bidentata* after at least two days (Chapman 1869). When a chrysid oviposits in a freshly provisioned cell, the brief duration of the egg stage permits the first-instar larva (Fig. 25c) to seek out and destroy the eumenid egg or young larva which it does by mangling it with its small but effective mandibles. Feeding by the young larva is essentially a sucking process following puncturing of the prey cuticle, the more mature chrysid larva later chewing the tissue of the flaccid prey.

There are four larval moults, one every two days, so that the larva is fully grown within 6 to 8 days (Chapman 1869). The mature larvae spin cocoons of which the outer layer is attached to the cell wall or, in the case of *Chrysis bidentata*, the cocoon of its host (Chapman 1869). Chrysids overwinter as larvae, pupation taking less than three weeks, the emerging adults cutting circular holes at the end of the cocoon prior to emergence from the cell.

Predators

Few predators of eumenid wasps have been recorded, although the earwig, *Forficula auricularia* L., often destroys the outer partitions of stem nests before devouring the contents of the cells (Danks 1971a).

Robber flies (Asilidae), such as *Machimus atricapillus* (Fallén), have been recorded preying on *Odynerus* spp. (Séguy 1927).

Little data on the populations of solitary aculeates and the effects of parasites and predators on their numbers have been published, probably because of the generally low population levels of the group which makes their study somewhat intimidating for the student of animal populations. The use of hollow tubes or pieces of bamboo, strategically placed as trap nests, has permitted more effective studies on the population structure and mortality of the stem-nesters (Krombein 1967). For example, Danks (1971b), in a study of a wide range of stem-nesting bees and wasps at Silwood Park near Ascot, found that mortality due to failures during development was about 30 per cent (some of which was caused by unsuccessful parasitism), and parasitism was also about 30 per cent. The comparatively high rate of successful emergence coupled with a high potential fecundity should, theoretically, lead to a rapid increase in their population density but this does not occur. Danks suggests that the controlling factors are probably the limits imposed by restricted nesting sites, and the loss of a suitable site if taken over by another female of the same or different species – a common occurrence known as supersedure.

Fye (1972) has studied the effects of sustained attack by defoliating insects and also logging operations on the populations of aculeates in Canadian forests. When a forest area is opened up to light penetration, there follows an increase in the variety and numbers of flowering plants and a subsequent increase in aculeate populations. Colonization by solitary bees and wasps is due to the abundant floral forage and herbivorous prey together with suitable nesting sites such as broken branches and well-drained sandy banks where roads have been constructed. However, with the closing in of the forest canopy following regeneration, these sites become less favourable and the bee and wasp populations decline.

CHAPTER 4

THE BEGINNINGS

A convenient stage at which to begin a description of social wasp biology is the winter period when queen wasps produced during the preceding autumn are dormant in their winter quarters. At this point in their annual cycle, there is little to distinguish the social wasps from the solitary members of the family. Overwintering is not a social activity and only rarely and fortuitously does it appear gregarious, when numbers of queens may be found in the same location. With their awakening in the spring, the activities of all wasps are basically similar – the foraging for food and, with the development of the female's ovaries, nesting drives become apparent and a search for nest sites is begun.

The social wasps build single cells or groups of cells in which the young are reared, and during the early period of colony development the activities of the queens are not unlike their solitary relatives. Queens construct small nests entirely on their own, foraging for building materials and the food with which to feed their growing larvae. However, the emergence of the first few daughter wasps, the workers, marks the beginning of the social phase.

The workers take over foraging and building activities while the queen performs her reproductive functions in the comparative security of the nest. While many other activities characterize sociality in the Vespinae, it is this co-operation between daughters and a long-lived parent which defines them as being truly social.

The life cycle of wasps in the temperate climate of the British Isles is a seasonally dominated series of events in which the cold conditions of winter cause the final disintegration of colonial activities, only the hibernating queens surviving until weather and supplies of food improve during the spring. Overwintered queens of the social species make their appearance at about the same time during April and May, although the social parasite, *Vespula austriaca*, is found considerably later (Fig. 26). This chapter describes the preparatory activities of

77

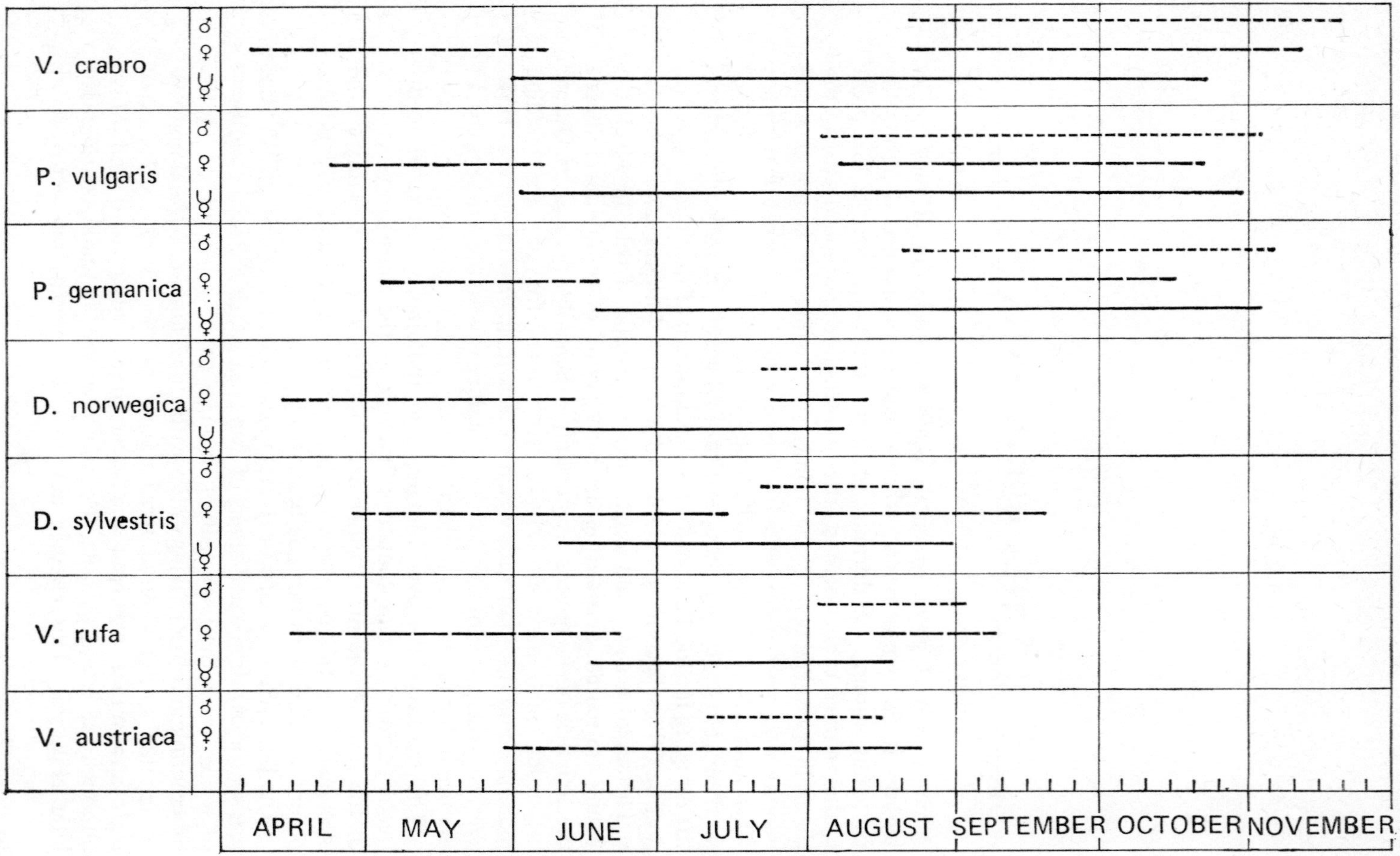

Figure 26. Flight period of British Vespidae (original)

queens before they enter hibernation; the adaptations necessary to overwinter successfully; an account of the early, crucial steps in the establishment of a nest by the solitary queen; and a description of the developmental stages of the wasp, from egg to adult.

HIBERNATION

The young queens produced in late summer and autumn when seasonal and colony conditions are optimal, are faced with the prospect of several months of unfavourable weather and severely limited food supplies. These adverse conditions of winter necessitate changes in their behaviour and physiology.

The major responses by queens to ensure their survival are a general quiescence in overall physical activity and a delay in ovariole development. The first response results in a typical winter dormancy, a phenological condition generally brought about by sub-optimal conditions such as low temperature. The second response is a true diapause for ovariole development is completely arrested for the duration of the dormant period, even if winter temperatures rise sufficiently to cause periods of flight activity.

It is well established that young queens begin to enter hibernation quarters before the onset of cold weather (Wailes 1860, Duncan 1939), indicating that dormancy is not directly brought about by harsh winter conditions. Roubaud (1929) concluded that hibernation in wasps was independent of temperature changes. Because all young queens begin hibernating before the advent of winter it might be suggested that they have an obligatory diapause which is genetically determined, but contemporary workers on insect diapause (see Norris 1964) increasingly favour the concept of a facultative diapause induced by environmental factors acting on the diapause-susceptible stage. The most likely candidate factor is day-length or photoperiod, a consistent component of seasonal change which can give advanced warning of impending changes. A point in favour of a facultative mechanism of diapause in wasps is the overwintering of *P. germanica* colonies in New Zealand (Thomas 1960) and Tasmania, Australia (unpublished observations), where many nests remain active during the winter following re-queening in late autumn. These colonies continue to produce offspring throughout the winter and, in the relatively mild climate of Australasia, the reproductive diapause is apparently dispensed with.

Ovariole diapause is also a caste characteristic for worker's ovaries will rapidly develop in the absence of the founding queen, the response being independent of seasonal or other physical factors. Similar changes do not occur in young queens in temperate Europe where ovariole development is completely arrested until the following spring.

To ensure successful overwintering, queens rely on food supplies stored in their much enlarged fat bodies. A marked reduction in their metabolic activities conserves these reserves. The fat body consists principally of storage cells called trophocytes which are filled with fat (=lipid), glycogen (the storage form of carbohydrates), and possibly some protein. Mature adult queens which leave the nest in search of hibernation sites, have about 40 per cent of their dry weight in the form of fats, but workers of a comparative age have less than 10 per cent (Table 7) (Spradbery 1963). These results have been confirmed by using the monophasic extraction technique of Hanson and Olley (1963) on fresh material. The proportion of lipids extracted was 18 per cent of the fresh weight in mature queens, but only 4 per cent in mature workers. Newly emerged queens and workers, however, contained 8-9 per cent lipids, demonstrating that queens lay down depot fat after their emergence and prior to entering hibernation, while workers burn up much of their reserves during their brief adult lives. Further analyses were undertaken to determine the quantity of phospholipids present in the wasp because these complex lipids are components of cell membranes and can thus indicate the density of cells in the body. There was no difference in the phospholipid content of callow and mature queens, showing that the enormous build up of depot fat is not accompanied by the differentiation of more storage cells. The queens' capacity to lay down adequate fat reserves is one of the major features which distinguishes them from workers. Workers have, however, been found hibernating occasionally (Thomas 1960).

The movement of queens to hibernation sites occurs in small groups or singly, there being no evidence of any mass movements or migrations amongst autumnal queens, although Rau (1941), in his studies on temperate zone *Polistes* in America, suggests that there is an indication of 'swarming' in late summer as the queens move by slow stages to hibernation sites, masses of them being found in different places before they finally enter permanent hibernaculae. The places in which wasps hibernate are legion, for example in England, *P. vulgaris* and *V. rufa* have been found near the surface of banks (O. W. Richards, personal communication), *P. vulgaris* under slates in Cumberland (Wailes 1860), *P. germanica* under the loose bark of a felled oak (Billups 1882), elm (unpublished observation), ash (Sandemann 1936), and unidentified wasps under the split bark of a silver fir which had been struck by lightning (Haworth-Booth 1896). Duncan (1939) has recorded American wasps hibernating under roof shingles, between books in a case, in cracks or beetle holes in wood, cracks in rocks, and in leaf litter. In New Zealand, Thomas (1960) found *P. germanica* queens hibernating in a wide variety of places including the original nest, in a coal-carrying railway truck, under corrugated-iron sheeting and beehive lids. Their

VI. British social wasps
(top row) *Paravespulis vulgaris*, (middle row) *P. germanica*, (bottom row) *Dolichovespula sylvestris* (male, queen, workers, from left to right).

occurrence in houses and outbuildings, clinging to curtains or sacking, for example, is widespread. In Japan, many species of hornet dig out small individual hibernaculae in soil or rotten wood, plugging the entrance with earth or wood (Matsuura 1966), and similar habits have been recorded for *Vespula* in America (Rau 1934a). Not all of these hibernaculae have common physical attributes which could be described as typical or even appropriate, many recorded sites being wet, others dry, some exposed to the elements and others completely protected. It would seem that well-insulated places with moderate humidity would be most suitable, but there are as many examples of wasps successfully hibernating in rotting, moist wood as in dry locations.

Aggregations of queens within hibernaculae have been frequently recorded, for example Billups (1882) found 38 *P. germanica* under loose bark, Haworth-Booth (1896) found 68 queens of the same species under ash bark, Sandemann (1936) found 10 *V. crabro* queens hibernating together inside the rotten wood of a dead ash tree, and Free and Butler (1959) have published an excellent photograph of a very large aggregation of *P. germanica* in their original nest. Up to 400 queens of *P. germanica* have been seen hibernating together in New Zealand (Thomas 1960). In Japan, Yamane (personal communication) has found clusters of 2,000 to 3,000 *Polistes* queens hibernating under eaves or in disused hornets' nests. These aggregations are probably a reflection of suitable hibernating conditions rather than an example of sociality among the queens.

The hibernating attitude of the queen (Plate Va) is very characteristic among the different species and genera of wasp, the female generally gripping tightly on to a suitable part of the substrate with her mandibles, although if the hibernaculum is small, she may lie loosely within the cavity. The antennae are folded ventrally along the body and the legs extended posteriorly and held against the body, with the wings folded and tucked between the hindlegs and propodeum. As pointed out by Figuier (1868), the characteristic hibernation posture of the adult is remarkably similar to the pupal stage. When *Polistes* and *Mischocyttarus* wasps are in repose at night, they adopt a similar attitude while worker wasps remaining out of the nest at night also share the same hibernation posture (unpublished observations).

Although wasps may be exposed to freezing temperatures and even be covered in a layer of frozen water (Billups 1882, Sandemann 1936), they are unaffected by these extreme conditions and will revive within a few minutes if placed at higher temperatures. This suggests that the quiescent state may be maintained by low temperature if not initiated by it. In fact during warm days in winter, queens can be roused from their hibernation and take to the wing before re-entering hibernation in different places. These midwinter appearances of queens in Britain have been recorded on 15, 18 January (Scott 1920), 20 January (Billups 1882), and 13 February (Smith 1858) for *Vespula* species, and *V. crabro* has been seen in flight on 26 December and 7 February (Latter 1913).

The duration of hibernation depends on the species of wasp and the vagaries of climate. Queens of *V. rufa*, *D. norwegica*, and *D. sylvestris*, which complete their annual cycle in mid to late summer (Fig. 26), probably spend one or more months longer in hibernation than *P. vulgaris* and *P. germanica* which may produce queens as late as October or even November (Goodall 1924). In Britain, the period of hibernation varies between 5 and 8 months, while in America, Duncan (1939) considers the dormant period to be 2 to 8 months depending on species of wasp, seasonal conditions and locality – especially its altitude.

POST-HIBERNATION ACTIVITIES

The warm weather of spring gradually awakens the queens (Fig. 27) which begin to make short exploratory and feeding trips, collecting nectar from flowers or in the case of hornets, the sap of trees. By the time the queens become active in the spring, much of their stored food

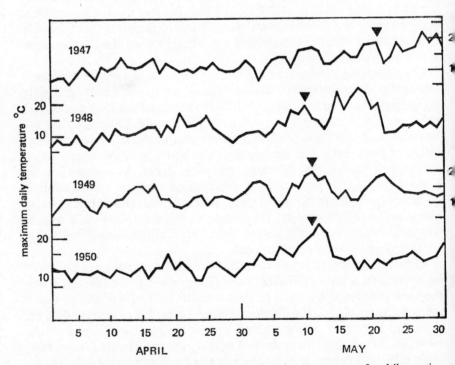

Figure 27. First appearance of *Dolichovespula sylvestris* queens after hibernation, Scotland (after Brian and Brian 1952).

reserves have been used up and their fat content depleted to about 10 per cent of the dry weight, a loss of nearly 30 per cent (Spradbery 1963). In Japanese *Vespa*, the live weight of queens decreased by 38 per cent during hibernation, from 3.46 ± 0.21 g to 2.14 ± 0.22 g (Matsuura 1969).

The dispersal of queens from winter quarters has been recorded infrequently, those of *Polistes* in America being described by Rau (1930) as moving in 'an unorganized mass' to the original nesting areas where clusters are formed before their final dissemination when nest building begins. C. B. Williams (in Rudebeck 1965) records instances of individual queens of *P. vulgaris*, *D. sylvestris*, and *V. crabro* being sighted at lightships off the coast of Britain during the spring. Rich sources of nectar frequently attract large congregations of queens and in Ireland one year a gardener killed more than a thousand queens which were feeding at a Cotoneaster bush (Pack-Beresford 1899).

A remarkable series of observations on the mass movement of *V. rufa* queens in Sweden has been recorded by Rudebeck (1965). During a period of warm weather between 16 and 20 June in 1957, thousands of queens were seen flying towards the coast, reaching a maximum of about 4,800 wasps per hour, all flying in the same direction (WSW). These queens had probably flown at least 50 km, for numbers of wasps were observed 50 km north-east during the period 9 to 15 June. This migration continued during calm conditions and also when light winds blew from different quarters, but was interrupted when the temperature dropped as a cold front passed through the area. When the wasps reached the coastline, their behaviour was very similar to that of migrating birds when presented with a large expanse of water, for they became concentrated along the coast and flew parallel to it, the coastline acting as a leading line. However, when the wasps reached a south-west tip of land which jutted into the North Sea, some changed direction through 150° while the majority, with some apparent hesitation, flew out to sea in a WSW direction. Rudebeck considers that the queens would have reached Denmark only 25 km away. The reasons for this migration are not known but Rudebeck suggests that it may have been a response to the large numbers of queens in the original locus and these flights could therefore be considered an irruptive migration.

Whether or not a queen is fecundated prior to entering hibernation seems to play no part in successful hibernation, for Matsuura (1969) discovered that queens of the largest Japanese hornet, *Vespa mandarinia* Smith, frequently fail to be inseminated (more than 30 per cent in two successive years) yet they overwinter successfully. However, during the following spring, they feed at tree sap long after the fecundated queens have founded colonies and, despite an initial development of the ovarioles, the mature oocytes degenerate. The nest-building drives are apparently absent for these females never founded nests. However, Ormerod (1868) cites the case of a *D. norwegica* colony which produced wholly male brood and adults, presumably established by an uninseminated queen.

During the period following hibernation, when queens feed at flowers and tree sap, their ovaries begin to develop. There is evidence that ovariole development is associated with activity in the neurosecretory cells of the wasp's brain. Workers and hibernating queens have very small amounts of a secretion, 'Gomori's substance' (chorme – haematoxylin-ophilous granules), in the brain cortex but, just prior to oocyte maturation, this substance accumulates and a high level is maintained throughout the oviposition period (Takamatsu 1955, 1956).

In Britain the period of activity between hibernation and nest initiation takes place in May and lasts for 2 or 3 weeks, followed by a further few weeks when embryo nests are built and the first crop of workers are produced. This period of springtime activity by queens is well illustrated by the results of catching wasps with suction traps at Rothamsted Experimental Station given in Fig. 61 (p. 170).

The search for a suitable nest site is an individual endeavour in the Vespinae, although large groups of queens may be seen in favourable localities. For example, Walton (1934) recorded 30 *P. germanica* queens searching along 6 metres of hedgerow between 2 and 12 May one year. Queens which build subterranean nests are characterized by their slow, swinging flight low over the ground, any round dark object or depression which may indicate a hole in the soil, attracting the attention of the wasps (Potter 1965). The choice of site is little understood for many queens select locations which are either unsuitable from the outset or, when enlarged, would become so, while others are in such exposed situations that bad weather or marauding animals could easily wreak havoc with the nest.

There are records of queens being killed when competing for nest sites (Brian 1965) which suggests that suitable nesting places may be a limiting factor in the abundance or scarcity of wasps (see Chapter 7 for a more detailed treatment of this topic). The minimum requirement for a nest site is probably a suitable surface from which to suspend the foundations of the nest.

As the ovaries begin to develop, the nesting drives probably intensify until a stage is reached when the first available site will be selected, but the neuro-hormonal mechanisms involved have not been studied so far.

THE EMBRYO NEST

Once a nest site has been discovered and considered suitable, the queen makes a thorough locality study during an orientation flight.

In *P. vulgaris* the queen flies to and fro in front of the site entrance in a slow, hovering flight which continues until she is some distance from the entrance, the flight arc increasing to about 2 metres and taking the form of a figure of eight. When some 17 metres from the site, she suddenly flies off to collect the first load of wood pulp for construction (Potter 1965). During this flight, the relative positions of certain landmarks near the nest site are presumably fixed in the wasp's brain.

Construction of the nest may begin without delay (Duncan 1939) or after several exploratory surveys of the site (Brian and Brian 1948). Pre-treatment of the spot where the first load of pulp is attached does not occur in *D. sylvestris* (Brian and Brian 1948) but has been recorded in *Dolichovespula media* (Retzias) in France by Janet (1895b) who saw a queen coating about 5 cm of a chosen twig with a glutinous substance which probably serves some adhesive function. Some wasps begin building in one spot while others (notably wasps of the tree-nesting genus, *Dolichovespula*) apply loads of pulp to a number of different places in the same area, finally selecting one spot from which to suspend the nest (Brian and Brian 1948).

Details of the initiation of nests by queen wasps have been rarely recorded, the notable descriptions being those by Brian and Brian (1948) on *D. sylvestris* in Scotland, Potter (1965) on *P. vulgaris* in England, Darchen (1964) on *V. orientalis* in Israel, and Janet (1895a) on *V. crabro* in France. It is on these observations that I have based the following account of embryo-nest construction.

Several loads of wood pulp are applied to the under surface of the chosen spot to form a sheet of paper - the preliminary buttress - before a spindle-like pillar of paper is constructed downwards (Fig. 28). While building the buttress and first part of the spindle, the queen clings on to the supporting structure with her mid and hind legs, using the fore tarsi to help manipulate the load of pulp in her mandibles. As the spindle is lengthened, the queen clings to it rather than the support. When the spindle has been extended to about 12 mm, the next few loads of pulp are used to form the cup-like bases of the first two cells. In *P. vulgaris*, two loads of pulp were utilized to form the base of the first cell before the queen began the second cell, which was made slightly below and to the side of the first cell. In *D. sylvestris*, the second cell was slightly above the first.

When the first two cells have been initiated, the queen begins to construct the envelope, an umbrella-like structure which eventually surrounds the cells and provides some protection and insulation for the future brood. The distance between the base of the cells and the point of attachment of the envelope is approximately the width of the queen's body (5 mm in *D. sylvestris* and *P. vulgaris*) and this area becomes the major resting place for the queen which curls itself round

TABLE 7

Fat content of queen wasps (after Spradbery 1963)

SPECIES	STAGE	DATE	NO. SAMPLES	NO. PER SAMPLE	DRY WEIGHT PER QUEEN (mg)	PERCENTAGE FAT OF THE DRY WEIGHT	S.E.
P. germanica	young adults	September	3	10	133·2 (131–151)	40·7 (39·7–41·3)	±0·41
P. vulgaris	hibernating	20 February to 20 March	3	1	85·7 (89–91)	26·8 (21·2–29·7)	±2·20
P. germanica	founding colony	3, 8 June	2	1	75·0 (74–76)	9·3 (8·1–10·5)	±0·62
P. vulgaris	from mature colony	25 July to 27 August	6	1	68·3 (56–76)	5·6 (4·2–7·0)	±0·43
P. germanica	from mature colony	13 August to 14 September	4	1	85·2 (71–92)	6·7 (5·2–7·6)	±0·46

ranges in parentheses

TABLE 8

Foraging trips by a *P. vulgaris* queen (after Potter 1965)
(Number of trips observed during 2 hours' observation each day)

DAYS SINCE NEST WAS FOUNDED	6	7	8	9	10	11	12	13	14	15	16	17	18	19	20	21	22	23	24	25	TOTAL
Wood pulp	5	7	5	5	3	1	1	1	0	0	0	0	0	1	0	0	0	0	1	0	30
Fluids	2	0	3	3	4	6	5	5	4	4	4	7	6	4	4	4	3	2	3	1	74
Insect flesh	0	0	0	1	1	2	2	2	2	3	2	0	0	3	1	0	1	1	0	0	21
TOTAL	7	7	8	9	8	9	8	8	6	7	6	7	6	8	5	4	4	3	4	1	125

the spindle (Fig. 29c). *D. sylvestris* queens took 3 hours to prepare the buttress, $1\frac{1}{2}$ to 2 hours to construct the spindle, and 1 hour to make each of the first two cells, thus spending $6\frac{1}{2}$ to 7 hours before commencing envelope construction.

After two days from the start of building, embryo nests of *Vespula* species have 4 to 6 cells, with 5 to 9 cells after three days, 13 cells after nine days, and 21 cells after thirteen days (see Fig. 57). The rate of cell building varies among individuals of the same species and also between species. For example, the number of cells in a nine-day-old *V. crabro* nest was 8, with 11 cells after thirteen days. The number of cells built by the queens before the emergence of the first workers in several wasp species is given in Table 9.

TABLE 9
Mean numbers of cells in embryo nests

SPECIES	NO. CELLS	SOURCE
V. crabro	39	Janet 1895a
P. vulgaris	23	Potter 1965
P. germanica	30	Unpublished record
V. rufa	33	Smith 1856
D. norwegica	24	Unpublished record
D. sylvestris	21	Brian and Brian 1948

After about three days *P. vulgaris* will have completed its first envelope umbrella and begun the second one (see Plate Vb), but the number and rates of construction of umbrellas vary a great deal. For example, one *D. sylvestris* queen built five umbrellas within seven days while another queen built only three in the same time (Fig. 29). When a hornet builds its nest in a hollowed-out tree it does not normally build an envelope (Duncan 1939) but will do so if the site is exposed or subterranean, the aerial nest studied by Janet having two umbrellas when completed. When the queen returns with pulp for envelope building she invariably enters the nest first and spends a few minutes resting, grooming, and masticating the load before crawling out of the nest to apply the pulp. The distance between successive umbrellas is generally about half the width of the queen's body and is caused by the method of envelope construction: while building the second, third, and subsequent umbrellas, the queen adds pulp to the edge of the envelope while keeping one side of her body in contact with the inner umbrella, the latter acting as a kind of template or 'yardstick'. As the comb is extended with the addition of cells around its periphery, the inner umbrellas are torn down and incorporated into cells and new umbrellas.

When nest building begins, the queen forages exclusively for pulp until the eggs hatch and the larvae require feeding. The durations of

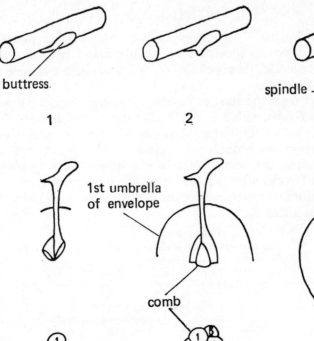

buttress.

1

2

spindle

3

1st umbrella
of envelope

comb

4

5

6

7

8

Figure 28. Initial stages of nest building by a *Paravespula vulgaris* queen (after Potter 1965).

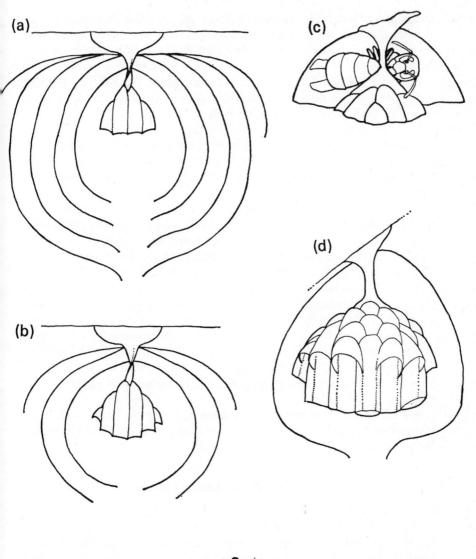

Figure 29.   Embryo nests: (a) (b) nests of *Dolichovespula sylvestris* (after Brian and Brian 1948); (c) nesting position of queen, *Vespa crabro;* (d) mature embryo nest of *V. crabro* (after Janet 1895a).

pulp-foraging trips made by a *P. vulgaris* queen were 6 and 8 minutes for loads collected from two different sources. The time difference was probably due to the distance between the two pulp sources and the nest, or the relative ease of working one of the sources. When not foraging or building, the queen rests in her characteristic position around the spindle, the time spent foraging being considerably shorter than the resting periods. For example, in two *D. sylvestris* queens, the times spent in and out of the nest were 9·1 and 13·4 minutes in the nest, and 6·9 and 7·9 minutes on foraging trips. The differences in the time spent in the nest were probably due to the fact that one queen built five umbrellas and the other only three.

With the eclosion of eggs some 5-6 days after nest initiation, there is a progressive change in the foraging activities of the queen as she begins to collect fluids and a little insect prey to feed the larvae. Pulp collection is maintained however, and cells continue to be built. An indication of these changes in foraging activity is given in Table 8. The large number of pulp-collecting journeys is largely replaced by fluid and flesh trips. Fluid collecting in *P. vulgaris* queens tends to be a morning activity (38 fluid trips compared to 8 flesh trips) with an increase in flesh collecting in the evening (35 fluid trips compared to 13 flesh trips), and is similar to the activity patterns of *D. sylvestris* workers (Brian and Brian 1952). Fluid is the dominant forage, however, with 74 fluid loads and only 21 flesh loads observed during days 6-25 since nest founding by the *P. vulgaris* queen.

When the first batch of larvae pupate, flesh collection by the queen declines and finally ceases while fluid collection is severely reduced. The reduction in foraging activity of the queen at this time is similar in both *D. sylvestris* and *P. vulgaris* and is probably of general occurrence.

A consideration of cell-building rates and population growth in the embryo nest will be found in Chapter 7 in which seasonal changes in the population of colonies are discussed.

DEVELOPMENTAL STAGES

Oviposition (Plate XXIVa)

During the early stages of the incipient colony, the queen lays an egg in each cell soon after its initiation as a shallow cup, the egg being fixed to the corner of the cell nearest to the central axis of the comb. One reason for placing the egg in this particular position is because the inner 'corner' is the first to be built and is angular compared to the outer part which tends to be rounded and without corners. In older cells, the queen usually oviposits in one of the corners nearest the central axis, fixing the egg from a half to two thirds down the cell. According to Potter (1965), when the queen lays in these older cells, she inserts her abdomen fully into the cell and then moves the rest of her body on to the surrounding comb until she locates one of the angles in which to fix the egg. The curvature of the cells towards the periphery of the comb (see Fig. 34) tends to help the queen 'align herself preferentially along the radius of the comb', resulting in the characteristic orientation of eggs in cells.

Fertilization of the egg takes place after the egg has passed from the ovariole and into the common oviduct where sperm are released from the spermotheca. Entry of the sperm is effected through the micropyle, a small, funnel-shaped canal passing through the egg shell or chorion.

The Egg

The eggs of wasps are typically sausage-shaped and slightly pointed at the caudal end which is fixed to the cell wall (Fig. 30a, Plate VIIa). The egg is slightly curved and projects into the cell at an angle of about 45°. Milky white in colour, it is enclosed by a very thin, fragile chorion. The size of eggs is roughly proportional to the size of the wasp species with the eggs of hornets being the largest (Iwata 1960).

The incubation period of the egg is somewhat variable, most information having been obtained from incipient colonies where fluctuating temperatures and other factors cause considerable disparity in the duration of the developmental stages. In incipient colonies of *P. vulgaris*, I found the average incubation period to be 5·3 days (range 3·4-6·7) and in Potter's colony, the period was 5·2 days (range 5-7). In *V. crabro*, the incubation period in young colonies varied from 5 to 18 days, but by July and August, the duration was more constant at 5 days (Janet 1895a). In the seven colonies of *D. sylvestris* studied in 1948-9 by Brian and Brian (1952), the first 10 eggs or so hatched in 5 days, but there was an apparent prolongation of the incubation period in the latter stages of the incipient colonies. It would appear that a 5-day incubation period is fairly general in wasps during the early stages of colony development, but it seems likely that the duration may be reduced as the colony increases in size and higher and more constant temperatures prevail in the nests.

Larvae

In *Vespula* species there are five larval instars, of which the first three are fixed to the cell wall at the point of egg attachment. These larvae face into the lumen of the cell with their mouthparts pointing away from the centre of the comb and their abdomens remaining within the split chorion (Fig. 30). Brian and Brian (1952) called these larvae the outward-facing stage. According to du Buysson (1903), the larvae attach themselves to the egg shell with a viscous secretion. When the larva moults into the fourth instar, it becomes free of its attachment to the wall and is able to move freely, preventing itself dropping out of the cell by means of the pleural lobes and dorsal ridges (Fig. 30e). During this and the final, fifth instar, the larva gener-

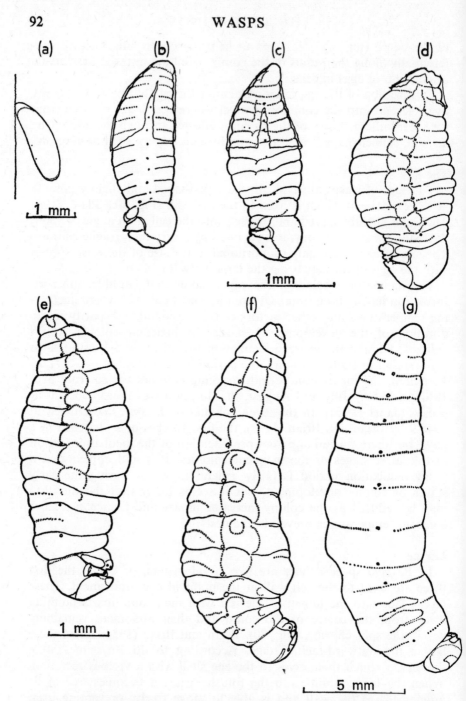

Figure 30. Developmental stages of *Paravespula vulgaris* (after Potter 1965): (a) egg; (b) first-instar larva; (c) second-instar larva; (d) third-instar larva; (e) fourth-instar larva; (f) mature fifth-instar larva; (g) pre-pupa after cocoon spinning.

ally orientates itself so that it faces towards the centre of the comb (inward-facing stage). It is during the fifth instar that the greatest increase in size takes place so that the larvae fill the cells in which they were reared. Details of larval feeding and an indication of their diet will be found in Chapter 6.

Wasp larvae of different species are similar in general appearance, being soft-bodied and apodous, with a head bearing simple mouthparts. There are three thoracic and ten abdominal segments. The respiratory system opens to the exterior through ten pairs of spiracles. The mature larva has been described by Reid (1942) and his account of the generalized vespid larva forms a basis for the following description. The head has few visible landmarks, the Y-shaped epicranial groove being more obvious in genera with more heavily sclerotized head capsules such as *Vespa* and *Polistes*. This groove is the line along which the larval cuticle splits during a moult and is sometimes called the ecdysial cleavage line. Small deep depressions, the anterior tentorial pits, which mark the point where the tentorium is attached, are readily visible (Fig. 31). The antennae are represented by simple discs on which three, small, circular sensillae occur. A pair of well-defined bands of unknown function, the temporal bands, are characteristic features of

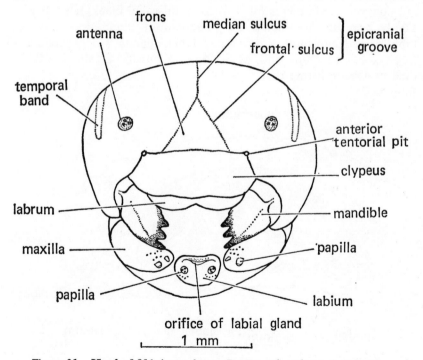

Figure 31. Head of fifth-instar larva, *Paravespula vulgaris* (original).

the vespid head capsule. The mandibles are sclerotized; more heavily so at their distal ends where the margin is toothed. There are numerous sensory papillae on the maxillae and labium, and a sensory seta between the labial papillae and the opening to the salivary-gland duct. Several other sensory setae are found on the labium, maxillae, labrum, and other parts of the capsule where they have some importance in the classification of larvae. Conical sensillae are found on the upper and lower surfaces of the labrum. The thorax bears spiracles between the pro- and meso-thoracic, and meso- and meta-thoracic segments, and there are paired spiracles on the first eight abdominal segments. The thorax and abdomen have a series of dorsal and lateral protuberances – the dorsal ridges and pleural lobes – which help the larva retain its position in the cell. Differences between larvae of some wasp species have been described and reviewed by Reid (1942), but the work to date is insufficient to provide a key to the British species. Some of the specific differences that have been noted include 3-toothed mandibles in *P. vulgaris* and *P. germanica*, but only a single tooth in *D. norwegica;* 3-labial palpi in *P. vulgaris* and 4 in *P. germanica;* and a number of differences in the structures found on the walls of the spiracular atria.

The gut is of considerable interest because wasp larvae store the indigestible remains of their food in the midgut until, at the time of pupation, the lumen is filled with a semi-solid, black mass (Fig. 32). The larva is also notable for the possession of functionless malphigian tubules, and enormously developed labial glands which produce the trophallactic secretion and, at the time of pupation, fabricate the silk used in cocoon formation.

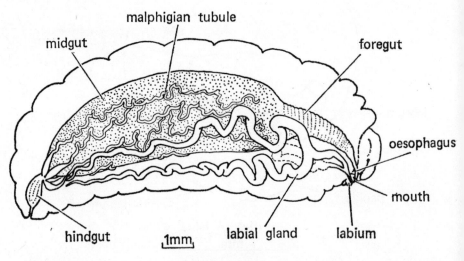

Figure 32. General anatomy of fifth-instar larva, *Paravespula germanica* (original).

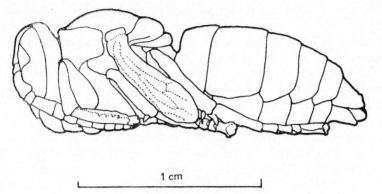

1 cm

Figure 33.   Paravespula germanica worker pupa (original).

The duration of larval life is variable. During the incipient colony stage, the first three, fixed instars are as short as 3 days (generally 4 to 5 days) or as long as 11 days in *P. vulgaris* (Potter 1965). Instars four and five occupy 6 to 7 days according to Potter, and in *D. sylvestris* were 3 days in some cases, normally 6 days, but with a maximum of 16 days. Other figures for the duration of the larval stage are 15 days in an incipient *P. vulgaris* colony (Spradbery 1963), and 14·5 days (range 12 to 18) in early and late season *V. crabro* colonies with an average of 12 days during the midsummer period (Janet 1895a).

In a nest of *P. vulgaris* which was maintained at 32°C, duration of larval life was 9 days. It was extended to 17 days during a period of bad weather even though nest temperature was kept at 32°C (Potter 1965).

Pupae

After completing feeding, the mature larva begins to spin its cocoon, the silk being produced by the labial glands. To produce the pupal capping the larva moves round and round, attaching the silken thread to the rim of the cell to produce a fringe and, by working towards the middle, it finally closes the open end of the cell completely (Plate VIIc). A thinner silken lining is also spun around the walls of the cell, the larva turning over until its head is at the base of the cell (Potter 1965). Like other insect silks, the material is proteinaceous in composition. With the cocoon complete, the larva re-orientates with its head facing towards the centre of the comb. The faecal mass which accumulates in the midgut during larval development is now voided (Plate VIId) and applied to the base of the cell as a thick, cup-shaped disc. Occasionally the faeces are found at the capped end of the cell, the larva having evacuated its gut while in the inverted position. These pupae normally perish.

With the voiding of the faeces, the pre-pupal stage is reached and the larva begins its metamorphosis into the pupal form. One of the significant changes at this time is the marking off of the pupal thorax and the separation of the first abdominal segment which is incorporated into the thoracic region as the propodeum (Fig. 30g). Within three days of finishing the cocoon, the change to pupal form is complete and after pupation, the change to adult form takes some two to three days before emergence from the cell (Plate VIII) (Potter 1965). The duration of the entire pupal period (from start of spinning to emergence) in young *P. vulgaris* colonies was 15·1 days (range, 14·3-17·8) (Spradbery 1963), and 11 days (8-14) (Potter 1965); in *D. sylvestris* colonies it was 7 to 22 days (Brian and Brian 1952); 10 days in *V. rufa* (Nixon 1934a); and in *V. crabro* it was 13·9 days (13-15) (Janet 1895a). Details of the changes in the alimentary system of wasps during pupation have been described by Green (1933), and changes in the development of the labial gland by Ochiai (1960).

Exit from the cell by the teneral adult is effected without assistance from other wasps. When the callow is ready to emerge, it begins to chew at the pupal cap with its mandibles, gradually tearing it away until there is a sufficiently big hole through which it can escape. To facilitate tearing the cap, the wasp softens the cocoon with a salivary secretion which does not, however, digest the silk. I have not found any evidence that proteinases are present in adult saliva during emergence. The entire operation of adult emergence takes only a few minutes, the wasp having an occasional rest between bouts of chewing.

A stage in colonial life has now been reached when the worker force makes its appearance. Succeeding chapters describe some of the major activities of wasps as they enlarge the nest and forage for food and building materials.

CHAPTER 5

NESTS AND NESTING

The building of large, complex nest structures by the social wasps is probably one of the most creative activities performed by any invertebrate, while the aesthetic qualities of nests have for long excited the entomologist and frequently been the source of artistic inspiration. I have seen ceramics in Japan which were based on hornets' nests; their form, colour, and textures finding expression in the clay on a potter's wheel.

The construction and maintenance of the nest involve the expenditure of considerable energy by the inhabitants during their search for and collection of building material for incorporation into the nest structure. In the subterranean nesters, building is also accompanied by massive excavation activities as the wasps hollow out the earthen cavity to accommodate the growing nest. Although the queen initiates the colony and builds the embryo nest single-handed, the workers which are later produced perform the major task of construction. As their numbers increase, the original queen-built comb is enlarged with the addition of cells around its periphery and further combs are added, suspended below each other by pillars. With the increase in size and number of combs, the envelope which surrounds the nest is torn down on the inside and rebuilt on the outside. The nest is the focal point for the social activities of the community and the rearing of brood, and forms a well-defined territory which is vigorously defended whenever threatened.

The engineering and logistic problems involved in the production of a mature wasp nest are remarkable, but as yet hardly understood. The integration of the activities of a few thousand adult wasps so as to produce a nest structure containing perhaps 12,000 cells in a little more than four months is an extraordinary achievement, particularly when it is realized that communication amongst the members of a colony is limited. The behavioural sequence which results in the pro-

H

duction of a few square millimetres of carton by a wasp is perhaps explicable in terms of anatomy, physiology, and the integration of nervous activity, but the collaboration of several thousand such workers to produce the whole structure is an extraordinary example of co-operative behaviour in an insect society.

Before describing the mechanics of construction and the seasonal changes which result in the building of a mature nest, a description of a typical subterranean nest is appropriate at this stage for purposes of terminology.

The typical *P. vulgaris* nest which is illustrated in Fig. 34 was built in a disused rodent hole, the burrow becoming the entrance tunnel to the nest. The nest structure is composed of 'wasp paper' or carton, a papier mâché material which results from the drying out of moist wood pulp. The original embryo nest was attached to an overhanging root by the founding queen, but with its enlargement, much of the original envelope has been torn away, although the rudiments are found incorporated into the upper part of the worker-built envelope. The envelope of the mature colony is quite different from the smooth sheets of umbrella-shaped carton found in the incipient colony, for it is composed of numerous shell-like structures, each enclosing an air space so as to form an insulating wall around the combs. The original spindle or pillar of the embryo nest has been strengthened and additional support provided in the form of stout pillars or sheets of carton connecting the upper part of the envelope to the walls of the cavity.

Access to the combs is provided by a small entrance hole of 2-3 cm diameter at the bottom of the nest although in some nests it may be somewhat higher up the envelope. The original rodent burrow has been excavated during the course of the season to permit expansion of the nest, and the walls of the cavity have become relatively smooth. There is a sufficient gap between the walls of the cavity and the envelope to allow the wasps to manoeuvre in the space while excavating the soil and building the envelope.

New combs have been suspended from older ones by means of pillars – an initial mainstay centrally placed with further pillars scattered between the combs. Occasional pillars are constructed which connect the comb to the envelope but these are few and, generally speaking, the combs hang freely within the envelope. The average size of the worker-cells in each comb increases with successively built combs and there are two combs of large queen cells at the bottom of the nest. When queen-cell building begins, there is a sudden and irreversible switch in building behaviour so that queen cells are frequently built on the periphery of worker-cell combs and between the two types, intermediate-sized cells occur. With the successive use of cells for rearing, the earlier-built ones have become filled with faecal pellets which make them unsuitable for further brood rearing and they are papered over with carton. This habit possibly helps insulate a part of the nest no longer in use and seals off a likely source of disease due to decomposing faecal material.

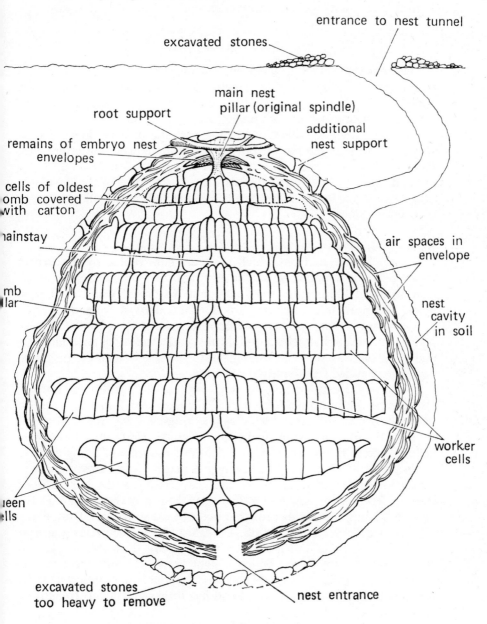

Figure 34. Typical *Paravespula vulgaris* nest (original).

Stones which were too heavy to be dragged out of the entrance tunnel during excavation activities have accumulated at the bottom of the cavity. Smaller stones which were light enough to be removed from the nest site are found around the entrance hole, with a gradation from large to small stones with increasing distance from the hole.

Nest Building

The construction of a wasp nest involves the collection of wood pulp, its mastication during which water and probably saliva are added, and its subsequent application to the nest structure. In subterranean nesting species, the underground cavity must be enlarged by excavation. Other modifications of the nest site may be demanded of all species such as the removal of roots or shoots which interfere with the growth of the nest. The principal elements of nest building are the collection of building materials, the construction of the envelope, the initiation and lengthening of cells, and the building of pillars between successive combs.

Building Materials

The raw materials from which nests are constructed by the British wasp species are mainly vegetable in origin, the principal sources including wood fibres from the sound but weathered wood of fences, posts, and dead trees; decayed wood; fibres derived from the cortex of non-woody plants such as dead brambles and stems of umbelliferous plants; the bark of living trees and shrubs; and a variety of miscellaneous materials such as paper, clothing, and the ragged remains of pupal cappings trimmed from vacated cells.

V. crabro collects rotten wood (Newport 1842) although hornets also scrape the inner bark from dead (Walker 1901) and living trees, particularly lilac and ash, which they may ring-bark with the subsequent death of the branch (Donisthorpe 1929, Kemper 1961). Bromley (1931) includes birch, rhododendron, and dahlias as sources of living cortical material, all of which may be severely damaged. Some observers (e.g. Reeks in Walker 1901) consider that hornets gnaw the bark of live trees to feed on the sap flow rather than collect cortical material for nest building, but it seems probable that at least some bark from living trees is used in nest construction. *V. crabro* also incorporates grains of soil or sand into its nest fabric (Ormerod 1868). Both the hornet and *P. vulgaris* produce carton which is light brown or buff coloured and exceptionally brittle, presumably because the source of building material is rotten rather than sound wood and has little mechanical strength or suppleness.

All other species build grey-coloured nests, the source of material being dead but sound wood which produces a more pliable carton with greater tensile strength. Nicholson (1917) has observed *D. norwegica* collecting sound wood, and I have frequently seen *P. germanica* collecting the grey, weathered wood of chestnut palings and soft-wood fences and posts. *D. norwegica* also collects the woolly pubescence from rhododendron leaves (Laidlaw 1930). Acolat (1953) has examined the carton of several wasp species and considers that the dark grey zones of carton are due to the wood source being impregnated with a blue-stain fungus, *Botrytis cinerea*. The shade and uniformity of colour, particularly in envelope structure, is a useful feature when classifying wasp nests.

The use of unusual sources of material for building has been frequently noted. For example, the use of blue paper has been recorded in *D. sylvestris* and *D. norwegica* (Walsh 1929) resulting in the production of vivid blue nests, and red nests were produced from cedar wood by American *Vespula* species (Howard 1915). Benson (1946) records a case of *P. vulgaris* incorporating woollen garments into a nest, and Lith (1956) found three colonies of the continental wasp, *Dolichovespula saxonica* (F.), which were made from cotton fibres taken from curtains. An interesting case of adventitious foraging for pulp is the multi-coloured *D. norwegica* nest made from confetti collected in the grounds of a church near Kirby Moorside (Walsh 1929).

Collecting Wood Pulp

When collecting wood fibres from a fence or post, the wasp aligns herself with the wood grain and moves slowly backwards, loosening a strip of pulp by biting and scraping the surface with the mandibles (Plate XVe). The scraping produces a distinctive noise which is often clearly audible, especially when the wasp is working dry material. With continued scraping, a ball of wood fibres builds up which is secured behind the mandibles. A little fluid is generally worked into the pulp as it is collected. When sufficient pulp has been obtained — often a ball the size of the head – the wasp flies off to the nest with the pulp held in the mandibles and kept in position with the maxillae and palpi (Plate XVIb). At the nest, the pulp is thoroughly masticated and mixed with saliva.

Paper Making

Whether building cells or extending the envelope, the wood pulp is always laid down in narrow strips and the following description applies to both these major elements of building behaviour. The construction of pillars is somewhat different and will be described later.

Once a position for applying the pulp has been selected, the wasp attaches it to the edge of a cell or the envelope by clamping it on with its mandibles. Holding the edge of the nest with the forelegs, the wasp then moves fairly rapidly backwards, continually biting the pulp and threading it out between the mandibles in a coarse ribbon of wet pulp (Plate XVIII). When the bolus of pulp is used up, the wasp moves back to the original point of application and then works the wet pulp into a flatter, more uniform strip, repeating the process until a thin strip of carton is produced. The strip dries after a minute or two to form the typical wasp paper. There is much interlacing of the wood fibres between individual strips, although the adhesive quality of the carton is probably derived from the wasp's saliva acting as a size.

Envelope Building

The outer covering of the nest, which protects the combs from the elements, insulates the inhabitants and enables a fairly constant temperature to be maintained in the colony. The envelope differs in its architectural details according to the species of wasp, *D. sylvestris* and *D. norwegica* having several layers of smooth, broad overlapping carton, while the envelope of *V. crabro, P. vulgaris,* and *P. germanica* is formed of numerous, shell-like pockets which give the structure a distinctly scalloped appearance. The envelope of *V. rufa* is somewhat

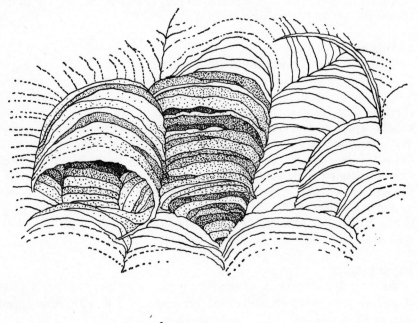

1 cm

Figure 35. 'Shells' from *Paravespula vulgaris* envelope illustrating individual strips of carton (original).

intermediate between these two types, having fairly broad sheets of carton with a few shell-like structures (Plate XIg).

In all species however, the sheets or shells are composed of the individual strips of paper applied by each wasp. In the aerial nesters (*D. sylvestris* and *D. norwegica*) the individual strips are added to the lower margins of existing sheets in roughly straight lines. New sheets are begun above existing ones so that they overlap like the tiles of a roof, conferring a degree of waterproofing to the combs within. The scalloped envelope of the remaining species is made up of overlapping shells, begun on their uppermost edges with distinctly crescent-shaped strips of carton such that the central part is horizontal but with the edges directed downwards at their margins (Fig. 35). With the near-completion of a shell, the last strip or two may be completely circular.

Cell Building

A wasp cell is hexagonal in cross section and becomes wider at its open end and is thus, geometrically speaking, a truncated pyramid

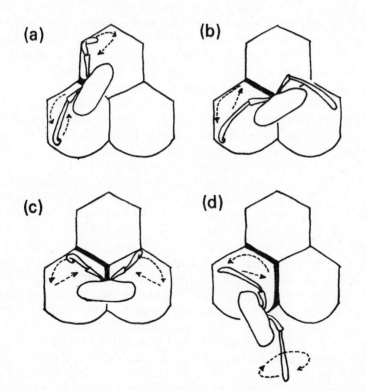

Figure 36. Rudiments of cell-building behaviour (based on *Polistes* species, after Eberhard 1969).

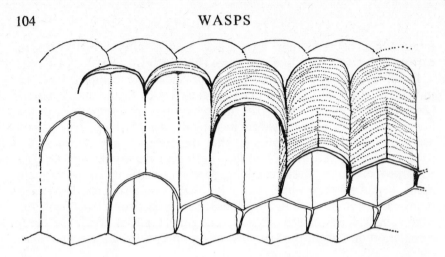

Figure 37. Sequence of pulp application in cell building, *Paravespula vulgaris* (original).

rather than a regular prism (Réaumur 1740). Although the typical wasp cell is hexagonal, the first-formed, isolated cells of a comb are round (Waterhouse 1864), the hexagonal form being assumed when surrounded by other cells. Several bizarre theories have been suggested in the past to explain how the shape is attained, one arm-chair pundit going so far as to state that the pressure exerted by surrounding cells forced the hexagonal shape upon the original cylinders!

The essential prerequisite for the production of the hexagonal cell was first proposed by Waterhouse in 1858 who considered that contact with adjoining cells was the all-important factor. The observations of Eberhard (1969) on *Polistes*, using frame by frame analysis of cine-film, have further elucidated the techniques of cell building.

When a cell is initiated, strips of pulp are applied in the angle between adjacent cells to form an arched ridge which is later expanded, with the addition of more strips, into a cup-like shelf which becomes the base of the cell (Fig. 37). The base is then lengthened to produce a cell, with the walls in contact with existing cells being straight and parallel, the outer wall remaining circular until, with the addition of further cells, it assumes the hexagonal shape. Eberhard's studies have demonstrated the importance of the antennae in cell building for, throughout cell construction, they are in continuous movement, rapidly palpating the sides of adjacent cells. While the wasp applies wood pulp to a wall between two cells it strokes the walls of the adjacent ones by sweeping the antennae forwards along the wall then backwards through the middle of the cell (Fig. 36a). When the pulp strip reaches an intersection between cells, it is continued along the next wall and one antenna moves into the cell adjacent to the new wall (Fig. 36b, c). If building on the periphery of the comb, the wasp completes a wall between existing cells and then continues the strip along the peripheral edge. Because the outer antenna has no cell to touch, it waves about in a circular movement and the resulting wall is circular in outline (Fig. 36d). The peripheral cell may be straight-walled if the adjoining cells – the 'guide cells' – are well-defined hexagons.

Eberhard (1969) points out that the truncated pyramid shape of the cell indicates that the antennae are used to determine the distance between cell walls relative to pre-existing cell surfaces rather than measuring absolute distances. The input of signals from a cell wall are probably perceived by one antenna which stimulates the application of pulp at a constant distance from the wall, a circular wall resulting if the surface is round or absent, and a straight parallel wall if the surface is planar. Stimuli perceived by both antennae results in a straight wall between the guiding surfaces. When cell building, a pulp load is generally used to construct three sides, two sides of one cell, the third side of an adjoining cell, the consequent interlocking of strips providing much strength and rigidity to the comb.

In a series of publications, Deleurance (1947, 1955b, 1957) analysed the building activities of *Polistes* under experimental conditions. The two major components of cell-building behaviour were the initiation or multiplication of cells and the subsequent lengthening of the cell wall ('surélévation'). By removing the ovaries of queens, it was shown that ovariectomized females ceased building new cells but, when the larvae in cells grew larger, the walls of the cells were extended. It appears that cell initiation results from some innate drive controlled by the ovaries but extension of existing cells is stimulated by the developing larva. Deleurance also discovered that cell building in *Polistes* tended to occur in cycles or phases of sustained activity.

Pillar Building

The structures from which the combs are suspended are of two basic types – vertical ribbons and stout pillars (Fig. 48). These structures are always made of more solid, inflexible carton than either cells or envelope. With the initiation of a new comb, the first structure to be built is the mainstay, a centrally positioned pillar with its foundations attached along two or more edges of a cell. From this foundation the carton is extended downwards, becoming concave centrally, and then expanded to form a base for the first two cells of the new comb. In cross section, the new pillar is ribbon-like but with increase in size and numbers of combs the pillars are strengthened until they become much stouter (Plate IXb).

Supplementary support for the comb in *V. crabro*, *P. vulgaris*, and *P. germanica* nests is provided by pillars similar to the first-built, central pillar, although ribbon-styled supports of 1-2 cm are occasionally built (Plate XIXa). The numbers of such pillars is variable but their quantity and robustness are related to the area of comb to be supported and the numbers of combs suspended below them so that there are more pillars per unit area in upper compared to lower combs (unpublished data) (Fig. 48c). The carton from which pillars are made is of a much stronger and harder texture than other parts of the nest while the pulp is very compacted and without gaps or spaces. It is common to find the remains of pupal cappings incorporated into the pillars although they are rarely found elsewhere in the nest structure. It is probable that their inclusion is a regular feature of pillar construction, lending added strength to those parts of the nest which support the weight of brood-filled combs.

In *V. rufa*, *D. sylvestris*, and *D. norwegica* nests, supplementary support for the combs is provided in the form of ribbons of compactly built carton. In effect, they are similar to the early stage of the central pillar structure but, instead of constructing numerous ones and strengthening them by adding carton around them, the initial thin pillar is continued lengthwise to form a series of meandering walls linking successive combs (Fig. 48a).

Occasionally, the pillar foundation is built over a cell opening during enlargement with the eventual entombment of the immature resident.

Excavation of Nest Site

With the growth of the colony, the nest site generally requires some modification, from the considerable amount of earth-moving in the subterranean species to minor adaptations of the site in aerial nesting wasps. The excavation of soil is continued at the same rate as the increase in volume of the nest so that a narrow gap of 1-2 cm is maintained between the surface of the cavity and the nest envelope (Weyrauch 1937). To remove pellets of soil, wasps probably use water in much the same way as the Eumenidae, softening the earth as it is

Figure 38. Downward elongation of cells following inversion of comb (after Montagner 1964a).

scraped away by the mandibles. Weyrauch (1937) considers that the larval saliva collected by adult wasps may also be used to soften the earth. Pellets of soil (see Plate XVIc, d) are removed by dropping them at various distances from the nest entrance during brief flights, while stones too heavy to fly with are dragged to the entrance where they may accumulate in small piles (Plate XVIa). Larger stones loosened during excavations fall to the bottom of the nest cavity.

Some of the excavated earth is used to fill holes in the soil and to maintain the tunnel at an appropriate size (Plate XXIIa). For example, if the mouth of the tunnel is very large, the wasps may use excavated earth to decrease its diameter. *V. crabro* uses pulp to narrow the entrance hole in hollow trees (Janet 1903). Obstructions in the ground such as roots are frequently chewed away, although large roots or stones are usually left in place and the nest built around them. In some situations such as rocky ground, the various obstructions may impose unusual shapes on the nest such as lobed combs jutting into the various spaces excavated by the wasps. Kemper (1961) illustrates a *V. crabro* nest which had three of its eight combs alongside the earlier-built combs because it was impossible to continue downwards (Fig.

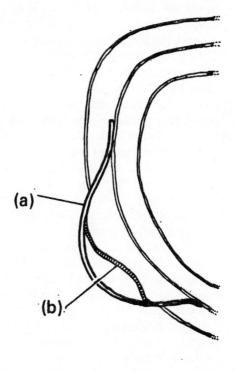

Figure 39. Envelope building in *Dolichovespula media* following introduction of a band of paper *a* resulting in the building of a new envelope sheet *b* to maintain constant distance between envelopes (after Vuillaume and Naulleau 1960).

(a)

(b)

0.5 cm

45). Janet (1903) records that *V. crabro* may enlarge the cavities of hollow trees by gnawing away the wood from the inside. A *P. vulgaris* nest which I found sharing a cardboard box with a robin's nest, had been extended downwards following the excavation of considerable quantities of superphosphate contained in a bag at the bottom of the box.

To excavate the cavity for an average wasp nest, Ritchie (1915) computed that each wasp must remove about $8 \cdot 2$ cc. ($0 \cdot 5$ cu. in.) of soil.

Obstructions some distance from the nest may also be modified, particularly when they interfere with the flow of foraging wasps leaving and returning to the colony. Grass growing in the vicinity of the entrance hole is trimmed back regularly (see Plate XXIIa), and Step (1932) has recorded the case of a *P. germanica* colony which repeatedly cut holes in a twine netting fence to improve the flight path to and from the nest entrance.

Nest Repair and Replacement

If a nest is damaged or destroyed, the wasps will generally repair it or construct a new one. In view of the considerable work entailed in the construction of a nest, it is not surprising that the inhabitants have the capacity to repair the structure or rebuild it, and thereby prevent the total loss of a colony.

Although Rau (1928) considered that *Polistes* queens seldom rebuild the embryo nest if it should be destroyed, Stone (1864b) induced two queens of *P. germanica* to build two and three embryo nests respectively after removing the original nests. Similarly, Stone (1864a) obtained a series of six nests built by 300 workers after putting the wasps in boxes with a few pieces of comb at intervals of a few days. If a mature *Polistes* nest is destroyed, the remaining workers will readily rebuild, constructing large numbers of shallow cells in which the queen lays eggs. The cell walls are extended as the larvae grow so that the original brood density may be quickly regained following the loss of the old nest. Similarly, Matsuura (personal communication) has observed several Japanese hornets which swarm and establish new nests if the old one is destroyed. These nests are built very rapidly and may be built some distance from the original site.

I have seen an unusual example of the adaptability of wasps following damage to their nest. A colony of *P. vulgaris* under observation in a wood near Wrexham, was attacked by a badger one night, the predator destroying about two thirds of the subterranean nest. Over a period of two weeks the remaining wasps covered the exposed remains of the nest with a new envelope and built a roof of soil. This roof was made from moist pellets of earth added piece by piece to the edge of the gaping hole until it had extended over much of the rebuilt nest (Fig. 40).

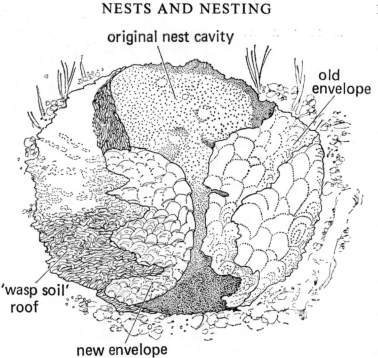

Figure 40. Nest repair in *Paravespula vulgaris* following predation by a **badger** (original).

If a nest is removed together with the queen, the remaining workers will build a nest structure at the original site or around pieces of comb which may be left behind. Janet (1903), after removing a *D. sylvestris* nest, noted that about 50 workers which were not caught had built a small nest very similar to an embryo nest within four days. After 26 days, a 39-cell comb had been built surrounded by several layers of envelope. A group of *Dolichovespula media* workers rebuilt a nest three times, cells being built on each occasion (Janet 1903). After I had collected a *P. vulgaris* nest on one occasion, the workers which were not trapped adopted a piece of comb left near the old nest site and, within a week, had covered the comb with paper and soil. Twenty-five days later the original comb had been broken down and a small comb of 16 cells had been built with an egg in each (Plate XVIIIb). A group of orphaned *V. rufa* workers built three replacement nests containing cells with brood (Stone 1864a).

Groups of orphaned workers building nest structures do not always construct cells, however, and Edgeworth (1864) obtained a series of four nest structures built by a group of *D. norwegica* workers, but in no instance were cells built. In the autumn when the social life of the colony disintegrates, groups of workers sometimes leave the parental colony and establish small groups which make paper structures with little architectural plan, often covering areas of walls with formless sheets of carton. These structures may result from an inherent building drive for they appear to serve no functional purpose in the life of these groups.

Experimental Studies of Building Behaviour

Although the nest is such a conspicuous component in the life of wasps, experimental studies on building behaviour are few and many of these have little relevance to the normal building activities of wasps. Weyrauch (1936a, b, 1937a) has examined aspects of building in *P. vulgaris* and *P. germanica* by cutting holes in the envelope or inserting pieces of cardboard with a variety of perforations into the envelope and observing the repairing activities. The principal results of these studies were that the various parts of a nest which require repair or expansion tend to vie with one another for the work of the wasps, especially when the parts are in close proximity. Where light enters a nest through a hole in the envelope, this hole will stimulate greater activity than other envelope defects, while the damp paper of newly built work is preferred, leading to a congregated effort in nest repair. One important result of Weyrauch's work was that comb containing larvae will stimulate considerably more energetic repair work than empty comb or cells containing pupae. The introduction of variously shaped pieces of cardboard apparently demonstrated a 'tactile-kinaesthetic' sense whereby wasps can distinguish the contours of various objects in the dark. These shapes and holes stimulated the wasps to join up the edges around perforations or projections so that a relatively uniform, smooth structure resulted. The underlying building instincts apparently result in the economical use of wood pulp in the construction of envelopes.

Vuillaume and Naulleau (1960) made similar experiments on the aerial nester, *D. media*, in France and showed that natural and artificial obstacles may be incorporated into the envelope as integral parts of its structure. One constant feature of envelope construction in the aerial nesting species is that the large sheets of overlapping carton tend to be parallel so that uniform spaces occur between them. The introduction of a convex piece of card into the envelope stimulated the building of an extra sheet within the bulge so as to maintain the air-space distance (Fig. 39).

SEASONAL CHANGES IN THE STRUCTURE OF NESTS

To accommodate the increasing volume of combs which are made during the season, the inner envelopes are constantly being torn down and the outer parts built up, this recycling of envelope carton being readily seen in *D. sylvestris* nests (Fig. 47c) where the bases of the earlier built envelope remain. In subterranean sites, the excavation of the cavity precedes extension of the envelope and it is a familiar sight when observing the tunnel entrance to see wasps dragging out large pellets of soil and stones or flying off with manageable quantities of earth (Plate XVIc, d). Even those species which build aerial nests must frequently modify the site to permit enlargement of the nest, although these changes often involve little more than cutting away a twig or leaf which has become an obstacle to further nest growth. The seasonal changes in the numbers of combs and cells has been studied in *P. vulgaris* and *P. germanica* by the destructive sampling of 89 colonies during a single season (Spradbery 1971). The numbers of combs and cells were counted and worker and queen cells distinguished. The value of sampling a large number of colonies during one year is that overall trends in nest growth and populations changes may be obtained, and a picture of the annual cycle of growth for a typical wasp colony may be drawn up.

Number of Combs and Cells

Throughout much of the season, cells are added to the periphery of combs and new combs suspended below older ones so that the volume of the nest increases.

In *P. vulgaris*, the combs in June and early July colonies were two or three in number, increasing to an average of five combs by the end of July and seven in late August. By the end of September, when nest-building has reached its climax, the average number of combs was nine, although one colony which had built its nest in the confined space of a cavity wall had constructed fourteen combs by the time of its capture in August. From two to four of the lower combs were composed of queen cells (Fig. 41a). *P. germanica* colonies were, on average, slightly smaller than *P. vulgaris* with four combs per nest in July, six in August and from seven to eleven combs (mean 8·4 combs per nest) by the end of the season with two to four queen-cell combs (Fig. 41b). In New Zealand and Australia where the accidentally introduced *P. germanica* is well established, perennial colonies may build nests with some thirty combs or more (see Chapter 7).

When the foundress queen is building the nest and foraging on her own, the number of cells never exceeds fifty, and with the emergence of the first few workers in May, the increase in number of cells is still low. For example, I found a *P. vulgaris* colony in early June with 12 workers present and with two combs of 101 and 8 cells, a stage similar to the nests figured in Plates XIII and XIXa. With the increase in numbers of workers in June and July, there is a very rapid expansion

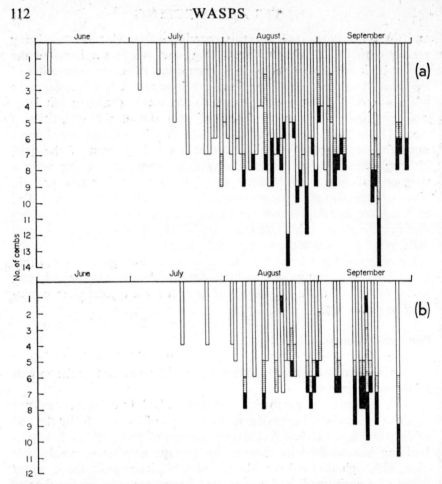

Figure 41. Number of combs per colony in (a) *Paravespula vulgaris* and (b) *P. germanica* (from Spradbery 1971). Open columns = worker-cell combs; closed columns = queen-cell combs; hatched columns = mixed-worker and queen-cell combs.

of the nest structure, with the mean number of cells per colony increasing from about 1,000 at the beginning of July to 7,000 by the end of the month (Fig. 42). The number of worker cells per colony does not increase after the commencement of queen-cell building in early August, by which time a maximum of 12,944 and 11,961 worker cells per colony were found in *P. vulgaris* and *P. germanica* respectively.

During August, 53 per cent of *P. vulgaris* and 62 per cent of *P. germanica* colonies contained queen cells and, by the end of the month, all colonies had begun queen-cell construction. Once queen-cell building begins, worker-cell construction ceases abruptly and is not normally resumed during the remainder of colony life. Combs com-

Egg attached to wall.

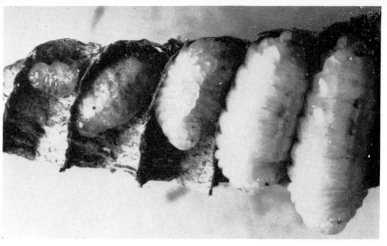

(b) Second to fifth-instar larvae of *Paravespula germanica*.

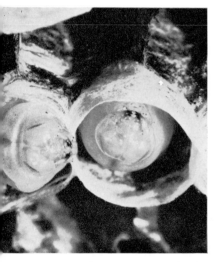

Mature larvae of *P. germanica* spinning oons.

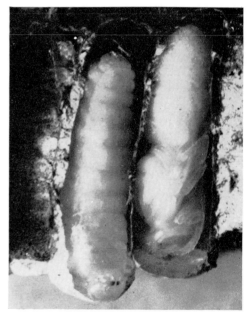

(e) Pre-pupa (left) and pupa of *P. germanica*, note faecal pellet at base of cell.

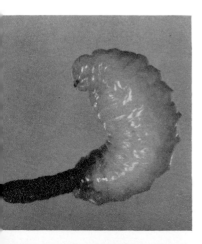

(d) Post-spinning stage larva evacuating faecal material from midgut.

VII (*a–e*). Developmental stages (*see also VIII*).

(a) Section of *Paravespula vulgaris* comb to illustrate increase in the pigmentation of pupae.

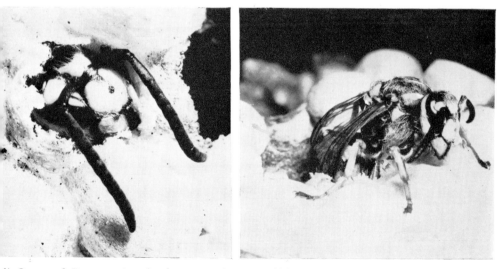

b) Queen of *P. germanica* chewing away the upal capping,

(c) Same queen emerging from cell.

III (*a–c*). Developmental stages (*see also VII*).

IX (top). Subterranean nest of *Paravespula germanica, in situ*, (bottom) pillars from which combs are supported, same nest.

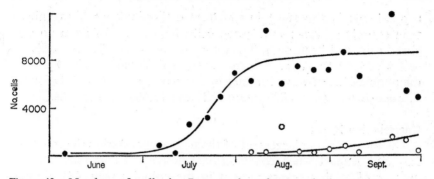

Figure 42. Number of cells in *Paravespula vulgaris* colonies (5-day means)
● = worker cells; ○ = queen cells (from Spradbery 1971).

posed exclusively of queen cells are built, although queen cells are
also added to the periphery of worker combs – the building of queen
cells around the edge of worker combs occurring in 43 per cent of
P. vulgaris nests and 87 per cent of *P. germanica* nests. There were

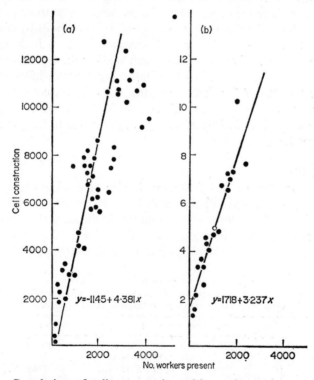

Figure 43. Correlation of cell construction with number of adult workers per
colony using June-August data only (from Spradbery 1971): (a) *Paravespula
vulgaris*; (b) *P. germanica*.

I*

two colonies in this study in which an earlier-built worker comb had been entirely replaced with queen cells, and in one of them no other queen cells had been built. The maximum number of queen cells in a nest was 3,888 in *P. vulgaris* and 2,886 in *P. germanica*. In a study of the populations of wasp colonies in Germany, Kemper (1961) found a *P. vulgaris* nest with 4,028 queen cells and 17,664 worker cells.

Construction Rates

The most rapid enlargement of the nest occurs during the months of July and August when constructional activity is correlated with the number of adult workers present in the colonies (Fig. 43). By early August, however, the major constructional activities are complete and the relative increase in number of cells is very small. Archer (1968), in studies on *P. vulgaris* and *P. germanica* colonies, estimated that the rate of construction, based on the number of cells built per worker per day, is 0·42 in the early season when nests were increasing rapidly in size, falling to 0·09 when colonies reached their maximum size in August, and only 0·04 when queen rearing was underway. Based on my own data, the mean number of cells built per worker per day was 0·07 throughout the season, an average of 1·2 cells built by each worker during its life. Because of the rapid increase of cells in July and August, the mean number of cells built by each worker during this period was calculated at 2·4 cells per worker, assuming a mean life span of 16·1 days (see Chapter 7 for details of longevity). Thus, construction rates vary according to the period of colony development, with maximum activity taking place in July and August, just prior to the production of queen brood.

Size of Cells

Apart from the marked difference in size of worker and queen cells, there are also seasonal differences in the relative size of cells in successively built worker combs. For example, in *P. vulgaris* colonies, there was an 11·4 per cent increase in width and a 17·0 per cent increase in depth of worker cells between the first and fourth combs (Table 10).

TABLE 10
The size of worker and queen cells in five *Paravespula vulgaris* colonies
(50 cells from each comb were measured) (after Spradbery 1971)

CELLS	COMB	DEPTH OF CELL (mm)		WIDTH OF CELL (mm)	
		mean	range	mean	range
Worker	I	12·48	11·4–14·0	4·30	4·0–4·5
	II	13·39	12·5–15·0	4·43	4·0–4·7
	III	14·40	13·2–15·5	4·52	4·1–4·9
	IV	14·62	12·7–17·3	4·79	4·3–5·1
Queen	V	14·18	12·8–15·3	6·27	6·0–6·5

In mature colonies, brood rearing in the upper, earlier-built combs is at a low level and there are many empty cells (see Fig. 59). The walls of these vacant cells are generally broken down and the carton is presumably incorporated into other parts of the nest. As will be seen later (Chapter 9), the progressive increase in size of the cells is probably related to an increase in the average size of adult workers which occurs during the year. It is likely that larger workers produce larger cells which in turn would aid in the rearing of still bigger wasps.

There was no difference between the depth of queen cells and the most recently built worker cells, but queen cells were 31 per cent wider, while the volume of carton was 40 per cent greater than in the largest worker cells.

PHYSICAL CONDITIONS WITHIN THE NEST

Wasps in common with all other insects are poikilothermic – cold-blooded animals whose body temperatures are close to ambient temperature such that body temperature varies with surrounding temperature. But the metabolic activities of wasps, from wing beating in adults to feeding in larvae, can raise the temperature of a nest appreciably above ambient temperature. Evaporation of water causes a heat loss because of the principle of latent heat of vaporization. Thus, despite the poikilothermic nature of wasps, there exists the capacity to regulate body and colony temperatures independently of external temperature.

Himmer (1932), in a review of temperature regulation in social Hymenoptera, showed that the body temperature of a wasp may be increased several degrees above that of its surroundings. In *P. vulgaris*, for example, queens, workers, and males could increase their body temperature by 10·48, 7·46 and 6·24°C respectively. The developmental optima for brood in *P. vulgaris* was determined at 29·5-32°C, and for *V. crabro* it was 29·8-31·8°C (Himmer 1932). To maintain these optimum temperatures, wasps must necessarily have a capacity for temperature regulation within the colony. The studies of Himmer (1927, 1931, 1932) and Ishay, Bytinsky-Salz and Shulov (1967) have demonstrated that wasps and hornets can maintain the temperature of their nests above ambient and, in the event of high external temperatures, they can reduce nest temperature to within the optimum range (Fig. 44). Nevertheless, temperature control in wasp colonies is less constant and uniform than the 35°C of a honeybee colony which fluctuates less than 0·5°C during the summer months.

The regulation of nest temperature is accomplished by a combination of factors, one of the most important being the nest itself. The combs

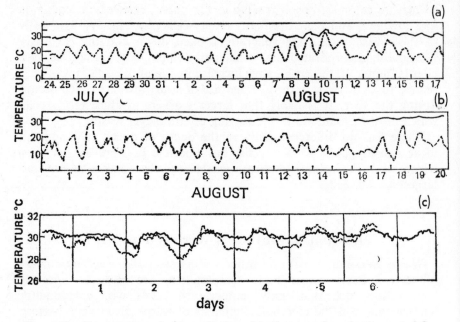

Figure 44. Temperatures inside colonies: (a) *Paravespula vulgaris* nest (after Himmer 1927); (b) *Vespa crabro* nest (after Himmer 1932); (c) *V. crabro* colony (after Ishay and Ruttner 1971).
Solid line in (a) and (b) = nest temperature; broken line in (a) and (b) = outside temperature; solid line in (c) = temperature in pupal cells; broken line in (c) = temperature in larval cells.

of a colony are surrounded by an envelope of variable thickness which depends largely on the nest site – more exposed sites stimulating the building of thicker envelopes. It is well established that diurnal temperature fluctuations decrease with increasing depth underground. For example, there is a fluctuation of more than 10°C at a depth of 5 cm and less than a 5°C variation at 30 cm. This physical characteristic is reflected in the thickness of the envelope. Examples are illustrated in Plate XI in which an underground nest of *P. germanica* with a 2 cm thick envelope is compared with a nest of the same species from an aerial situation in which the envelope was 6 cm thick. Potter (1965) points out that thermoregulation is dependent on colony size, heat production being proportional to the amount of adults and brood, while heat loss would be proportional to the surface area of the nest. Assuming a nest to be spherical, the larger the nest the lower the surface area to volume ratio, such that heat conservation would be more efficient in larger nests. It is interesting to note that small or immature nests have proportionately much thicker envelopes than the larger, mature nests. The common physical attribute of the envelope, irrespective of its architectural details, is the numerous air spaces between leaves or shells of carton, a 'multi-glazing' structure with excellent insulation qualities. With such a wall surrounding a nest, thermoregulation can be more effectively carried out. In the exposed combs of *Polistes* nests, heat accumulation and metabolic heat regulation are absent (Himmer 1932). Even vespine nests without brood or adults have less fluctuating temperatures due to the air spaces in the envelope and the empty cells which help insulate the nest from the influence of external temperature (Ishay, Bytinski-Salz and Shulov 1967).

To maintain a constant temperature within the well-insulated nest, wasps must be able to increase and decrease temperature above or below ambient. The generation of heat by the movements of adults and the wriggling, feeding, and growth of the larvae may increase nest temperature. The massing of adult hornets on the combs at night apparently helps increase nest temperature, especially around combs containing brood (Ishay and others 1967). Ishay and Ruttner (1971) in a detailed study of temperature control in *V. crabro* colonies, showed that around pupae, a very constant 30°C was maintained, although diurnal fluctuations in larval cells was much greater (Fig. 44c). One possible reason for this differential attention to pupae and larvae is the inability of pupae to raise the temperature within their cells due to their comparatively lower metabolic rate (Gaul 1952c). By introducing honey into a colony, the subsequent food intake by *P. vulgaris* and *P. germanica* adults causes a noticeable increase in nest temperature (Roland 1969). The movements of larvae and their metabolic activities can create sufficient controlled heat to maintain reasonable thermoregulation in nests even in the absence of adults (Ishay and Ruttner 1971). Thus, wasps and hornets have well developed methods of heat generation whereby they can raise nest temperatures above ambient, the maintenance of higher temperatures being aided by the insulation qualities of the nest structure.

If nest temperature increases above the optimum, the adults respond initially by fanning their wings (Gaul 1952d). As the temperature increases, more and more wasps begin fanning, suggesting that they have different fanning thresholds which would be an advantage if this type of graded response leads to a finer control of nest temperature. The wing-beat frequency during fanning in *Dolichovespula maculata* (L.) was 35 strokes per second compared to their flight frequency of 95 strokes per second (Gaul 1952d). Even when temperatures are below the optimum, there is a constant but low level of fanning activity, presumably creating convection currents to aid in heat distribution (Ishay and others 1967). As the temperature increases above the optimum and more adults begin to fan, they arrange themselves in a line between the nest and the tunnel entrance, thus creating a flow of air between the nest and the outside. If the temperature continues to rise, the adults collect water (Gaul 1952d, Ishay and others 1967) or even use larval secretions (Weyrauch 1936a) which they apply to pupal cappings or cell walls. The evaporation of the liquid causes a reduction in temperature due to the latent heat of vaporization being withdrawn from the carton. In *V. orientalis* the nest entrance may even be enlarged to permit greater ventilation if the temperature within the nest rises too much (Ishay and others 1967).

A further consequence of nest temperature is its influence on foraging activity for, as will be seen in Chapter 6, low nest temperature stimulates an increase in pulp foraging for envelope building (Potter 1965).

To conclude, it is apparent that one of the assets of sociality in wasps is the capacity of a colony to regulate the temperature of its domestic environment, with the attendant advantage of more efficient brood rearing.

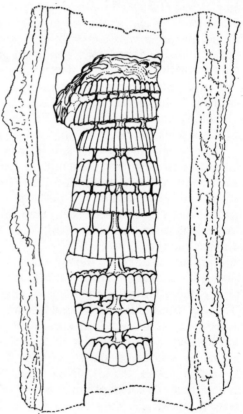

⌞10 cm⌟

Figure 45. *Vespa crabro* nest in hollow tree trunk (after **Beutenmuller** 1898).

BRITISH WASP NESTS

The following accounts describe the nesting sites, sources of building materials and details of nest architecture of the British social wasps. A Key to separate the nests according to species will be found in Appendix 2.

Vespa crabro (Plate XIa). Typically, the hornet *V. crabro* builds its nest in hollow, dead trees such as aspen (Lloyd 1942), elms and oaks (Beutenmuller 1898), but the roofs of thatched cottages (Walker 1901), barns (Simpson 1948, H. G. Hurrell personal communication), abandoned bee hives and holes in walls (Guiglia 1948) are also utilized. Professor O. W. Richards (personal communication) has found hornets' nests in a pollarded willow and in a felled elm tree, the latter having its entrance tunnel in the grass some 20 cm from the trunk. Underground sites are rarely encountered but they have been recorded from time to time (Walker 1901).

Being the biggest of British wasps, it is not surprising that hornets' nests tend to be large with cells much wider than the other species. For example, the mean width of the cells in the first-built comb of a hornet's nest is 7·4 mm while those of *P. vulgaris* are 4·3 mm. The recorded diameter and length of some representative nests are as follows: 38 × 56 cm (Ormerod 1868), 38 × 48 cm (Walker 1901), and 18 × 61 cm (Beutenmuller 1898), the dimensions depending very much on the shape and size of the nesting cavity. Where the site imposes no

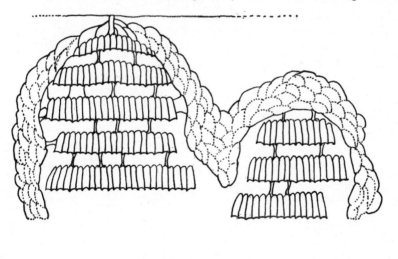

10 cm

Figure 46. Vespa crabro nest with the most recent combs built alongside earlier combs due to an obstruction at base of nest (after Kemper 1961).

restriction on nest building, they tend to be more oval than round in shape.

The carton of hornet's nests is brittle, composed of rather coarse fragments of masticated wood (Plate XIVa). The major source of wood pulp is rotten wood, although some bark fragments may be incorporated into the nest fabric (Simpson 1948) while Ormerod (1868) points out that sand is frequently mixed with the wood pulp. Ishay (1964) found that sand and small stones form large proportions of the nest fabric in *V. orientalis*. The use of rotten wood was also noted by the celebrated naturalist, Gilbert White, in the eighteenth century. Although very fragile, the envelope paper has considerable water-proof qualities and in unprotected sites, a full envelope is built around the combs, sometimes as much as 10 cm thick (Berland 1931). If the nest is built in a hollow tree where it would be largely protected from the elements, there is generally a rudimentary envelope or simply a small cap at the top of the nest (Fig. 45). Where a large concavity occurs in the interior walls of the hollow tree, this hole may be screened off with a few layers of envelope. The envelope, where it exists, is composed of elongated shells or tunnels of carton which are readily distinguishable from the smaller, scalloped structures of the *P. vulgaris* envelope. The colour is predominantly yellow or brown, but like *P. vulgaris* it has a rather variegated appearance if looked at closely. The individual strips of carton being white, grey, yellow, brown, and sometimes

TABLE 11

Distribution of nests in relation to site (after Spradbery 1971)

SITE	% OF NESTS		NUMBER OF NESTS
	Paravespula vulgaris	*Paravespula germanica*	
A. Subterranean			
a. Banks, hedge-rows	35	32	38
b. Open fields, soil borders	25	50	36
c. Rockeries, stony ground	4	6	5
d. Compost, refuse heaps	13	3	12
Total	77	91	91
B. Miscellaneous			
a. Sheds, outhouses	4	3	4
b. Boxes	2	0	2
c. Bee hives	1	3	2
d. Trees	9	0	7
e. Straw bales	4	3	4
f. Cavity walls	3	0	2
Total	23	9	21
Total number of nests examined	82	30	112

almost black – emphasizing the variety of sources used by hornets when collecting pulp.

The number of combs in a mature nest varies from 6 (Janet 1903, Kemper 1961) to 9 (Beutenmuller 1898), although their number is partly determined by the width of the nest cavity and consequently the size of combs they are able to build. Queen comb, in common with *P. vulgaris* and *P. germanica*, occupies the lower two to four combs of an average eight-comb nest. Combs are suspended by a much-thickened mainstay pillar and a variable number of supporting pillars similar in shape to the mainstay.

Paravespula vulgaris (Plate XIc, d). In a survey of wasp nests in Hertfordshire, I found that 77 per cent of the 82 *P. vulgaris* nests were in subterranean sites, the remainder in a variety of places such as attics and cavity walls of houses, empty beehives, and attached to the branches or trunks of trees (Table 11). Similar findings were recorded by Weyrauch (1935) in Germany (Table 12). *P. vulgaris* nests have been found in hedges (Stelfox 1930) and one was discovered in a disused hot-house stove, the wasps using the chimney and grate as entrance holes (Oudemans 1901). Sandemann (1936) found several nests in hollow trees, one sharing the same tree with a hornet's nest only 6 metres away. I have found a *P. vulgaris* nest in a cardboard box which also contained a robin's nest, and a correspondent in the *Daily Telegraph* recorded the association of a wasp colony and wren's nest in a nesting box. A. D. Johnston (personal communication) found a *P. vulgaris* colony which had been built in an abandoned house-martin's nest, the wasp nest overflowing the bird's nest during its development. Edgeworth (1864) discovered a *P. vulgaris* colony and a field mouse sharing a common tunnel, an association fraught with a certain amount of danger for the mouse.

TABLE 12

Nesting sites of social wasps (from Weyrauch 1935)

SPECIES	FREE HANGING			ENCLOSED SPACE			
				aerial		subterranean	
	on tree branch	in dense bushes	partially sub-terranean	large space	small space	banks	level ground
P. vulgaris	0	0	0	2	11	56	19
P. germanica	0	0	0	2	2	29	31
D. sylvestris	7	3	2	2	2	16	2
D. norwegica	—	very frequent	frequent	very rare	rare	rare	—

The shape of an unrestricted nest is globular and, like *P. germanica*, tends to be slightly flattened at the poles. The colour of the carton is very similar to *V. crabro*, and like the hornet's nest is distinctly fragile. The wide variety of weather-beaten or decomposed wood used in carton construction gives the nest its attractively variegated appearance (see Plate Xc). The overlapping, shell-like structures of which the envelope is composed are quite pronounced, each shell enclosing a pocket of air in much the same way as the cavity-wall of a domestic house. The envelope tends to be relatively thin in underground or other well protected sites being about 2 cm thick, but in more exposed situations the envelope may be 8 cm thick.

The combs, which are supported by pillars similar to the central mainstays, are slightly convex in the middle although the remainder of the comb is horizontal (Fig. 47b).

Paravespula germanica (Plate XIe, f).   The majority of *P. germanica* nests are in subterranean situations (Table 11 and 12) and only 6 per cent of the colonies in my Hertfordshire survey were in miscellaneous sites compared to 19 per cent of the *P. vulgaris* colonies. This difference may mean that *P. germanica* is less opportunist and more dependent on underground sites, although aerial nests have been recorded (Weyrauch 1935, Acolat 1953). In New Zealand, this species sometimes builds enormous, perennial colonies attached to tree trunks (Thomas 1960). The mature nests are generally about 25 cm in diameter although I have found nests in unrestricted sites such as attics which have grown to 36 cm in diameter. Newstead (1891) records a subterranean nest of 39 cm diameter. Perhaps the biggest nest recorded in Britain is the specimen on display in the University Museum at Oxford (Plate XIb). This nest was dug out of the ground in 1857 when only 12 cm in diameter and suspended from the wall of a house where sugar and beer were offered to the wasps to supplement their normal diet. Apparently the workers from two nearby colonies deserted their nests joined forces with the first colony, thus helping to increase its size to a prodigious 46 cm diameter and 61 cm length during a single season.

In common with other subterranean nesting species, the nest cavity is rarely more than a few cm beneath the surface of the ground (see Plate IXa), O. W. Richards (personal communication) recording depths of 5-15 cm in six colonies of *P. germanica* with entrance tunnels of 8-76 cm length.

Although the shape and size of *P. germanica* and *P. vulgaris* nests are very similar (Fig. 47) there can be no confusion in distinguishing the two species. The carton (Plate XIVc) is considerably more supple and less friable in *P. germanica*, and the colour is a relatively uniform, light slate-grey. The shells which make up the envelope are more

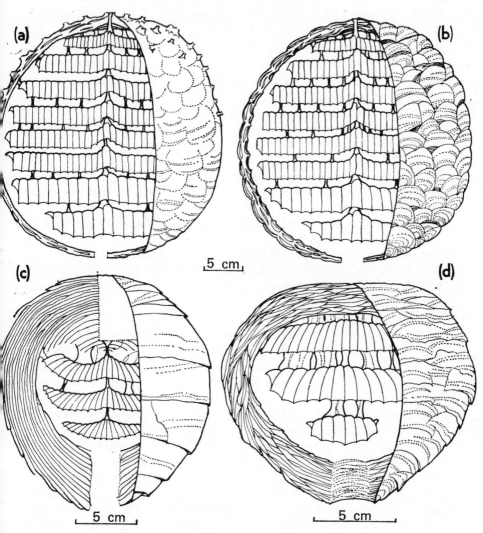

Figure 47. Wasp nests: (a) *Paravespula germanica*; (b) *P. vulgaris*; (c) *D. sylvestris* (after Janet 1903); (d) *V. rufa*.

flattened, the individual shells appearing as boss-like structures studding the surface. In common with the remaining species, the source of pulp is dead but sound wood scraped from fences, posts and trees.

Vespula rufa (Plate XIg, h). Nests of *V. rufa* are invariably subterranean with the nest cavity very close to the surface of the ground or even superficially located under moss in dry banks (Edgeworth 1864). Smith (1856) records an embryo nest in a small (7·5 cm diameter) hole which was 23 cm deep in the side of a bank. Janet (1903) describes and figures a nest which had been built in a bank shared by a colony of the ant, *Lasius niger* (L.). Nests have also been found in old tree stumps (Morley 1935) and beneath the roots of a tree (Pack-Beresford 1904). *V. rufa* often builds in cup-shaped hollows in the earth with the nest suspended from the roots of grass. This species is reputed to be a poor excavator of soil (Edgeworth 1864).

Nests of *V. rufa* are considerably smaller than the preceding species, recorded diameters and lengths of four nests being 16 × 7 cm (Janet 1903), 11 × 6 cm (Oudemans cited in Janet 1903), 12·7 × 12·0 cm (R. C. Watkins, personal communication), and 13·5 × 11·5 cm (personal data). The shape of the nest varies from a flattened sphere to an apple-shape.

The envelope of *V. rufa*, tends to be intermediate in style between that of *P. germanica* and the aerial nester, *D. sylvestris*, the outer covering being composed of more or less continuous leaves of carton with the lower edges fixed down in several places. The shell-like structures of the envelope are virtually absent (Fig. 47d). The envelope may be composed of 4-5 sheets in a subterranean nest site (Janet 1903) or as many as 13 sheets in an aerial nest, with the entrance at the bottom where the sheets are trimmed to form a circular hole (Fig. 47d and Plate XIIIb). The carton is loosely woven with large spaces occurring between individual wood fibres throughout much of the envelope (Plate XIVd). The colour is predominantly grey with occasional whitish or brown strips of carton.

Mature nests have 3 or 4 combs, the lower two being wholly or partially composed of queen cells (Smith 1852, unpublished data). In the one nest I have examined in detail, there were three combs of 9, 8, and 3·5 cm diameter, flat in side view, with 387 worker cells in the first comb, and 238 and 52 queen cells in the remaining two combs. Pack-Beresford (1904) found a *V. rufa* nest with two combs, the upper one being composed of about 200 worker cells, the lower one with 100 queen cells, both combs having a diameter of 6·5 cm. The maximum number of combs is five (R. C. Watkins, personal communication). The carton of the cells is also loosely woven with many small holes, although the comb carton is of much stouter texture than the envelope.

The supplementary support for the combs is provided by ribbon-like sheets of carton (Fig. 48a).

Dolichovespula sylvestris (Plate Xb). Although *D. sylvestris* is usually described as a typical aerial-nesting species, recorded nest sites suggest that it is as often found in partially subterranean sites as in aerial situations. For example, 18 of the 34 nests found by Weyrauch (1935) were underground (Table 12), and there are many other

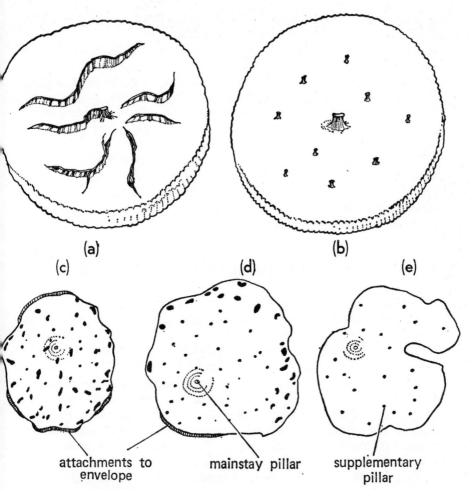

Figure 48. Comb supports (a) central mainstay pillar and additional ribbon support in *Vespula rufa*; (b) column pillars in *P. vulgaris*; (c) (d) (e) first, second, and tenth combs from a *P. vulgaris* nest to show decreasing number and size of pillars per unit area (c-e after Kemper 1961).

records of underground nests of *D. sylvestris* (Pack-Beresford 1903, 1904; Stelfox 1930; W. D. Hamilton, personal communication). Hollow trees, caves, beehives (Scott 1917), hedgerows (Ormerod 1868), old walls (Sandemann 1938), and an empty barrel (Palmer 1925) have been recorded as nest sites. Frohawk (1935) has described a nest which was built alongside a house-martin's nest under the eaves of a building, both communities continuing their activites without interference. When a nest is built in a tree or bush, *D. sylvestris* does not normally incorporate surrounding leaves into the nest fabric.

D. sylvestris nests are small (17-20 cm diameter, Janet 1903, Scott 1917) and constructed of supple carton, flexible in texture, and without holes or spaces in the envelope carton (Plate XIVf). The colour is characteristically a uniform light grey. The envelope is composed of numerous broad sheets of carton, normally attached at the top of the nest, each sheet overlapping the one beneath it like a series of umbrellas (Fig. 47c). The lower edges of the sheets are not fixed and are straight-edged. The entrance hole is normally at the bottom of the nest or slightly to one side.

There are generally three combs in mature colonies although four have occasionally been encountered (Berland 1931), their shape in cross-section being very characteristic, the central part being convex above, with the edges of the comb upturned. The combs are of small diameter with 230-435 cells per comb (Weyrauch 1935), although data on the proportion of worker and queen cells are lacking.

The combs are suspended by the usual spindle-like mainstay, but additional comb support is provided by ribbon-like sheets of carton.

Dolichovespula norwegica (Plate Xa). Nests of *D. norwegica* are most frequently built in low bushes such as gooseberry and currant (Smith 1852, Walker 1901), and I have taken a nest from a hawthorn hedge in East Kilbride, Scotland. Edgeworth (1864) has recorded a nest suspended from the lower branches of a fir tree, and found colonies in disused nests of a sparrow and a wren. Occasionally, *D. norwegica* builds its nest in higher aspects such as the top of an apple tree (Ormerod 1868), while Bignell (in Walker 1901) found a nest more than 10 metres high in the branches of a horse chestnut tree. Nests have also been located in haystacks (Nicholson 1917), attached to a window frame (Walsh 1929), in a beehive (personal observation), under a garden seat (Hey 1909), and occasionally in heather bushes or even underground on exposed moors in Cumberland (Routledge 1933).

The nests are typically pear-shaped and similar in size to *D. sylvestris* nests. Guiglia (1948) records a nest of 18 cm diameter and 22 cm length in Italy, and Winckworth Allen (1938) records a nest of 22 cm length containing 4 combs with a total of 1,534 cells. There are more contrasting shades in the greyish carton of *D. norwegica* compared to *D. sylvestris*, and the carton is of coarser texture. According to Weyrauch (1935), the envelopes, which are built in broad sheets, do not overlap markedly but form more or less continuous sheets down to the ventro-lateral entrance hole. In the nests I have seen, the sheets are either continuous or pressed down and attached in a few places to underlying sheets. The lower margins are characteristically flounced (Plate Xa) and not straight edged. The envelope is composed of several sheets of carton (12-15 according to Guiglia, 1948) and leaves are frequently incorporated into the structure where their inclusion replaces carton (Edgeworth 1864). The entrance hole has a horn-like porch of paper on its upper edge (Ormerod 1868).

A maximum of 4 combs has been recorded (Weyrauch 1935), the combs radiating downwards and outwards, while the combs are suspended by 'tape-like suspenders' (Winkworth Allen 1938).

CHAPTER 6

FEEDING AND FORAGING

There are many stimuli which, in various ways and to varying degrees, release and control foraging activities in social wasps. The needs of the colony in the form of nest construction and repair, the demands of the brood, and the influence of the queen are probably all directly implicated in determining the type and frequency of foraging trips. These varied stimuli impinge on the individual wasp in such a way that its behaviour will be determined by colony factors, but modified by the individual's genetic, physiological and age characteristics.

FORAGING THRESHOLDS

The conditions which determine the limits within which foraging is possible are principally physical but social factors also play their part in promoting foraging activities. The three major factors which stimulate flight are light intensity, temperature, and the social conditions prevailing in the colony.

Light Intensity

The illumination on a summer's day is about 10,000 lumens per square foot, while on a clear but moonless night, the light intensity is only about 0·002 lumen per square foot. Within this wide range of illumination, Blackith (1958a) determined that *P. vulgaris*, *P. germanica*, and *V. rufa* had similar thresholds of illumination above which flight may take place, although *V. crabro*, which frequently flies on moonlit nights, had a considerably lower threshold (Table 13). Blackith discovered that the first sorties at dawn are released by a lower illumination than that which prevails when foraging ceases at dusk. The explanation for this difference in threshold values is the probable reluctance of the wasp to leave the nest in the evening if the critical level of illumination necessary to navigate home should occur during the trip.

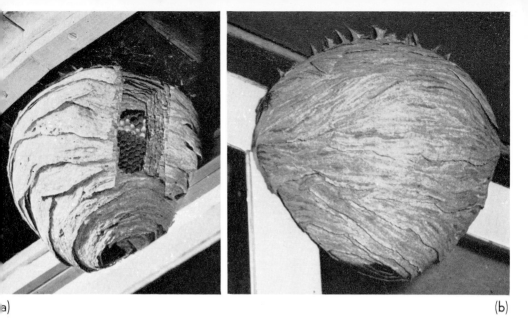

(a)

(b)

(c)

(d)

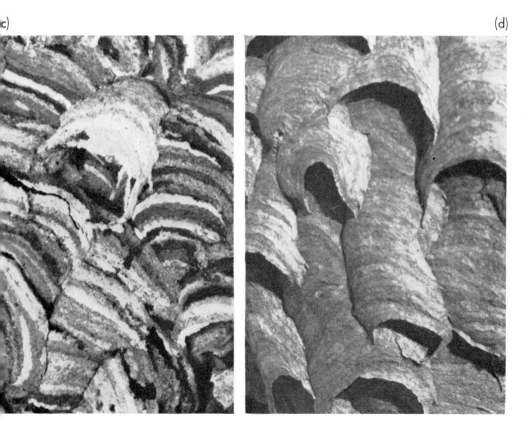

X (*a*). Nest of *Dolichovespula norwegica* built in a disused beehive, (*b*) nest of *D. sylvestris* hanging from a veranda, (*c*) detail of envelope of *P. vulgaris* to illustrate the scalloped design and individual strips of carton, each strip representing a single load of woodpulp, (*d*) detail of *P. germanica* envelope from aerial nest.

XI (a–h). Nests of British wasps.

(a) Immature nest of *Vespa crabro*.

(c) Aerial nest of *P. vulgaris* in attic.
(scale in inches)

(e) Subterranean nest of *P. germanica*.

(g) Aerial nest of *Vespula rufa*.
(scale in inches)

(*b*) Large *Paravespula germanica* nest from the Oxford University Museum (*see* p. 122).

(*d*) Same nest with envelope partially removed, note thickness of envelope.

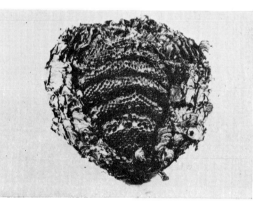

(*f*) Aérial nest of *P. germanica*.

(*h*) Same nest with envelope partially removed.

TABLE 13
Light thresholds and eye-length in worker wasps (after Blackith 1958a)

SPECIES	MEAN ILLUMINATION (lumens per square foot)			MEAN LENGTH OF COMPOUND EYE (mm)
	first sorties	last sorties	last entry	
P. vulgaris	—	1·77	0·22	2·337
P. germanica	0·15	3·64	0·25	2·478
V. rufa	0·34	3·37	0·55	2·445
V. crabro	0·010	0·0150	0·0027	3·933

In the evening when the workers are flying at the limits of their visual sensitivity, they frequently collide with small obstacles, including other wasps, during their attempts to locate the nest tunnel entrance (Blackith 1958a). If there is a misty dawn, the wasps will begin flying when the critical illumination is attained but, in the absence of visible landmarks, they do not leave the vicinity of the nest until the visibility improves. Wasps which are out foraging when the threshold level is reached at dusk, are unable to return and spend the night outside the nest. When observing colonies at dawn, the first recorded flights are invariably those of returning overnight foragers (Gaul 1952a, Blackith 1957, and personal observations).

Gaul (1952a), in his experiments on the American species *Vespula maculifrons* (Buysson), concluded that light was the basic factor in wakening a wasp colony and initiating flight, and that flight could be stimulated below the normal temperature threshold if the light intensity was greatly increased.

The influence of the moon's illumination on foraging activity in *V. rufa* has been studied by Edwards (1968). Comparison of the first sorties of the day at different times of the lunar cycle revealed marked differences in foraging activity depending on the phase and position of the moon above the horizon. With a full overhead moon, foraging began 1½ hours before sunrise compared to only 10-45 minutes when there was no lunar illumination. A similar increase in diurnal foraging time probably occurs in the evening if the moon rises above the horizon before solar illumination decreases below the threshold level.

Barlow (1952) proposed that the sensitivity of the hymenopterous compound eye is proportional to its length. Blackith (1958a) measured the eyes in *P. vulgaris*, *P. germanica*, *V. rufa*, and *V. crabro* and showed that there were specific differences which were paralleled by their illumination thresholds such that the threshold was inversely proportional to eye-length (Table 13).

Temperature
Observations on nests of *P. vulgaris* by Potter (1965) have shown that

K

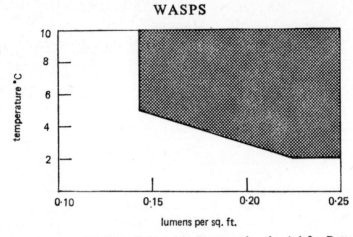

Figure 49. Flight thresholds (shaded area) in *Paravespula vulgaris* (after Potter 1965).

workers will not forage at temperatures below 2°C irrespective of light intensity, and that between 2 and 5°C, there is a distinct reluctance to leave the nest. It is probably quite infrequent for the temperature to fall below 2°C during the major part of colony life and therefore, with temperature above the threshold level, the dominant factor limiting flight would be light intensity. Threshold values for *P. vulgaris* with respect to light and temperature are shown in Figure 49. It is likely that the temperature threshold is of some geoclimatic relevance for, in America, the northerly species, *D. maculata*, has a threshold of 5°C while the mid-eastern species, *V. maculifrons*, has a value of 8·5°C (Gaul 1952a).

In a study of the effects of temperature on insect flight, Taylor (1963) analysed the results obtained by catching *P. germanica* queens with suction traps. The analysis was based on queens trapped in May when they are founding their colonies and their numbers could be considered reasonably constant with no recruitment to the population. The use of suction traps, which directly measures aerial density during the period of flight activity, indicated that there was a lower flight threshold of about 15°C above which increase in temperature caused no further increase in flight activity. The large disparity in thresholds between workers and queens is somewhat curious; perhaps there are different caste thresholds, or perhaps workers, which have the advantage of living in a warm nest, have body temperatures above the minimum limit for flight when outside temperatures are relatively low. Herold (1952) determined a temperature threshold of 14°C for *P. germanica* workers while above 20°C, flight activity apparently increased.

There is obviously much scope for future field and laboratory studies on flight thresholds in wasps which may, one day, clarify some of the more anomalous results so far published.

Social Factors

In observations at the nest entrance of wasp colonies, Blackith (1957) noticed that the sorties from and entries to the tunnel were in some instances non-random, the workers' passage through the entrance occurring in short bursts of activity. Blackith developed the theory that workers have an innate inhibition to leave the nest entrance and that this inhibition may be overcome by the accumulation of other workers at the entrance. His analogy of a queue of cars at traffic lights is enlightening — the response of the automatic lights depending on the numbers of cars and the period for which each was delayed. The flight of the first worker in the accumulated group (equivalent to the green traffic light) acts as a releaser for the remainder, thus producing a burst of flight activity.

This type of activity has been called social facilitation and describes the behavioural responses resulting from the proximity of companions during the performance of a particular duty. The presence of another individual may therefore produce an increase in an activity or perhaps improve the performance of the action. In the *V. rufa* colony studied by Blackith, it was calculated that the average inhibition of a wasp was just overcome by the presence of three other wasps, and that 90 per cent of the workers had an inhibition to leave the nest entrance which could be overcome by the presence of one to five other wasps.

This social facilitation at the nest entrance is of considerable importance to the colony, particularly in young colonies or in those species which have small worker populations, because of the loss of effective foraging time. Indeed, in the *V. rufa* colony examined by Blackith, it was estimated that about 10 per cent of the day may be lost in this way, although in the more populous *P. vulgaris* and *P. germanica* colonies, inhibition to forage, if it does occur, is not obvious during the height of the season.

FACTORS CONTROLLING FORAGING ACTIVITY

The stimuli which initiate and control foraging activity must be predominantly colony factors – the requirements of the nest-building programme, the feeding of larvae, and the underlying influence of the foundress queen.

Building Activity

When Potter (1965) destroyed the envelopes of a *P. vulgaris* nest in which the foraging rate had been constant, the response was a slight increase in foraging rate, the increase being entirely for wood pulp. The repair of the nest was slow, however, with little increase in the total number of foragers. As will be seen later, there is evidence that the workers collect most pulp when they begin their foraging life, and that the proportion of pulp-collecting sorties decreases with advancing age. Therefore, the recruitment of extra pulp collectors in the event of damage would be difficult to achieve if young adults are the principal carton makers. Potter suggested that decrease in the capacity to fabricate the carton may be correlated with a degeneration of the salivary glands.

Physical factors such as temperature, humidity and light intensity within or immediately surrounding the nest, may also control certain foraging activities. For example, reconstruction of the envelope following damage or removal is probably a response to decrease in temperature or (in aerial situations) penetration of light.

When the temperature of a *Paravespula vulgaris* nest was artificially reduced (from 32°C to 28°C) the proportion of sorties for pulp increased by 30-40 per cent, although reducing the temperature below 26°C caused a decrease in pulp collecting (Potter 1965). In another experiment, Potter maintained a nest at the optimum of 32°C in the dark and, despite removing the entire envelope, the wasps made little carton and this at a very dilatory rate. If light was not excluded, the wasps rapidly built a very thin layer of carton around the combs.

Brian and Brian (1948) suggested that the number of envelope layers in embryo nests of *D. sylvestris* was related to light intensity, there being more layers in nests situated in exposed places. Although light undoubtedly plays a part in envelope construction, it is more likely that temperature plays the dominant role, for the thickness of envelope in mature nests is related to the degree of site exposure, nests in well insulated places having thin envelopes and *vice versa* (see Plate XI). It would appear therefore that the thickness of envelope depends on temperature, although the rate of construction may be much influenced by light intensity.

Brood

When the amount of brood in a mature *P. vulgaris* colony was experimentally increased by inserting an extra comb containing about 700 larvae, the foraging rate was significantly increased (Potter 1965) (Fig. 54). The greatest increase was for fluid and flesh loads. In another experiment, all the larvae were removed from the combs with the result that foraging virtually ceased until larvae started to hatch from eggs laid in the empty cells by the resident queen.

The Queen

The removal of a queen from a *P. vulgaris* colony caused a marked reduction in overall foraging activity (Fig. 54c) even when brood and other colony stimuli remained unchanged (Potter 1965). The decrease in foraging was associated with an almost complete cessation of pulp and flesh collection so that larval and nest demands were ignored. With the replacement of the queen a day later, there was a resumption of normal foraging activity. In queen-less colonies or parasocial groups of workers, foraging takes place, nest construction (and frequently cell building) continues, and larvae are provisioned although foraging rates and the proportions of the different loads are undoubtedly different from normal, queen-right colonies.

It is apparent that the foraging wasp is stimulated by colony factors and not primarily by endogenous drives. The demands for pulp created by nest damage cause a small increase in the rate of pulp collecting, but this increase is limited by the numbers of wasps capable of constructional work, while the demands of growing larvae create a greater intensity of foraging which is maintained until the demand is satisfied. The means of communication between hungry larvae and adult workers will be discussed in Chapter 8.

On the available evidence, the role of the queen seems all important for, without her influence, other colonial factors fail to stimulate much foraging activity, although the queen-less replacement nests described in the previous chapter indicate that foraging, albeit at a low level, may be maintained in her absence.

FLIGHT AND FORAGING

Orientation

Before the young worker begins foraging it makes one or more orientation flights, similar to that of the queen previously described. The detailed description of orientation flights in American *Vespula* workers by Gaul (1951) is of particular interest, however, and form the basis of the following account.

When the wasp leaves the nest it flies straight from the tunnel entrance for about 25 cm then turns round so as to face the entrance before moving from side to side in a yawing, arc-like flight. The angle formed by the ends of the arc and the entrance is at first 90 degrees, increasing to nearly 280 degrees as the wasp flies further from the nest until it is about 75 cm from the entrance (Fig. 50). The wasp makes about 20 of these side-sweeping flights during the course of the first orientation flight which occupies about 15 seconds. During the flight there is a slight vertical movement, the amplitude of which rarely exceeds 50 cm.

At the completion of the flight, the wasp returns immediately to the nest but then re-emerges and begins a second orientation flight which may take it some 9 metres from the nest. Another flight, identical to the second flight, may take place. On the third flight, or more rarely

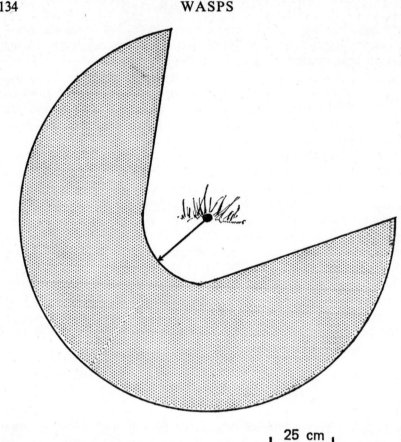

Figure 50.   Surveyed area (shaded) during orientation flight (drawn from data of Gaul 1951).

the second, the trip culminates in an abrupt flight away from the nest for the first foraging sortie. With the return from the first trip, the wasp generally makes several sweeping flights until the entrance is located. After five or twelve such return flights, the nest locality is learnt and the wasp thereafter flies directly to the entrance without any sideways movements. When Gaul moved a colony to a different site, the entire foraging population made similar orientation flights before the new locality was memorized. The locality study normally occupies from 100 to 300 seconds flying time.

In common with most other homing insects, landmarks in the vicinity of the nest are the points of reference in the locality study, the addition of new landmarks frequently stimulating fresh orientation flights by workers which had previously completed their orientation study (Gaul 1951). The orientation flight appears to be a response to unfamiliar

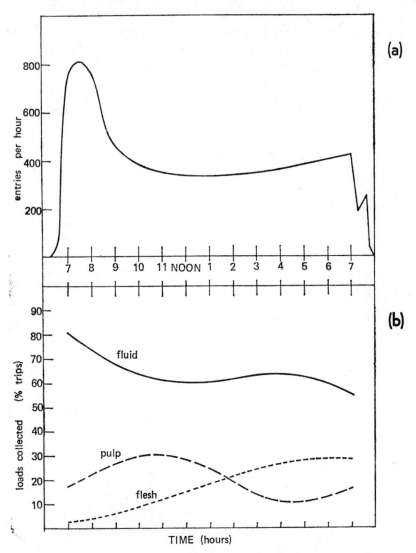

Figure 51. Diurnal foraging activity by *Paravespula vulgaris* colony (after Potter 1965): (a) foraging rate; (b) proportion of fluid, pulp, and flesh loads.

landmarks and may take place regardless of the age of the wasp. Wasps apparently have a navigation mechanism requiring a detailed locality study within about 9 metres of the nest, while orientation outside this area is probably in the form of light compass navigation, although there is no evidence yet of an appreciation of polarized light pattern which has been found to occur in ants and bees.

Influence of Weather

It is well known that the vagaries of weather influence foraging activity in honeybees (Kalmus 1954), but the social wasps are not as sensitive to meteorological adversities and will forage normally in light rain or moderate winds (Herold 1952). Cool conditions, high winds and heavy rain may reduce the foraging population temporarily but these conditions have little effect on overall diurnal activity (Blackith 1958a).

Gaul (1952b) in his study of wasp flight in relation to weather, did not detect any anticipation of impending storms by foraging wasps. The foraging rate was not correlated with pre-storm conditions such as changes in temperature, humidity, light intensity, barometric pressure or electrostatic factors. During stormy weather, when torrential rain and high winds prevail, foraging may temporarily cease – often preceded by a hurried return of foragers to the nest (Potter 1965)

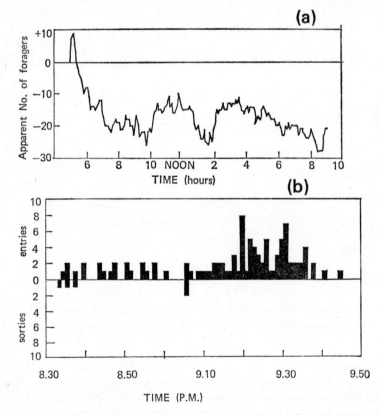

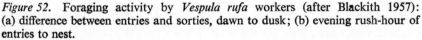

Figure 52. Foraging activity by *Vespula rufa* workers (after Blackith 1957): (a) difference between entries and sorties, dawn to dusk; (b) evening rush-hour of entries to nest.

(Fig. 53). When the storm passes, there is an apparent reluctance to forage, despite the return of calm, dry conditions. Gaul (1952b) suggests that foraging recommences when a wasp leaves the tunnel entrance and does not immediately return, thus releasing flight activity among the large numbers of wasps which crowd into the tunnel during a storm.

Flight and Load Capacity

The flight speed of the foraging wasp is determined by many factors, of which the weight of load and size of wasp are the major considerations. Ishay and others (1967) determined flight speed in *V. orientalis* workers at 2·6-3·8 metres per second (5·8-8·5 miles per hour) although lower speeds were recorded when the workers flew with heavy loads.

In his studies of *P. germanica*, Herold (1952) calculated that a worker is capable of carrying a load equal to half its body weight (70-85 mg) or sometimes in excess of this value. During three days of predation on *Pieris* larvae, two wasps collected 15-20 gm of butterfly meat. *V. orientalis* workers, which weigh 0·3 gm on average, collected 2·2 gm of adult honeybee prey per day (Ishay and others 1967). The

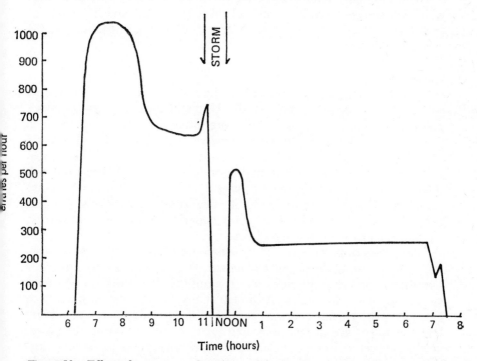

Figure 53. Effect of a storm on foraging activity by *Paravespula vulgaris* workers (after Potter 1965).

individual weights of loads carried by the *V. orientalis* workers included 0·1 gm of honeybee body, 0·3-0·5 gm of fish and beef, while soil particles of 2·5-3·7 gm were carried short distances during nest excavations. Some indication of the numbers of prey brought back to the colony on a daily basis will be given elsewhere in this chapter.

According to Herold (1952), larger workers are able to carry heavier loads and make more sorties per day than smaller workers. Signs of foraging fatigue became apparent earlier in smaller foragers, so it appears that for maximum foraging efficiency, the larger the wasp the better. As will be seen later (Chapter 9) there is a progressive increase in the mean size of adult workers during the course of the season which would be of considerable benefit to the colony, especially during the queen-rearing period.

Little is known of the territorial limits of foraging wasps but Arnold (1966) found that workers of *V. rufa* and *D. sylvestris* may forage up to 900 metres (1,000 yards) from their nests.

FOOD SOURCES

There are many references in the literature to the species of flowers which wasps visit to collect nectar (Table 14), and the species of arthropod prey which foragers collect for subsequent distribution to the larvae (Table 15).

Carbohydrates

Sugars are frequently obtained in the form of nectar from flowers with exposed nectaries such as the Umbelliferae (e.g. cow parsley), or the extrafloral nectaries on the vegetative parts of the plant (e.g. the fronds of Bracken, *Pteridium aquilinum*) (see Plate XVA). Carbohydrates are also collected in the form of 'honey-dew', the sweet excretions of aphids, psyllids, and coccids, frequently licked from oak (*Quercus robur*), hawthorn (*Crataegus*), and lime (*Tilia*) which are the principal host trees of the honey-dew producers. Wasps will also rob honeybee hives and collect sweet materials from a host of diverse sources such as jams and fruit juices.

The species of flowers visited by wasps are determined by the flowering period, spring-flowering *Cotoneaster* being a favourite shrub for the young founding queens while the autumn-flowering ivy (*Hedera*) is popular with the males. Although many flower species have been listed as carbohydrate sources (Table 14), there is always the possibility that the wasps are in fact searching for insect prey visiting the flower heads for nectar. For example, O. W. Richards (personal communication) has observed *P. vulgaris* preying on *Chrysogaster solstitialis* (Fallén) and *Chilomyia barbata* (Loew) flies at flowers of *Pastinaca*

TABLE 14

Some plants visited by social wasps for nectar

WASP SPECIES	PLANT SPECIES	COMMON NAME	SOURCE
V. crabro	Angelica sylvestris L.	Wild angelica	Walker 1901
	Acer sp.	Sycamore	Kemper and Döhring 1967
	Tilia sp.	Lime	„ „ „ „
P. vulgaris	Scrophularia aquatica L.	Water betony	Brown 1925
	Daucas carota L.	Wild carrot	Fahringer 1922
	Heracleum sphondylium L.	Cow parsnip	P. F. Yeo (pers. comm.)
	Hedera helix L.	Ivy	Free 1970
	Epipactis latifolia (L.)	Helleborine	Kemper and Döhring 1967
	Fuchsia sp.	Fuchsia	„ „ „ „
	Calluna vulgaris (L.)	Heather	Laidlaw 1934
	Centaurea nigra L.	Lesser Knapweed	„ „
	Symphoriocarpus rivularis Suksdorf	Snowberry	Kemper and Döhring 1967
	Scrophularia nodosa L.	Figwort	Laidlaw 1934
P. germanica	Scrophularia aquatica L.	Water betony	Brown 1925
	Hedera helix L.	Ivy	Free 1970
	Angelica archangelica L.	Angelica	Kemper and Döhring 1967
	Heracleum sphondylium L.	Cow parsnip	„ „ „ „
	Syringa vulgaris L.	Lilac	„ „ „ „
	Origanum vulgare L.	Marjoram	„ „ „ „
	Solidago sp.	Golden-rod	„ „ „ „
	Artemisia abrotanum L.	Southern wood	„ „ „ „
	Calendula officinalis L.	Pot marigold	„ „ „ „
	Centaurea nigra L.	Lesser Knapweed	Laidlaw 1934
V. rufa	Scrophularia aquatica L.	Water betony	Brown 1925
	Pastinaca sativa L.	Wild parsnip	Nicholson 1917
	Cotoneaster sp.	Cotoneaster	Hey 1909
	Symphoricarpos rivularis Suksdorf	Snowberry	„ „
	Pyrus japonica L.	Flowering cherry	„ „
	Heracleum sphondylium L.	Cow parsnip	P. F. Yeo (pers. comm.)
	Angelica sp.	Angelica	Kemper and Döhring 1967
	Hedera helix L.	Ivy	„ „ „ „
	Epipactis latifolia (L.)	Helleborine	„ „ „ „
	Salix sp.	Willow	„ „ „ „
	Berberis vulgaris E.B.	Barberry	„ „ „ „
	Ribes nigrum L.	Black Currant	„ „ „ „
	Conium maculatum L.	Hemlock	Laidlaw 1934
	Centaurea sp.		„ „
	Solidago virgaurea L.	Golden-rod	„ „
	Ulex europaeus L.	Gorse	„ „
	Ribes grossularia L.	Gooseberry	Kemper and Döhring 1967
	Rubus idaeus L.	Raspberry	„ „ „ „
	Rhamnus sp.	Buckthorn	„ „ „ „
	Foeniculum vulgare Mill.	Fennel	„ „ „ „
	Azalea sp.	Rhododendron	„ „ „ „
	Vaccinium myrtillus L.	Whortleberry	„ „ „ „
	Scrophularia nodosa L.	Figwort	„ „ „ „
D. norwegica	Pastinaca sativa L.	Wild parsnip	Nicholson 1917
	Scrophularia aquatica L.	Water betony	Brown 1925
	Heracleum sphondylium L.	Cow parsnip	Hey 1909
	Angelica archangelica L.	Angelica	Kemper and Döhring 1967
	Ribes nigrum L.	Black Currant	„ „ „ „

TABLE 14 continued

WASP SPECIES	PLANT SPECIES	COMMON NAME	SOURCE
D. norwegica	*Ribes uva-crispa* L.	Gooseberry	Kemper and Döhring 1967
	Vaccinium myrtillus L.	Whortleberry	,, ,, ,, ,,
	Melampyrum sp.	Cow-wheat	,, ,, ,, ,,
	Symphoriocarpus racemosus Auct.	Snowberry	,, ,, ,, ,,
	Rubus idaeus L.	Raspberry	Laidlaw 1934
	Rubus sp.	Bramble	,, ,,
	Centaurea cyanus L.	Cornflower	,, ,,
	Azalea sp.	Rhododendron	,, ,,
	Scrophularia nodosa L.	Figwort	,, ,,
D. sylvestris	*Sambucus ebulus* L.	Danewort	Fahringer 1922
	Scrophularia nodosa L.	Figwort	Laidlaw 1934
	Symphoricarpos rivularis Suksdorf	Snowberry	Hey 1909
	Scrophularia aquatica L.	Water betony	Brown 1925
	Pastinaca sativa L.	Wild parsnip	Nicholson 1917
	Rubus sp.	Bramble	Brian and Brian 1952
	Crataegus sp.	Hawthorn	,, ,, ,, ,,
	Rhododendron sp.	Azalea	,, ,, ,, ,,
	Heracleum sphondylium L.	Cow parsnip	P. F. Yeo (pers. comm.)
	Angelica sylvestris L.	Wild angelica	,, ,, ,, ,, ,,
	Salix sp.	Willow	Kemper and Döhring 1967
	Mahonia sp.	Mahonia	,, ,, ,,
	Prunus padus L.	Bird-Cherry	,, ,, ,, ,,
	Vaccinium myrtillus L.	Whortleberry	,, ,, ,, ,,
	Berberis vulgaris E.B.	Barberry	,, ,, ,, ,,
	Ribes nigrum L.	Black Currant	,, ,, ,, ,,
	Ribes uva-crispa L.	Gooseberry	,, ,, ,,
	Epipactis latifolia (L.) All.	Broad Helleborine	,, ,, ,, ,,
	Rubus idaeus L.	Raspberry	,, ,, ,, ,,
	Conium maculatum L.	Hemlock	Laidlaw 1934
	Oxycoccus palustris Pers. E.B.	Cranberry	,, ,,
	Rhamnus sp.	Buckthorn	Kemper and Döhring 1967
	Azalea sp.	Rhododendron	,, ,, ,, ,,
	Vaccinium myrtillus L.	Whortleberry	,, ,, ,, ,
	Ballota sp.	Horehound	Smith 1858
	Scrophularia nodosa L.	Figwort	Kemper and Döhring 1967
	Symphoriocarpus rivularis Suksdorf	Snowberry	,, ,, ,, ,,
Vespula spp.	*Ribes uva-crispa* L.	Gooseberry	Watson 1922
	Alyssum alyssoides (L.)	Sweet alyssum	,, ,,
	Ilex aquifolium L.	Holly	,, ,,
	Prunus avium L.	Wild cherry	,, ,,

Latin names from *Flora of the British Isles* by Clapham, Tutin and Warburg 1952

which Nicholson (1917) lists as a nectar source for *V. rufa*, *D. norwegica*, and *D. sylvestris*. Similarly, Nicholson (1917) records *V. rufa* preying on flies which visit *Heracleum*, which Fahringer (1922) lists as a source of carbohydrate for wasps.

It is well known that *V. crabro* feeds at the exuding sap of oak and elm trees, and will gnaw the bark of living trees to obtain the sap (Reeks in Walker 1901). O. W. Richards (personal communication) has also observed swarms of *P. vulgaris* and *P. germanica* on the trunk of an elm, groups of up to twelve workers feeding at the small exudations of sap which resulted from the tunnelling activities of the bark beetle, *Scolytus scolytus* (=*destructor*) (F.). The nutrient value of sap has not been investigated, but it undoubtedly contains large quantities of carbohydrate. If allowed to ferment, the sap has a remarkably alcoholic effect on the visiting wasps and many die a drunken death as a result.

Wasps which visit plants for nectar may help to pollinate the flowers and there are several instances of wasps having orchid pollinia attached to their heads and presumably contributing to orchid pollination (Schremmer 1961, K. G. Preston-Mafham (personal communication)).

Protein

The versatility of wasps as predators on a wide range of arthropod prey can be seen in Table 15. Wasps will also rob other animals of their prey and Chevalier (1924) records the case of a wasp stealing a paralysed caterpillar (*Agrotis segetum* L.) which had been left at the burrow entrance of the sphegid wasp, *Ammophila hirsuta* (Scopoli) just before the prey would have been dragged into the burrow by the rightful owner. Similar instances of robbing have been recorded by Eltringham (in Poulton 1934) who observed a wasp cut the web of a spider to remove a tipulid fly, and Bristowe (1931) records a *P. vulgaris* worker pull a struggling fly from the web of the spider, *Epeira diademata*. I have frequently seen wasps foraging for insects trapped in spiders' webs and on one occasion a wasp simply cut open the abdomen of a trapped honeybee and fed on the contents of the honey stomach (Plate XVf).

A remarkably detailed survey of the prey of *P. vulgaris* has been carried out in Holland by Brockhuizen and Hordijk (1968) who developed a capture apparatus which enabled returning foragers to be trapped and their prey removed for examination. In the four colonies studied (which were all in the same locality) the enormous range of arthropod prey is perhaps the most striking result of the survey. More than 30 species of insect from eight different orders and 8 species of spider were recorded, together with larvae of Lepidoptera, Symphyta, and Diptera. The dominant prey were adult flies, some colonies collecting as much as 83·5 per cent of flies in the daily catch, although spiders figure highly in some colonies (up to 44·1 per cent). Larval insects represented up to 43·7 per cent in some instances. Kemper and Döhring (1962) have analysed the prey collected by a *P. germanica* colony and of the 546 loads examined, 63 per cent were flies of which

TABLE 15
Insect prey of British Social Wasps

PREY	WASP SPECIES	SOURCE
DERMAPTERA		
Forficula auricularia L.	P. vulgaris	Killington 1932
ORTHOPTERA		
Meconema thalassinum (Degeer)	P. vulgaris	Broekhuizen and Hordijk 1968
Grasshopper sp.	Vespula sp.	Smythe 1882
Tettigonia viridissima L.	V. crabro	Forel 1895
ODONATA		
Sympetrum striolatum (Charpentier)	Vespula sp.	Robbins 1938
HEMIPTERA		
Jassidae	P. vulgaris	Watson 1922
Cercopidae	P. germanica	Fox Wilson 1946
Philaenus spumarius (Fallén)	P. vulgaris	Broekhuizen and Hordijk 1968
LEPIDOPTERA		
Vanessa atalanta (L.)	V. crabro	Lucas 1905
Pieris napii (L.)	Vespula sp.	Newport 1836
Pieris rapae (L.)	Vespula sp.	Newport 1836
Pieris brassicae (L.)	P. vulgaris	Killington 1940
Pararge aegeria L.	Vespula sp.	Lucas 1905
Bupalus piniaria (L.) larvae	P. vulgaris	Broekhuizen and Hordijk 1968
COLEOPTERA		
Polydrusus mollis (Stroem)	Vespula sp.	Hardy 1876
Phyllobius sp.	P. vulgaris	Broekhuizen and Hordijk 1968
HYMENOPTERA		
Apis mellifera L.	V. crabro, P. germanica	Andrews 1882
	D. sylvestris	Black Hawkins 1911
		Watson 1922
Vespula sp.	V. crabro	Tooner 1883
Bombus sp.	Vespula sp.	Eales White 1911
Pteronidea ribesii (Scopoli)	P. germanica, V. rufa, D. norwegica	Cuthbert 1914
Paravespula germanica	P. germanica	unpublished data
DIPTERA		
Tipulidae		
Tipula paludosa Meigen	P. vulgaris	
Bibionidae		
Bibio sp.	D. sylvestris	Brian and Brian 1952
Dilophus febrilis (L.)	P. vulgaris	Broekhuizen and Hordijk 1968
Syrphidae		
Chilomyia barbata (Loew, H.)	Vespula sp.	O. W. Richards (pers. comm.)
Eristalis nemorum (L.)	P. vulgaris	Davis 1833
Syrphus vitripennis (Meigen)	P. vulgaris	O. W. Richards (pers. comm.)
Chrysogaster solstitialis (Fallén)	Vespula sp.	O. W. Richards (pers. comm.)

TABLE 15 continued

PREY	WASP SPECIES	SOURCE
Asilidae		
Laphria marginata (L.)	*Vespula* sp.	Séguy 1927
Calliphoridae		
Protophormia groenlandica (Zetterstedt)	*P. vulgaris*	Malloch (unpublished)
Lucilia sericata (Meigen)	*D. sylvestris*	Brian and Brian (1952)
Muscidae		
Musca domestica L.	*Vespula* sp.	Eales White 1911
Fannia canicularis (L.)	*P. vulgaris*	Lucas 1929
Polietes lardaria (F.)	*P. vulgaris*	Lucas 1929
Mesembrina meridiana (L.)	*P. vulgaris*	Brockhuizen and Hordijk 1968
Phaonia sp.	*P. vulgaris*	Brockhuizen and Hordijk 1968

the majority were *Musca domestica L*, 14 per cent were various Lepidoptera, while honeybees and spiders accounted for 4 and 2 per cent respectively. Only 4 beetles were brought back to the colony during the period of study.

In many parts of the world the predation of hornets on honeybees can be a serious problem for beekeepers (Rivney and others 1949, Ishay and others 1967, Matsuura, personal communication), and there are several records of *V. crabro* preying on honeybees in Britain (Andrews 1882, Black-Hawkins 1911). The hornet will also take species of *Vespula* (Tooner 1883), while species of *Bombus* are reputedly preyed upon by wasps (Eales White 1911). In the Oriental and Indo-Malayan regions, various subspecies of the hornet, *Vespa tropica* (L.), prey on other wasps such as *Polistes, Parapolybia, Ropalidia* and *Stenogaster* (Sakagami and Fukushima 1957a, Van der Vecht 1957, Ward 1965).

Benefits may also accrue from the predation of wasps and they have occasionally been used in biological control projects (see Chapter 12). The cabbage white butterflies, *Pieris rapae* (L.) and *P. napii* (L.) are frequently taken by wasps (Newport 1836). *V. crabro* will take the large grasshopper *Tettigonia* (=*Locusta*) *viridissima* L. (Forel 1895) and other species of unidentified grasshoppers (Smythe 1882). Their depredations on economically important flies (e.g. *Musca domestica, Fannia canicularis* (L.), *Stomoxys calcitrans* (L.), and *Tabanus bromius* L. (Kühlhorn 1961, Viewig 1896)) should help ameliorate the wasp's otherwise bad reputation.

Although arthropods provide the major source of protein for feeding to larvae, wasps also obtain meat from butchers and fish shops, while Rau and Rau (1918) give a macabre list of meat sources which includes chicken bones, dead cockroaches, the decapitated head of a cockerel, and the eyes of a dead rat. In north America, *D. maculata* has been seen attacking the adult hummingbird, *Selasphorus rufus*, while other species of wasp were predatory on this bird's nestlings (Grant 1959). In Britain, Wild (1927) has observed *D. sylvestris* workers flying around the nest of a blackcap (*Sylvia atripilla*) which contained three newly hatched young. The parent birds were apparently forced to evacuate the nest while the wasps gnawed at the young nestlings to obtain loads of meat.

Perhaps Lucas' (1905) commentary on the fate of a red admiral butterfly caught by a wasp, might provide a fitting if sober footnote, *'Sic transit gloria mundi!'*

Food Preferences

In his studies on *P. vulgaris*, Kemper (1963) offered various sugar solutions and other foods to workers in an attempt to determine feeding preferences. The minimum level of perception of sugars was 1 per cent saccharose, 2-4 per cent glucose, and 10-30 per cent fructose, while the wasps preferred strong sugar solutions to weak ones although aqueous (20-80 per cent) solutions of honey were preferred to pure honey.*

Ishay and others (1967) compared food preferences in the Oriental Hornet, *V. orientalis*, using protein foodstuffs. Their main conclusions were that hornets preferred bees to hornets, ground beef to fish; and that boiled insects lost much of their attractiveness as food. By offering honeybee adults and pupae to *P. vulgaris* and *P. germanica* workers, Free (1970) showed that wasps preferred pupae to adults and, among adults, the newly emerged bee was preferred to older ones. These preferences were probably associated with the ease of dismembering soft-cuticled material. Free also noted that wasps could be enticed from protein collecting if they were offered sugar syrup.

Although food preferences undoubtedly exist in wasps, the wide range of protein and carbohydrate sources utilized by foragers would undoubtedly overcome problems accruing from the depletion of a preferred food source.

FORAGING BEHAVIOUR

It is likely that wasps commence a foraging trip in response to colony stimuli and that they leave with a specific objective – the collection of wood pulp, fluid, or flesh, depending on the requirements of the colony. How the demands of the colony might be perceived are unknown and any attempt to explain foraging motivation in terms of neural or hormonal communication would be entirely speculative. One signal which may stimulate foraging is the hunger call of larvae which scratch

*The by-products of sucrose fermentation by yeasts are highly attractive to foraging wasps (J. L. Madden, personal communication).

their cell wall with their mandibles to attract the attention of workers (see Chapter 8 for details), but this stimulus is probably directed towards adults which have already returned with food or those to which food was distributed by the returning forager.

Wasps of an appropriate age will forage more for pulp if the nest is damaged, and food will be collected with greater vigour if the numbers of larvae are artificially increased. Foraging for a particular type of material is, as will be seen later, influenced to some extent by the age of the wasp, the time of day when foraging occurs, and the individuality of the forager. Nevertheless, if wasps leave a colony with a specific foraging objective, they can readily divert their attention to a different activity. For example, Brian and Brian (1952) have circumstantial evidence that foraging *D. sylvestris* workers which fail to catch insect prey divert to fluid collecting, and Free (1970) has noticed a wasp change from nectar collecting on ivy flowers to preying on a fly, during the course of a single trip. Free points out, however, that wasps collecting carbohydrates are generally reluctant to hunt prey although flesh foragers are more readily diverted to fluid collecting.

The complex of stimuli which initiate foraging and the conditions which limit these activities have occupied much of this chapter so far, but once in the field, a different range of stimuli come into play which enable the wasp to locate, recognize, and collect food materials.

Food Finding

It is clear that wasps which search for carbohydrates respond primarily to odours as they move slowly from flower to flower or examine the leaves where honey-dew producers are present (Brian and Brian 1952). Gaul (1952e) has shown that wasps fly upwind to honey baits but are unable to detect glucose (which is odourless) from a distance. Attraction to some nectar-producing flowers is likely to be a combination of chemotaxis at long range, and a response to visual clues such as honey guides on petals or glistening areas of exposed nectaries at shorter range. Upwind flights to the source of odours emanating from carrion are well documented (Gaul 1952e).

By contrast to the search for static sources of food, the search for insect prey is characterized by a more rapid and agile flight as the wasps search for material frequenting hedgerows and walls or that feed at flower heads. Visual stimuli are probably the most important when seeking prey (Kemper 1962) and wasps are quite capable of seeing flies at windows of buildings and entering them to prey on the flies (Kühlhorn 1961). Although wasps generally seek prey while flying, there are records of them lying in wait for insects to land on dung pats or similar situations (Rau 1934b). In the majority of cases, it is the movement of the prospective prey which attracts the wasp, although Duncan

(1939) records seeing wasps pouncing on dark nailheads in a white washed wall, mistaking the nails for flies.

Prey Capture

When a wasp locates its prey, it normally pounces vigorously on to the victim, frequently knocking it to the ground from the flower or wall on which the prey had been feeding or sunbathing. The wasp kills by biting into the neck of the victim, often decapitating the prey within seconds. Only in rare instances does the wasp use its sting when grappling with prey and then only when it is particularly large or struggles sufficiently to free itself from the wasp's grasp. O'Rourke (1945) has described a *P. vulgaris* worker capture a fly, which it attempted to sting while chewing at the neck of the prey. Decapitation took five minutes. Although the wasp does not normally use its sting, Pack-Beresford (1931) records a *P. vulgaris* killing a bumble bee by stinging, and Bordas (1917) observed *V. crabro* use its sting to immobilize a large grasshopper before dismembering it. Ishay and others (1967) note that the Oriental Hornet uses its sting to paralyse honeybees.

Moffat (in O'Rourke 1945) observed *Vespula* species taking butterflies (*Pieris rapae* and *Pararge aegeria* L.) while on the wing. As soon as wasp and prey reached the ground, the butterfly's wings were snipped off with the mandibles. Apart from immobilizing prey, the severing of the head, wings, and legs is normal preparatory work before the muscle-filled thorax is carried back to the colony. When presented with fresh but dead honeybees, there is sometimes an apparent conflict of interests between the protein-rich thorax and the honey-filled crop in the abdomen (Free 1970). Wasps and hornets will capture bees and tear the abdomen open to feed on the crop contents.

Ishay and others (1967) have described the remarkable behaviour of *V. orientalis* workers in Israel when foraging for honeybees. If hunting alone, the hornet approaches a hive and, by executing a characteristic retreating flight, entices a bee to follow in pursuit. As the defending bee leaves the hive and becomes isolated from the other members of the colony, the hornet turns round and pounces on it.

Wasps are independent hunters and are unable to communicate food sources to other members of the colony (Kalmus 1954, Kemper 1962), although Ishay and others (1967) have observed groups of 3 or 4 workers leave a nest and remain together until they locate a rich source of food. The individual foragers then take it in turns to collect the food until the source is depleted. This 'group foraging' does not occur when wood pulp is being sought. Similarly, when *V. orientalis* forage for honeybees at the entrance of hives, collaboration frequently takes place. One hornet will draw the bees from the hive while the other hornets attack the bees as they leave the entrance. When a hive has been successfully taken, a few hornets will guard the entrance to prevent an invasion of hornets from other colonies.

Not all conflicts between wasps and other insects lead to successful prey capture, for the pouncing wasp frequently misses the intended victim or, by persistent struggling, even a butterfly may break loose and regain its freedom (Moffat in O'Rourke 1945). Hobby and Killington (1932) have observed that *V. crabro* was intimidated by the threat display of a red admiral butterfly (*Vanessa atalanta* (L.)), and after three attacks, the hornet flew away. Duncan (1939), in observations on *D. maculata*, noted that sometimes up to a dozen attempts to catch flies were made before the wasp was successful. Wasps also pounce on each other while searching for prey, but they are quickly released.* It would appear that it is the appropriate size and movement of the prey which releases the pouncing reaction.

Once the prey has been caught and perhaps partially or wholly dismembered (Plate XVB), the wasp invariably flies to a nearby tree or other suitable resting place, and begins to malaxate the food before returning to the nest (Newport 1836, O'Byrne 1934). If the prey is large and several trips are required to utilize it fully, the wasp makes an orientation flight over the remains of the prey before flying off with the first load (Duncan 1939).

Learning Behaviour

There is evidence that wasps benefit from previous foraging sorties and learn from these experiences. Free (1970) has described the behaviour of some wasps which learn how to deal with insect prey, their first attempts being frequently frustrated by loads that were too cumbersome or heavy for them. The more experienced workers would speedily remove thoracic appendages from bees before flying off with a manageable load, although there was much variation in the individual wasp's expertise and capacity for work.

Unlike honeybees, wasps are more difficult to train to visit feeding dishes for they apparently have little or no appreciation of time. Learning a food source, however, is very soon accomplished and wasps will return repeatedly to the same place to collect food or wood pulp (Broekhuizen and Hordijk 1968), the frequency with which they return depending on the attraction of the source (Free 1970). Hornets soon recognize the location of a food source and during repeated trips form an 'association' which remains for at least two days after the source is depleted or removed (Ishay and others 1967). In one experiment, Ishay and his co-workers found that if a honey dish is moved several metres away following locality imprinting, the hornets

---

*In Tasmania, where dense populations deplete the insect fauna around a nest, wasps will prey on each other (personal observations).

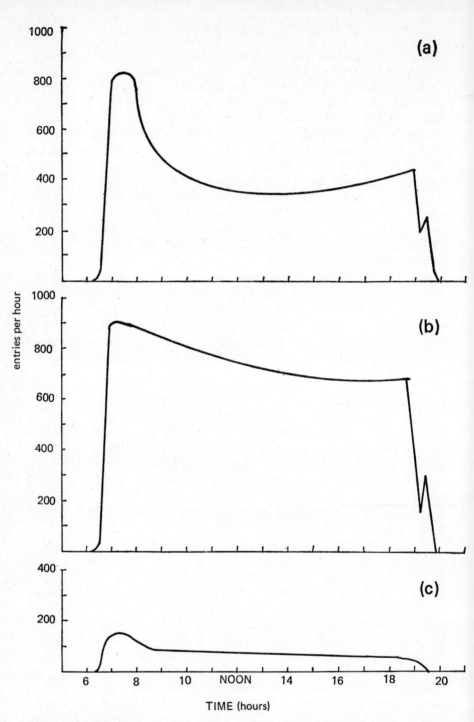

Figure 54. Experiments on foraging activity by *Paravespula vulgaris* workers (after Potter 1965): (a) normal foraging activity; (b) foraging activity 4 days after implantation of 700 extra larvae; (c) foraging activity following removal of the foundress queen.

maintain a route from colony to old locality to new locality, returning by the same route. It is only after a couple of days that the hornets establish a new and more direct flight path between the colony and the new food site.

Kalmus (1954) has demonstrated that wasps are unable to communicate the position of a food source to other wasps. Wasps however are highly flexible in their foraging activities and are better adapted to discovering small, isolated food sources which are exploited by the individual, rather than working large resources of food in a few places like the honeybee.

FORAGING ACTIVITY

Diurnal Activity

The typical daily foraging activity of a colony is remarkably similar among the different wasp species studied by Blackith (1958a), Potter (1965), and Edwards (1968) in Britain, and Gaul (1952a) in America. When temperature and light intensity are above threshold levels, there is an initial peak of entries into the nest as workers which failed to navigate home the previous night, return to the colony (Figs. 51a, 52a). Blackith and Stevenson (1958) have trapped more than 100 wasps which were returning to their colony in the early morning.

Within one or two hours of colony awakening, the foraging rate increases very rapidly to its highest level of the day and, after a brief period at this rate, it declines to a fairly constant level which is maintained for much of the day (Fig. 51a). As threshold levels of illumination are reached at dusk, the foraging rate declines sharply but, shortly before illumination falls below the threshold for successful navigation, there is a burst of activity (the evening 'rush hour') as foragers return to the colony while there is still sufficient light (Fig. 52b).

Gaul (1952a) has suggested several possible reasons for the early morning peak of sorties, namely the need to feed larvae after a night without food, the necessity to release excretory products which have accumulated overnight, or even exercising flights for those wasps which normally behave as brood nurses or domestics. The pattern of peak activity which extends over an hour or two would seem to be a response to the food demands of the larvae so that most foragers capable of collecting food maintain an intense level of foraging until the demands of the brood have been satisfied. Potter (1965) further suggested that there is a spate of exploitive foraging for fluids due to the availability of early morning dew and an abundance of nectar following the morning nectar rise.

An examination of the type of load brought back by returning foragers indicates that fluid collection is the dominant activity in the early morning (Brian and Brian 1952, Potter 1965) (Fig. 51b). Fluid collecting trips at the beginning of the day were always of shorter duration than at other times which suggests that fluids are also easier to collect at this time. For example, a fluid collecting sortie by *P. vulgaris* in the early morning took 6 minutes, while at midday, the duration had increased to 12-15 minutes (Potter 1965).

It appears therefore, that the early morning peak of foraging activity is probably a response to the demands of larvae, allied to the relative ease of fluid collection at this time. There also exists the possibility that the larval demand stimulates a greater proportion of the worker force to forage, for increase in numbers of larvae (=larval demand) stimulates an increase in the numbers of foragers and their activity levels.

The diurnal variation in the proportion of fluid, pulp, and flesh collection are given in Figure 51b which illustrates the decrease in fluid collection from its early morning peak, and a steady increase in the rate of flesh collection which reaches a peak in the evening. Pulp collecting is principally a morning activity. The proportion of trips for fluids was always higher than either flesh or pulp collecting in *P. vulgaris* (Potter 1965) and *D. sylvestris* (Brian and Brian 1952). In the latter, the proportion of fluid collecting trips was between 40 and 50 per cent of the total.

The duration of a foraging trip depends on the nature of the load and was 10·9, 8·5, and 6·1 minutes for fluid, pulp, and flesh collecting respectively, by *D. sylvestris* workers. The queens of *D. sylvestris*, when founding incipient colonies, were apparently more efficient foragers for their trips occupied 8·1, 5·6, and 3·1 minutes for fluid, pulp, and flesh (Brian and Brian 1952). The brief duration of a flesh-collecting trip may be due to the workers which fail to capture prey soon after leaving the colony, diverting their attention to fluid collection. Pulp collecting was of consistently short duration and is probably due to the fact that once a source of wood pulp has been discovered, it may be visited regularly for brief periods of concentrated work. Before collecting wood pulp, the wasp generally collects water (Plate XVc) which is presumably used to soften the substrate and aids in the mastication of the wood fibres.

The time spent in the nest between foraging journeys was 4·5±0·19 minutes in *D. sylvestris* and was very constant, irrespective of the type of load brought to the nest.

In his studies of *V. crabro* in Japan, Matsuura (1967b) observed that the workers spent 14·5 per cent of their time foraging with 4·1 per cent devoted to collecting nest-building materials, 1·8 per cent when foraging for prey, 2·4 per cent while collecting tree sap, and 5·8 per cent for collecting the water used in nest cooling. Orientation flights occupied 0·4 per cent of foraging time.

The numbers of prey brought back to the colony have occasionally been recorded. Black-Hawkins (1911) observed an orphaned colony of 50-60 *P. germanica* workers collect 227 flies in one hour, and Janet (1903) found that a *D. sylvestris* colony captured more than 100 flies within half an hour. It is clear that in densely populated colonies of wasps, the depredations on insects, especially flies, must be enormous.

Seasonal Changes in Foraging Activity

With the emergence of the first few adult workers in the incipient colony, the foraging activities of the queen slacken off and finally cease. In the case of *D. sylvestris*, this stage is reached some 30-33 days following the initiation of the nest, although in one colony in which the adult workers disappeared, the queen continued to forage more than 50 days after nest founding (Brian and Brian 1952). In *P. vulgaris*, the period between nest initiation and emergence of the first workers was 23-33 days (Potter 1965). Verlaine (1932) has described the situation in one *D. media* colony in which the queen continued to forage for two months following the emergence of the first worker, but the number of workers during this period never exceeded twelve. In *P. vulgaris* and *P. germanica*, the queen normally ceases building activities, foraging, and feeding of the brood as soon as workers appear, Verlaine (1932) noting that once four or more workers were present, foraging by the queen ceased completely. The first batch of workers begin foraging on the second or third day after emergence in *P. vulgaris* (Potter 1965), and only one day after emergence in *D. sylvestris*, although a few do not start foraging until the second day (Brian and Brian 1952). As the season progresses, the pre-foraging period tends to increase in duration. In observations on a young *P. vulgaris* colony in June, it was noted that the mean pre-foraging period increased from 2·1 days in the first week of June to 6·4 days by the end of the month (Spradbery 1963). These data are similar to Potter's findings on the same species in which the pre-foraging period increased from 2·5 days among the first emerging workers to 3·0 days during the period of rapid colony growth, and 8 days during the period of slow colony growth which precedes queen rearing. During queen production, the pre-foraging period decreased to 3 days.

The intensity of foraging varies during the season on both an individual and colony basis. For example, Potter noted that *P. vulgaris* workers not only start foraging earlier during the period of rapid colony growth (see Table 16), but also forage more (7-8 trips every 2 hours) with only brief periods of rest between flights. During the period of slow increase in colony growth, they began foraging later in life and made fewer trips (2-2·5 trips every 2 hours). With the advent of queen rearing, there is a general tendency to revert to the earlier level of activity associated with the period of rapid colony expansion.

A further consequence of the changing seasons on foraging activity is the decrease in effective foraging time due to the reduction in day length from about 17 hours in midsummer to only 10 hours by early November (Blackith 1958a). In a study of a *V. rufa* colony (Edwards 1968), it was found that the earliest recorded sortie was made at 0250 (British Summer Time) in the morning and the latest entry at 2224, a potential foraging day of nearly 20 hours. It must be emphasized however that the extreme times were unusual and partly due to the presence of a full, overhead moon.

Ontogenetic Changes

During the life of an adult worker, certain changes in foraging activities take place which are related to the age of the wasp. As mentioned above, the pre-foraging period tends to fluctuate, depending on the stage of growth and needs of the colony. During this period, the wasps perform a number of domestic duties after spending the first few hours of adult life being fed by more mature workers (Plate XXIb) and imbibing the salivary secretions of the larvae. After this feeding period, during which time the cuticle hardens and the pale, downy appearance of the callow begins to disappear, the young adult becomes involved in the economy of the colony. The first duties include

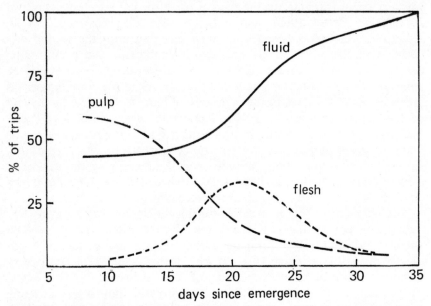

Figure 55. Ontogenetic changes in foraging activity of 30 *Paravespula vulgaris* workers (after Potter 1965).

feeding the larvae on pieces of malaxated insect prey distributed to them by returning foragers, and breaking down the internal parts of the envelope, carrying the pulp from the nest, and extending the envelope on the outside (Brian and Brian 1952).

When the young workers begin foraging, they first perform orientation flights. During the first few days the dominant activity is the collection of woodpulp, older workers spending more time on fluid collection (Fig. 55). The *D. sylvestris* workers, studied by the Brians, made 59 per cent of their trips for pulp during the first three days of foraging, but only 15 per cent by the eighth or ninth foraging day. The proportion of trips for fluid, pulp, and flesh in the first three days being 18 : 43 : 5, compared to 40 : 26 : 28 after eight days. It is interesting to note that the pattern of decrease in pulp collecting and increase in predatory activities during worker life, is very similar to the pattern of activity engaged in by the founding queen. Predatory activities of foragers tends to occupy the middle period of their adult life, with a progressive increase in fluid collecting throughout their life span (Fig. 55).

The longevity of workers is related to the amount of foraging they perform for, during the period of rapid colony growth in July when foraging is intense, the mean longevity of a worker is 13·6 days (range, 2-27 days), the length of life of August workers, when foraging activity decreases, is 22·3 days (range, 8-37 days), decreasing to 17·4 days (range 4-29 days) during the queen-rearing period (Potter 1965).

Within a few days of the commencement of foraging, the rate of sorties increases slightly although the duration of a trip remains the same (Fig. 56). With advancing age, however, there is a progressive decrease in foraging activity allied to an increase in the duration of a trip and also the time spent in the nest between trips (Fig. 56). These observations are of particular interest for they suggest that repeated foraging induces fatigue with an attendant decrease in foraging efficiency. The increase in duration of foraging trips is probably emphasized by the increase in proportion of fluid-collecting trips with age (Fig. 55), for they are of longer duration than flesh- or pulp-collecting journeys. Wasps more than 30 days old rarely leave the nest and spend much of their time at the nest entrance where they perform as guards.

There is considerable worker individuality according to the observations of Brian and Brian (1952) on *D. sylvestris*. Despite minimal variation in total activity, some workers collected more insect prey than others, while there was substantial variation in the duration of trips, reflecting individual differences in their relative efficiency or expertise at particular foraging duties. There is also the likelihood that these differences may be due to age, or simply the exploitation of a rich source of fluid or prey once it has been located.

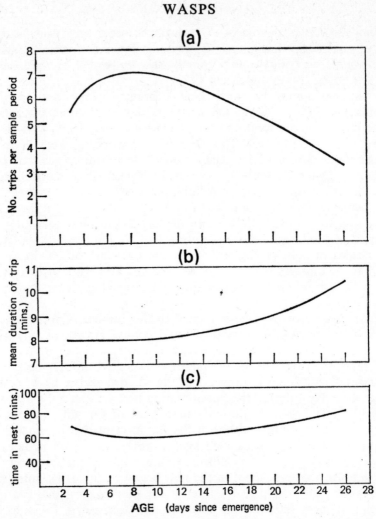

Figure 56. Ontogenetic changes in foraging activity of *Paravespula vulgaris* workers (after Potter 1965): (a) activity; (b) duration of trips; (c) time spent in nest between foraging trips.

DIVISION OF LABOUR

The establishment of an insect society provides the opportunity for differentiation of its members into groups whose efficiency would undoubtedly benefit from some form of work distribution. In primitive societies, division of labour could be on a purely functional or behavioural basis (polyethism) which might in time lead to the discrimination of specialized labour groups having structural modifications (polymorphism). The termites (Howse 1970) and ants (Sudd 1967) have achieved advanced societies in which groups of morphologically distinct individuals have become highly adapted for reproduction, foraging, or colony defence.

The principal development in the evolution of work distribution in vespine wasps is the production of a morphologically distinct worker caste which is responsible for all colony duties except oviposition, which is normally the exclusive function of the queen. The emergence of the first few workers in early summer creates the initial segregation of labour, for the queen then ceases to forage as she devotes herself to the reproductive needs of the colony, while the workers carry out all other duties. Despite a lack of polymorphism among the workers, there may occur several forms of polyethism, namely those based on age, physiological condition, and size.

The variety of work which engages the attention of wasps is wide, domestic duties including the distribution of food to larvae, and clearing of cells which involves the removal of the ragged remains of pupal cappings and the extraction and disposal of dead larvae to the midden at the bottom of the nest cavity or to the outside. Continuous rounds of reciprocal feeding between adults and larvae and among the adults occupies the inhabitants at all times and, in the case of *V. orientalis* at least, the formation of resting circles or royal courts around the functional queens. Many workers help cool the nest by creating convection currents during their wing-fanning activities. The defence of the colony is ensured by the presence of groups of guard wasps at the nest and tunnel entrances. Outside the nest, foraging activities include the collection of sugary liquids, the capture of insect prey, and the collection of water for site excavation and nest cooling, and woodpulp for nest building. In a large, populous colony there is obviously some integration of activities which, collectively, enables the building of a complex nest structure and the rearing of thousands of brood. Some indications of how this is achieved have already been discussed in this chapter, namely the response to larval demands, or to decrease in temperature following nest damage. To succeed in these objectives, there must be a capacity at all times to carry out the variety of work required in colony development, and this may be brought about by either the formation of discrete labour groups specialized in a particular duty, or a capacity for an unspecialized population to perform all or most of the work demanded by a developing colony.

As outlined earlier, there is a fairly well defined age polyethism in wasps, the newly emerged worker remaining in the nest distributing food and helping in envelope reconstruction, followed by a lengthy foraging period, and concluded by a post-foraging phase when older workers act as guards. During the foraging period, definite trends in the relative proportions of fluid, flesh- and pulp-collecting have been determined, young foragers being dominantly pulp collectors, middle age is occupied with predatory activities, and at the end of their foraging lives, the wasps are almost exclusively fluid collectors. With a population composed of different aged foragers, there would be a labour pool available for all foraging duties. But, because polyethism is not rigidly defined in wasps, there exists the capacity for the recruitment of more workers for a particular duty if conditions warrant it. On a colony rather than an individual basis, there are seasonal trends in the division of labour, allied to the intensity of foraging activity and the relative longevity of adults, which are determined by the cyclic nature of colony development. The proportion of workers which forage varies during the season, there being more foragers (53-56 per cent) in young colonies, and a smaller but fairly constant foraging population in mature colonies (37·4 per cent foragers in *P. germanica* and 37·6 per cent in *P. vulgaris*) (Spradbery 1963). Blackith and Stevenson (1958) estimated that 44·8 per cent of the workers in a September colony of *P. vulgaris* were foragers, and Gaul (1948b) determined that 40 per cent of the workers were foragers in *Dolichovespula arenaria* (F.), an arboreal nesting species. It is likely, therefore, that a temporal division of labour on a seasonal basis occurs in wasp colonies, dictated by the demands of nest building and brood rearing.

The flexibility of wasp behaviour is a characteristic of the Vespinae, for they are far less constant to a particular duty compared to honeybees (Kalmus 1954), and frequently switch from one activity to another, even during a single foraging trip (Brian and Brian 1952, Free 1970). Indeed, during the course of one day, a worker wasp may perform a whole series of different duties from foraging to feeding, and building to practising nest hygiene.

FEEDING

The food of adult and larval wasps differs markedly for adults are capable of ingesting only liquid or, at the most, semi-liquid food because of the narrow oesophagus and the restrictions placed on the alimentary canal by the narrow neck and petiole. Larvae are fed on both liquid and solid food.

Adults

The adult insect requires an energy-producing rather than a body-building diet and their food is principally carbohydrate in origin. The food sources, as detailed above, include nectar, honey-dew, juice from ripe fruits, and a variety of manufactured foodstuffs such as jams and fruit preserves. An adult hornet, when starved for 24 hours, will imbibe 0·02 to 0·05 ml of glucose solution (Gitter and others 1971).

According to Ishay and Ikan (1968), adult *V. orientalis* do not normally possess the necessary enzymes to deal with proteins although I have evidence that proteases are produced by the midgut in adult *P. germanica* workers (see Chapter 8). There are several records of adult wasps ingesting protein food. For example, Bordas (1917) recorded *V. crabro* sucking up yellow juices derived from the abdominal muscles of a grasshopper, and Chapman (1963) observed an American *Vespula* species chewing up winged ants but not returning to the colonies with the carcass. Van der Vecht (1957) cites several similar cases in tropical hornets. Adults probably store protein fluids and other products in their crops for transportation to the colony and subsequent dispersal to the larvae. Queen wasps require considerable protein for ovogenesis and they may derive amino acids for protein synthesis from their body fat or haemolymph during the spring, although captive queens will readily devour the thoraces of flies if they are offered (Watson 1922). When the colony is established much of the protein requirement may be obtained from the salivary secretions of the larvae (see Chapter 8).

Larvae

The larvae in their cells are fed by the adult workers which constantly inspect the brood by putting their antennae into the cell. The larvae are then fed a drop of liquid food or a small piece of malaxated meat, after which they invariably secrete a drop of saliva which is swallowed by the tending adult. Frequently, the larva attempts to hold on to the nurse wasp by gripping it with the mandibles. Larvae are visited by tending adults throughout the day in *V. orientalis*, the duration of visits to small and medium-sized larvae lasting 1 to 3 seconds while large larvae occupy from 2 to 13 seconds of the adult's time (Ishay and others 1967). The size of the protein food bolus, and its degree of mastication by the adult, is variable. *V. orientalis* larvae were offered pieces 1·5-2·0 mm in diameter which took 3 to 4 minutes to ingest. *D. sylvestris* larvae are apparently offered less well-masticated morsels for they reject small pieces of uningested food which fall to the bottom of the nest (Brian and Brian 1952). These 'rejection pellets' must be due to the pre-treatment afforded to the prey and appears species specific, for a food bolus masticated by *P. germanica* caused no such pellet rejection when experimentally offered to *D. sylvestris* larvae. Pellets were ejected by *P. germanica* larvae if offered a food bolus prepared by the *D. sylvestris* queen. The pre-treatment by *D. sylvestris* took 1 minute while *P. germanica* spent 2 to 3 minutes masticating a *Lucilia sericata* (Meigen) fly.

The total food intake and relative proportions of solids and fluids is unknown and difficult to determine under natural conditions.

Returning foragers share their loads with other adults in the colony and they in turn apportion some of it to yet other workers, thereby achieving a rapid dissemination of food to the larvae. The quantity of food given to and assimilated by larvae is related to colony factors such as the presence of the queen, number of workers available for nursing duties and the size of cells. Montagner (1967), by using radio-active tracers, found that the quantity of food in the crop is related to the size of larva, and that older and larger larvae stimulated greater feeding than small larvae. The influence of cell size was determined by transplanting deep cells from the centre of combs to the edge where they are normally shallow. Larvae in the deep cells were given more food despite there being identical-sized larvae in both types of cell. Nest temperature also influences the feeding régime with a four-fold increase in food intake when the temperature was increased from 12 to 28°C. The maximum feeding level occurred when the nest was main-tained at 30°C and is possibly related to an increase in the number of brood nurses when fewer workers are engaged in thermal regulation duties. Montagner also discovered that removing the queen caused a sharp decrease in the feeding of larvae. The age of tending workers is also critical for old wasps (17 to 24 days) rarely feed larvae while young ones (0-2 days) fed larvae well but not as abundantly as the middle-aged ones (3-16 days). This ontogenetic variation in feeding behaviour may be allied to degeneration of the adult's glands, for Deleurance (1950) found that after a certain age, *Polistes* were in-capable of feeding their brood due to an apparent deterioration of the salivary glands. Once a larva is replete it will close its mandibles firmly and refuse food, the provisioning of larvae being regulated by larval demands. The soliciting for food is an auditory stimulus, for they scratch the walls of the cells with their mandibles to attract the attention of the workers (more details in the 'Communication' section of Chapter 8).

The larval gut does not communicate with the rectum, the lumen between mid and hind gut being occluded until cocoon spinning is completed. Examination of the accumulated waste products in the midgut, which comprise 25-30 per cent of total body weight in mature larvae (Ishay and others 1967) shows that it is composed of a thick, dark brown or purplish mass with traces of insect cuticle derived from the prey. Occasionally, plant remains are found which are probably ingested when plant-feeding prey such as caterpillars are offered to larvae (Hüsing 1954, 1956). Ishay and others (1967) also demonstrated the presence of the bacteria, *Staphyloccus aureus* var. *albus* and *Proteus vulgaris* in the midgut of *V. orientalis* larvae.

CHAPTER 7

WASP POPULATIONS

The major parameters in population studies are the 'quality' of the individuals which constitute a population, their numerical density and biomass, and the manner in which their numbers fluctuate or patterns of distribution vary. The social insects present particularly interesting and challenging subjects for such investigations due to their ability to regulate colony conditions despite fluctuations in the physical environment. Similarly, the communal effort in foraging and defence, allied to variations in the proportion of workers and queens, may confer a high degree of survival and reproductive potential on colonies.

Population studies in social wasps may be conveniently divided into two major categories, the seasonal changes in populations of individual colonies and the year to year fluctuations in the numbers of colonies. The interactions between numbers of colonies, their growth rates, and population densities, will determine annual fluctuations in the numbers of wasps.

Wasp colonies may be considered to combine some of the characteristics of plants and animals for they are sedentary, yet extra-colonial foraging extends the range of activities well beyond the nest site, while the mature colony may attain a size and metabolic rate comparable with some mammals and birds (Brian 1965).

Seasonal Changes in Population Structure

The life history of social wasps in Britain is governed by the cyclic changes of the temperate climate – hibernation of queens during the long months of winter, followed by the establishment of incipient colonies in the spring, and the explosive increase in the size of the nest and numbers of inhabitants in the summer. During a brief climactic stage in midsummer and early autumn, the reproductives are reared, before the final demise of the society with approaching winter (Table 16).

TABLE 16
Stages in the growth and development of *Paravespula* colonies

STAGE	COMPOSITION OF COLONY	PERIOD
1. Incipient colony (Solitary stage)	Foundress queen with embryo nest	April–June
2. Juvenile colony (period of rapid increase followed by a period of slow increase in population)	appearance of adult workers, explosive increase in numbers of cells, brood and adults	June–July
3. Mature colony	(1) Male production initiated	August
	(2) Queen cells constructed and queens reared	August–October
	(3) Emission of reproductives	September–October
4. Declining colony (period of senescence)	Physiological break-down of queen followed by her death, disintegration of colony both socially and physically	October–November

The development of individual colonies during the year is difficult to follow because much of their activity is hidden from the investigator by the envelope, and manipulation of nests is treated with considerable intolerance by the inhabitants. Direct observations on the early stages of colony development have, however, been recorded by Janet (1895a) in his classic paper on *V. crabro* in France, by Brian and Brian (1948, 1952) in their meticulous studies on *D. sylvestris* in Scotland, and Matsuura (1971) on hornets in Japan. Changes in the population structure of more advanced colonies of *P. vulgaris* and *P. germanica* have been determined by the destructive sampling of many colonies throughout one year (Spradbery 1971).

There are several accounts of population census of individual colonies (e.g. Weyrauch 1935, Blackith and Stevenson 1958, Kemper 1961, and Kemper and Döhring 1961) which are intrinsically of great interest, but they rarely concern the less common species. A disadvantage of these studies is that the time of sampling often produces data which gives little indication of population potential, especially if colonies are taken before queen rearing begins. Nevertheless, careful analysis of mature or even expended colonies can be very productive of information because the numbers and kinds of cells and their frequency of use can indicate the total population produced.

It is more convenient and logical to begin a description of seasonal changes in wasp populations with the emergence of queens from their winter quarters followed by an account of the development of incipient colonies – the solitary phase – and to conclude with a history of the maturing colony.

Spring Queens

The period of queen wasp activity in the spring is similar among the

XII. British social wasps.
(top row) *Dolichovespula norwegica;* (middle row) *Vespula rufa;* (bottom row) *V. austriaca* (males in left-hand column). N.B. — no worker caste in *V. austriaca*, the social parasite.

XIII. Juvenile and mature nests.

(*a*) Juvenile nest of *Paravespula vulgaris*.

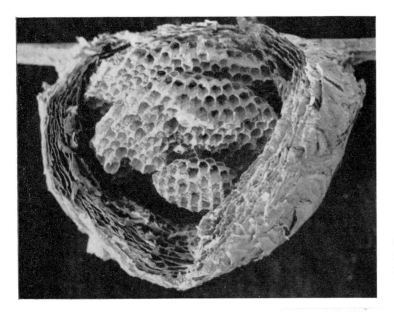

(*b*) Mature *Vespula r[...]* nest to show details [...] multi-leaved envelope.

Errata

PLATE XIV: Details of carton structure
This plate is now facing p.176.

Wasps p.161.

XIV (*on opposite page*). Details of carton structure. (top left) *Vespa crabro;* (t[op] right) *Paravespula vulgaris;* (middle left) *P. germanica;* (middle right) *Vespula ru[...]* (bottom left) *Dolichovespula norwegica;* (bottom right) *D. sylvestris.* All to sa[me] scale of magnification (×6).

British species, although queens of the social parasite, *V. austriaca*, appear later, coinciding with the founding of colonies by the host, *V. rufa* (Fig. 26).

The number of queens encountered during the period between leaving hibernation in mid-April and the juvenile colony stage in June, may be very high. Barrington and Moffatt (1901) published records of the number of queens killed by a gardener in Fassaroe, Ireland (Table 17). Over a period of eight years he collected 1,155 wasps which included all the British species except the hornet (which does not occur in Ireland), giving a good indication of the relative abundance of the different species in the area. At the peak of a five-day long migration of *V. rufa* in southern Sweden, more than 35,000 queens were recorded passing an observation post in one day (Rudebeck 1965). A detailed account of this migratory movement is given in Chapter 4.

TABLE 17
Numbers of queen wasps collected during the spring in Fassaroe, Ireland
(from Barrington and Moffatt 1901)

SPECIES	YEARS								TOTAL
	1893	1894	1896	1897	1898	1899	1900	1901	
P. vulgaris	39	42	82	60	26	109	118	112	588
P. germanica	0	8	6	25	0	11	35	30	115
D. norwegica	7	13	16	23	3	11	16	20	109
D. sylvestris	1	15	21	69	22	48	10	21	207
V. rufa	12	2	4	23	0	50	9	19	119
V. austriaca	3	0	1	4	0	6	1	2	17
TOTAL	62	80	130	204	51	235	189	204	1155

By using suction traps to catch queens of *P. germanica* at Rothamsted (Fig. 61), Taylor (1963) determined that their aerial density during the spring of 1960 was constant at 14·5 queens per 28,320 cubic metres (10^6 cubic feet) of air, when temperatures were above the threshold for flight. A positive correlation between the daily catches of queens and the number of hours per day when the temperature was above the flight threshold of 15·5°C, strongly suggests that daily fluctuations in the numbers trapped are brought about by the amount of time available for flight. After emerging from hibernation, there is no further recruitment of queens to the springtime population and fluctuations in their numbers were slight, the fall-off in early June coinciding with the confinement of queens to their colonies.

Although the flight period of spring queens in the British Isles occupies little more than two months, in the milder climates of New Zealand and Tasmania, founding queens may be active in the field for up to four months (Thomas 1960, and personal observations). By using various baits, Thomas trapped 3,000 *P. germanica* queens during the spring of 1950/51, and in a three-month long eradication campaign

M*

in 1948, 118,000 hibernating queens were discovered, more than 7,000 by one enterprising schoolboy.

By mid-June, founding queens are no longer seen on the wing (Fig. 61) because successful ones remain in their growing nests while the others have perished during their attempts to establish colonies. We now turn to the first stage in the growth of colonies – the crucial period of embryo colony development – when the queens attempt to establish nests and rear their first few daughters.

The First Forty Days – early colony growth
in *Dolichovespula sylvestris*

This account of the growth of the incipient colony up to the time when the first workers are produced is based on the studies of Brian and Brian (1948, 1952) on a number of *D. sylvestris* colonies in Scotland.

The initial activities of queens when establishing embryo nests are the construction of cells and envelopes, and their almost immediate oviposition in the newly prepared cells. The rate of nest construction is more intense during these first few days, one queen building 15 cells in the first few days, each cell containing an egg. With the hatching of eggs from the fifth day onwards, the building and oviposition rates decreased, probably necessitated by the larval demand for food. It is well established that in *Polistes* colonies the feeding demands of newly hatched larvae cause a delay or halt to cell construction (Morimoto 1954a, b, c). This appears to be an effective stimulus which limits the size of the incipient colony to the foraging capacity of the founding queen. However, cell construction and oviposition in *D. sylvestris* continued sporadically throughout the period of the Brians' observations (Fig. 57).

With the pupation of mature larvae after two weeks, cell construction was even more severely curtailed or even halted in some colonies, and not resumed until the first adults had emerged. Throughout this period, cells are rarely vacant, oviposition taking place as soon as a new cell base is prepared, a cell vacated by an emerging adult, or following removal of dead brood.

The first eggs to be laid were generally highly fertile with an incubation period of five days but later, the rate of development of eggs increased markedly, some cells being occupied by eggs for up to fifteen days. The Brians suggested that the increase in the apparent incubation period could be caused by low egg viability for physiological reasons, or perhaps replacement of eggs following cannibalism. There were also increases in the duration of the larval and pupal stages following the queen's success in rearing the first batch of workers.

In the more successful colonies of *D. sylvestris*, the founding queens made about 40 cells with some 15 eggs, 20 larvae, and a few pupae

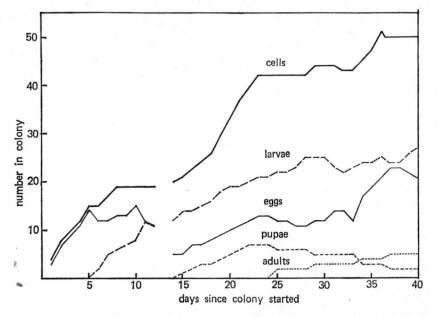

Figure 57. Population changes in incipient colonies of *Dolichovespula sylvestris* (data from 2 colonies) (after Brian and Brian 1952).

by the time the first workers emerged (Fig. 57). However, incipient colony success was the exception rather than the rule, for of 12 colonies under observation, only one succeeded in producing a viable group of foragers. The reasons for colony failure are difficult to pinpoint, loss of queens from predation or other causes contributing in some measure, but there were other failures which may have arisen from defects in the physiology and behaviour of queens. As the Brians pointed out, more efficient regulation of the building, oviposition, and rearing patterns would contribute most to colony success.

It appears that there is some, as yet unexplained, factor underlying early colony development such that the first batch of brood is successfully reared to maturity, but the remainder suffer periods of inanition which result in reduced viability, prolonged development, and the production of smaller adults. The queen-reared workers are, however, much smaller than those produced later in the year (see Chapter 9), their diminutive size probably favouring a more rapid development than would occur if much larger workers were produced at this time. To ensure the success of a colony it would seem that a more defined brood-rearing cycle would be an advantage. For example, if the queen built only 15 cells initially and fifteen large workers were reared to maturity as quickly as possible, it would be better than attempting to rear too many, which results in very few large workers and increased mortality and times of development of the remainder. In *D. sylvestris*, the rearing pattern seems to be a compromise between an oscillating and continuous cycle during the incipient colony stage but, in common with all the other social wasps in Britain, once a worker force is established, the cycle becomes markedly continuous, with a fairly steady flow of workers being recruited to the adult population every day.

To succeed, the incipient colony must produce an effective worker population rapidly during this the most vulnerable phase of colony development. When the first few workers have been reared, they soon begin foraging and the queen remains within the nest, protected from predators and relieved of foraging duties. With her frequent insertion of the abdomen into cells to oviposit, the wings of the queen soon become frayed (Plates XX, XXIV) and, allied to massive ovariole development, she eventually loses her ability to fly.

Seasonal Changes in the Populations of *Paravespula* Colonies

Investigations of the day-to-day changes in the numbers of brood and adults in a maturing wasp colony are virtually impossible without disturbing the nest too much. A solution to the problem is to collect and sample several colonies during the period when population data is required. In this way it is possible to determine average population trends with the added bonus of finding the extremes of population density in both large and small nests.

During studies at Rothamsted Experimental Station in 1961, I collected 59 colonies of *P. vulgaris* and 30 colonies of *P. germanica* from early June to mid-October. After killing a colony, it was excavated and brought to the laboratory for a detailed census. The numbers of combs, cells, immature stages, and adults were counted, while the type of cell and male, queen and worker, pupae and adults were distinguished. The generations of wasps reared in each cell were determined by counting the number of faecal pellets at the base of the cells. A maximum of four pellets per cell was discovered, indicating that four adults had been reared in the one cell, although Parker (1928) found five pellets in a cell of an American *Vespula* species. The founding queen in each colony was dissected and her ovariole eggs counted to give an indication of egg-potential or fecundity. This measure was used in studies on bumble bees by Cumber (1949) who called the number of eggs in the ovaries which were equal in size to or larger than the adjacent nurse cells, the 'ovariole index'.

The changes taking place in *Paravespula* colonies during the course of the year are more easily described if numbers of eggs and oviposition rates, numbers and types of brood (larvae and pupae), and the adult populations are presented separately.

Fecundity and Oviposition. In mid-April, when queens leave their hibernation quarters and start searching for nest sites, their ovariole index was less than 20, increasing to nearly 60 by the end of June when colonies were producing workers, and 97 by early July. At the end of July it was 400, a value which remained relatively constant until mid-October (Fig. 58). From July onwards, the abdominal cavity of the queen is almost completely filled with eggs and the gaster very distended (see Plate XX). The mean ovariole index of queens during August and September was 391 (Range, 361-527) in *P. vulgaris* and 433 (295-546) in *P. germanica.*

TABLE 18

Numbers of eggs in colonies (from Spradbery 1971)

PERIOD	Paravespula vulgaris			P. germanica		
	NO. OF COLONIES	MEAN	RANGE	NO. OF COLONIES	MEAN	RANGE
June	1	36	—	0	—	—
Mid-July	3	464	77–954	0	—	—
Late-July	8	1122	542–1573	2	637	492–782
August	37	821	334–1573	18	727	284–1653
September	9	739	140–1171	9	823	454–1362

Assuming a five-day incubation period for the eggs (see Table 19), the daily oviposition rate was calculated by dividing the number of eggs in a colony (Table 18) by five.

The daily oviposition rate thus derived increased from 7 in early June to 72 in early July, reaching a peak of 225 in late July followed by a decline to 120 by the end of September (Fig. 58). Archer (1972b) found a similar variation in oviposition rate in *P. vulgaris,* with a maximum of 185 eggs per day during the period of male brood production, the rate decling thereafter until the end of the season. From my census, the maximum oviposition rate was 330 in a *P. germanica* colony.

Comparison of ovariole index and oviposition rate suggests that in the early stages of colony growth (June to early July), oviposition is possibly limited by the number of ovariole eggs available, although there are very few empty cells at this time and any potential increase in oviposition could not be realized. From mid-July, however, the great increase in number of ovariole eggs is not paralleled by a similar increase in oviposition rate, although the rate does rise. By early August, the number of vacant cells increases, suggesting that oviposition is not limited by the availability of cells. For the rest of the season, oviposition is apparently not limited by either the number of ovariole eggs or lack of empty cells. However, there is a progressive decline in the use of the older cells (Fig. 60), probably because they become too

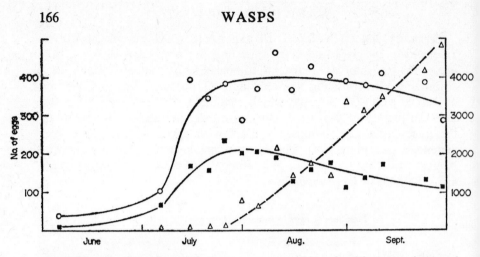

Figure 58. Number of ovariole eggs per queen (○), oviposition rate, (■), and number of empty cells (△) in *Paravespula vulgaris* colonies, 5-day means (from Spradbery 1971).

fouled with faecal material. It is also possible that the queen spends more of her time in the lower and more recently constructed combs where empty cells are few in number.

There was a linear relationship between oviposition rate and cell construction during the early part of the year (5 June to 20 July) but thereafter, the number of cells increased without any corresponding increase in oviposition rate. There were also positive correlations between numbers of eggs in colonies and the numbers of larvae and pupae. A similar situation was recorded in bumble bee colonies by

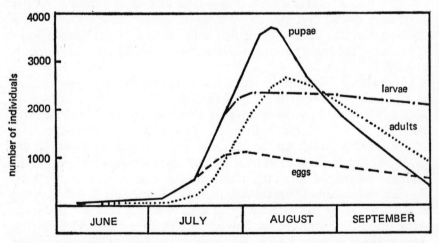

Figure 59. Number of immature stages and adults in colonies of *Paravespula vulgaris* (5-day means) (after Spradbery 1971).

TABLE 19
Longevity of immature and adult workers (in days) (from Spradbery 1971)
(a) Estimates based on proportion of eggs, larvae, pupae, and adults per colony, assuming an egg-period of 5 days.

SPECIES	NO. OF COLONIES	EGGS	LARVAE	PUPAE	ADULTS	AUTHOR
P. germanica and P. vulgaris	4	5	13·0	15·0	—	Kemper and Döhring 1961
P. germanica	27*	5	13·35	15·90	11·20	Spradbery 1963
P. vulgaris	50*	5	15·75	17·60	16·45	Spradbery 1963

*Data from colonies collected after 25 July

(b) Observed longevity

SPECIES/ PERIOD	EGGS	LARVAE	PUPAE	ADULTS	AUTHOR
P. vulgaris					
June	5·28 (3·4–6·7)	15	15·14 (14·3–17·8)	12·42 (5–26)	Spradbery 1963
June	5·2 (5–8)	10 (9–17)	11 (8–14)	—	Potter 1965
July	—	—	—	13·55 (2–27)	Potter 1965
August	—	—	—	22–32 (8–37)	Potter 1965
September	—	—	—	17·37 (4–29)	Potter 1965
—	8	13	10	21–28	Ritchie 1915
August	—	—	—	11·6 (3–33)	Roland 1969
D. sylvestris					
May	5	10	7–22	—	Brian and Brian 1952
V. crabro					
May–September	10·0 (5–18)	14·5 (12–18)	13·9 (13–15)	19·5 (2–>41)	Janet 1895
July–August	5	12	13	—	Janet 1895
V. orientalis	—	—	—	36·1 (12–64)	Ishay et al. 1967

Brian (1951) who found that the number of eggs laid was related to the number of cocoons present, supporting her hypothesis that the queen lays eggs in proportion to the number of pupae and thus ensures an adequate worker force (recruited from the pupal population) to tend the larvae (recruited from the eggs).

The Brood. During the early part of the season, the numbers of eggs and larvae are approximately the same (Fig. 59), but the duration of the larval stage is considerably longer than the incubation period of the egg, so that larvae tend to accumulate until, by the end of July, some 2,000 are present in a colony. With the levelling off in the oviposition rate and its decline from August onwards, the number of larvae does not increase much after early August. The maximum number of

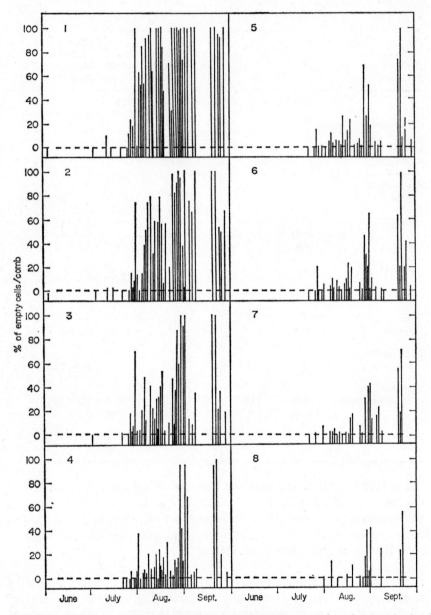

Figure 60. Percentage of empty cells per comb in *Paravespula vulgaris* colonies. Combs 1-8, numbered in decreasing age (from Spradbery 1971).

larvae found in a colony was 3,421 in *P. vulgaris* and 2,771 in *P. germanica*.

The number of worker pupae was small in June and early July, reaching a maximum of 3,500 in early August and thereafter declining rapidly during the latter half of August and throughout September (Fig. 59). I found worker pupae in colonies as late as 26 October and, during mild winters, worker production may even continue into January (Barrington 1900). The increase in the numbers of pupae relative to larvae would suggest that pupal development is of longer duration than the larval period, but the meagre data available (see Table 19) do not show this clearly. Perhaps the larval period is reduced during the August-September period due to improved feeding conditions, without a corresponding reduction in pupal duration. The maximum numbers of worker pupae per colony was 5,524 in *P. vulgaris* and 4,458 in *P. germanica*.

Male pupae first appear at the end of July in *P. vulgaris* (Fig. 59) and early August in *P. germanica*, with many of the queen cells at this time being used to rear male brood. The proportion of male pupae to all pupae present increased from less than 10 per cent in August to 50 per cent by the end of September, the majority of them being reared in the lowermost worker combs (Table 20), where oviposition activity by the queen is greatest. The maximum numbers of male pupae in colonies were 2,014 in *P. vulgaris* and 1,289 in *P. germanica*.

Queen pupae were found in colonies from mid-August, reaching their numerical peak in mid-September, when they accounted for nearly 30 per cent of all pupae present. The maximum numbers of queen pupae in colonies were 866 in *P. vulgaris* and 1,002 in *P. germanica*.

Adult Wasps.   The recruitment of adults to the colony begins within three or four weeks of nest establishment (Fig. 57), but their numbers

TABLE 20
Density of male pupae in worker combs (from Spradbery 1971)

COMB		*Paravespula vulgaris* (nineteen colonies)		*P. germanica* (eighteen colonies)	
		No. combs	% male pupae	No. combs	% male pupae
(Lower)	1	19	39·7	18	26·7
	2	19	33·3	18	23·1
	3	19	29·3	18	31·4
	4	19	25·2	18	19·8
	5	19	13·2	17	12·2
	6	18	3·7	13	2·9
	7	12	0·9	3	3·3
	8	6	0	1	0
(Upper)	9	2	0	1	0

increase very slowly during the early part of juvenile colony development. In early June, I found a *P. vulgaris* colony which had produced only 15 workers, of which 12 were still alive and by early July there were generally less than 100 workers in a colony. The successful *D. sylvestris* colony studied by Brian and Brian (1952) produced 31 workers within 45 days of nest initiation. The population explosion occurs between mid-July and mid-August with an increase to 1,500 workers per colony in late July and 2,500 by mid-August. Thereafter, the number of workers declined to about 1,000 by late September (Fig. 61). The maximum number of adults occurs about one month after the peak in number of eggs, reflecting the duration of the immature stages which is 25 to 35 days. The maximum number of worker adults which were found in a colony was 5,268 in *P. vulgaris* and 2,894 in *P. germanica.*

A crude measure of the daily recruitment of adult workers to a colony was obtained by counting the number of emerging wasps during the 24-hour period following the collection of a nest. A peak emergence

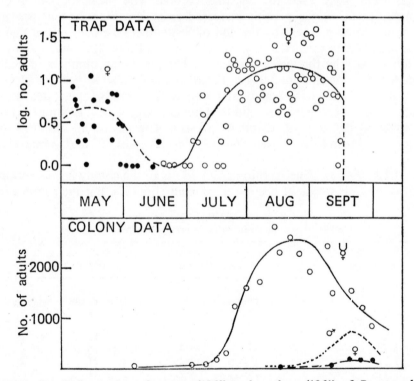

Figure 61. Daily catches of queens (1960) and workers (1961) of *Paravespula germanica* from suction traps (trapping ceased on 16 September, 1961) compared to total adults per *P. vulgaris* colony (1961) (after Spradbery 1971).

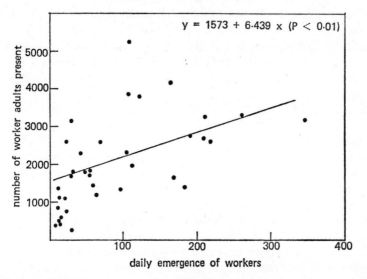

Figure 62. Relation between number of workers present per colony and the daily emergence of adults, data from *Paravespula vulgaris* colonies (after Spradbery 1963).

of 207 workers per day took place in early August, the rate declining gradually until the end of the month, followed by a sharp drop to about 40 per day in September. A maximum emergence of 346 wasps was recorded in a *P. vulgaris* colony collected in early August. These emergence rates are closely related to seasonal changes in the number of adults present in the colony (Fig. 62), and also to pupal density. Archer (1972b) found emergence rates of 36-54 per day during the juvenile colony stage, with an increase to 96-176 when the colony was mature, followed by a decrease to 30-45 during the latter stages of colony development.

The collection of wasps with suction traps indicates day to day changes in the relative abundance of foragers. A graphical comparison of the daily catches of *P. germanica* workers with the total adult population in *P. vulgaris* colonies shows that the two curves have similar peaks (Fig. 61). Trapped foragers, however, will be a reflection of several interacting factors, rather than a simple measure of the density of total wasps in a given area. Populations of adults in individual colonies and the number of colonies in the district will of course provide the major contribution to the trap catch. But the intensity of foraging activity, the proportion of adults which forage, and prevailing climatic conditions will all govern the density of foragers and, thereby, the numbers trapped. Details of foraging rates, proportion of foragers during the season, and their rates of foraging have been dealt with previously (Chapter 6) and these parameters must be borne in mind when interpreting trap catches. There is obviously still much work to be done on foraging rates and the interactions between the density of wasps in colonies and the aerial density of foragers, taking into account such variables as the development stage of the colony and phenological conditions.

The effects of wasp predation on populations of prey have been little studied, although Morris (1972) found a relationship between per cent predation by vespid wasps and the population density of the Fall Webworm, *Hyphantria cunea* Drury, in Canada. However, when this caterpillar pest of trees is at high population levels, predation becomes inversely related to density, a situation which is characteristic of many avian predators and insect parasitoids.

Diurnal variation in the number of foraging wasps has been described in some detail in Chapter 6, the maximum foraging rate taking place early in the day (between 0600 and 0900 hours) with a fairly constant but lower rate being maintained until the evening when the light intensity drops below the threshold for successful navigation (Fig. 51).

Adult males make their appearance in colonies during late July and their numbers, though fluctuating, increase until the end of the season (Fig. 61). The fluctuations are probably due to individual colony differences, although the behaviour of males is such that many may leave the parental colonies in search of nubile queens. The maximum number of males found in a colony was 1,049 in *P. vulgaris* and 1,293 in *P. germanica*.

Adult queens began to emerge from the pupal cells by the end of August in *P. vulgaris* colonies and in early September in *P. germanica*. The maximum number of adult queens found at any one time was 235 in a *P. vulgaris* colony and 603 in *P. germanica*, the ratio of males to queens being approximately 1 : 1.

The numbers of males and queens found in colonies during my survey do not of course indicate total production, for the reproductives leave the colonies when males are sexually mature and the queens receptive to mating. I have, however, seen both males and queens return to their nests after periods outside the colony when they may be found feeding at flowers or mating (see Chapter 10 for further details). Furthermore, if colonies are collected before queen production is complete, a low estimate of queen productivity will be obtained. Further comment on productivity will be found later in this chapter.

POPULATIONS OF MATURE COLONIES OF BRITISH SPECIES

There is remarkably little information on the population structure of mature wasp colonies in the British Isles, apart from the census of

TABLE 21

Population structure of mature *Paravespula* colonies (from Spradbery 1963)

DATE COLLECTED	COMB	NUMBER OF						NUMBER OF ADULTS					
								EMERGED			PRESENT		
		CELLS	EGGS	LARVAE	PUPAE (female)	PUPAE (male)	EMPTY CELLS	(1)	(2)	(3)	♀	♂	♀
(a) *P. vulgaris* 25 September	1	456	0	26	0	0	430	430	430	370			
	2	700	81	220	46	21	332	697	284	26			
	3	1230	274	455	139	118	247	1245	865	116			
	4	1530	319	706	149	238	119	1524	779	106			
	5	1323	277	714	73	150	109	1297	414	0			
	6	180	14	121	4	6	35	160	0	0			
		(483)	(175)	(138)	(87)	(3)	(81)	(202)	0	0			
	7	(629)	(11)	(241)	(361)	(1)	(15)	(230)	0	0			
	8	(81)	(20)	(54)	0	0	(7)	0	0	0			
TOTAL { 8		5421 (1625)	965 (206)	2242 (433)	411 (448)	533 (4)	1272 (103)	5353 (432)	2772 / 0	618 / 0	1277	681	143+1
(b) *P. germanica* 13 September	1	560	0	0	0	0	560	560	560	273			
	2	1003	0	51	5	0	947	1003	1003	327			
	3	1225	123	398	324	41	339	1225	550	51			
	4	1277	252	508	73	378	71	1277	314	0			
	5	1384	179	475	212	466	52	1323	1256	98			
	6	892	95	535	11	203	48	965	621	17			
		(129)	(9)	(36)	(61)	(1)	(23)	(23)	0	0			
	7	(654)	(60)	(189)	(288)	(1)	(116)	(153)	0	0			
	8	(431)	(38)	(217)	(160)	0	(16)	(24)	0	0			
TOTAL { 8		6341 (1214)	649 (107)	1967 (442)	625 (509)	1088 (1)	2017 (155)	6353 (200)	4304 / 0	766 / 0	1820	477	147+1

N.B. 1. Figures in parentheses denote queen cells or the contents of queen cells.
2. Emerged (1) (2) (3) refer to the first, second, and third generations of adult produced per cell, determined by counting the faecal pellets per cell.

P. vulgaris and *P. germanica*. It seems extraordinary that, despite the many records of the nesting habitats of the rarer species, no-one has published detailed accounts of nest architecture, the composition of brood, productivity, and reproductive potential.

To illustrate the typical population structure of mature *Paravespula* colonies, I have enumerated the 'raw data' from a *P. vulgaris* and *P. germanica* colony sampled during the Hertfordshire census in Table 21. The similarities between the two species are obvious. The disuse of older cells in the first comb or two is typical of colonies at this time, reflecting an accumulation of faecal material after two or three generations of wasps have been reared. Queen cell building in both nests began when comb 6 was being extended so that a peripheral ring of large cells are found enclosing worker cells, subsequent combs being exclusively of queen cells. It is characteristic that there are proportionally fewer queen cells compared to worker cells. The estimate of the number of wasps produced per colony demonstrates the massive mortality of workers during the course of the season, the proportion of surviving adults being 15 per cent in the *P. vulgaris* colony and 16 per cent in the *P. germanica* colony.

These data also give an idea of the amount of information to be obtained by the examination of wasp colonies, and it is hoped that comparable information on the less common species will one day be published.

Available data on the populations of the rarer species is summarized in Table 22. Populations in *V. crabro* colonies are considerably smaller than *Paravespula* species, the number of workers rarely exceeding a thousand. It would appear a characteristic of the genus *Vespa* that hornet colonies are smaller in population size than *Paravespula* species (Matsuura 1968d), although the large size of adults results in nests, and possibly biomass, of a similar volume.

The subterranean nester, *V. rufa*, and the aerial nesting *D. sylvestris* and *D. norwegica* all produce comparatively small nests of a few hundred cells and their populations are correspondingly low. The markedly early production of males and queens and termination of activities by late August or early September (Fig. 26) further emphasizes the exiguity of their colonies.

The density of colonies of the different wasp species and their relative abundance in different parts of the British Isles are almost completely unknown. Records of the distribution of the various species will be found in Appendix 4, but they do not indicate relative abundance or the density of colonies within their geographical range. It is quite obvious that *P. vulgaris* and *P. germanica* are the dominant species, both in individual colony size and the numbers of colonies per unit area. During my studies in Hertfordshire, 141 wasp nests were dis-

TABLE 22
Population census of some wasp colonies

SPECIES	NUMBER OF COLONIES	NUMBER OF					TOTAL ADULTS	SOURCE
		COMBS	CELLS	WORKERS	MALES	QUEENS		
V. crabro	1	2 ♀+♂ / 4 ♀+	790 / 1090	<2000 / <1000		<1000	<3000	Janet 1903
	1	—	500 / 2000			<2000	<3000	Simpson 1948
	8	4·6 (3–7)	—	99 (10–400)	67 (4–270)	39 (12–80)	205 (38–730)	Kemper and Döhring 1961
	1	—	—	142	—	29	—	Cory 1931
	1	—	1700	—	—	—	3,600 produced	Bodenheimer 1936
D. sylvestris	5	2·8 (2–3)	—	114 (40–180)	31 (5–60)	30 (9–50)	152 (96–220)	Weyrauch 1935
	1	—	—	—	58	191	—	Scott 1917
	4	—	395 ♀ (80–1000)	—	—	—	—	Arnold 1966
D. norwegica	2	3 (2–4)	—	50 (40–60)	36 (10–63)	13	93 (70–116)	Weyrauch 1934
	1	—	—	15	20	100	135	Smith 1852
	1	4	1534	166	162	—	328	Winckworth Allen 1938
V. rufa	1	3	387 ♀+♂ / 290 ♀+	—	—	—	655 ♂ + ♀ produced / 169 ♂ + ♀ produced	personal data
	3	—	—	246 (97–395)	—	32	—	Kemper and Döhring 1961
	2	—	270 ♀ (190–350)	—	—	—	—	Arnold 1966

covered during two years and only one, a *V. rufa* colony was not a *Paravespula* species. Wasp nests were systematically destroyed in the Royal Horticultural Society's Gardens in Surrey between 1921 and 1945 but records of the individual species were not kept (Fox Wilson 1946). However, the relative numbers of colonies of the different species did not differ markedly from year to year, although the proportion of *P. vulgaris* and *P. germanica* varied annually. The rarest species were *D. norwegica* and *D. sylvestris* with never more than five nests of the latter and that in a year when more than 80 wasp nests were located. *V. rufa* was apparently fairly abundant.

OVERWINTERED COLONIES OF *Paravespula germanica*

The European wasp, *P. germanica*, became established in New Zealand in 1945 (Thomas 1960) and in Tasmania during 1959 (Anon 1962). The rapid dissemination of the wasp and the occurrence of overwintering colonies are of major interest in studies of the invasive capabilities and reproductive potential of this species. Only a small, but as yet unknown, proportion of colonies survive the winter, however, the majority following the normal course of events which take place in Europe.

No colonies have yet been found which were more than two seasons (18 months) old, yet the prodigious size of these nests is testimony to the productivity of the social wasp if the precarious and slow-growing incipient stage is by-passed. Colonies surviving the winter start the annual cycle with a profound advantage over those being established by unaided queens.

Maintenance of a colony during the winter depends on the re-queening which takes place in the late autumn. I found two colonies in Tasmania which had reached this crucial step, the nests being structurally identical to mature colonies under European conditions with the old founding queen still alive, but with an additional 20 and 22 laying queens in each nest. Most of these queens showed signs of having been egg-layers for a month or more (see Chapter 9 for details of physogastry and ageing in queens). Throughout the winter, brood rearing is maintained and, perhaps surprisingly, males and queens are produced in large numbers despite sub-optimal climatic conditions and a decrease in available food supplies. Thomas (1960) has determined that the majority of winter brood is queen brood. By early spring, the size of nests has not increased significantly, but during the next few months, they may be enlarged ten times or more (Fig. 63).

The largest nests recorded are those in aerial situations where lack of restrictions on building activities may lead to nests 4·6 m (15 ft) in length, and 2·4 m (8 ft) wide with perhaps 180 combs present (Thomas

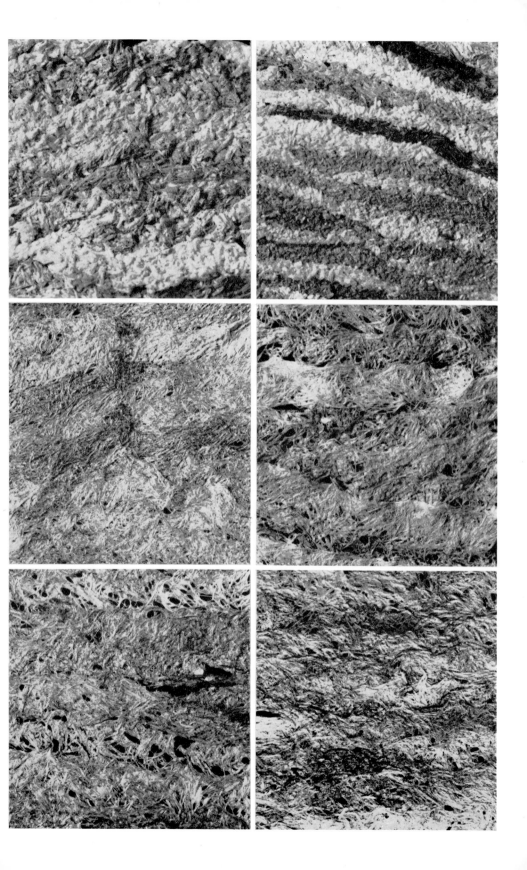

XV–A. Collecting nectar.

XV (A–F). Foraging activities are shown above and on following pages; *see* also Frontispiece.

XV–B. Severing the wing of a fly after its capture and prior to carrying the prey back to the nest.

XV–C. Obtaining water prior to pulp-collecting.

XV–D. Scavenging on remains of a crushed snail.

XV–E. Collecting woodpulp from a post.

XV–F. Dissecting abdomen of bee trapped in spider's web to obtain the honey-filled crop.

XVI. Activities at the nest tunnel entrance of a *Paravespula germanica* colony.

Returning foragers, note excavated pellets of soil at entrance.

Forager returning with woodpulp.

Two pictures of workers with excavated soil leaving the nest entrance.

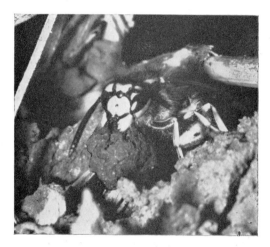

Guard wasps around the nest entrance at night.

XVII. British species of Vespoidea. (1st row) male, queen, and worker of *Vespa crabro*; Eumenidae (2nd row). *Eumenes coarctatus*; (3rd row) *Ancistrocerus parietum*; (4th row) *Pseudepipona herrichii* (males left, females right).

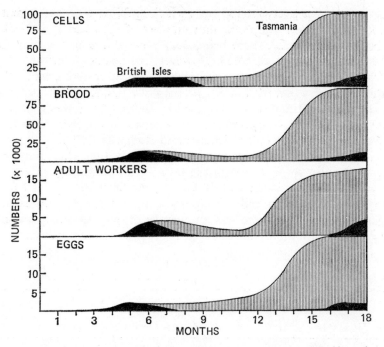

Figure 63. Comparison of population changes in European (black) and over-wintered Tasmanian colonies (hatched) of *Paravespula germanica* (original).

1960). The biggest subterranean nest I have so far examined was built in sawdust near Hobart, Tasmania, the girth being 1·8 m (6 ft), height 0·8 m (2½ ft) and projecting 1·2 m (4 ft) deep into the sawdust. This nest had 30 combs with an estimated 1·5 million cells, while the largest New Zealand nest had an estimated 3 to 4 million cells. A New Zealand nest of 117 × 100 × 95 cm (47 × 40 × 38 inches) weighed 45 kg (100 lb), from which it may be deduced that the largest nest probably weighed 450 kg (1,000 lb).

With the reduction in brood and numbers of workers during the winter, many cells and even entire combs are papered over with carton, possibly to conserve heat by increasing the insulating qualities of the nest. When cell-building activities begin in the spring, only worker cells are made which may result in some combs having a core of worker cells surrounded by queen cells with a further ring of worker cells around the periphery. The building of queen cells begins again in mid to late summer as usual.

There are comparatively few empty cells during the second season's development (Table 23), no doubt due to the many egg-laying or functional queens in each colony. The maximum number of queens that were found in a colony was 71, and there are generally more than

N*

25, even in those overwintered nests which are little bigger than mature European colonies. The maximum number of eggs was in the colony described in Table 23, there being 26,023 compared to the maximum I recorded in Europe of 1,653. However, the average number of eggs laid per functional queen was only 366 and it appears a characteristic of these colonies that with many queens present, oviposition per queen is reduced. This situation is paralleled by the polybiine wasps of South America in which oviposition rate per queen is inversely related to the number of queens present (Richards and Richards 1951).

Another feature of overwintered colonies is the large number of excess eggs and young larvae in the cells – with an average of 2·6 eggs per cell in the nest which had 71 queens, and in another nest I found 20 eggs in one queen cell! Comparable figures for *P. germanica* in England showed that there was an average of only 13 cells per colony (range, 1-55) with more than one egg. There is undoubtedly considerable

TABLE 23

A typical perennial colony of *P. germanica* in Tasmania (collected 19 November 1971)

COMB	NUMBER OF CELLS		CELLS WITH EGGS	NUMBER OF EGGS PER CELL	TOTAL EGGS (eggs per cell)	LARVAE	PUPAE		EMPTY CELLS
	Worker	Queen					Worker Cells	Queen Cells	
I	493	—	136	1·7	231 (1–4)	323	34	0	0
II	1111	—	333	2·0	666 (1–4)	663	115	0	0
III	1673	—	424	2·4	1018 (1–4)	1064	162	0	23
IV	2118	—	324	2·2	713 (1–6)	1308	457	0	29
V	1040	573	269	2·8	753 (1–13)	925	198	191	30
VI	862	921	363	3·0	1089 (1–7)	908	170	312	30
VII	1700	562	602	2·5	1505 (1–6)	1023	378	238	21
VIII	2766	463	748	2·3	1720 (1–5)	1537	803	123	18
IX	2449	581	551	3·3	1818 (1–6)	1384	803	277	15
X	2406	1352	785	2·7	2120 (1–5)	2022	612	325	14
XI	5127	909	718	4·0	2872 (1–12)	3887	1155	265	11
XII	3001	834	607	3·0	1821 (1–7)	2248	634	304	42
XIII	967	916	647	3·7	2394 (1–6)	629	199	375	33
XIV	4188	—	607	2·8	1700 (1–5)	2780	773	0	28
XV	4018	—	2949	1·9	5603 (1–3)	795	185	0	89
				average: 2·59					
TOTAL	33919	7111	10063		26023	21496	6678	2410	383

Queens—Functional	71
—Young adults	543
Workers	4724
Males	1008
Total adults	6346
Total brood (eggs, larvae and pupae)	40647
Total adults and brood	46993 (assuming 1 egg per egg cell)
Larva : worker ratio	4·6

pressure on functional queens to oviposit, even if two thirds of the eggs which they lay are doomed. The excess eggs or young larvae they give rise to are probably fed to growing larvae, thereby circumventing wastage.

There is only one instance recorded so far of overwintering by another vespine wasp, that of a *P. vulgaris* colony in California, U.S.A., which had 22 functional queens (Duncan 1939). The more southerly range of *P. germanica* in the northern hemisphere (being the only *Paravespula* species found in North Africa for example) may help explain its success in Australasia where the climate is less extreme than much of Europe, and where arthropod prey is generally available during the winter months.

With the apparent exemption from an ovariole diapause, re-queening in the autumn is possible and this combination of circumstances has helped create a situation where reproductivity surpasses the limits normally found in regions where the wasp is indigenous.

PRODUCTIVITY OF COLONIES

In any biological system, the criteria for success may be judged by the relative efficiency of environmental exploitation, the growth of the organism or community, and the realization of reproductive potential. Wasps which produce annual colonies are of considerable interest in productivity studies for the efficiency of a colony and, ultimately, its capacity to produce new queens is a product of the successful and timely establishment of the incipient colony, the rearing of a sufficient worker population to permit an adequate flow of adults into the foraging population, and the construction of an appropriate number of queen cells. The balance between available workers and an adequate reservoir of worker brood, numbers of queen cells and brood, and the timing of queen production will determine the relative success of the colony.

Richards (1971a) has pointed out that productivity in wasps consists of two principal components – the reproductive performance of the individual colony, and the rate of successful establishment of new colonies by the young queens. This section will be concerned with productivity at the colony level, with a consideration of reproductive success at the species level in the section on population regulation.

Gross Productivity

Because there is normally only one egg-laying queen in a vespine colony, the total progeny produced during the season is equivalent to the fecundity of the queen – if one ignores brood mortality and any contribution to male production by laying workers. This situation is quite different in most of the tropical wasps, such as the Polybiini of

South America, in which several laying queens may be found in a colony (Richards and Richards 1951). Similarly, the overwintered colonies of *P. germanica* in Australasia with their numerous functional queens will have a different set of values for queen fecundity.

By counting the brood and estimating adult emergence from faecal pellet counts, gross production has been determined for the Hertfordshire nests. In *P. vulgaris*, the average production per colony was 16,739 with a maximum of 25,154, and in *P. germanica* the average was 14,938 with a maximum of 25,302. These maximum values, if converted to number of eggs laid per day throughout the three- to four-month period of maturing colony life, give a daily oviposition rate of 200 to 300 – approaching the peak daily rate estimated from the number of eggs found in colonies. These high fecundity values are necessary if the colony is to maintain an adequate flow of workers to the adult population, for longevity of adults is brief and their turnover correspondingly high.

Data for the other species of social wasps are meagre, the total production in one *V. rufa* colony I examined was 823 and in a colony of *V. crabro*, Janet (1903) estimated a production of 3,600 adults during the season. Colonies of *Dolichovespula* species probably produce less than one thousand adults during the year (see Table 22).

There is some evidence that the average size of colonies decreases from the south to the north of England, the average number of worker cells in mature *P. vulgaris* colonies being 8,000 in Hertfordshire, 7,400 in Derbyshire, and 5,900 in Yorkshire (M. E. Archer, personal communication).

Cell Utilization

Each cell may be used to rear three and occasionally more generations of adults and the utilization of worker cells may therefore be expressed as the 'percentage cell productivity':

$$\frac{(\text{number of brood present} + \text{total adults produced})}{\text{number of cells} \times 3} \times 100$$

Cell productivity in the Hertfordshire colonies of *Paravespula* always exceeded 33 per cent, indicating that all cells were used at least once, the value increasing to more than 70 per cent by the end of the season (Table 24). The percentage of cells used to rear a first, second, and third generation shows that 100 per cent are used for a first, 60 per cent for a second, and only 10 per cent for a third generation (Fig. 64). Most worker cells are constructed during June and July, the building rate decreasing thereafter, coinciding with a rise in the number of empty cells. Thus, occupation of cells prior to the decline in construction rate is almost complete but, with a reduction in oviposition rate in late

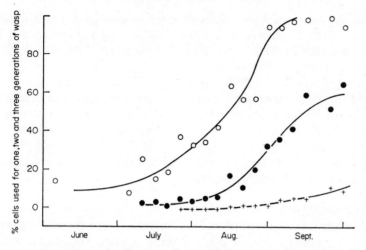

Figure 64. Percentage of cells per colony which were used to rear a first (○), second (●), and third (+) generation of adult workers in *Paravespula vulgaris* (5-day means) (from Spradbery 1971).

July, empty cells increase in number, cell construction rate is reduced, and the existing worker cells suffice for the rearing requirements of the colony. Despite the possibility of rearing three complete generations of adults per cell, the many cells relative to the progeny produced seem necessary to maintain an adequate worker population during the short period of colonial life.

Building Activity and the Number of Queen Cells

The number of queen cells that are built will depend on the number of adult workers produced and, indirectly, on the number of worker cells previously constructed. Thus, the amount of worker-cell construction necessary to produce a queen cell (number of worker cells : queen cells) should give a measure of the relative efficiency of colonies. This criterion, like all other productivity estimates, depends on the time of colony sampling and in this instance shows a progressive decrease until the end of the season (Table 24). *P. germanica* was apparently more efficient than *P. vulgaris* in producing queen cells, there being fewer worker cells constructed per queen cell, although in one *P. vulgaris* colony there was one queen cell for every two worker cells. Kemper (1961) gives a value of 1·4 worker cells per queen cell in a very large colony of *P. vulgaris* which contained 5,200 queen cells. Colonies which begin queen-cell construction too late in the season have insufficient time to construct large numbers of queen cells for rearing their queen brood during the period when optimum conditions prevail. Conversely, colonies which begin queen-cell production very early, may not have attained other requisites for queen rearing, such as an adequate worker force (or larva : worker ratio), and there is evidence that in these rare cases, the first generation of brood to be reared in the queen cells is exclusively male.

According to Janet (1895a, 1903) and Simpson (1948), the nests of hornets have proportionally more queen cells than are found in *Paravespula* colonies, there being 1·4 to 4 queen cells per worker cell (Table 22). In *V. rufa*, the number of worker cells per queen cell is about 1·3 (Arnold 1966 and personal data). It seems that the more 'primitive' species are more 'efficient' in their construction of queen cells than the *Paravespula* species.

Queen Production

The ultimate criterion of colony success is the number of young queens it produces (Table 24). I have estimated the productivity of queens in the *Paravespula* colonies by counting the adult queens present and brood in queen cells. This estimate would include males in those colonies which had built some queen cells in early August, but these colonies were few in number. Some of the queen brood counted in the census may not have emerged successfully as adults but, in view of

TABLE 24
Productivity estimates from colonies (from Spradbery 1971)

TIME	NO. OF COLONIES	'% CELL PRODUCTIVITY' (see text) Mean	Range	NO. OF WORKER CELLS/QUEEN CELL Mean	Range	NO. OF QUEENS PRODUCED/ COLONY Mean	Range
(a) Paravespula vulgaris							
First half June	1	37·9	—	—	—	—	—
First half July	3	38·1	35–41	—	—	—	—
Second half July	8	42·9	40–47	—	—	—	—
First half August	16 (5)	44·6	34–60	144	2–518	673	15–2461
Second half August	21 (14)	56·2	45–73	113	7–779	317	8–1379
First half September	4 (4)	69·9	66–74	25	10–48	286	45–767
Second half September	6 (6)	71·2	63–81	11	4–23	830	121–1831
(b) P. germanica							
Second half July	2	36·3	35–37	—	—	—	—
First half August	6 (2)	42·3	40–47	43	23–62	146	59–233
Second half August	12 (10)	50·3	43–65	51	7–244	234	17–407
First half September	7 (7)	66·9	50–83	7	4–17	1285	156–2759
Second half September	2 (2)	63·9	57–71	6	3–8	2439	2005–2873
First half October	1 (1)	79·1	—	12	—	402	—

Figures in parentheses denote colonies with queen cells present

the normally low brood mortality, coupled with the fact that all colonies, even in late September, were obviously very healthy units, error accruing from this source is probably not too great. A further criticism of these estimates of queen productivity could be due to the fact that the year during which the survey was carried out was a particularly favourable one for wasps. However, in my experience, the absolute size of mature colonies does not vary a great deal from year to year, although the number of colonies may fluctuate within wide limits. This opinion is reinforced by the studies of Archer (1972b) made on *P. vulgaris* during other years.

Because there is usually only one laying queen in a nest, the figure for total queen production per colony will be the same as the number of queens produced per queen per year. The values determined in my survey were from 8 to 2,873 the latter being considerably in excess of those which occur in the more primitive genus *Dolichovespula* which probably have less than 200 queens per queen per year (Table 22). They are also much greater than the values of 107 in *P. vulgaris* and 384 in *P. germanica* recorded by Kemper and Döhring (1961). In Archer's (1972b) analysis of *P. vulgaris* colonies, nests were classified as small or large, the small colonies producing an average of 746 queens, while the large colonies reared more than 1,120.

A rather different way of presenting queen productivity is to express it in terms of the number of queens produced per laying queen per day (Table 25). This value can then be compared with those from colonies of tropical wasps which have several queens and no defined seasonal cycles and also with other social insects. High queen productivity is associated with social insects which emit independent sexuals while those which swarm tend to have lower values. This difference

TABLE 25
Queen production in colonies of bees and wasps

SPECIES		NUMBER OF QUEENS PER QUEEN PER DAY	SOURCE
Vespidae:	Polybiini	0·06	Richards and Richards 1951
	Dolichovespula spp.	0·035–0·16	Weyrauch 1935
	D. sylvestris	0·54*	Arnold 1966
	V. rufa	0·37*	Arnold 1966
	V. crabro	1·49–2·74*	Janet 1903, Simpson 1948
	P. vulgaris	2·04–3·07	Archer 1972b
	P. vulgaris	1·68	Spradbery 1971
	P. germanica	4·22	Spradbery 1971
Apidae:	*Halictus marginatus*	0·04	Plateau—Quénu 1962
	Bombus spp. (Europe)	0·25	Cumber 1949
	Bombus sp. (S. America)	1·23	Ihering 1903
	Apis mellifera L.	0·014	Brian 1965

* Based on 50 per cent production of queens from queen cells, data from Table 22

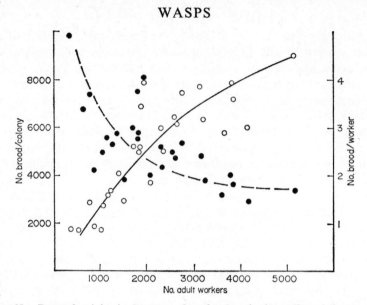

Figure 65. Reproductivity in *Paravespula vulgaris* colonies collected during 11-31 August 1961: ● = number of brood per adult worker, ○ = number of brood per colony (from Spradbery 1971).

presumably reflects the greater hazards to which a single queen is exposed compared to the degree of protection given to a queen or queens in a swarm, plus the fact that a swarm can establish a nest quickly.

Productivity in the perennial colonies of *P. germanica* in New Zealand and Tasmania is of considerable interest because of their multi-queen or polygynous organization. Few colonies have been examined critically, but it seems clear that the reproductive potential, by virtue of the numerous egg-laying queens and a winter devoted primarily to the production of sexuals, is of a very high order. For example, in the colony with 71 functional queens there were twice as many queen cells compared to a large European colony, and more than seven thousand queen brood and adults present (Table 24). This colony was taken during the spring and it is intriguing to speculate on the number of queens that would have been reared if the colony had been allowed to continue for the rest of the year.

The reproductive efficiency in various social Hymenoptera has been reviewed by Michener (1964) who based his comparisons on the production of reproductives and immature stages, and their relationship to the size of the colony as measured by the number of queens (or total females). In general, the larger the colony, the more reproductives were produced, although reproductivity per female decreased with increase in number of females. *P. vulgaris* has similar trends, the large colonies producing most queens, with a relatively greater increase in prospective reproduction (the immature stages) with increase in numbers of adult workers per colony (Fig. 65). The number of immature stages per adult worker – a measure of female efficiency in rearing brood – decreases with increase in numbers of workers. Greater reproductivity per female is attained by a single queen rather than groups of queens and, as Michener suggests, this may well be responsible for the haplometrotic societies (one queen per colony) of the more advanced social insects.

ANNUAL FLUCTUATIONS IN THE NUMBER OF WASP COLONIES

Most people are familiar with the occasional years when wasps abound in home and garden. These 'wasp years' seem to occur in irregular cycles without any marked periodicity. Gilbert White recorded one such year in Selbourne in 1783. By sifting through the entomological journals for the period 1864 to 1931, Beirne (1944) found that there were records of marked abundance or scarcity of wasps on twenty occasions during the 67-year period. In 10 years, wasps were abundant and in a further 10 they were scarce, with two to sixteen years between 'wasp years'.

Records of the density of wasp nests in a defined area are few, while year-by-year accounts are almost non-existent. One notable exception is the description of the number of nests destroyed at the Royal Horticultural Society's Gardens at Wisley, Surrey, between 1921 and 1945 (Fox Wilson 1946). The cycles of abundance and scarcity occurred every two to four years with the number of nests varying from 1 to 84 per year (Fig. 66b). The gardens at Wisley occupy a 40·5 hectare (100-acre) site so that density was 0·048 to 1·99 nests per hectare (0·002 to 0·83 nests per acre). The Wisley records are based on the nests of all species, which included *P. vulgaris*, *P. germanica*, *D. sylvestris*, *D. norwegica*, and *V. rufa*. The most common were the *Paravespula* species, *V. rufa* was fairly abundant, *D. sylvestris* nests varied from one to five per annum, and *D. norwegica* was the rarest. An interesting observation by Fox Wilson was the fact that year-by-year fluctuations in density covered all the species, there being no particular predominance of one species during a 'wasp year'.

A further feature of the Fox Wilson account is the spatial distribution of nests during a six-year period (Fig. 66a). Virtually all the nests were found alongside hedges, ditches, and paths and none was found in open situations such as fields or lawns. The clumping of nests in suitable sites is a feature of wasp-nest distribution and, as will be seen in the map, groups of up to seven nests were found within a few

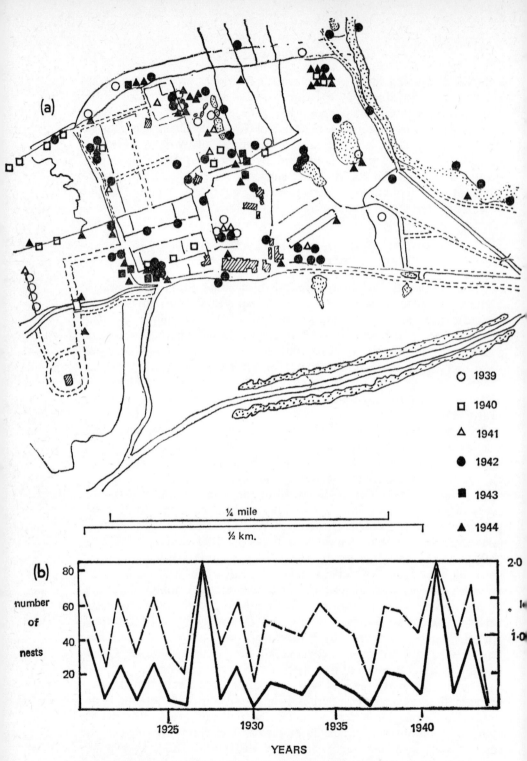

(a)

○	1939
□	1940
△	1941
●	1942
■	1943
▲	1944

¼ mile

½ km.

(b)

number
of

nests

80
60
40
20

2·0

1·0

1925   1930   1935   1940

YEARS

Figures 66 a *and* b. Wasp nests in the Royal Horticultural Society's gardens at Wisley, Surrey.
(a) Map of area to show distribution of nests;
(b) Annual numbers of nests (solid line = arithmetic; broken line = logarithmic presentation) (after Fox Wilson, 1946).

yards of one another. During my 1961 survey, I found four colonies of *P. germanica* within 9 metres (10 yards) of each other.

Years of marked wasp abundance have also been reported from continental Europe, Leclercq (1944) coining the phrase, '*années à guêpes*', to describe the phenomenom. In 1942, Belgium and the Rhine Valley were subjected to a particularly bad 'wasp year', Leclercq noting that on one small farm which usually had about 3 wasp nests per year, more than 40 were located.

Other records of the abundance of wasp nests include Nicholson's (1921) report of 400 nests which were destroyed on a 1,822 hectares (4,500-acre) estate near Epping Forest, which gives a density of 0·22 per hectare (0·09 per acre). In the north island of New Zealand in 1951, the numbers of discovered *P. germanica* colonies was 6,048 over an area of 31,565 square miles (Thomas 1960). The maximum density recorded in New Zealand was in 1945, with 0·0017 per hectare (0·0007 per acre) over a 15-square-mile (3,887 hectares) area.

When quoting figures of nest densities, it must always be borne in mind that the numbers recorded apply only to those nests which are detected and, except for the Wisley records, published accounts almost certainly underestimate the total number of nests in an area.

REGULATION OF POPULATION

General Concepts of Population Changes in Wasps

Before examining the various factors which are likely to control populations of wasps, some aspects of general population ecology will be outlined to provide a background for a more detailed discussion.

The Growth Curve. The growth of wasp colonies, in common with other insect societies and populations of non-social organisms, tends to follow an S-shaped or sigmoid curve, if the arithmetic increase in numbers is plotted against time (Bodenheimer 1937). Typically, this curve shows a slow rate of increase at first followed by a rapid increase until the population reaches a saturation point with respect to the carrying capacity of the environment. At this point, the growth rate diminishes and the population either remains numerically static or declines. The simplest mathematical expression for idealized population growth, given constant mortality, and a rate of increase proportional to the numbers present at a given time and also to the carrying capacity of the habitat, is the logistic equation:

$$\frac{dN}{dt} = rN \frac{(K-N)}{K}$$

where the differential function dN/dt is the net rate of increase at time t; r is the innate capacity for increase (equal to instantaneous birth rate minus instantaneous death rate); N is the umber present; and K the maximum number the habitat can carry. K−N is, therefore, the 'degree of unsaturation' of the habitat. If plotted on semi-log paper the transformed data will form a straight line, illustrating that the rate of growth is multiplicative.

By solving the original differential equation, it is found that:

$$N = \frac{K}{1 + e^{a-rt}}$$

(where e is the base of the Naperian or natural logarithm, and a/r is the time at the inflexion K/2).

This equation was fitted to data from *P. vulgaris* colonies collected between early June and mid-August, the period of population increase (see Fig. 59). Values of K and r were determined, using a modified Gauss-Newton method for non-linear least square estimation. The carrying capacity of the environment K was 3,084 ($\pm$1,766) and the innate capacity for increase r was 0·117 ($\pm$0·108). Despite large standard errors, due no doubt to the considerable variation in worker populations in different colonies at the same time of the year, these estimates appear to be reasonable predictions. It must be borne in mind, however, that this equation can only hope to approximate population change in a fairly crude way using field-collected data of this kind. My estimate for r compares favourably with the value of 0·1 for polybiine wasps which Brian (1965) calculated from Richards and Richards (1951) data. In the ant, *Myrmica*, Brian estimated r = 0·001 and in the bumble bee, *Bombus agrorum* (F.), r = 0·03, considerably lower values for population increase than found in wasps, although Archer (1972b) derived low values of r for *P. vulgaris* colonies.

Mortality and Survival Rates. The high rate of reproduction in *Paravespula* colonies with one or two thousand queens produced per colony would require a mortality of 99·9 per cent to maintain the same numbers of colonies from year to year. Although the annual density of colonies does fluctuate widely (Fox Wilson 1946) a year of marked abundance is generally succeeded by one of scarcity so that the attrition of queens and young colonies must be very high. The factors which may contribute to this massive mortality will be dealt with in the following section, but some indication of the survival rates of incipient colonies, brood and adults will be outlined here.

The failure of colonies to become established is a major source of mortality in wasps. The incipient colony is the most vulnerable stage in colony development for published records (e.g. Scott 1944) indicate that very few survive the hazards of nest initiation to reach a stage when a viable worker force relieves the queen of foraging duties and can protect the colony against marauders. For example, survival of the *D. sylvestris* colonies studied by Brian and Brian (1948, 1952) was extremely low, only 1 in 12 establishing an adequate worker population. The situation in *Polistes* is similar, Yoshikawa (1962) finding that of 69 colonies only 2 survived, and Yamane (1969) found only 5 of 43 colonies matured successfully.

Data for the survival of immature stages in colonies are meagre. In the incipient colony larval mortality may be high (Brian and Brian 1952), but once a colony has passed this precarious stage, mortality of brood is very low. The evidence for this is circumstantial. The brood in vespine colonies occurs in concentric rings of eggs, larvae, and pupae, with up to three or more such rings in a comb (Plate XIXc). Gaps in brood rings indicate where mortality has occurred and, with subsequent oviposition, 'out of phase' brood is found in these cells. Examination of the combs in Plate XIX reveals a total of 72 'gaps' in the 2,042-cell nest, an estimated brood mortality of 3·5 per cent. In more mature nests, the pattern of brood rings is disrupted because oviposition in the older combs is reduced (see Fig. 60). Comparable figures for brood mortality in bumble bees is 53 per cent and in the ant, *Myrmica*, it is 67 per cent (Brian 1965). Nevertheless, considerably more data on brood mortality are required before more definite conclusions on survival of eggs, larvae, and pupae can be made.

It has been emphasized before that the turnover of adult wasps is very high, with an average life span during the season of 12 to 22 days (Table 19). When the proportion of surviving workers per colony is plotted against time, the resulting survival curve (Fig. 67) appears

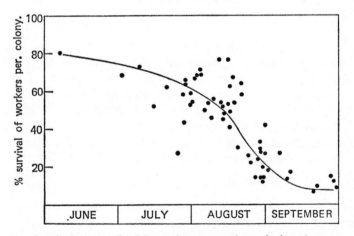

Figure 67. Survival curve of adult workers per colony during the course of the year, *Paravespula vulgaris* data (after Spradbery 1963).

intermediate between Slobodkin's (1961) survival curve I, which is typical of honeybees in which mortality is concentrated in the older workers, and curve II which describes the situation when animals die off at a constant rate irrespective of their age structure or population size. However, adult survival varies during the season with heaviest mortality occurring before and after queen rearing when foraging rates are high, while the lowest mortality takes place during the early stages of queen rearing. The brevity of adult life in *Paravespula* necessitates massive worker-brood production so that the level of the worker population can be increased or even maintained.

Factors Controlling Wasp Populations

The large fluctuation in wasp density from year to year are the consequence of various factors acting on the population which help to promote or suppress their numbers. Although the annual cycle of development of the individual wasp colony is subjected to pressures of various kinds, the seasonal pattern of growth at the colonial level probably does not alter appreciably, from year to year. The regulation of wasp populations is essentially the cause and effect relationship which governs year to year fluctuations in the number of successful colonies, with the unit of selection being the colony or queen.

From personal experience with *Paravespula* species, it is clear that once a colony is established with an adequate number of workers, its success is virtually guaranteed, so that the major causes of population regulation must be acting during the period between emission of queens from autumnal colonies, and the juvenile colony stage. The big exception is the influence of man, for it appears that only he can destroy mature vespine wasp colonies effectively, although the predatory activities of the badger may contribute to losses of some mature nests.

The annual fluctuations are of such magnitude that the regulatory processes may be unrelated to density (density independent), although with their high rates of natality (=queen production), Southwood (1967) suggests that a very sensitive density-dependent mechanism may be operating which promotes these oscillations in numbers of colonies (Fig. 66b). In this survey of the factors which may affect wasp populations, emphasis will be placed on those processes which regulate queen or colony numbers rather than the relative size of the individual colony (Fig. 68).

Nest Sites. Some nest sites are patently unsuitable for successful colony growth, particularly where physical restrictions impose a limit to nest expansion, or subterranean nests are built below the normal water-table, and in situations such as hayricks which would be disposed

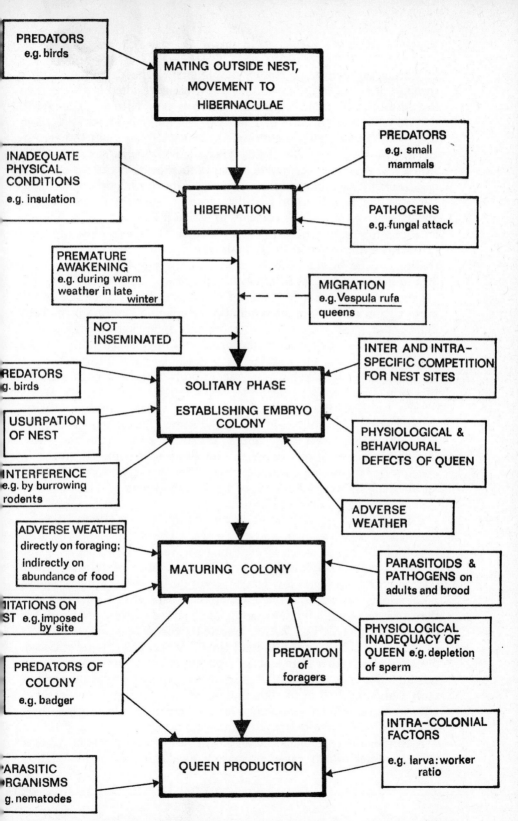

Figure 68. Flow chart of factors which influence the abundance of wasps (original).

of during the course of colony development. The depletion of sites through progressive urbanization has probably resulted in the marked decrease in the hornet, *V. crabro*, which is now virtually confined to the New Forest and parts of East Anglia, although Lloyd (1942) and Lloyd and Benson (1945) considered the hornet to be not too rare in Hertfordshire during the 1940s. Those subterranean nesting species which rely primarily on rodent burrows to provide a site for embryo-nest building, are likely to be influenced by the incidence of small, burrowing mammals, although a list of nest sites shows that *P. vulgaris* and *P. germanica* have the capacity to utilize a wide variety of different locations for nesting purposes (see Chapter 5). Where nests are built in burrows, the original inhabitants could destroy colonies by either feeding on the brood of an embryo nest, or simply dislodging nests during their movements through the tunnels.

Limitations on the availability of nest sites is likely to be one of the most significant factors in population regulation, especially if large numbers of queens are competing for sites following a year of wasp abundance. It is well known that queens will fight each other for the possession of a nest site, and bodies of dead queens in entrance tunnels bear witness to such behaviour. Where both competing queens perish this would lead to extreme over-compensation. Matsuura (1970) has observed queens of *V. crabro flavofasciata* Cameron attempt invasion of embryo and juvenile colonies of the same species, but on the five occasions noted, the foreign queen was either killed or driven away. During the observations of Brian and Brian (1952) on *D. sylvestris*, one queen repelled an invading one, although she and the queen of another colony were later usurped by foreign queens.

Climatic Factors. Beirne (1944) and Fox Wilson (1946) have attempted to relate annual changes in wasp density to meteorological conditions. Despite some correlation between low rainfall during the period of colony establishment and the abundance of colonies, there was no correlation with low temperatures during these months. Beirne pointed out however that there were many years when higher or lower than average rainfall did not result in any marked scarcity or abundance of wasps. Similarly, Fox Wilson detected a correlation of low numbers of wasps with high spring rainfall (in 16 of the 24 years of scarcity), although in a further four years of high rainfall, the number of colonies was high. Heavy spring rainfall in some years caused a rise in the water-table which resulted in the flooding out of some subterranean embryo nests and in one year, following a fall of 5 cm of rain in 13 days, three *P. vulgaris* nests were destroyed as a direct result of flooding.

A further meteorological factor might be periods of warm weather in late winter which cause premature awakening from hibernation

XVIII (top). *Paravespula germanica* worker adding a load of wet woodpulp to the envelope, note the glistening strip prepared by the mandibles; (bottom) nest structure produced by a group of *P. vulgaris* workers without a queen, the 16 cells each have one egg in them (viewed from below).

XIX. Nests, cells, and combs of *Paravespula germanica.*

Juvenile nest of *P. germanica.*

Comparison of queen and worker cells of *P. germanica.*

Four combs from a young *P. germanica* colony to show the rings of brood and gaps where mortality of an egg or larva has occurred.

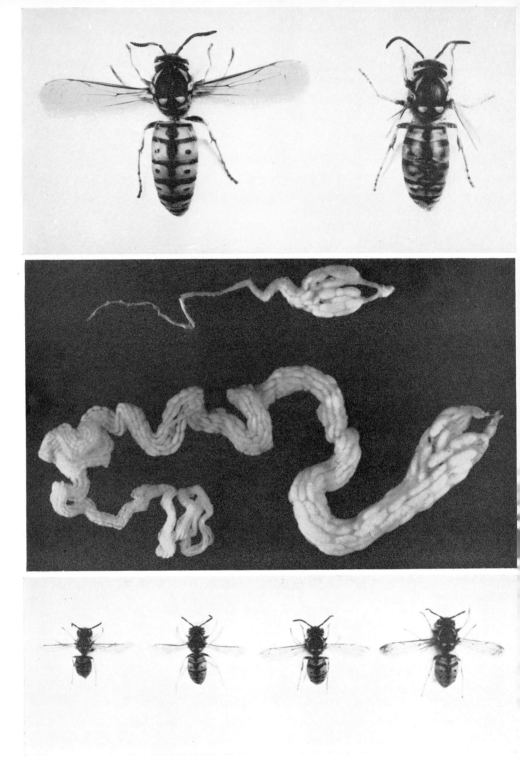

XX (top). Comparison of a young (left) and old foundress queen (right) of *Paravespula germanica*, note the frayed wings and discoloration of the gaster in the old queen; (middle) ovaries of spring queen (above) and mature foundress queen (below) of *P. germanica*; (bottom) range in size of workers from a *P. germanica* colony.

which, if followed by severe frosts, could prove fatal to queen wasps. Beirne's data did not, however, show any correlation between the number of queen wasps flying in the spring and the abundance of colonies subsequently established. Both Latter (1895, 1898) and Walker (1898) concluded that climate does not altogether influence wasp abundance, and that numbers of spring queens were not correlated with density of colonies later in the year. Döhring (1960), in her analysis of wasp populations in Berlin during a fifteen-year period, considered that cold, wet winters had no apparent effect on abundance but sudden cold periods during April and May severely curtailed the numbers of colonies, while a prolongation of warm weather in the autumn tends to encourage 'wasp years'.

It is apparent that weather conditions may influence mortality of queens and hinder the establishment of colonies but the conflicting meteorological evidence outlined above suggests that weather does not play a dominant role in population control.

Parasites, Predators and Pathogens. A wide range of natural enemies of social wasps has been recorded, from parasitoid Hymenoptera and parasitic nematodes, to a range of vertebrate and invertebrate predators (see Chapter 11 for details). The incidence of bacterial and virus diseases, however, has never been confirmed, although Stone (1865) found colonies in which brood had apparently died from a bacterial infection. Except in weakened colonies, biotic agents have little effect on wasp density, levels of parasitism being generally low and the number of affected colonies small. To regulate wasp populations on an annual basis, colonies must be severely weakened or destroyed before queen production gets under way, or predation and parasitism must be directed at the queen brood or adults. Although parasitism of *Polistes* may reach high levels, and whole West Indian island populations have been wiped out (Ballou 1934), heavy parasitism of *Vespula* and *Vespa* is rare. Nevertheless, the moth, *Aphomia sociella* (L.), destroyed a *D. saxonica* colony in Germany (Reichert 1914), and the ichneumonid, *Sphecophaga*, occasionally parasitizes large numbers of wasp larvae (Reichert 1914, Gauss 1968), but these are apparently exceptions to the general rule. Nematode infection of queens may be a significant factor in some circumstances (Blackith and Stevenson 1958).

Other factors. Failure to hibernate successfully may cause heavy losses of potential founding queens either through predation by birds or mammals, death due to growth of fungus in the hibernaculum (especially when hibernating in the crevices of dead or rotten wood, or under loose bark), and extremes of temperature and humidity if the hibernation site is inadequately insulated.

Queens which do not succeed in mating may overwinter successfully but they do not attempt to establish colonies and die during the spring (Matsuura 1969).

As emphasized by Brian (1965), most mortality in social wasps occurs before nests are built or during the period of colony initiation, mortality decreasing markedly as the colony becomes established and its defences stronger. The survival rate would be a negative exponential curve.

The cause of failure at this stage is not known. Loss of queens from accident or predation may be a factor, although Brian and Brian (1952) noticed that most colonies which failed had queens that were weak fliers or did not appear attentive to larval demands. The underlying cause of such behaviour could be physiological or even genetic, and might follow a year of wasp abundance. There is a need for more knowledge on the subject of genetic variability and what attributes make for 'successful' queens.

Competition for available food, particularly as wasps are secondary consumers (in the larval stage at least), might play a part in limiting the population size of individual colonies and, hence, the production of queens. However, the varied sources of food available to wasps (see Chapter 6) would tend to mitigate against food limitation being an important regulatory factor. Scarcity of food during nest founding, however, would necessitate more prolonged foraging and therefore increased exposure to the hazards which beset foraging queens.

When the density of spring queens is high there may be emigration from a region of high density to other areas (Rudebeck 1965) although normally, the queens rarely disperse more than half a mile or so (Thomas 1960).

There is obviously a great deal more information needed, not only on numbers of wasps of different castes at different times, but also on their behaviour, before a better understanding of population regulation is acquired. Interpretation of population change demands a greater understanding of wasp biology and this appreciation will undoubtedly determine the manner and timing of sampling. Nevertheless, sufficient data is available for reasoned speculation and a start has already been made in charting the changes in wasp populations by the use of mathematical models.

POPULATION MODELS

By using reasonable values for various parameters which describe wasp populations, it is possible to construct mathematical models illustrating and predicting the growth of colonies. Richards and Richards (1951) were the first to attempt a mathematical description of colony growth, using data from South American Polybiini. These authors used a series of algebraic equations employing known or assumed values for the numbers of queens and workers in the founding swarm, duration of adult and immature stages, and the cell-building rate (number of cells constructed per worker per day). Oviposition rate was assumed to be limited only by availability of cells. The results of this mathematical exercise revealed that, with the passage of time, population growth followed the logistic curve with a slow initial rate followed by a rapid increase in adults. One feature of the model was the change in larva : worker ratio. Due to the mortality of founding workers and increase in number of larvae, the ratio increased during the first 30 days but, with recruitment of the new workers, the value fell suddenly to near unity by day 45. The timing of male and queen production and the efficiency of queen production (i.e. number of new queens per founding queen per day) were also evaluated with the model and the derived values were close to those that could be verified by sampling colonies.

With the time limit imposed on temperate-zone wasps by the climate, the initiation of queen production (or, in Vespinae, queen-cell construction) is crucial if sufficient queens are to be reared under optimum colonial and climatic condition. Lövgren (1958) has constructed a mathematical model which attempts to predict the optimum time for starting queen rearing. Various biological assumptions were made, the most important being the choice of constant values for the proportions

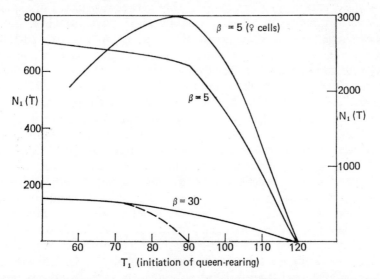

Figure 69. Population model : estimation of the time (T_1) when queen production should be initiated using different values for the constant β (ratio of worker eggs : queen eggs) (after Lövgren 1958). See text for details.

of worker and queen eggs laid per unit time, worker and queen cells built per unit time, and empty worker cells. Constants for cell-building rates and for the number of workers required to tend brood were also employed. Although Lövgren concedes that these assumptions may not be biologically very accurate (especially the first assumption), their validity when expressed as average values over the season seems reasonable for the purposes of model making. After working through a series of more than one hundred equations, Lövgren made a computer analysis of $N_1(T)$ as a function of T_1, where N_1=number of queens produced, T=time when colony breaks up (equivalent to swarming in the tropics) and T_1=time when the first queen-producing eggs are laid. T_0 was the time the first queen-reared workers emerged. By choosing different values for β (proportion of worker-producing : queen-producing eggs), N_1 (T) was computed as a function of T_1 (Fig. 69). With values for β ranging from 0·2 to 10, T_1 was optimal at 90 days. Where β=5 and no special queen cells are built, queen rearing can begin any time before 90 days without loss to the economy of the colony. Where queen cells are built and β=5, they must be initiated by day 86, four earlier. It was found that with low values of β, the timing of queen rearing had to be precisely set so that sufficient workers remained to rear the queen brood.

Data from my *P. vulgaris* census show that β=10·3 (in colonies just starting queen rearing) and T_1=approximately 75-85 days, although T_1 probably varies within a species according to local climatic conditions and it certainly differs considerably between species. For example, in *Dolichovespula* spp. T_1 is probably 45-55 days (see Fig. 26). In *Dolichovespula*, T is only about 90 days, compared to 120-150 in *Paravespula* and early queen rearing would require a high value for β. Lövgren's curve, using β=30 is given in Fig. 69 and I have also indicated (broken line) the observed duration of season for *Dolichovespula* species. This genus also has much lower queen productivity (0·4 queen/queen/day) compared to *Paravespula* (2·8) although it appears that *Dolichovespula* and also *V. rufa* colonies generate more queens per worker than the larger *Paravespula* colonies (see Table 22).

Lövgren then calculated that, when T_1=90 and β=5, a colony would produce 15,768 cells and 671 queens, with 3,474 workers present during queen rearing, a worker : cell ratio of 0·22, and total adult worker production of 15,213. My observed values from *Paravespula* colonies were 8,914 (3,794-15,383) cells; 1,053 (45-2,873) queens from September colonies; 2,026 (481-5,268) workers present; worker : cell ratio of 0·227; and total worker production of 15,835. Despite some major differences between Lövgren's chosen values and my results (notably adult worker longevity), his mathematically derived wasp population closely follows many of the observed parameters.

Brian (1965) has developed a predictive-type model, based on his studies of ant populations. The principal interest of Brian's model is the widely differing growth curves which are produced by varying only slightly the value of the variable which describes the rate and timing of queen emission. Three major growth curves were obtained. The first was an 'explosive' type characterized by a short season, a rapid growth rate, and a sharp decline following queen emission. The second was more steady with oscillations coinciding with queen emission and the third showed a gradual rise in population until a steady state was attained. Wasps have an explosive growth rate, culminating in the production and emission of queens which appear to act as a density-dependent negative feedback phenomenom, causing the rapid decline of the colony. A more oscillating-type of growth curve would describe the overwintering colonies of *P. germanica* in Australasia.

Population models which stimulate colony growth in wasps are likely to be a productive exercise in the future. Increased knowledge of the parameters which describe population growth will permit more information of greater accuracy to be built into the model so that, by adjusting certain variables, a greater understanding of the mechanics of population change are likely to be appreciated.

CHAPTER 8

SOCIAL ORGANIZATION

By definition, social organization in an insect community is an association of the parental female (queen) and her offspring (workers), and their co-operation in the production and rearing of brood. The interactions between the queen and her offspring, between adults and larvae, and among the workers determine the levels of sociality, the degree of integration and, ultimately, the relative efficiency of the group as a reproductive unit. In this chapter, emphasis will be placed on these three interactions, although of course, virtually every activity performed by a wasp, be it building, foraging, guarding the nest, or tending the larvae can be considered to influence the social organization of the colony.

In this chapter I will outline the major studies which have illuminated aspects of social organization in wasps, but I wish to emphasize that the behaviour of more primitive subfamilies or even closely related genera are unlikely to be universal in all wasp societies. Although our knowledge of the social life in British wasp colonies is increasing, it is still very fragmentary and for a better understanding of the processes whereby social life is established and maintained, heavy reliance must be placed on the studies of wasps in other parts of the world. The first detailed investigation of social organization in wasps was made in northern Italy by Leo Pardi (1941-51) working on *Polistes* species, although Heldmann (1936) pioneered such studies. It was Pardi who demonstrated that a dominance hierarchy prevails among adult wasps which is analagous to the 'pecking order' described originally in domestic fowl but now known to regulate the social life of many animals including the higher apes and even man. Similar dominance relationships have been recorded in *Paravespula* species by Hubert Montagner in France who studies the complexities of reciprocal feeding among the adult wasps.

The studies of C. G. Butler and his associates on 'queen substance' in the honeybee provided solutions to many of the mysteries of colonial life in bees and prompted a search for similar pheromones in the social wasps. In Israel, Jacob Ishay and his colleagues made a detailed study of the Oriental Hornet, *V. orientalis*, discovering and synthesizing a pheromone analogous to honeybee 'queen substance'.

There is little doubt that exchanges of food and chemical stimuli (pheromones) among the members of a society are of major importance in maintaining the colony as a group, with examples found in most insect societies, from ants and termites, in which adults lick off the exudates secreted through the skin of larvae, to wasps which feed their larvae and receive in return salivary secretions. It is apparent that the evolution of insect societies has resulted in a variety of solutions to the problem of social integration.

SOCIAL HIERARCHIES

In many species of social wasp, notably the members of Polistinae, caste differences are weakly defined and the major distinctions between egg-laying females (queens) and non-laying females (auxiliaries or workers) are based on the psycho-physiological interactions between the adults. The investigations of Pardi (1940-51) and Pardi and Cavalcanti (1951), showed that the discrimination of a principal egg-layer (an α individual) was achieved by its dominance behaviour towards the other females. By reason of size, posture, and generally more aggressive behaviour (see Table 26) one female gains a dominant position in the small society.

When a colony is founded by two or more females, as frequently occurs in *Polistes* species from Mediterranean or tropical climates, only one of them becomes the queen and the others disperse or remain as sterile females behaving like workers. The co-operative founding of a nest has been called 'pleometrosis' by Bequaert (1930) and 'social colony foundation' by West (1967).

Pardi (1948) considered that one of the most important factors influencing dominance behaviour was the relative size and activity of the ovaries, finding that there was a correlation between the development of the ovaries and the position in the linear hierarchy or pecking order. Females with larger ovaries were more dominant and, because of resorption and development of oocytes (Strambi 1963), wasps with more advanced oocytes (ascending phase) dominated those undergoing oocyte resorption (descending phase).

Once dominance has been established by a female, its behaviour patterns alter. There is much reduced foraging activity, a monopoly on oviposition and a greater share of the regurgitated food from the subordinate females. Having become 'top wasp' various processes enable

TABLE 26

Behavioural and anatomical differences between dominant and subordinate *Polistes* wasps
(from Richards 1971, based on several authors)

DOMINANT	SUBORDINATE
1. larger size	frequently smaller size
2. posture during exchanges: raised up on legs	posture depressed
3. palpates subordinate with antennae	antennae depressed
4. often aggressive by running at, biting, or threatening to sting the subordinate	submissive or flying from nest
5. abdomen pressed against comb and wagged to produce an audible vibration	no wagging
6. position in nest: on centre of comb	back of comb or nearby objects
7. receives wood-pulp, and food	gives pulp and food
8. if foraging, usually collects only wood pulp	collects pulp and food
9. ovaries more developed	ovaries less developed, if developed, later regress
10. eats eggs of other wasps but not her own (differential oophagy)	eats fewer eggs

it to maintain its dominant rank – advantages in trophallactic exchange (discussed in more detail in the next section), more developed ovaries, and probably a more generally active neuro-secretory system. Pardi found that the ovaries of dominant females were invariably well developed and contained mature eggs compared to the underdeveloped or regressing ovaries of the subordinates. However, Deleurance (1948) severed the ovaries of *Polistes* females and, on being returned to the nest, the original hierarchical position of the ovariectomized females was maintained. Gervet (1956) extended the work of Deleurance and determined that a decrease in oviposition, either naturally or by putting the queen at low temperatures at night, created an increase in empty cells with a corresponding renewal or increase in the ovariole activity of auxiliary females. The position of the queen was maintained, principally because she ate the eggs of any auxiliary attempting to usurp her position. Gervet (1964b) called this behaviour 'differential oophagy.' These results are in keeping with work on other insects in which extirpation of ovaries or testis cause little change in behaviour or even sexual development, suggesting that insects do not produce sex or gonadal hormones. Further details of the factors which influence fecundity in *Polistes* are given by Gervet (1957a and b, 1962, 1964a).

When *Polistes* colonies are founded by a single female (haplometrosis), the founding queen establishes her dominant position over the workers as they emerge. As the nests become populated with the emergence of more workers, there is a constant interchange of dominance behaviour. The position of individuals in the hierarchy continually alters, factors such as those listed in Table 26 determining the pecking order. Dominance behaviour is directed principally towards the female immediately below it in the social order and rarely towards females several positions below it, thereby maintaining position with the minimum of aggressive action. Because of the brevity of adult life in wasp colonies, the position of workers in the hierarchies is constantly changing, probably on a day-to-day basis.

Although dominance hierarchies are better understood in *Polistes*, similar behaviour among workers in *Paravespula* colonies has been described (Montagner 1966d). By careful observation of marked wasps and the use of ciné film, Montagner was able to distinguish individual workers and note the interactions among them. Although details of their behaviour will be dealt with later in this chapter, the major outcome of these studies revealed that loosely defined dominance hierarchies exist in *Paravespula* even when several thousand workers are present in a colony. Aggressive dominance behaviour tends to be fairly benign, however, compared to the clashes between founding *Polistes* queens.

TROPHALLAXIS

In a society, it is the interaction between the constituent members which promotes and maintains sociality and enables the community to operate efficiently. In a wasp colony, the relationships between adults and larvae and among the workers provide the foundations for social life, the interactions being on an essentially trophic level with a constant exchange of food among the individuals. Anyone who observes a brood-filled wasp comb and attendant adults will be impressed with the high level of contact between adults and larvae – workers visiting the cells and eliciting drops of fluid from the larvae, and the mouth to mouth contact between adults which adopt characteristic postures as food passes between them (Plate XXI).

It was du Buysson (1903) and Janet (1903) who first described the larval secretions of *Polistes* and *Vespula*, both remarking on the sweetness of the secretion, believing it to be highly attractive to the adults. Based on his observations on *Belonogaster* wasps in Africa, Roubaud (1911) suggested that the sociality of wasps was a direct result of these larva/adult food exchanges so that adult wasps were encouraged to breed and tend larvae in order to obtain their secretions. The famed American entomologist, William Mortimer Wheeler (1918) proposed the name 'trophallaxis' to describe this reciprocal food exchange in wasps (and ants), and later developed his concept of the insect society being a 'superorganism', the exchange of food involving the transmission of social stimuli in much the same way as the circulatory system of higher animals translocates food and hormones throughout the body.

There followed two decades of armchair research on the subject of trophallaxis with the concept being widened to include virtually all types of gustatory, tactile, and other sensations between individuals of a group; one eminent entomologist going so far as to describe a scientific Congress as a form of 'intellectual trophallaxis'. In his review of organization and communication in social insects, Michener (1953) proposed restricting the application of the word trophallaxis to those cases where there is an exchange of food, secretions, or other materials in both directions.

Because the exchanges between adults and larvae and among the adults of a colony are different, these two major forms of food exchange will be dealt with separately.

Larva – Adult Trophallaxis

A wasp larva secretes a drop of liquid, the salivary or trophallactic secretion, when approached by an adult wasp or otherwise stimulated. For example, the secretion may be elicited by touching the head of a larvae with a straw. The liquid, which is colourless and slightly viscous, is secreted by the large labial gland (Fig. 32) and passes out through a duct to appear on the labrum as a droplet of variable size. The quantity of secretion is roughly proportional to the size or instar of larva (Table 27) and is related to the amount of food previously eaten. Although du Buysson (1903) and Janet (1903) wrote that they were able to detect sweetness in the secretion, Brian and Brian (1952) did not support these findings. The analyses of Ishay and Ikan (1968b) have shown that the labial secretion of *V. orientalis* larvae contains 5·5 per cent carbohydrates (as glucose, fructose, sucrose, maltose, trehalose, 4G$\propto$-glylosyl-sucrose and oligosaccharides), 0·21 per cent total nitrogen, and 0·13 per cent nitrogen of free amino acids.

Brian and Brian (1952) were the first to carry out experimental work on trophallaxis in wasps during their studies on *D. sylvestris*. They collected the saliva of larvae and offered it to adults but found that it was not intrinsically attractive to them, particularly when offered

TABLE 27

Saliva obtained from wasp larvae (*Vespa orientalis*) after 12 hours isolation from adults
(after Ishay and Ikan 1968a) (data based on 60 larvae in each instar)

LARVAL INSTAR	MEAN WEIGHTS OF LARVA (mg)	MEAN VOLUME OF SALIVA (ml)	MEAN VOLUME OF SALIVA PER LARVA (ml/mg)
I	4·4	0·0004	$9·1 \times 10^{-5}$
II	23·4	0·0018	$5·9 \times 10^{-5}$
III	178·0	0·0025	$1·4 \times 10^{-5}$
IV	292·6	0·0051	$1·7 \times 10^{-5}$
V	919·3	0·0024	$2·6 \times 10^{-6}$

with a choice of dilute sucrose in preference tests. The Brians noted that larval secretion resembled water excretion in other insects and was closely related to fluid intake, and if the secretion was not removed, the larvae became conspicuously distended only releasing the fluid when offered food or stimulated to do so by the tending adult.

They suggested that excess water, fed in the form of dilute carbohydrates and/or animal juices was voided by the larva via its labial gland, the secretion being controlled by the tending adult to prevent wetting of the paper fabric of the nest. Larvae are certainly fed on quantities of fluid and, unlike the larvae of solitary wasps which are mass-provisioned with insect prey without additional fluid in the diet, some means of osmotic control is probably necessary. Because the hindgut is occluded and the malphigian tubulus apparently functionless, excretion is not possible in the usual way, and the salivary secretion would appear an eminently suitable means for disposing of excess water and perhaps other excretory products (ammonia was detected in the saliva but at low concentrations, Brian and Brian (1952)).

The rate of production of labial exudate and its relation to fluid intake was studied by Morimoto (1960c) by feeding larvae of *Polistes* with a radioactive-labelled solution and determining the radioactivity of the saliva subsequently produced. None was detected after 30 minutes but after 3 hours there was distinct radioactivity in the saliva, the rate increasing between 18 and 24 hours after feeding. In another experiment, the larvae were offered to adult workers for trophallactic exchange and after 24 hours, the adults had become strongly radioactive, confirming the passage of labial exudate from larva to adult.

Ikan and Ishay (1966) concluded that the larval secretion of *V. orientalis* constitutes a powerful attraction for adults, especially during periods when foraging is prevented or reduced, and they drew attention to the similarities in the sugar content of wasp saliva and aphid honeydew, the latter being a much sought-after form of carbohydrate. Ishay and Ikan (1968) made several experiments to determine the role of larval saliva in the social organization of the hornet. When empty combs were offered to a laying queen with workers, the combs were abandoned after 6 to 11 days, despite oviposition by the queen in the empty cells. The queen invariably died within a few days and in some experiments workers left the larva-less combs and joined nearby colonies which had larvae present. If combs with larvae and pupae were separated from the adults by transparent nylon sheets to prevent trophallaxis, the queens died and the workers abandoned the combs within 4 days, but if mosquito nets were used to separate comb from adults, the newly-emerging workers tranferred larval saliva through the holes in the netting. These colonies survived and within 2 days new cells were built with subsequent oviposition by the queen. Thus it

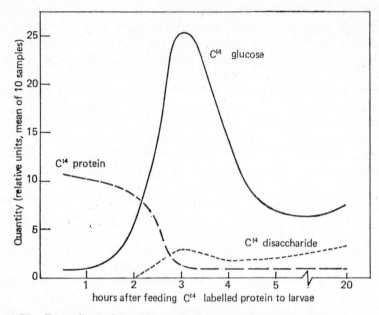

Figure 70. Degrading of isotope-labelled protein by larvae of *Vespa orientalis* (drawn from data after Ishay and Ikan 1968b).

appears that the presence of larvae and the intake of larval secretion is of paramount importance in maintaining sociality among workers and for the survival of the queen.

When Ishay and Ikan (1968a, 1968b) fed larvae on C^{14} labelled proteins, they detected radioactivity in the glucose and disaccharide from the saliva 3 hours after feeding (Fig.70) demonstrating that some of the protein food ingested by larvae is degraded and reformed as sugars which are subsequently 'returned' to adults via the saliva. During periods of intense trophallactic activity, the carbohydrate concentration of the larval haemolymph was considerably reduced (by up to 26 per cent) indicating a drain on the carbohydrate reserves of the larva. When adults were similarly fed, no radioactive sugars were later detected, and incubation of adult, pupal, and larval homogenates (prepared by macerating the whole insects) with C^{14} protein demonstrated that only larval homogenates caused a degradation of the protein and production of glucose. Ikan, Bergmann and others (1968), Sonneborn and others (1969), and Hagenmaier (1971) have identified several proteolytic enzymes from the midgut of *V. orientalis* larvae, but no protease activity was demonstrated in adult saliva. It would appear therefore that only the larvae have a capacity to degrade proteins and reconstruct sugars from them, this ability being lost at the time of pupation.

However, I have determined the presence of proteolytic enzymes in the midguts of both larvae and adults in *P. germanica* using the gelatin strip technique and the colorimetric method of Charney and Tomarelli (1948). Proteolytic activity in the saliva of *P. germanica* larvae was also demonstrated. The apparent differences in the distribution of enzymes between *V. orientalis* and *P. germanica* adults is possibly a reflection of their taxonomic position, although Ishay (personal communication) tells me that adult *V. orientalis* workers will fabricate proteases in the absence of the queen. It appears that the biochemical story of enzyme systems in wasps and hornets is an involved one, particularly if some enzyme activity is controlled by the queen. This research field should prove an intriguing and fruitful one for future investigations.

Analyses of *V. orientalis* larval saliva by Ishay and Ikan (1968a) showed that there were 5·5 per cent sugars and 1·3 per cent 'proteins' (total nitrogen × 6·25) present, while in *P. vulgaris, P. germanica* and *V. crabro* saliva, Maschwitz (1965) determined that 8·9 per cent was sugar and 1·8 per cent was 'protein'. Using a specific colorimetric technique (ninhydrin assay) with *P. germanica* material I determined that there is 1·4 per cent free amino acids in larval saliva (unpublished data).

Although Brian and Brian (1952) detected little glucose in the larval saliva of *D. sylvestris* and considered the quantities too small to be attractive to adults, there is little doubt that the amounts of carbohydrate and protein are of great nutritional value to adult wasps. Ishay and Ikan (1968a) point out that human milk contains only 7·2 per cent sugar and 1·5 per cent protein, proportions very similar to those found in wasp saliva.

The importance of sugars for utilization by the foraging adults hardly requires mention, their energy expenditure requiring a relatively large carbohydrate component in the diet.

Sugars in the larval saliva may help increase its attractiveness to adults, or be a means of disposing excess protein by converting it to sugars, or perhaps an unavoidable 'leak' in the metabolic system. What is quite certain, however, is the benefit gained by the adults which supplement their diet with these salivary secretions. Moreover, during periods of inanition the adults may exploit the larvae for their saliva, the newly emerged adults feed almost exclusively on saliva, and, as will be seen later, males derive much of their alimentary needs from this source. More importantly, the queen drinks large quantities of saliva (which contains amino acids) enabling her to maintain the high level of nitrogen metabolism necessary for egg production. For example, Ishay and Ikan (1968a) estimated that a *V. orientalis* queen produces about 4,000 eggs weighing about 8,000 mg during the course of the season. This is four to eleven times the total weight of the queen when she leaves hibernation, while the weight of the ovaries increases from 9–10 mg in the spring to 153 mg by September, a fifteen-fold increase in weight.

To summarize, wasp colonies do not exist satisfactorily without the secretions of the larvae, for workers abandon broodless comb and queens fail to survive. Larvae are fed on proteins (and some carbohydrate) and they produce a saliva which is relatively rich in carbohydrates and various elements of protein metabolism including protein-degrading enzymes. The saliva is an important and probably essential component of the adult diet, while the queen derives much of the protein for ovogenesis from larval secretions. Wasps may even use larvae as food reservoirs when foraging outside the nest is prevented or curtailed. Salivary secretions may also be an oral means of osmotic control for the larvae. In vespine wasps the trophallactic relationship can be regarded as a symbiosis between adults and larvae.

Trophallaxis among Adults

Food exchange among the wasps in a colony is widespread, from the distribution of food to larvae and adults by returning foragers, to the continuous round of trophallactic contacts among the remainder. One of the features of adult trophallaxis is the circulation of larval saliva which possibly contributes to the colony as a whole acquiring a characteristic odour. In his detailed studies on *Paravespula* species, Montagner (1963, 1964b, c, 1966d) has described the elements of food exchange among adult wasps and demonstrated the importance of trophallactic exchange in the social organization of the colony.

The passage of food from the crop of one adult to another is stimulated by the behaviour of the soliciting wasp which lowers its body slightly in a recumbent posture and, with the head lowered and turned to one side, strokes the mouthparts of the prospective donor with its antennae (Plate XXIb). With one antennae stroking the glossa between the donor's mandibles to elicit the regurgitation of fluid, the other antenna is used to maintain contact by stimulating the maxillary and labial palps. The palps of the soliciting wasp are also used to stimulate the donor. During the period of regurgitation, the donor remains relatively passive under the influence of the stimuli applied by the solicitor's antennae. When the exchange has come to an end, the donor signals the completion of contact by pushing its antennae against the mandibles of the other wasp and thereby stopping the flow of stimuli to its mouthparts. Frequently, a third worker joins in a trophallactic exchange, and at other times adult males attempt to 'steal' the regurgitated fluid as it passes between two workers.

The behaviour pattern which enables a wasp to elicit food successfully is not innate but must be learnt by the newly emerged adult during a one- or two-day period of trial contacts with other workers.

One of the important results of Montagner's studies was the discovery of a social hierarchy among the adult workers which is emphasized during trophallactic contacts. For example, a worker which is more dominant in the hierarchy behaves in a characteristic manner when demanding food which is different from the behaviour described above. On approaching a subordinate wasp, the dominant individual does not lower its body or turn the head to one side but faces forwards, using its antennae to stimulate the palps on either side of the mandibles of the donor or forcing the mandibles apart and thereby gaining access to the glossa. The dominant may even hold down a subordinate with its legs or climb on to its body and nibble at the wings and other parts of the body until its demands are met. A feature of the trophallactic behaviour of the dominant is its capacity to elicit food more easily and maintain the contact for a longer time, thus deriving a greater trophic advantage at the expense of the subordinates. As mentioned earlier, the brevity of adult life in wasp colonies probably causes daily changes of position in the hierarchies.

The foundress queen also obtains food from workers during trophallactic exchanges and her behaviour towards the workers is characteristic of a dominant individual, although at the end of the season when the young queens are maturing, her dominance declines and she must resort to soliciting rather than demanding. The young queens are dominant individuals and readily obtain food from workers. The males, however, are unable to establish successful trophallaxis with workers because their antennae, which are relatively long, cannot be articulated sufficiently to stimulate the mouthparts of workers. Before the appearance of young queens though, the workers will feed the males quite readily but thereafter they must obtain food from larval secretions or by robbing the fluid passing between workers engaged in trophallaxis.

Trophallactic exchanges probably contribute to the acquisition of a specific colony odour whereby colony members may recognize each other. Montagner and Courtois (1963) fed radioactive gold to adult workers which were separated by gauze screens from workers or larvae taken from their own colony and also from another colony. Radioactivity determinations showed that more food was regurgitated to workers and larvae from their own colony. If the perforations in the gauze were increased in size so that trophallactic contact could be more easily accomplished, the adults and larvae from their own colony were fed correspondingly more. Wasps are therefore able to distinguish strangers from sisters, this capacity for recognition being emphasized when the amount of contact between them is increased. When alien workers or brood comb are added to another colony, the strangers apparently acquire the host colony's odour within three or four days (Montagner 1967).

ROLE OF THE QUEEN IN VESPINE SOCIETIES

The dominance hierarchies which are so characteristic of the primitive social wasps such as *Polistes* do not appear to have the same significance and importance in the more populous vespine colonies. Here, the differences between queen and workers are more distinct, based on size as well as physiological and behavioural factors, and the societies are typically haplometrotic – the queen initiating the colony alone. The vespine queen is a dominant individual, being the only or at least principal egg-layer, and confined to the nest with no foraging duties to perform after worker emergence. As recent research is beginning to show, she co-ordinates the activities of workers through the agency of pheromones rather than dominance behaviour.

In most species of hornet so far studied, the workers cluster around the queen when she pauses between bouts of oviposition and feeding. Ishay (1964) has described the situation in *V. orientalis* where groups of 2-30 workers surround the queen, the first arrivals orientating towards the head and thorax, the later ones clustering around the abdomen. These 'resting circles' are very similar to the 'royal court' in honeybees where the queen is surrounded by large numbers of workers which continually lick her body. The hornet workers, especially those at the anterior end of the queen, lick her body, palpate their antennae on her sclerites and even place their forelegs on her. Several of these workers tap their abdomens on the cells of the comb and Ishay and Schwarz (1965) suggest that this may be a means of communication, enticing the queen to renewed oviposition or perhaps attracting the attention of other workers to the presence of the queen. At the end of the season, the workers form more frenzied clusters around the queen, licking her vigorously and even causing her death by gnawing at her body. If the queen dies, the workers continue to lick and palpate her corpse for up to two days after her death (Ishay 1964). Similar royal courts have been described for several Japanese hornets, including *V. crabro*, although this behaviour was not seen in the very small colonies of *V. tropica* and rare in small colonies of *V. analis* (Matsuura 1968a). Ishay and others (1970) observed that workers in *V. crabro* colonies lick the queen's body, paying special attention to the abdominal region.

The presence of a physiologically competent queen produces a general calm among the workers but in her absence a state of unrest develops in the colony, skirmishes break out between workers, brood-care activities are disrupted, and many workers leave the nest and roam about outside the colony (Ishay, Ikan, and Bergmann 1965). If a queen is removed from a colony for two days and then returned she is invariably attacked and killed. When a queen is taken away or dies, the ovaries of the workers develop rapidly and they begin ovipositing some days later. All these facts point to the presence of a pheromone being produced by the queen which regulates worker behaviour and inhibits their ovariole development.

When wads of cotton wool soaked in ethanolic extracts of queen hornet's bodies were presented to queenless colonies of *V. orientalis*, the workers gathered round the cotton wool and licked it, the extract having a marked tranquillizing effect on the colony. An analysis of the extract revealed a strongly acidic component which appeared to have a potent effect on the behaviour of the hornets (Ishay, Ikan, and Bergmann 1965). The final isolation of the *V. orientalis* pheromone and its identification as δ-n-hexadecalactone was carried out by Ikan and others (1969). Apart from its tranquillizing properties when introduced into queenless colonies, the lactone stimulated the construction of queen cells – a phenomenom which occurs only in queen-right colonies. The pheromone was identified in extracts from the head of the queen, but the thoracic and abdominal extracts had no biological activity. The situation is very similar to the honeybee suggesting that the pheromone is produced by glands in the head of the queen which the workers obtain by licking her mandibular region, and subsequently spread throughout the colony during trophallactic exchanges.

The situation in *Paravespula* colonies with their thousands of adult workers is somewhat different for there have been no observations of workers clustering around the queen and licking her, in fact the reverse has been frequently recorded (Marchal 1896, Spradbery 1963, Potter 1965, Montagner 1967). Archer (1972b) has confirmed that no licking of queens takes place in *P. vulgaris* and that a queen does not have clusters of workers round her, although she may join groups of workers from time to time.

The significance of the queen in regulating the behaviour of workers and suppressing their ovariole development was first recorded by Marchal (1896) in his studies on *Vespula* species, although Siebold (1871) had earlier recorded that workers of *Polistes* and *D. sylvestris* lay eggs in the absence of the queen and that their progeny is exclusively male. Marchal also records that, after removing the queen, the ovaries of the young workers develop most rapidly and they begin ovipositing within 10 days. Generally, 25-60 per cent of the workers in queen-less colonies were found to have developed ovaries containing mature eggs.

Perhaps one of Marchal's most interesting findings was that workers' ovaries developed in the presence of a competent queen if she was

P

prevented from ovipositing should all the cells be filled. This suggests that an ovary-suppressing pheromone may be produced or emitted during the act of oviposition. Similarly, when a live *P. vulgaris* queen failed to oviposit for only 2 days, the workers began ovipositing shortly afterwards (Potter 1965). Nevertheless, in one queen-less colony of *P. vulgaris* which I examined in mid-September, not one egg was discovered despite a worker population of 1,200 and more than 7,000 empty cells. Montagner (1967) has shown experimentally that the presence of a queen in *Paravespula* colonies assures the continued and regular feeding of larvae, while the removal of a queen results in reduced feeding after 35-40 hours. By putting the corpse of a queen with a group of workers, Montagner found that it did not prevent ovariole development.

It seems clear that a queen-producing pheromone governs the initiation of queen-cell building in wasps for Potter (1965), in experiments on *P. vulgaris*, transferred a queen from a colony not engaged in queen-cell construction to one which was building queen-cells, causing a change to worker-cell building in the latter. The reverse transfer caused the immature colony to begin queen-cell building immediately. The almost total lack of physical contact between workers and queens in *Vespula* colonies suggests that the pheromone produced by the queen permeates the colony by diffusion. If this is so, the pheromone must be highly volatile which may well make its extraction and identification very difficult. Proposed sites of pheromone production will be dealt with in Chapter 9.

OTHER MEANS OF COMMUNICATION

Virtually any contact between two insects can be considered a form of communication, from the visual and audible signs which attract the sexes for mating, to various displays during courtship or aggression, and the symbolic language used by bees to communicate the sources of nectar or pollen. In a populous insect society, there is a greater need for communication between its various members so that the building, foraging, and defence activities may be efficiently integrated. From the studies on social facilitation, trophallaxis, and pheromones it is clear that communication of social stimuli is well established in social wasps although there are other forms of communication in their colonies.

Lindauer (1961) has discussed the perception of sound in the honeybee, pointing out that bees can respond to solid-borne sounds through the substrate, but there is no distinct response to airborne sonic stimuli. However, the wax combs of the honeybee are acoustically inert whereas wasp carton can act as a sounding board. The studies of

Ishay and his colleagues on *V. orientalis* have demonstrated that a range of sounds is produced by a hornet colony, of which some have definite cybernetic properties.

The sounds in hornet colonies are produced both by adults and larvae, the latter producing distinctly audible scraping noises which were originally noted by Chapman (1870) who deduced that they were a 'call for food'. These noises are produced by fourth- and fifth-instar larvae which extend their bodies so that their mandibles reach the rim of the cell then, by contracting the body, they scrape the mandibles across the bands of carton which make up the wall, producing a rasping noise. The whole operation lasts some 1·6-1·7 seconds of which about one third of the time is occupied with producing the scraping noise. Schaudinischky and Ishay (1968) described the sound as a 'hunger signal' for, if recorded on magnetic tape and played back through a vibrator attached to a part of comb with empty cells, the workers were stimulated to 'feed' the empty cells. Under natural conditions, when a larva makes the scraping signal a worker adult approaches the cell, touches the larva with its mandibles and leaves a drop of food near the larva's mouth. The larva then secretes a drop of saliva which is licked up by the adult, after which the larva bends its head towards the thorax, picks up the food in its mandibles and chews it before finally swallowing it. The smaller larvae (instars one to three) are unable to reach the opposite wall and there is some evidence that by bending away from the wall to which they are attached and swinging the head back sharply, they produce a perceptible knock on the wall behind them, although the significance of this sound as a hunger signal has not been confirmed. Montagner (1964) noted that workers will adopt a piece of comb if larvae are present, and he suggested that they were attracted to the comb by the scraping noises produced by the hungry larvae.

Ishay and Schwartz (1971) provided evidence that worker, male, and queen larvae have different sound frequencies and that there are also species differences, the sounds produced by *V. crabro* larvae differing markedly from *V. orientalis*. An attempt has been made to determine the communication code used by larvae to attract adults (Ishay and Landau 1972).

Anyone standing near an aerial wasp nest or a large subterranean colony with only a short tunnel cannot fail to be impressed by the incessant buzzing noise of the inmates. These airborne sounds are chiefly produced by the vibrating wings of the wasps, but there are other adult noises such as those produced when they gnaw food and crush woodpulp. The carton of a wasp nest conducts solid-borne sounds and to help isolate adult noises from larval hunger signals, the adults dangle from the combs by their hindlegs which helps attenuate the sounds they produce while chewing or vibrating their wings. The air-borne sounds of adults were rarely picked up as solid-borne sounds during simultaneous recordings, demonstrating that adult sounds are not transmitted to the comb. The adult-produced sounds may have some communicative function among the adults in the colony. Nixon (1934d) has observed a queen stimulate the mass exodus of workers from a *P. germanica* colony when she buzzed her wings in apparent alarm.

There is some evidence that wasps may produce an 'alarm substance', possibly associated with their venom, which stimulates a general state of alarm in the colony and releases aggressive behaviour towards an intruder (Evans and Eberhard 1970).

Despite a lack of symbol communication which is found in the honeybee, returning foragers frequently excite other wasps in the nest and may even stimulate foraging activity (Spieth 1948). Naumann (1970) has evidence that the polybiine wasp, *Protopolybia pumila* (Saussure), makes 'departure dances' which stimulate activity among potential foragers.

In an investigation of colony recognition in *P. vulgaris*, Butler and others (1969) determined that wasps departing and returning from the nest leave a 'footprint substance' around the nest entrance which, when deposited on an artificial entrance tube, was attractive to the adults. This substance probably helps in recognizing the nest entrance and stimulates wasps to enter, and is somewhat analagous to the trail scents of ants and termites.

There is evidence that pupal wasps emit a pheromone which stimulates the adults to warn them (Ishay 1972).

A consideration of sex pheromone will be found on page 246.

Inter- and Intra-specific Relationships

Social organization within the colony has dominated the discussion of social life in wasps in this chapter, but an examination of animosity and tolerance between colonies of the same and different species provides some interesting features which may help our understanding of integration in the wasp community.

The nature of dominance hierarchies within a colony has been dealt with at some length already, but similar relationships among wasps and hornets foraging at food sources also occur. In Japan, Sakagami and Fukushima (1957) have described the interspecific dominance order which is established between hornet workers feeding at sap exudations from oak trees. The hierarchy is based primarily on size, the larger species dominating the smaller. A very similar relationship was noticed by Matsuura (1969) among queen hornets in the spring –

linear dominance orders being established among the queens of one species and also between different species. The dominance order among the species was the same for queens and workers. The antagonism of wasps and hornets when foraging is probably a manifestation of territorial defence (Free 1970) for wasps are individualists when foraging, and aggressive behaviour at a food source would be an advantage if the wasps were from different colonies and therefore competing for available food (Kalmus 1954). Moreover, there is evidence that workers from the same colony do not behave aggressively towards each other at a food source (Matsuura, personal communication).

Apart from the interactions between wasps outside their nest territory, there are many observations of usurpation or adoption of another colony by queens or workers of the same and different species. Desey (1922) has observed queens of *P. germanica* and *D. sylvestris* adopt embryo nests of their own species if they contained viable larvae.

Nixon (1934a, b, 1935, 1936) in a series of experiments with *P. vulgaris* and *P. germanica* has shown that the queen of either species will adopt a nest of their own or the other species. When a *P. germanica* queen was put into a small *P. vulgaris* nest containing a few original workers but no queen, the colony thrived, eventually becoming an all *P. germanica* population with a typical *P. germanica* envelope extending from the original nest. Similarly, when callow *P. vulgaris* workers were added to a queen-right *P. germanica* colony, the two species worked together despite occasional antagonism during the initial stages of introduction. When the two species are present in the same colony, the envelope becomes a patchwork of light brown and grey stripes, representing the carton-making efforts of the two species. Yoshikawa (1956) was able to produce combination nests of *Polistes jadwigae* Dalla Torre by putting several colonies close together until they formed a compound nest. Under these circumstances, the workers from all colonies worked co-operatively but antagonism between the queens resulted in the death or disappearance of all but one of them.

Ishay and others (1970), in experiments with *V. orientalis* were able to combine colonies towards the end of the season, and in one instance, five such colonies were joined, the queens and their respective offspring functioning normally with a typical 'royal court' around each queen while on one occasion, a single royal court formed around two queens which were close together on the same comb. The tolerance between queens and workers at this time is in stark contrast to the period before mid-August when queens, if introduced to queen-right embryo colonies, are quickly chased away or killed by the rightful owner. When workers are present in the maturing colony, they attack the prospective usurper.

Co-operation between several queens in one colony is a distinctive feature of the overwintered *P. germanica* colonies in Tasmania, for by the recruitment of young queens in the autumn and possibly throughout the mild winter and spring, enormous nests can be produced. In one colony I found 71 functional queens and total adult populations of 11,000 per colony are not uncommon (unpublished results).

The usurping of another colony by a queen wasp has been observed by Nixon (1936) who described a *P. germanica* taking over a *P. vulgaris* embryo nest. During their studies on *D. sylvestris*, Brian and Brian observed the attempted usurpation of an embryo colony by a queen. The same colony was successfully taken over by a foreign queen some days later but she was herself displaced by yet another queen. In a second colony, usurpation took place on two successive occasions. Matsuura (1970) has recorded queens and workers of *V. crabro flavofasciata* Cameron invading nearby colonies of the same species. The intruders are generally driven off by the original queen and workers but occasionally the foreign workers are accepted. The reasons for invasive behaviour are not known but it is possibly prompted by the loss of an original nest or is a form of competition for a nest site. The behaviour of a queen which usurps or adopts the nest of another wasp may be described as a form of parasitism and it possibly indicates a stage in the evolution of social parasites.

PARASITIC SOCIAL WASPS

True social parasitism may be defined as an obligatory usurpation of the colony of one wasp species (the host) by another species (the parasite), the latter having no worker caste and relying on the host species' workers to forage and tend her brood.

There is only one species of parasitic social wasp in the British Isles, *V. austriaca*, which is found predominantly in the north and west. Its discovery in the last century led to considerable speculation about its biological and taxonomic status, many entomologists confusing it with its host, *V. rufa*. For example, Carpenter and Pack-Beresford (1903) concluded that in some instances 'the old *austriaca* queen was the foundress of the nest, and that both the *rufa* and *austriaca* forms are her offspring'.

The first biological information on a social parasite was deduced from the contents of a *V. rufa* nest taken in Ireland by Robson (1898). In late July a *V. rufa* worker was seen dragging the dismembered corpse of a queen out through the entrance of the nest. By early August, the colony had virtually completed its development and it was excavated. Inside were 6-8 young *V. austriaca* queens and 44 *V. austriaca* male pupae together with a few male pupae and about 20 adult workers of *V. rufa*. Robson deduced that the dead queen being removed in July was the *V. rufa* queen which had been usurped by the *V. austriaca* queen. A similar nest was found by Carpenter and Pack-Beresford (1903) in which the old *V. austriaca* was present together with males and queens of the parasite species, and one male and five workers of the host species. A *V. austriaca* queen was reputedly found in a feeble colony of *D. norwegica* (Harrison 1915).

Another interesting example of parasitism by *V. austriaca* has been recorded by Yamane and Kubo (1970) who found a colony of *V. rufa schrencki* Radoszkowski with an old but active *V. austriaca* queen, and a further two parasite queens which were dead, one in the nest and the other in the entrance tunnel. The dead *V. rufa* queen was also found in the nest. From these data it is possible to reconstruct the sequence of events which led to successful parasitism. In the nest described by Yamane and Kubo, the *V. rufa* colony was invaded by one parasitic queen which killed the founding queen, but the colony was subsequently twice invaded by *V. austriaca* queens, leading to the death of two of them. It is impossible to determine whether the first parasite maintained her position by killing the further intruders or was herself usurped.

When the *V. austriaca* succeeds in locating its host's nest and killing or chasing away the *V. rufa* queen, she oviposits in the cells and relies on the *V. rufa* workers to tend the brood. Only males and queens are produced, there being no worker caste.

The parasite is better adapted for combat than its host for the cuticle is thicker, the abdominal sclerites fit more closely together (for protection) and they have a curved sting which can more easily be plunged through the intersegmental membranes of the host.

Weyrauch (1937b), Taylor (1939), and Scheven (1958) have described the other parasitic social wasps of Europe and North America, including *Polistes* (=*Sulcopolistes*) parasites.

Taylor (1939) has described the possible phylogenetic stages in the development of social parasitism and I use his scheme in this discussion of the evolution of a parasitic species.

Stage 1

Intra-specific, facultative temporary parasitism. When a queen invades a colony of the same species and deposes the original queen or perhaps replaces a lost queen, the parasitic stage is only temporary for, as soon as the progeny of the second queen emerge as adults, the parasitic state ceases. Several instances of this relationship have been recorded, including the observations and experiments made by Nixon (1934-1936) on *Paravespula*, Janet (1903) on *V. crabro*, and Yoshikawa (1955) on *Polistes*. The conditions leading to this type of association are either an inhibition of the queen to build her own nest or the destruction of a nest if previously initiated.

Stage 2

Inter-specific, facultative temporary parasitism. In this stage an identical situation to that found in Stage 1 occurs, except that two different but generally closely related species are involved. The case of a *P. germanica* queen taking over a *P. vulgaris* colony cited by Nixon (1936) is an example of this type of association. Taylor (1939) illustrates this stage with an American example, and Sakagami and Fukushima (1957) have described a similar relationship between *Vespa dybowskii* André which, despite a capacity for founding its own colonies, frequently usurps those previously constructed by *V. crabro* and occasionally those of *Vespa xanthoptera* Cameron. *V. dybowskii* leaves its hibernation quarters much later than the other hornet species which probably facilitates this kind of behaviour. These authors report that the workers of both species collaborate before the host workers finally die off and the colony becomes exclusively *V. dybowskii* in brood and adults.

Stage 3

Inter-specific, obligatory temporary parasitism. This theoretical association was suggested as a necessary transitional step towards full, worker-less parasitism. Taylor suggested that a queen may lose its ability to found a colony and must therefore usurp the colony of a different species, the emergence of its own workers terminating the parasitic phase.

Stage 4

Inter-specific, obligatory permanent parasitism. The fully parasitic stage is exemplified by *V. austriaca* in which one species is parasitic on another, there is no worker caste, and the reproductives of the parasite are reared by the host workers.

In a discussion of social parasitism, Richards (1971a), makes the point that if a geographical race of wasp begins to spread into an area occupied by an earlier nesting indigenous species, there exists the possibility for parasitism. This would be especially so if the prospective host wasp is a closely allied species rather than one more phylogenetically distant and more distinct with reference to colony odour. Late emergence from hibernation appears to be a necessary step in the evolution of social parasitism as exemplified by the month or more delay in the appearance of *V. austriaca* compared to its host *V. rufa* (Fig. 26), and the comparatively late appearance of *V. dybowskii*. The capacity and frequency with which free-living species usurp nests of their own or closely-related species makes it perhaps surprising that there is not a greater incidence of social parasitism among wasps. Nevertheless, the percentage of socially parasitic species is high with 14 per cent (1 of 7) in the British Vespinae, 12·5 per cent (2 of 16) in North American Vespinae, 2·7 per cent (4 of 150) in the Polistinae, and 11 per cent (23 of 200) in the South American polybiine wasp, *Mischocyttarus*.

CHAPTER 9

MALES AND FEMALES

The establishment of the wasp colony followed by the increase in size of nest and number of workers are a means to an end – the generation of reproductives, the males and queens. The survival of wasps can only be ensured by the production of queens, and the evolution of social wasps has probably been influenced by factors which favour the production of large numbers of reproductives, especially in those species which found colonies with unaided queens. Factors which stimulate and control the appearance and development of males and queens are diverse, resulting from interactions between the founding queen, the developmental stage of the colony, and the behaviour of the workers.

The males, which are produced from unfertilized, haploid eggs, play no significant part in the social organization of the colony, their sole function being the insemination of the young queens. Moreover, males do not forage or feed the larvae and contribute little to trophallactic exchange among the other adults, and they can thus be considered a somewhat parasitic group, feeding off larval secretions and regurgitated food passing between workers. However, Shida (1954) records a male *Vespula lewisii* (Cameron) masticating meat obtained from a returning forager and subsequently offering it to larvae.

Queens and workers develop from fertilized, diploid eggs. In Vespinae, special cells are constructed for queen rearing and their initiation at the appropriate stage in the seasonal cycle of colony development is one of the most significant happenings in the life of the colony. The timing of male and queen production is variable among the British species, *D. norwegica*, *D. sylvestris*, and *V. rufa* being the earliest with reproductives emerging in late July and early August, while in *V. crabro*, *P. vulgaris*, and *P. germanica*, they are produced from late August through to November (see Fig. 26).

The appearance of reproductives is a cyclic phenomenon, male production beginning before queen production, although they and

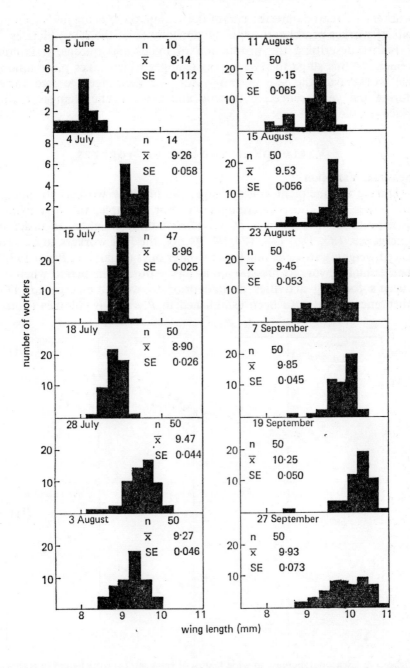

Figure 71. Histograms showing wing length of workers from *Paravespula vulgaris* colonies; n = number of wasps in sample; x̄ = mean; SE = standard error of mean (after Spradbery 1972).

workers are reared until the end of the season, there being no 'switching off' of worker production with the appearance of the reproductives.

Before describing the production of males and queens, it is convenient at this stage to recount the changes which takes place among the workers as the season progresses, for their average size varies during the year, reflecting trophic and other cyclic changes taking place in colonies.

VARIATION IN THE SIZE OF WORKERS

Seasonal Variation

During the incipient colony stage, the first few workers to emerge are larger than those emerging later. For example, the first wholly queen-reared workers in a *D. sylvestris* colony weighed, in order of emergence, 183, 185, 177, 124, 94, 94 mg, the first workers to be produced weighing twice as much as the later ones (Brian and Brian 1952). These smaller workers are starved as larvae during the period when the queen's foraging activities decline prior to worker emergence. This phenomenon has also been established in *P. vulgaris* colonies (Potter

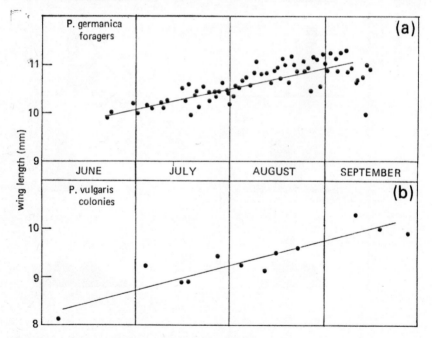

Figure 72. Seasonal increase in wing length of workers: (a) wing length of trapped foragers of *Paravespula germanica* (daily means); (b) wing length of workers from *Paravespula vulgaris* colonies (each point is the mean of a colony) (after Spradbery 1972).

1965). With the recruitment of workers and the attendant increase in foraging activities, the trophic conditions improve and the average size of adults then increases steadily for most of the season (Marchal 1896, Spradbery 1972).

The seasonal increase in worker size was established by measuring wing lengths and weighing adults from the *P. vulgaris* and *P. germanica* colonies that were used in the population census (Chapter 7). Although the average weight of workers fluctuated a great deal (probably due to their age and fat levels) the average wing length increased with time (Figs. 71, 72b). The smallest workers were the ten adults collected from a colony on 5 June which, as larvae, would have been tended by the queen. An indication of the range in size of workers from a colony is illustrated in Plate XXc. The size of foragers which were trapped at Rothamsted showed a similar trend during the season (Fig. 72a), although in common with samples from colonies, there are indications of a levelling off or even a decrease in average size at the end of the year.

How are these changes in the size of adults accomplished so rapidly during the development of the colony? One factor is the brevity of adult life. Because adults live for only two or three weeks, there is a constant replacement of old workers by new and little accumulation of the older, smaller ones. Thus, any changes which do occur will be quickly expressed.

It is obvious that the size of an adult insect is a reflection of the

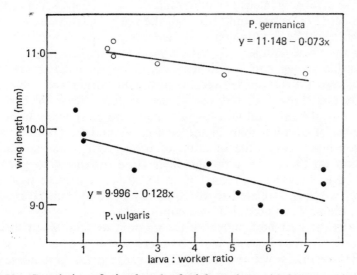

Figure 73. Correlation of wing length of adult workers with larva: worker ratio in *Paravespula vulgaris* and *P. germanica* colonies (after Spradbery 1972).

feeding régime enjoyed during larval life so that, in wasps, adult size can be used as a measure of trophic conditions prevailing in colonies some three weeks earlier. The number of adults available for foraging and feeding the larvae (the larva : worker ratio) probably gives a reasonable estimate of the availability and distribution of food. By plotting the size of adults against the larva : worker ratio of colonies 22 days earlier, I have shown that there is a significant correlation between these two parameters such that the size of adults increases with the decrease in larva : worker ratio (Fig. 73). The larger adults result from improved trophic conditions which take place when there are relatively more adults available to feed the larvae.

However, there are other factors which contribute to the seasonal size increase. It has been noted earlier (Chapter 5) that the average size of the cells increases with successively built combs so that, in a 4-comb nest for example, the most recently built cells are 11 per cent wider and 17 per cent deeper than those of the first comb. The volume of a cell must limit the size of the occupant so that bigger larvae can be reared in larger cells. This point has been neatly demonstrated by Potter (1965) who compared the size of male hornets reared in worker and queen cells (Fig. 74). Despite being genetically very similar, there is a distinct bimodality in the wing length of the males, illustrating how cell size can influence adult size. The studies of Montagner (1967) have shown that the quantity of food offered to larvae increases with the increase in size of cells, the height of the cell wall having the most influence. Therefore, a combination of larger brood cells and an increase in feeding intensity could result in larger wasps being produced.

Archer (1972a) has confirmed that the size of workers increases on a chronological basis although statistical analyses showed that the major correlation was with size of nest (as measured by the number of cells) rather than its age. Archer also measured the pupae to determine whether there were differences between combs and within the same comb. The results showed an increase in size of pupae from the top to the bottom of the nest and that larger pupae were more likely to occur on the edge of a comb than in the centre. Montagner (1967) found no relationship between the quantity of food given to larvae and their position on the comb, although their close proximity to pupal cells resulted in some larvae receiving up to 30 per cent more food. If the size of a pupa is related to the quantity of food it receives when a larva, the position occupied on a comb and the relative position of the comb in the nest both influence the amount of food given to larvae. These results may help explain why there is such a considerable range in size of workers within a colony. The range tends to increase as the season progresses so that in mature colonies, the greatest variation is found (see Fig. 71).

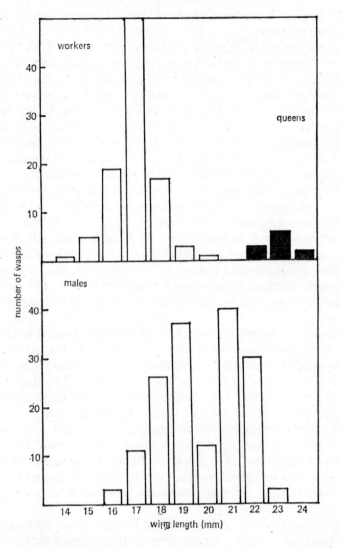

Figure 74. Frequency distribution for wing length of males, queens, and workers of *Vespa crabro* (after Potter 1965).

Size and Division of Labour

It is well established that in some bumble bee colonies about two thirds of the workers are constant to either foraging or household duties, although they can change their occupation if the requirements of the colony alter (Free 1955). In a few bumble bee species, these behavioural differences are paralleled by morphological differences such that larger workers tend to be foragers (Free 1961). There is some fragmentary evidence that a similar situation might occur in *Paravespula* colonies.

For example, in the *P. vulgaris* colony collected on 4 July (Fig. 71), only the foragers were used in the morphometric study and they proved to be significantly larger than the average of entire worker populations from colonies collected up to two weeks later. To determine whether foraging wasps were different from those remaining in the nest (the domestics), I collected foragers at the nest entrance with a hand-operated aspirator, sucking in the flying wasps until flight activity stopped or was severely reduced. This technique did not seem to disturb the colony and there was never a rush of guard wasps during the operation. After excavating the nest, samples of foragers, domestics and callows – the recently emerged, pale-coloured wasps – were obtained and their wings measured. No differences were found between foragers and domestics except in one colony of *P. germanica*, which was excavated in late September. In this colony, the foragers were significantly bigger than domestics and callows ($p < 0.001$) (Fig. 75). In four of the five colonies examined the callows were larger than the domestics, which would be expected if the average size of the adults was increasing with time.

In another experiment, I siphoned off foragers from a colony with the aspirator every hour until activity virtually ceased. Although the wing length of most samples was similar, the last workers to be collected were significantly smaller than the first few samples. This data could be interpreted as follows: with the depletion of the foraging force of large workers, smaller wasps, which would normally behave as domestics, were stimulated to forage due to the lack of food being brought back to the colony. Compared to a control colony a few metres away, the proportion of orientation flights (a measure of forager recruitment) was up to twenty times greater in the experimental colony, which suggests that, for many workers, foraging activities were only just starting.

Finally, a comparison of *P. germanica* foragers from the Rothamsted suction traps with samples from entire colonies showed that from mid-July to mid-August, the foragers were considerably bigger ($p < 0.01$-0.001) than the average for a colony.

Morphological differences between foragers and domestics will tend to be obscured because of the chronological increase in size, the youngest pre-foraging adults tending to be the biggest. Ideally, morphometric studies should be made on stabilized populations in which the size of adults is not increasing with time – a situation which occurs towards the end of the season. The one colony in which the foragers were larger than the domestics was taken during this period. Even in the bumble bee, *Bombus agrorum*, morphological differences between

XXI (top). *Paravespula germanica* queen feeding on the labial secretion of a larva, note larva on left which has disgorged a large drop of saliva; (bottom) trophallactic exchange among adult *P. vulgaris*, the pair above are establishing contact by means of antennal stimulation and below a newly emerged callow (right) obtaining regurgitated food from a mature adult, both adopting submissive postures.

XXII (top). *Paravespula germanica* worker adding pellets of moistened soil around the tunnel entrance, note the grass stem (right) pruned by wasps; (bottom left) pairing in *P. germanica* with one male attempting to insert its intromittent organ; (bottom right) queen nibbling gaster of male during copulation.

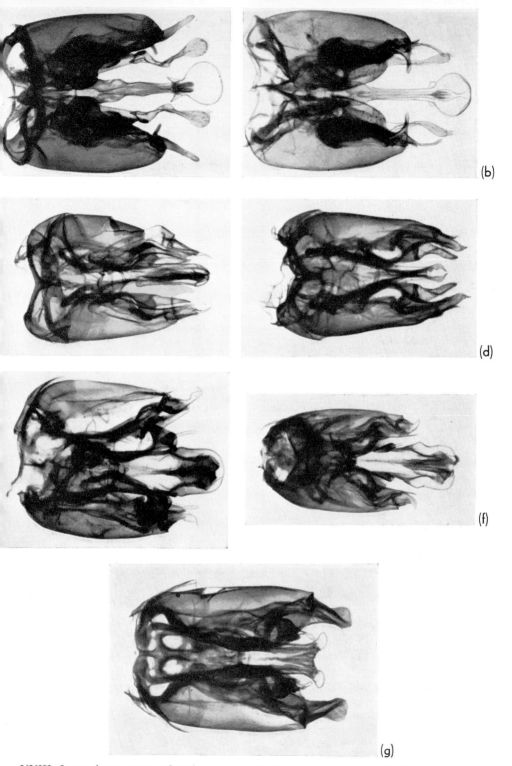

XXIII. Intromittent organ of male wasps: (a) *Paravespula vulgaris;* (b) *P. germanica;* (c) *Dolichovespula sylvestris;* (d) *D. norwegica;* (e) *Vespula rufa;* (f) *V. austriaca;* and (g) *Vespa crabro.*

XXIV (top) *Paravespula germanica* queen ovipositing; (bottom) copulation in *P. germanica*, the queen, left, nibbling the gaster of the male which beats its wings during pairing.

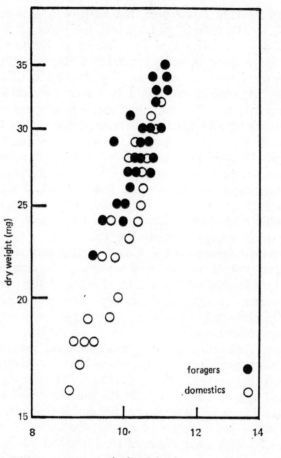

dry weight (mg)

foragers ●
domestics ○

wing length (mm)

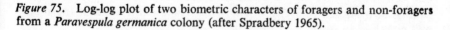

Figure 75. Log-log plot of two biometric characters of foragers and non-foragers from a *Paravespula germanica* colony (after Spradbery 1965).

foragers and brood nurses only become apparent after mid-August (Cumber 1949). Further study is necessary before the question of a morphologically biased division of labour in wasp colonies can be finally resolved.

MALES

In colonies of *P. vulgaris* and *P. germanica*, the first male-producing eggs are deposited in mid-July and account for 17 per cent of all eggs by the end of August, and 60 per cent by mid-September. Although the haploid origin of males is now well established, there is still an un-

Q*

resolved controversy concerning the relative contribution to male production, by the founding queen and the workers. Siebold (1871) was the first to establish that the ovaries of *Vespula* workers will develop in the absence of the queen and that they can lay male-producing eggs. By dissecting workers from *Vespula* colonies during the course of a season, Marchal (1896) found that their ovaries were relatively well developed during August, when males first appear, but the proportion of workers with developed ovaries decreased for the remainder of the season until, in September, none were found with ovariole development. It appears that workers' ovaries develop during the period characterized by a peak in the numbers of workers (see Chapter 7) when foraging rates are at their lowest level of the season (see Chapter 6). Perhaps ovariole development at this time is due primarily to the trophic advantages accruing from large adult numbers, allied to a decrease in energy expenditure. The converse situation – fewer workers to tend larvae and a high foraging rate – might prevent ovariole development by means of a work or nutricial castration, as suggested by Marchal (1897). In the absence of the queen, however, worker's ovaries develop within ten days, and subsequent oviposition is characterized by cells containing several eggs.

Since Marchal published his findings, many students of wasp biology have assumed that cells containing more than the usual single egg are proof that workers are ovipositing. I do not believe this to be universal, for Brian and Brian (1952), Potter (1965), and I have observed queens lay a second egg in a cell, while in the multi-queened colonies of *P. germanica* in Tasmania, several eggs per cell is the rule. For example, in one colony with 71 functional queens, the average number of eggs per cell was 2·7 with a maximum of 13. Ishay and others (1970) report that the queen in *V. orientalis* colonies may lay as many as 4 eggs in one cell. Therefore, on the evidence of supernumerary eggs in cells, it cannot be assumed that the workers are responsible or that these eggs will give rise to males.

Montagner (1966b) provides the most convincing evidence that workers contribute to male production by feeding queens on radioactive tracers which are taken up by the ovaries, and later exposing the egg-filled combs to sensitive plates. Radioactive eggs could be distinguished from other, non-radioactive and presumably worker-laid eggs. In studies on *Dolichovespula* and *Paravespula* species, Montagner (1966b, 1967) found considerable differences among colonies with respect to haploid egg production. In some the queen had apparently laid all the male eggs while in others none at all. In about half the colonies, workers had contributed about 75 per cent to male production and in the others they had possibly laid all the haploid eggs. Montagner noted that laying workers (=those with developed ovaries) were more likely to be found on the upper combs, well away from the queen which normally occupied the more recently built lower combs. The upper combs generally contain little brood and the workers tended to keep food to themselves rather than feed larvae. There was, incidentally, no obvious correlation between the degree of ovariole development of these workers and their position in the social hierarchy, contrary to the situation in *Polistes*. Finally, Montagner observed that when queens failed to lay haploid eggs, they frequently lost their dominant role in the social structure and were often ejected from the nest, or even killed. Montagner concluded that workers make a significant contribution to the male population, their ovariole development being related to colonial factors and/or the physiological age of the queen.

By dissecting workers from queen-right colonies and para-social groups (groups of workers on pieces of comb in the absence of the queen) towards the end of the season I found slight ovariole development in workers from some colonies containing a functional queen (Table 28). In the para-social groups, the proportion of workers with developed ovaries was considerable, and they had significantly more mature eggs

TABLE 28
Ovariole development in worker wasps (original)

COLONY DATA	DATE COLONY EXCAVATED	NO. DIS- SECTED	WASPS WITH DEVELOPED OVARIES		
			No.	percent	Mature eggs per wasp
P. vulgaris: foundress queen, young males and queen adults present.	17 September	31	1	3	1·0
P. vulgaris: foundress queen and male pupae present.	22 September	25	0	0	—
P. germanica: foundress queen, adult males and queen pupae present.	30 September	50	0	0	—
P. vulgaris: adult queens and males present. Foundress queen absent.	19 September	50	2	4	1·0
P. vulgaris: foundress queen, young males and queen adults present.	26 October	50	7	14	1·3
P. germanica: foundress queen, young males and queen adults present.	3 November	50	0	0	—
P. vulgaris: workers without queen for 25 days.	22 August	44	9	20	6·1
P. vulgaris: workers without queen for 15 days.	30 August	25	2	8	3·5

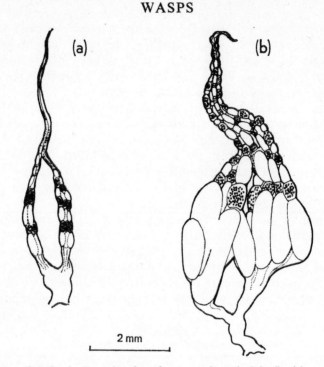

2 mm

Figure 76.   Ovaries in *Paravespula vulgaris* workers (original): (a) undeveloped;
(b) developed, following loss of queen.

in their ovarioles (Fig. 76). In one case, the original piece of adopted
comb had been destroyed and under a new envelope, a small comb of
16 cells had been built, each cell containing one egg (Plate XVIIIb).

If workers do contribute to male production, what proportion of the
male population is derived from worker eggs? Assuming a worker
population of 2,500 of which 4 per cent have developed ovaries, their
daily oviposition rate would be 100 if each laid one egg per day. From
the *Paravespula* population data, the oviposition rate in mid-September
colonies was approximately 150 of which 60 per cent (90 eggs) were
haploid. On this theoretical basis, the workers could have laid all the
haploid eggs.

In the absence of more substantial evidence, it is probably safer to
assume that both queen and workers contribute to the male population
under normal circumstances.

Unfertilized eggs are first deposited during the period of maximum
oviposition in mid-July and, if laid by the queen, might fail to be fertilized during their rapid passage down the oviduct. I have called this
possibility 'accidental haploidy'. A diminution of sperm in the queen's
spermotheca is an unlikely cause of male production because female
(fertilized) eggs continue to be laid until the end of the season, although

their proportion decreases. Flanders (1962) suggests that male production in Hymenoptera takes place 'when opulent conditions prevail in the colonies', full nourishment being associated with inactivation of the spermathecal gland. Because both haploid and diploid eggs occur throughout the latter half of the seasonal cycle, there seems little evidence for a direct control of sex by the environmental stimulation of the spermathecal gland. In honeybee colonies, Flanders (1957) considers that the large drone cells may stimulate haploid egg-laying, but in the social wasp, haploid eggs are laid in both worker and queen cells and it seems unlikely that cell size determines whether an egg is fertilized or not. Males are almost certainly produced in response to cyclic factors, perhaps the development stage of the colony or the physiological age of its queen, acting on the queen herself, the workers or both.

THE FEMALE CASTES

In social wasps, functionally different castes are restricted to the female sex – the queens and workers – the distinctions between them including morphological, anatomical, physiological, and behavioural characteristics. As Richards (1971a) points out in his review of social wasp biology, the distinctions between castes in many primitive wasps are not always obvious and the often subtle differences which do occur frequently lead to females which are intermediate between true queens and workers. The primary distinction between castes is that queens do most of the egg-laying and the workers carry out all other colony duties, although this major difference is not always adhered to. For example, queens initiate colonies single-handed, which involves foraging and building activities, and workers may lay eggs. In the Vespinae, larger cells for rearing queens are constructed and the size difference between castes is clear-cut although there are other features which distinguish them:

1. *Morphological.* The disparity in size between *Vespula* queens and workers is obvious, the variation between them being discontinuous. In his study of polymorphism in wasps, Blackith (1958b) measured various size parameters (e.g. wing length, width of head, thorax, and abdomen) and found that the difference between queens and workers was not just a matter of size, but also involved a difference in form. Although in most characters the size differences were isometric, the width of the abdomen in queens was disproportionally wider than workers – an allometric relationship. This difference is probably allied to the future massive ovariole development of the queen (Plate XXb). With the founding of the colony, further changes in the form and colour

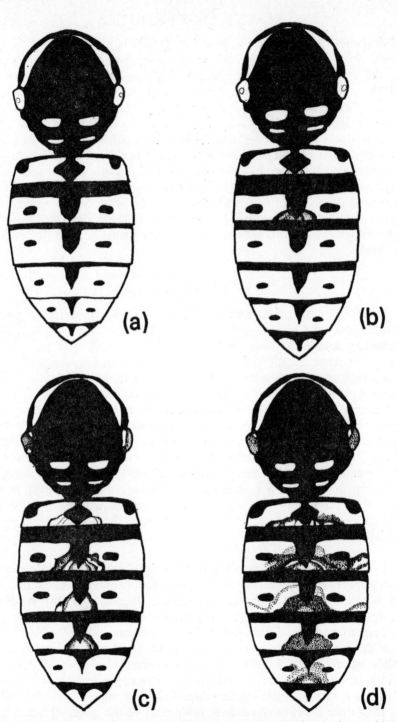

Figure 77. Abdominal distension (physogastry) and spread of cuticular markings with age in queens of *Paravespula germanica* (original): (a) incipient colony stage; (b) after 6 weeks; (c) after 10 weeks; (d) after 20 weeks.

of the queen take place. The abdomen becomes distended as a result of ovariole development, a phenomenon called physogastry. Through continued oviposition, the wings become frayed as they rub against the cell walls and may even be worn down to the tegulae (Plate XXa). In contrast to the bright and shining black and yellow markings of the young queen, the old ones look very shabby, the cuticle becoming greasy in appearance with the yellow areas very dull.

A further change in the appearance of the queen is the development of brown patches in the cuticle, beginning in the second gastral tergite but later found throughout much of the gaster and thorax (Fig. 77). Becker (1937) drew attention to their similarity to Liesegang Rings, rings of precipitation which occur spontaneously in colloidal solutions. The red-brown material was considered to be a pterine pigment which had been precipitated within the epidermal region. The pattern of pigmentation suggests a diffusion of pterines into the epidermis beginning at the distal margin of the sclerite. Becker thought that they might be caused through abnormal metabolic activity in the underlying tissue, and Marchal (1896) suggested they were a result of friction between sclerites during oviposition activity and he called these areas 'wear spots'. Pterines may be produced from the purine, uric acid, and in this form could be considered a form of storage excretion. Unpublished studies of the tergites of young and old queens, using a scanning electron microscope, have revealed a further possibility. The sclerites of young queens are covered in a dense layer of fine setae approximately 50μ long. In the old queen there is a bald area corresponding to the brown-pigmented region. Here the setae are broken off at the base to leave apparent holes through the exocuticle. It may be that these holes permit the diffusion of substances from the underlying epidermis or oxidation within the epidermis. Although queens which are prevented from founding colonies fail to develop the colour changes (unpublished observations), Marchal (1896) found two laying workers of *D. media* with brown coloration in their tergites. Browning of the cuticle has also been noted in termite queens, the discoloration being brought about by starvation, fungal infection or insecticide damage (Sannasi 1970). In termites, the cuticular colour change has been ascribed to the activity of the corpora allata (which produces juvenile hormone regulating metamorphosis and yolk deposition in eggs) or the corpora cardiaca (which controls the storage and release of certain hormones from the neurosecretory cells of the brain).

Gaul (1947) defined six female castes or phases in *Vespula* species, although his distinctions were based on size differences among workers (e.g. micrergate and gynaecoid were terms used to describe a diminutive worker, and a large egg-laying worker) and the presence or absence of wings. As is clear from a study of seasonal variation in the size of workers, it is quite improper to define caste phases on size alone, and apterous forms probably result from some malfunction during pupal development. For example, if combs are not maintained at optimal nest temperatures or even kept upside down, many emerging adults have deformed or rudimentary wings.

2. *Anatomical.* There are no major differences between queens and workers with regard to their reproductive anatomy although the spermatheca is disproportionally smaller in workers though structurally identical, and the alkaline gland is somewhat larger in workers.

A fundamental difference in the relative size of the corpus allatum (C.A.) in the brain has been detected by Takamatsu (1952) who found that the C.A. indices for queens, workers, and males of *V. lewisii* were 6·78 : 1·38 : 1, while other histological studies indicated a greater activity in the form of larger and more numerous nuclei, in the corpus allatum of the queen.

Although both workers and queens possess the Van der Vecht organ and associated glandular tissue, the gland area in workers is disproportionally smaller than that of queens (Fig. 10). The functions of Van der Vecht's organ have not been established, but if the queen's gland is associated with pheromone production of the 'queen-substance' variety, this would represent a further fundamental difference between castes. In workers, the gland could possibly produce a characteristic colony odour. It is well established that the same gland in the two castes of the honeybee can have different functions, and a similar situation could well occur in wasps with respect to Van der Vecht's organ.

3. *Ovariole Development.* A fundamental difference between castes is the magnitude of ovariole development in queens (Plate XXb) and the conditions which determine it. In the absence of a functional queen, the ovaries of young workers develop in two days, and those of older ones may develop within ten days (Fig. 76) (Marchal 1896). Under the climatic conditions of much of Europe and North America, the young queens undergo a lengthy ovariole diapause before the ovaries begin developing shortly after leaving hibernation and before initiating colonies. As discussed earlier (Chapter 4), the reasons for ovariole diapause are probably neurosecretory, the mechanism being controlled by some consistent feature of the environment such as photoperiod. The interrelationships between climate, neural activity and diapause should prove a rich field for future investigators.

4. *Hibernation and Fat Content.* In temperate zone wasps, hibernation provides only for the survival of queens and must be considered a major factor in caste differentiation. During development the amount

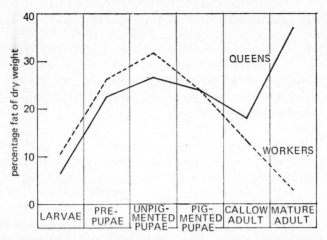

Figure 78. Fat content in queen and worker wasps of *Paravespula vulgaris,* expressed as percentage chloroform-soluble fat of the freeze-dried body weight (25 specimens in each sample) (original).

of fat in the body increases, reaching a maximum during the unpigmented pupal stage, then decreases a little by the time the adults emerge from their cells (Fig. 78). During the developmental stages and shortly after emergence the proportion of fat is approximately the same in queens and workers. The large amount of fat body in queens is deposited *after* adult emergence (contrary to the results of earlier studies, Spradbery 1963)). Before leaving the colony to enter hibernation quarters, the young queens feed on the secretions of larvae and regurgitated food from workers, and also food collected outside the nest during foraging trips. Much of this food is converted to fat and other tissue-stored reserves. Meanwhile the workers continue to forage and their fat content is depleted. By the time queens leave the colony, fat reserves account for nearly 40 per cent of their total dry weight. Evidently there is a fundamental physiological difference between the castes with respect to fat metabolism.

Fischl and Ishay (1971) record caste differences in the glucose levels and rates of carbohydrate autolysis of *V. orientalis* larvae which may originate from differences in their diet or enzyme levels.

5. *Insemination.*   There are no records of worker wasps being successfully inseminated, although males occasionally attempt to copulate with them. The intromittent organ of the male is too large to be inserted into the genital chamber of even the largest workers (Montagner 1967). Fecundated queens are therefore the only ones capable of producing the fertilized eggs which give rise to females. However, not all queens are inseminated prior to entering hibernation and the absence of

sperm in the spermatheca does not apparently influence the ability to overwinter successfully (Matsuura 1969). Nevertheless, these queens fail to found colonies in the spring despite some initial ovariole development, and it looks likely that the presence of sperm is a necessary prerequisite for colony founding, and further differentiates the two castes. The capacity to found colonies unaided could also, of course, be considered a criterion for queen status.

6. *Pheromone production.* Already proved to exist in *V. orientalis*, and likely to occur in all Vespinae, the pheromone(s) which controls the behaviour of workers and their ovariole development and stimulates the initiation of queen-cell building, must be a highly specialized biochemical attribute of the queen. Pheromones of the 'queen substance' type appear to be produced by all the larger communities of social insects such as ants, honeybees, and termites, and they are probably a necessity for the evolution of large, complex societies. In smaller groups such as bumble bees and *Polistes*, with fewer than one hundred adults in a colony, the behavioural control exercised by dominance hierarchies is apparently quite adequate.

In the Polybiini, which are relatively less advanced than the Vespinae, some species maintain large colonies of more than 11,000 adults (Richards and Richards 1951). Some of these species have a glandular organ in the gaster of females which produces a more copious secretion in the queens (Richards 1971a). This suggests that the populous colonies may be integrated through the agency of pheromones in much the same way as *Vespa* or *Vespula* species.

DETERMINATION OF QUEENS

There are several possibilities which may explain the differentiation of female castes in vespine wasps. In the preceding section, the differences between queens and workers suggest that, despite the relatively small distinctions involved, compared to honeybees and ants for example, their differentiation is unlikely to be a simple matter, and probably results from a combination of factors with possible reinforcement at different stages in their development or during the course of adult life.

Large females which emerge from queen cells are the future queens with a potential for founding a new colony, but they must acquire sufficient reserves of food to survive the hibernation period, and also be inseminated before they can establish a colony and realize their reproductive potential. The remainder of this chapter, however, will be concerned with the factors which lead to the differentiation of queens in mature colonies.

Determination at the Egg Stage

A theory of caste determination at the egg stage has been postulated by Flanders (1953, 1957), based principally on studies of solitary Hymenoptera and the honeybee. Briefly, Flanders suggests that yolk-replete eggs give rise to queens and eggs with a reduced amount of yolk become workers; differential absorption occurring in the oviduct with ovisorption being greatest when the oviposition rate is low. But most workers in *Vespula* colonies are produced in the earlier stages of the colony cycle when the oviposition rate is high, and queens when the rate has declined. In a modification of his theory, Flanders (1962) proposed that any diploid egg could produce a queen, providing the larva from an egg with reduced yolk was adequately fed. This means in effect that a predisposition for either caste at the egg stage may be reversed by subsequent treatment during the larval stage. It seems very unlikely that caste determination could be determined at the egg stage in social wasps, especially as the transfer of eggs from queen to worker cells results in progeny identical to workers in their morphology and behaviour (Montagner 1967).

Chronological Factors

In less specialized wasps, the age of the wasp may be an important feature in determining which females lay eggs and which perform other duties in the colony. Roubaud (1916) reported that in the polybiine wasp *Belonogaster*, immature females pass through a brood-nursing and foraging phase before becoming sexually mature. This is an extremely primitive form of differentiation because all females will have an equal status once they have matured. However, Richards (1969) found evidence of small morphological differences between the females, so perhaps *Belonogaster* does not rely entirely on an age-specific differentiation of castes as originally proposed. In *Polistes*, Pardi (1948) found that the dominance hierarchy among females was based primarily on their order of emergence, the first females to appear being the more dominant, at least in the early stages of colony development.

Cyclic factors of various kinds probably contribute to caste differentiation directly or indirectly. For example, Deleurance (1949) found that, under laboratory conditions, *Polistes* colonies will produce males and queens after a fixed period of time irrespective of the season. This is presumably due to a developmental cycle in the queen. Seasonal fluctuations in climatic conditions and the availability of food almost certainly play some part in the success of colony development and, ultimately, the production of the female reproductives.

Differential Feeding at the Adult Stage

In *Vespula*, where the caste status is distinct and irreversible, different feeding habits of the adult queens and workers could not determine caste, although they undoubtedly reinforce the existing polymorphism. For example, the deposition of fat by the queen results from feeding after emergence, while the cumulative effects of foraging activity and a small or inadequate food supply maintain the worker's ovaries in an undeveloped state.

In *Polistes* the regurgitation of food from subordinate to dominant wasps during trophallactic exchange plays an important part in their dominance hierarchies and enables egg-layers to maintain their dominant position (Pardi 1948).

Differential Feeding of Larvae

In those wasps with morphological or anatomical characters separating the castes, the differences must result primarily from variations in the quantity or quality of food received during the larval stage. In *Vespula* species, the queens are larger than workers with few structural differences between castes, although in one American species, *Vespula squamosa* (Drury), the difference in colour is sufficiently striking to have led early taxonomists to place queens and workers as different species. A difference in size rather than shape is most easily interpreted

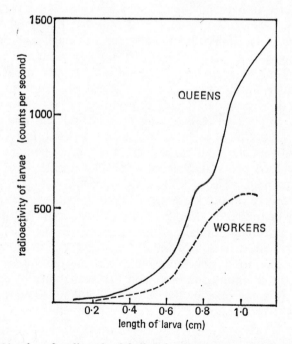

Figure 79. Uptake of radioactive-labelled food given by workers to queen and worker larvae (after Montagner 1967).

as resulting from differences in quantity or supply-rate of food, rather than its quality. Montagner (1963) has demonstrated a difference in food supply by labelling the adult food with radioactive tracers and measuring the subsequent radioactivity of worker and queen larvae of comparable size. It was discovered that queens received almost twice as much labelled food by the time the larvae had grown to 1·2 cm in length (Fig. 79).

It is not clear at what stage during development the female larva in a queen cell can be designated a queen, but the plasticity of caste status possibly continues throughout the first three larval instars for, during these stages, there is no difference in size between workers and queens. The major size increase occurs during the fourth and fifth instars (Potter 1965). Males as well as females are significantly larger if reared from queen cells (Fig. 74), the factors which promote the difference being stimulated more by cell size than the prospective caste or sex of the larva. Queen cells may stimulate workers to feed the larvae within them at a greater rate than the progeny in worker cells, or simply, that the larvae continue to grow, and be fed, until they fill the cell. Montagner's (1967) studies confirm the importance of cell size.

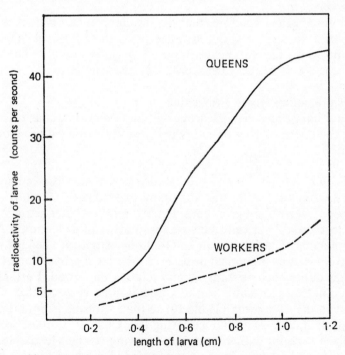

Figure 80. Uptake of radioactive-labelled secretions of workers by queen and worker larvae (after Montagner 1966a).

Hand rearing of larvae transferred from queen cells to worker cells resulted in typical worker-like adults as a result of under-feeding (Spradbery 1963), while Montagner (personal communication) succeeded in rearing queen-like adults from larvae removed from worker cells by feeding them lavishly. By transferring young larvae from queen to worker cells and *vice versa*, Montagner (1967) found that the adults produced from worker cells were identical to workers, although those from queen cells were somewhat intermediate in size and they lived no longer than 10 days. Montagner suggests that perhaps some vital element in the diet was lacking or in too small a quantity to produce a fully developed queen. On this evidence, it appears that to become a queen, the larvae must be exposed to 'queen-making' factors throughout most of its larval life.

In a significant series of experiments, Montagner (1966a) incorporated radioactive tracers into the adult's food until the tracers were taken up by their tissues. When larvae in queen and worker combs were offered to these adults, it was discovered that after 48 hours, the larvae became radioactive, the queens far more so than the workers (Fig. 80). The radioactivity detected in the larvae was probably derived from one of the glands, the secretion being inequally distributed to larvae in queen and worker cells.

It would appear, therefore, that the developmental divergence which results in a worker or a queen takes place during larval life, and is determined by a feeding régime imposed by the size of cell. The dietary differences are quantitative and probably also qualitative.

Factors promoting Queen Production

Several important changes occur within Vespine colonies before and during the queen rearing period which would favour the production of queens.

Division of labour. It has been shown earlier that the expansion of the nest structure, with the attendant expenditure of effort during excavation and building, is considerably reduced after early August, with less than a 2 per cent increase in numbers of cells during August and September. The decrease in nest building activities, when the worker population is at its numerical peak, releases a large proportion of adults for other duties such as foraging and tending the brood. Furthermore, the accumulation of adult workers at this time is associated with an increase in their longevity (Table 19) so that, with the temporal pattern of pulp, flesh, and then fluid gathering (see Chapter 6), there would be more food-foraging rather than pulp-foraging workers available.

The seasonal increase in the average size of workers permits heavier loads of food to be brought back to the colony, for Herold (1952) has demonstrated that the larger the wasp, the more it can carry, while a decrease in the wing-loading factor (weight/wing length) (Spradbery 1972) would emphasize this capacity. A possible result of the increase in numbers and size of workers is the differentiation of a distinct foraging force, larger in size than the workers remaining in the colony. The pre-foraging period of the young worker increases at about or just before the period of queen rearing (Potter 1965) so that a population of sedentary or 'brood-nursing' workers may build up and thereby provide better brood-tending conditions in the colony. Gaul (1948) suggests that there is a segregation of a 'brood-nurse' group during queen-rearing in American *Vespula* colonies.

The larva : worker ratio. During the early part of the colony's growth, the numbers of adults relative to larvae is high, such that each worker is 'responsible' for seven or more larvae. With the increase in the relative abundance of workers towards the end of July, the larva : worker ratio drops to unity (Fig. 81). To achieve the decrease in larva : worker ratio and thereby increase the trophic advantage of larvae, there must be an increase in the absolute number of adults or decrease in number of larvae. In the case of *Paravespula* colonies it is probably a combination of these factors which promotes the decrease. For example, the oviposition rate (and subsequently the number of immature stages) falls off after late July, but the decrease in number of adults would not be realized until considerably later (4-6 weeks at least, see Fig. 59). Perhaps a major contribution to the decrease in larva : worker ratio results from the marked increase in worker longevity from 12-14 days in June and July to 22 days in August (Potter 1965). The decrease in larva : worker ratio has also been noted in bumble bee colonies by Cumber (1949) and Polybiini by Richards and Richards (1951) and is probably one of the more significant cyclic changes occurring in social insect colonies at queen-rearing time. It is interesting that in the overwintering colonies of *P. germanica* in Australasia, queen rearing is also conducted throughout the winter months when food is not so abundant, and Thomas (1960) suggests that queen rearing may be a response to adverse conditions.

Where caste differences are weak, or based primarily on size, it is more likely that a quantitative difference is mainly responsible rather than special 'royal food' in the form of glandular secretions. With the high level of adult trophallaxis it would seem that any special glandular secretions of the workers might be widely spread in the colony, and it is difficult to visualize how a qualitative/glandular component could operate effectively, unless – as Montagner's work suggests – a gland, such as the hypopharyngeal, secretes a specific queen-promoting substance or enzyme complex which determines caste or enables better assimilation of a more abundant and richer food source.

The Initiation of Queen Cells. The Vespinae are the only wasps which construct special cells for rearing queen brood and these larger cells must represent the initial requisite for queen rearing for, without them, the colony is unable to produce queens even if all other physical and trophic conditions were satisfied. Thus, the crucial stage in the maturation of the wasp colony is the initiation of queen cells at the appropriate time. The construction of queen cells in individual colonies occurs at widely different times during the season (see Fig. 81) and it appears unlikely that their initiation is made in response to seasonal factors such as photoperiod. The size of the colony is probably not critical either because queen cells are found in colonies of widely

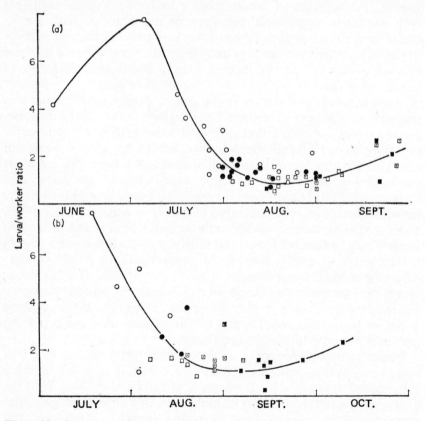

Figure 81. Larva : worker ratio in colonies of (a) *Paravespula vulgaris* and (b) *P. germanica*;

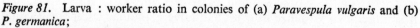

○ workers only; ● males present; □ queen cells present; ▣ queen pupae present; ■ young queens present (from Spradbery 1971).

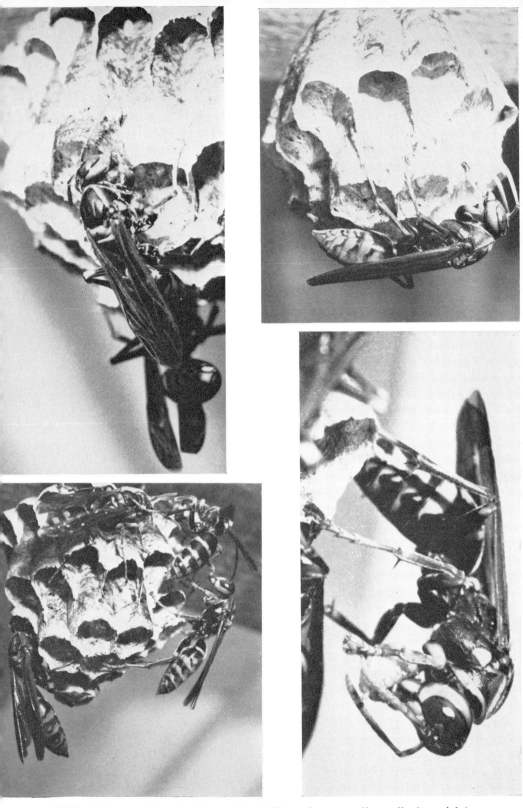

XXV. *Polistes jadwigae* in Japan: (top left) worker extending cell; (top right) foundress queen on embryo nest; (bottom left) same nest after emergence of workers; (bottom right) worker malaxating caterpillar prey after returning to nest.

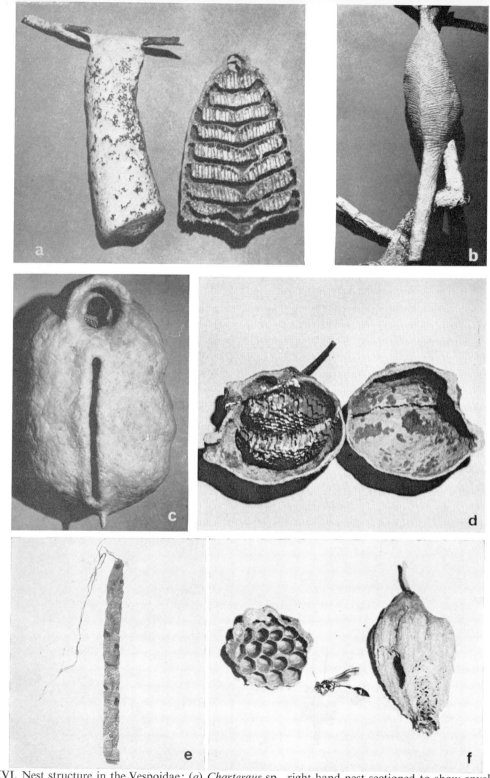

XXVI. Nest structure in the Vespoidae: (*a*) *Chartergus* sp., right-hand nest sectioned to show envelope fixed to combs and holes in centre of combs for passage-way; (*b*) *Parachartergus fraternus* (Grib.), with spout-like entrance; (*c*) *Polybia singularis* Ducke, clay nest with slit-like opening and ring above through which the supporting branch passed; (*d*) *Polybia emaciata* Lucas clay nest with lateral entrance hole; (*e*) *Parischnogaster striatula* (du Buysson), a rope-like nest suspended from a rootlet; (*f*) *Stenogaster micans* (Saussure), nest at left has envelope removed to show comb.

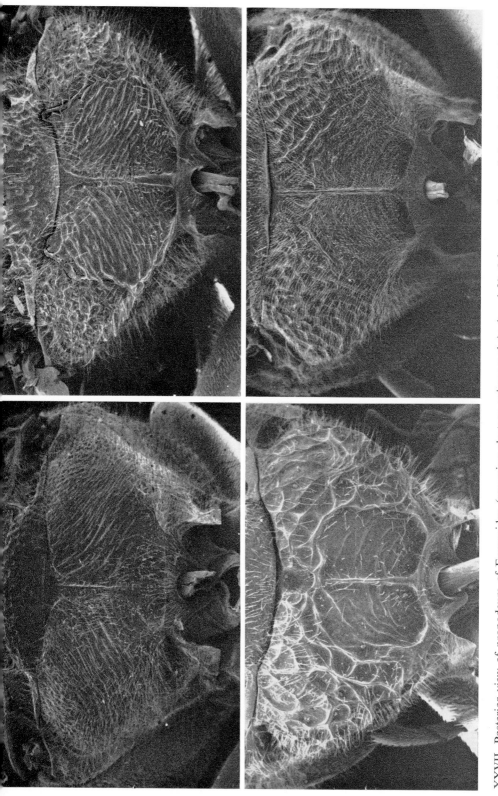

XXVII. Posterior view of propodeum of Eumenidae (scanning electron micrographs): (top left) *Odynerus melanocephalus*; (top right) *Euodynerus quadrifasciatus*; (bottom left) *Symmorphus gracilis*; (bottom right) *Pseudepipona herrichii*.

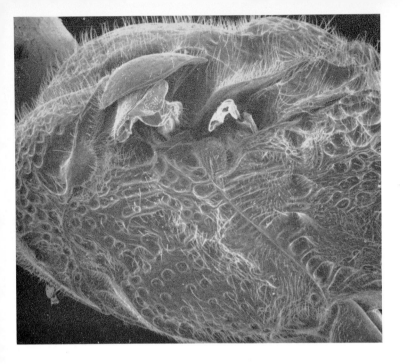

XXVIII. Lateral view of thorax of *Symmorphus* species; (above) *S. sinuatissimus;* (below) S. connexus.

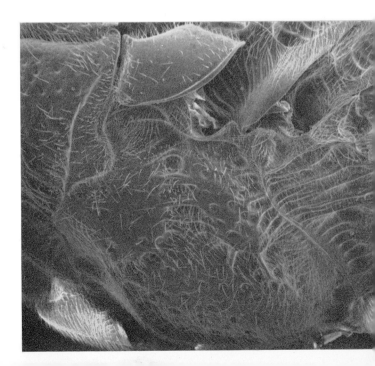

differing sizes, although there may be a minimum size below which they are unlikely to be constructed.

The building of queen cells coincides with the decrease in the larva : worker ratio and there could be some correlation between population changes and queen-cell initiation. However, several colonies with a larva : worker ratio of unity in late August did not have queen cells (Fig. 81), and when Potter (1965) artificially decreased the ratio by adding workers to a colony, the behaviour of the wasps did not change significantly and no queen cells were built for several weeks.

The studies of Ishay and his co-workers have demonstrated the existence of a queen-produced pheromone which stimulates the building of queen cells when offered to a colony in the absence of a queen. How this pheromone is produced and the details of its action on worker behaviour are not entirely clear. Presumably the queen emits the pheromone in response to endogenous factors – possibly her physiological age, or in response to external factors such as population density or a component of the population (e.g. pupal density). It is perhaps easier to visualize a pheromone being emitted during the early part of the season which would inhibit ovariole development in workers and prevent queen-cell building but, with its exhaustion due to ageing of the foundress, the lack of pheromone leads to queen cell initiation. This kind of situation is more redolent of the honeybee and may occur in *Vespula* species. A point which mitigates against this theory is that the removal of a queen, and hence the inhibiting pheromone, does not stimulate queen-cell construction by the workers. Nevertheless, the physiological age of the queen is likely to be the major influence in queen-cell initiation. Under normal conditions, once queen-cell building is begun, there is a complete cessation of worker-cell construction, but when Potter (1965) transferred a queen from a juvenile colony to a queen-producing colony, the workers reverted to worker-cell building and this behaviour was maintained for many weeks. When the queen from the queen-producing colony was transferred to the juvenile colony, the latter immediately began the construction of queen cells. It seems clear, therefore, that the queen is the dominant influence in queen-cell initiation, probably through the agency of pheromones.

Colonies which begin queen-cell building earlier in the season appear to limit the type and amount of brood, because a large proportion of the queen cells are left empty or, alternatively, the brood is predominantly or exclusively male. This suggests that in colonies which have not attained other queen-rearing requirements such as trophic or physical conditions, the queen is able to control the production of brood by differential oviposition.

In conclusion, it is seen that in the Vespinae, the initiation of queen cells is the most important event leading to queen production, but

R

other conditions such as relatively high and constant nest temperatures, and an adequate worker force to exploit the abundant food resources in midsummer and early autumn, must all contribute to provide optimum conditions for this the most crucial activity in the wasp's annual cycle.

CHAPTER 10

THE END OF THE SEASON

The males and queens which are produced towards the latter stages of the seasonal cycle, spend some time within the nest (about one week according to Gaul (1951) and two to six weeks in *V. orientalis* (Ishay and others 1970) and *P. germanica* (personal observations)) during which time they feed on larval saliva and the food brought in by the foragers. Queens also forage outside the nest for food, contrary to Gaul's (1951) observations on American Vespinae, for I have frequently seen young queens make typical orientation flights during the early autumn and up to 30 queens per hour returning to observation colonies. Males also make occasional orientation flights although I have never seen a male returning to the nest. Schultz-Langner (1954) records that males of *P. germanica* do not return to the parental nest but rest in groups in the open. The flight activity of the reproductives may last up to six weeks or more and during this time, the mating of wasps takes place and the social organization of the colony begins to break down until, finally, the old founding queen dies, the workers desert the nest or die, and the paper structure of the nest begins to crumble, hastened by the scavenging activities of other organisms.

DISINTEGRATION OF SOCIAL ORGANIZATION

With the appearance of young queens and the death or physiological breakdown of the old queen, the social life of the colony disintegrates. One of the features of this final phase in colony life is the destruction which occurs in the nest; larvae and even pupae are ripped from their cells and frequently carried outside to be dropped some distance away. Many workers simply leave the nest and may establish queen-less aggregations. I have seen several of these para-social groups in an outhouse at Rothamsted where aggregations of up to twenty workers were seen building formless carton structures, foraging for woodpulp

243

and food, and engaging in trophallactic activities. Nevertheless, these groups are not maintained for more than a few weeks and they soon die.

The stage when brood fails to be tended and social life breaks up has been called '*couvain abortif*' by the French entomologists Deleurance (1950) and Montagner (1966c, 1967) who studied this phenomenon in *Polistes* and *Paravespula* species respectively. This period is initiated when young queens begin to emerge, for they disturb the social hierarchies previously established so that dominance struggles break out between workers. These struggles may become quite violent and I

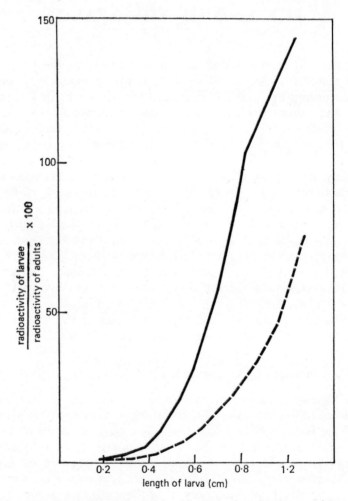

Figure 82.   Relative radioactivity (= food intake) of worker larvae of *Paravespula germanica* before (solid line) and during (dashed line) the abortive brood stage (after Montagner 1967).

have often seen workers fighting on the envelope of a nest, even attempting to use the sting in an attempt to establish dominance over another worker. One of the major results of these activities is the decrease in attention given to the larvae, especially those in worker cells. As Montagner showed, by maintaining adults on food containing a radioactive tracer, the quantity of food given to worker larvae during the abortive brood stage is reduced by a half (Fig. 82). Larvae in queen cells however are not neglected, indeed they are abundantly fed, but at the expense of brood in worker cells. With reduced feeding, many larvae remain in the same instar for two to three weeks before finally dying. It is these larvae which are defined as abortive brood.

The reasons for underfeeding the larvae are complex – dominance struggles among the workers occupy much of their time, but other factors contribute to the decrease in larval care. The decline in the queen's oviposition rate results in progressively fewer diploid eggs being laid in worker cells so that recruitment of workers to the adult population decreases. This results in an increase in the average age of adult workers. It was noted earlier (Chapter 6) that workers over the age of 15 days rarely feed the larvae, possibly because of a degeneration of certain glands implicated in larval feeding. With fewer workers and an increasing proportion of them ineffective as nurses, the larvae are inevitably neglected. A further consideration is the activity of males, for they constantly feed on larval secretions, draining them of resources given by the workers.

Brood from an aborting colony is itself unattractive to prospective nurse wasps. When offered to workers with brood from a pre-abortive colony it receives only half as much 'glandular food' from the tending adults (Montagner 1967). As conditions deteriorate in the colony, thermal regulation becomes less efficient and, with a drop in the optimum temperature, disturbances in development may occur. For example, A. D. Johnston (personal communication) has seen apterous wasps in colonies during the late autumn.

MATING BEHAVIOUR

Mating normally occurs on warm, bright days and is preceded by the nuptial flights of the males which frequently congregate around trees or shrubs, constantly flying in a series of figure-of-eights (Thomas 1960). These mating 'swarms' have been observed several times and seem to have a characteristic pattern. Wynne-Edwards (1962) found a group of several hundred *D. norwegica* males, attended by a few workers, on a rocky summit in Scotland, and Pack-Beresford (1901) caught 128 male *V. austriaca* which were flying round a fir tree in Ireland. Sandemann (1938) gives an account of the swarming of male

D. sylvestris in Wales. On a hot, cloudless day in August, males were seen flying round the gorse bushes (*Ulex* sp.) at the top of a cliff. About 50 males were involved in each swarm, and at least four such swarms were seen at the same time, each apparently 'occupying' a gorse bush. According to Yoshikawa (1959) the males and queens of several Japanese *Polistes* species leave their nests and aggregate in temporary shelters. Mating activity within these aggregations does not occur until they become sexually mature at which point the temporary associations disperse as mating activities begin. In a *Polistes* species in America, the males form tight clusters near the parental nest and await the young queens, copulation taking place near or even on the original nest (Rau 1929). I have seen swarms of male *V. rufa* in Dorset hovering around the taller trees in a pine plantation, but during cool or cloudy days these aggregations were never observed. The *V. rufa* males were active for a period of about three weeks in late August and on two occasions queens were seen flying rapidly into areas where males aggregated, their presence stimulating more intense flight activity by the males.

Mating probably occurs near the nest entrance from time to time. Hamilton (personal communication) has seen a tightly knit ball of male *D. sylvestris* near the entrance of their nest, and it can be confidently assumed that one or more queens were involved in the cluster, and A. D. Johnston (personal communication) has observed *P. germanica* pairing at the entrance to their nest.

In Sandemann's (1938) observations on *D. sylvestris* a queen was found on a gorse bush with a cluster of about 15 males forming a compact mass around her which eventually hid her from view. Males which congregate at selected sites may attract virgin queens by 'marking' the surrounding areas like bumble bees or emitting a characteristic odour or sex pheromone, but there is as yet little evidence for such behaviour in the social wasps. Queens certainly attract males at close quarters, for if a group of males is kept in a box and a queen is introduced, they immediately approach her and attempt to copulate (Plate XXIIb). After Sandemann had caught and killed the queen he had been observing in the mating cluster, he put the dead female on a gorse bush. At once, males arrived and attempted to copulate with the corpse, and eventually a group of 20 of them congregated around the queen's body. This observation shows that queens probably emit a sex attractant. The response threshold of males is quite low, however, for they will attempt to copulate with worker wasps or even passing honeybee workers (Schultz-Langner 1954). Thomas (1960) noted that males which have successfully inseminated a queen are frequently attractive to other males, the male possibly becoming contaminated with the queen's sex attractant.

There are no records of mating within the nest, but the ease of obtaining mating under confined conditions suggests that this may occur, while the records of large aggregations of hibernating queens in the parental nest (e.g. Free and Butler 1959) support this view although these queens could have returned after mating outside the nest.

The behaviour of mating wasps has been recorded infrequently and detailed accounts are few. One of the earlier and more detailed descriptions is that by Professor Sir Edward Poulton (quoted in Richards, 1937) who discovered a *P. germanica* queen *in copula* on a pavement in Oxford. Professor Poulton's delightful account which follows will be used as the basis for the description of pairing.

'This was the first time that I had seen a living pair of any wasp in the genus (*Vespula*), and I was anxious to capture them and observe the behaviour of both sexes. Disturbed by my attempts the pair, drawn by the fluttering wings of the female, moved fairly rapidly along the pavement but was unable to rise. Two or three times I managed to induce them to enter my hat, but the female, dragging the male, instantly climbed to the brim and flew, taking off at a height of two or three feet from the pavement, she was, however, quite unable to maintain this level and gradually sank until the ground was reached after a flight of several yards. The last of these attempts to escape ended in the road with its constant stream of motor traffic. This was a risk which I felt must not be repeated and accordingly pressed the hat against my body as soon as the wasps had entered it. Thus safely enclosed they were easily taken to my house which was near at hand. It was evident that *coitus* at this stage is not to be ended by repeated and very considerable disturbance. Within the house the female at once began a series of attempts to induce the male to withdraw. Her behaviour was characteristic. She assumed a position which enabled her to mount the back of the male and seize with her widely opened mandibles the dorsal surface of an anterior abdominal segment. "Seize" is an incorrect term, for the polished exoskeleton did not admit of seizure, but the closing mandibles would certainly cause a tactile stimulus. The female then withdrew to a slightly more posterior position where her mandibles again embraced and closed at the mid-dorsal line of the male's abdomen. Repeating this process many times and rapidly, the mandibles reached and worked upon the male intromittent organ. The armature was never visible. The impression was again that of tactile stimulus and not of attempt to sever or in any way injure the organ. The mandibles at this point opened and closed many times (unlike the single movement at each withdrawal posteriorly), but finally desisted when the efforts were fruitless. The whole process I have described occupied but a few seconds and I saw it repeated several times during the brief period of captivity in the box. In every instance the female mandibles embraced the dorsal surface of an anterior abdominal segment and reached the male organ after a series of backward movements and embracings. Finally, less than half an hour after the capture, the male withdrew at the close of an attempt which appeared to be precisely similar to others made by the female. I gained the impression that the male's behaviour was a voluntary response to tactile stimulus.'

Donisthorpe (1917) describes a similar encounter with *P. vulgaris* in a street at Putney. The wasps were unable to fly properly and the male was occasionally dragged along on his back behind the female. The most striking habit during copulation is the nibbling of the male abdomen by the queen (Plate XXII). When the male approaches a female, it is normally from behind, stimulating the queen with the antennae and fanning its wings as he climbs on to her back. Once the male has inserted the aedeagus into the female, thereby displacing the sting, the positions are reversed so that the queen appears to be mounting the male. It is in this position that the queen can then effectively grip the male with her mandibles. As suggested in Poulton's account, the nibbling action by the queen is most likely to be stimulatory for the action is maintained for much of the time during copulation, does not increase in intensity, and does not seem to terminate pairing. Males may copulate repeatedly while queens in captivity will pair several times with different males (Thomas 1960).

What happens to queens immediately after mating is not clear. Thomas (1960) suggests that they return to the nest for a brief period before their final departure in search of hibernation sites.

As winter approaches, social wasps are once more represented solely by queens. Some exceptions to this normal state of affairs have been reported from time to time, namely the occurrence of males as late as 1 January (Daecke 1905), while flourishing colonies have been recorded as late as mid-November in the Isle of Wight (Goodall 1924) and late December in Ireland (Barrington 1900). During every mild winter in Enniskerry, Ireland, Barrington reports that colonies continue into January but they suddenly die out following the first heavy frost. Where *P. germanica* has been accidentally introduced into regions with milder climates, successful overwintering of colonies may occur. In these cases, the end of the season imposed by the climatic régime of a European winter becomes a period of consolidation. Foraging activities are maintained and brood rearing continued for a further five months, although the nest structure is not enlarged appreciably. During most of this time, males and queens are produced, increasing the reproductive potential of these colonies many times compared to the European situation. With the approach of spring, the overwintered colony starts the new season with a massive advantage compared to the queen initiating a colony on her own, and this is reflected in the enormous size these colonies attain during the next six months or so of another season (see Chapter 7 for details).

CHAPTER 11

PARASITES, PREDATORS AND COMMENSALS

The Fauna Associated with Wasps and their Colonies

The wasp colony with its paper nest structure and large population of adults and brood, is a rich habitat for a wide range of associated organisms. Many arthropods of diverse habits frequent colonies of wasps, some predatory on adults or brood, others feeding on the dead remains of wasps in the midden at the bottom of the nest, while some utilize the moulds which develop on the carcass of wasps or the nest carton.

Numerous species of birds take adult wasps while mammals such as the badger frequently feed on brood-filled combs.

A wide range of parasitic organisms, from parasitoid Hymenoptera to nematode worms, are known to infest adult and immature wasps, and many of them are elegantly adapted for feeding at the expense of wasps without endangering their own lives in the hostile environment of the colony.

Wasps probably succumb to diseases from time to time although there is no firm evidence that pathogenic micro-organisms play an important role in the lives of wasps. Stone (1864b, 1865) reports that during a year of wasp abundance, many colonies became diseased with larvae and pupae turning black and decaying rapidly which suggests a virus or bacterial infection. Colonies of *Polybia* in South America may be affected by disease (Bruch 1936) and parasitic protozoa, gregarines, have been found in the guts of the adults (Richards and Richards 1951).

PARASITOIDS AND PARASITES

Under this heading will be included all those insects, mites, and nematodes which are either facultative or obligatory parasites living

on wasp adults or larvae without directly killing them, and parasitoids
whose eggs or larvae are deposited in, on, or near the host which is
then consumed by the larval stage. For convenience, the predatory
larvae of beetles are included here.

Insects

Lepidoptera. Although most Lepidoptera which have been recorded
in wasp nests are essentially scavengers (Table 29), there is one species
of moth, *Aphomia sociella* (L.), which destroys both brood and the
nest fabric. The caterpillars are found in the autumn, feeding on wasp
larvae within their cells. Reichert (1914) found a nest of *D. saxonica*
which had been so decimated by the caterpillars that most of the wasp
brood had been consumed, the colony dying out as a result before
queen production began. The caterpillars spin thick, protective cocoons
in the cells or between combs, the adults emerging the following June
and July.

TABLE 29
Lepidoptera associated with wasp nests

SPECIES	HABITS	SOURCE
PYRALIDAE		
PHYCITINAE		
Ephestia kuehniella Zell.	scavengers	Linsley 1944
Plodia interpunctella (Huebner)		Linsley 1944
GALLERIINAE		
Aphomia sociella (L.)	scavengers, and	Cumber (in Thomas 1960)
Achroia grisella (F.)	predators in	Linsley 1944
Galleria mellonella (L.)	weakened colonies	

A species of *Chalcoela* is predatory on *Polistes* in America and is
one of the most common enemies of this wasp genus in the United
States with between 40 and 48 per cent of colonies affected in some
areas (Nelson 1968). According to Ballou (1934), the moth, *Dicymolomia* sp., has eliminated *Polistes* from some islands in the West Indies.

Diptera. Numerous species of flies are found in wasp colonies with
a few being predatory on the developmental stages of wasps (Table 30).
The most familiar flies associated with colonies are the syrphids
('hover-flies'), *Volucella pellucens*, *V. zonaria*, and *V. inanis* (Fig. 83).
Although primarily a scavenger during larval life, *Volucella* may also
be predatory on larval wasps at the end of the season (Henslow 1849).
Blackith (1957) found that *Volucella* will devour live worker adults and
in one *V. rufa* colony, *Volucella* and a muscid fly had eaten all the
brood, including pupae and teneral adults. Nixon (1934a) has observed

(a)

(b)

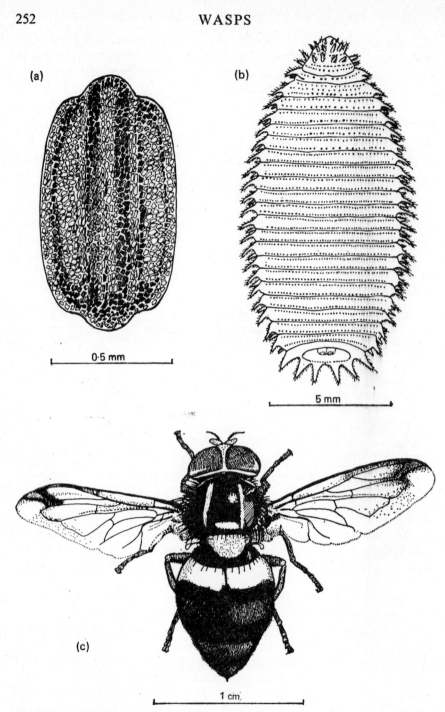

0·5 mm

5 mm

(c)

1 cm.

Figure 83. Volucella inanis: (a) egg (original); (b) larva (after Fraser 1946a);
(c) adult female (original).

V. pellucens females enter the nests of both *P. vulgaris* and *P. germanica* colonies. The fly is not challenged by the workers as it passes through the tunnel, and neither do they pay much attention when it walks over the envelope. The fly was seen sucking fluid from the recently applied damp carton of the envelope prior to ovipositing about 60 eggs (Fig. 83a) in groups of twos and threes. After hatching, the larvae migrate to the bottom of the nest cavity where conditions are very moist and remains of dead larvae, adults, and scavenging insects provide food. The larvae of *Volucella* (Fig. 83b) are covered in conspicuous spines (Fraser 1946a) which possibly aid locomotion for, as mentioned they are able to move from the midden to the combs above. Reichert (1914) has observed a *V. pellucens* larva feed on the saliva of a wasp larva which it previously squeezed to elicit the secretion. When the fly larvae are fully fed, they migrate into the soil beneath the nest and overwinter, pupating in March and April before emerging as adults in May and early June (Fraser 1946b).

TABLE 30
Diptera associated with wasp nests

SPECIES	WASP	HABITS	SOURCE
TIPULIDAE			
Ctenophora (= Dictenidia) bimaculata L.	Vespula sp.	Feed on decaying vegetation (wood)	Collart 1936
TRICHOCERIDAE			
Trichocera hiemalis (De Geer)	Vespula sp.	Feed on detritus and nest fabric	Collart 1936
T. regelationis (L.)	Vespula sp.		
SCATOPSIDAE			
Scatopse notata (L.)	Vespula sp.	Feed on decaying vegetable and animal remains	Collart 1936
SCIARIDAE			
Lycoriella vanderwieli (Schmitz)	Vespula sp.	Feed on decomposing vegetable matter and detritus	Collart 1936
MYCETOPHILIDAE			
Docosia gilvipes (Walker)	Vespula sp.		Collart 1936
PHORIDAE			
Gymnoptera vitripennis (Meigen) syn. genitalis Schmitz	P. vulgaris	Feed in decaying vegetation and nest material	Richards 1932
G. longicostalis Schmitz	Vespula sp.		Collart 1933
Conicera pauxilla Schmitz	P. germanica		Richards 1932
Triphleba lugubris (Meigen)	P. vulgaris		Richards 1932
Diploneura concinna (Meigen)	P. vulgaris		Richards (p.c.)
D. funebris (Meigen)	Vespula sp.		Collart 1933
Megaselia rufipes (Meigen)	Vespula sp.		Collart 1933
PLATYPEZIDAE			
Platypeza modesta (Zetterstedt)	Vespula sp.	Mycetophagous	Collart 1936

continued

SPECIES	WASP	HABITS	SOURCE
SYRPHIDAE			
Volucella pellucens (L.)	*P. vulgaris*	Feed on decomposing	Nixon 1934a
Volucella pellucens (L.)	*V. rufa*	material in midden;	Tuck 1896
Volucella pellucens (L.)	*P. germanica*	also predatory on	Bury 1920
V. inanis (L.)	*P. vulgaris*	larvae and pupae at	Step 1932
V. bombylans (L.)	*P. vulgaris*	end of season	Smith 1852
V. bombylans (L.)	*P. germanica*		Newstead 1891
V. zonaria (Poda)	*P. germanica*		Collart 1933
V. zonaria (Poda)	*P. vulgaris*		Fraser 1946b
Myathropa florea (L.)	*V. rufa*		Tuck 1896
CONOPIDAE			
Myopa sp.	*P. vulgaris*	Endoparasitic	Séguy 1927
Physocephala rufipes (F.)	*V. rufa*		Tuck 1896
Conops flavipes L.	*V. rufa*		Arnold 1966
SEPSIDAE			
Themira lucida (Staeger)	*P. vulgaris*	Saprophagous	Richards (p.c.)
HELOMYZIDAE			
Tephrochlamys canescens (Meigen)	*Vespula* sp.	Feed on decomposing animal remains	Collart 1936
T. laeta (Meigen)	*Vespula* sp.		Collart 1936
SPHAEROCERIDAE			
Paracollinella caenosa Rondani	*Vespula* sp.	Feed on decomposing vegetable and animal	Collart 1936
Crumomyia glacialis Meigen	*Vespula* sp.	remains	Collart 1936
Limosina caenosa (Rondani)	*P. germanica*		Richards 1932
L. palmata Richards	*P. germantica, P. vulgaris*		Richards 1932
L. moesta Villeneuve	*P. germanica*		Richards 1932
L. fungicola Haliday	*P. germanica*		Richards 1932
L. claviventris Strobi	*P. vulgaris*		Richards 1932
L. heteroneura Haliday	*Vespula* sp.		
L. flavipes Meigen	*Vespula* sp.		
MUSCIDAE			
Achanthiptera rohrelliformis (=*inanis*) (Robineau-Desvoidy)	*P. vulgaris*	Feed on decaying organic matter; some possibly carnivorous	Richards 1932
Achanthiptera rohrelliformis (=*inanis*) (Robineau-Desvoidy)	*P. germanica*	on wasp larvae and weakened adults or other dipterous	Newstead 1891
Fannia canicularis (L.)	*V. crabro, P. vulgaris*	larvae	Collart 1933
Fannia canicularis (L.)	*P. germanica*		Newstead 1891
F. hamata (Macquart)	*Vespula* sp.		Karl 1928
F. scalaris (F.)	*Vespula* sp.		Karl 1928
F. coracina (Loew)	*Vespula* sp.		Collart 1933
F. serena (Fallén)	*P. vulgaris*		Richards 1932
F. fuscula (Fallén)	*P. vulgaris*		Richards 1932
F. vesparia (Meade)	*P. germanica*		Newstead 1891
Muscina pabulorum (Fallén)	*V. rufa*		Richards (p.c.)
Muscina (=*Cyrtoneura*) *stabulans* (Fallén)	*P. germanica*		Newstead 1891
Phaonia populi (=*scutellaris*) (Meigen)	*Vespula* sp.		Collart 1933
Phaonia populi (=*scutellaris*) (Meigen)	*Vespula* sp.		Henslow 1849

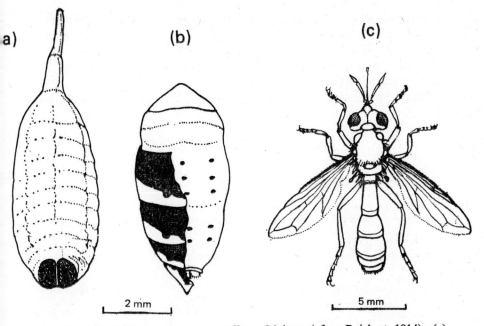

Figure 84. Conopid fly, *Conops scutellatus* Meigen (after Reichert 1914): (a) larva; (b) puparium in wasp abdomen; (c) male adult.

Several species of conopid flies are parasitoids of wasp adults, although only two species have been recorded from nests in Britain (Tuck 1896, Arnold 1966). The adult females congregate at the nest entrance of a wasp colony and dive on to returning foragers, the duration of contact being very brief (0·25 of a second according to Reichert (1914)). The wasps generally retaliate but do not pursue the flies, and during an hour's observation of such behaviour, Reichert did not see any flies caught by wasps. During the brief moment of contact an egg is deposited on the wasp, the resulting larva penetrating the intersegmental membrane and entering the host's abdomen. The larvae (Fig. 84a) have conspicuous spiracles which are reputedly attached to a large trachea or air-sac in the host. When the fly pupates, the puparium fills the distended abdomen of the host (Fig. 84b), the adult emerging via the anterior part of the dead wasp. Arnold (1966) found *C. flavipes* puparia in the abdomens of seven *V. rufa* workers in one nest, the adults emerging during the latter half of June the following year.

Nelson (1968) reports that the calliphorid fly, *Sarcophaga*, is a parasitoid of *Polistes* in America. The fly deposits larvae on the immature wasp which is then consumed prior to pupating in the cell.

F. Ennik (personal communication) has recently found a phorid fly, *Apocephalus* sp., parasitic on American vespine wasps.

Hymenoptera. All the Hymenoptera found in wasp colonies are parasitoids, either on the wasps themselves or the commensals inhabiting the nest (Table 31). The only exceptions are *V. austriaca* which is an obligatory social parasite, and the occasional occurrence of ants from nearby ant nests (see Janet 1903).

Several species of the braconid, *Aspilota,* have been located in wasp

TABLE 31
Hymenoptera associated with wasp nests

SPECIES	WASP	HABITS	SOURCE
BRACONIDAE			
Aspilota concinna (Haliday)	*P. vulgaris*	endoparasitoids of	Newstead 1891
A. vesparum Stelfox	*P. vulgaris*	commensals (Diptera, Phoridae)	Bigneli 1901
ICHNEUMONIDAE			
Sphecophaga vesparum (Curtis) (=*Anomalon vesparum*)	*P. vulgaris*	ectoparasitoids of wasp larvae	Stone 1862, 1865
Sphecophaga vesparum (Curtis) (=*Anomalon vesparum*)	*P. germanica*		Nixon 1935
Sphecophaga vesparum (Curtis) (=*Anomalon vesparum*)	*V. rufa*		Smith 1858
Sphecophaga vesparum (Curtis) (=*Anomalon vesparum*)	*V. crabro*		Reichert 1914
S. thuringiaca Schmiedeknecht	*P. germanica*		Perkins 1937
S. thuringiaca Schmiedeknecht	*P. vulgaris*		Potter 1965
S. thuringiaca Schmiedeknecht	*V. rufa*		Perkins 1937
PTEROMALIDAE—CHALCIDOIDEA			
Nasonia vitripennis (Walker)	*D. saxonica*	endoparasitoids of wasps and	Gauss 1970
Dibrachys vesparum (Ratzeburg)	*D. saxonica*	hypoparasitic on *Sphecophaga* spp.	Gauss 1970
PROCTOTRUPIDAE			
Proctotrupes sp.	*P. vulgaris*	parasitoids of	Newstead 1891
Proctotrupes sp.	*P. germanica*	commensals, especially beetle larvae	Newstead 1891
CHRYSIDIDAE			
Chrysis ignita (L.)	*V. rufa*	parasitoid of wasp larvae	Smith 1852
TIPHIIDAE			
Myrmosa melanocephala (F.)	*D. sylvestris*	parasitoid of wasps	Tuck 1896
VESPIDAE			
Vespula austriaca (Panzer)	*V. rufa*	obligatory social parasite	Robson 1898

colonies where they are endoparasitic within wasps or commensals such as the muscid fly, *Fannia canicularis* (L.) (Bignell 1901). The biology of *Aspilota* is presumably similar to the braconid, *Syntretus*, which parasitizes bumble bees (Alford 1968).

The most familiar hymenopterous parasitoids of social wasps are the ichneumonids, *Sphecophaga vesparum* (Curtis) and *S. thuringiaca* Schmiedeknecht, which have been recorded from several species of *Vespula* and *V. crabro* (Table 31). Remarkably little is known of the habits of *Sphecophaga*, particularly its mode of entry into the nest and its subsequent oviposition. This ichneumonid is possibly facultatively parthenogenetic for, of hundreds of specimens found by Reichert (1914), only one male was located, and Gauss (1968) found only 1·5 per cent males in a total of 933 adults. It is assumed that the female parasitoid deposits eggs on the wasp larvae in their cells, pupation taking place in characteristic cocoons within the cells (Fig. 85a). The two species both have two generations per annum, the cocoons made by the overwintering larvae of *S. vesparum* being characteristically different from those made by the summer brood (Potter 1965). Levels of parasitism by *Sphecophaga* can be high and Reichert (1914) records that

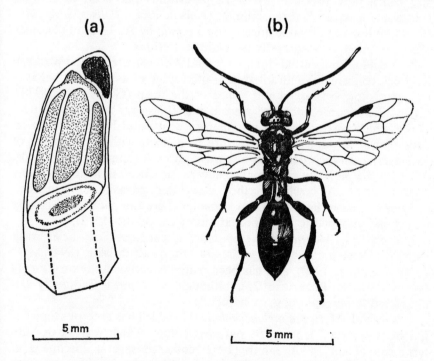

(a)   **(b)**

5 mm   5 mm

Figure 85. *Sphecophaga vesparum*: (a) pupal case in wasp cell (after Potter 1965); (b) adult female (after Reichert 1914 and specimens).

S

all of the pupae in a juvenile colony of *P. vulgaris* were parasitized, most cells containing 3 or 4 *Sphecophaga* pupae. Gauss (1968) found a 5,603-cell nest of *P. vulgaris* which was 20 per cent parasitized, more than one thousand *Sphecophaga* being present or having previously emerged. Biegal (1953) records levels of parasitism as high as 89 per cent with some combs being entirely parasitized. Adults of *Sphecophaga* are active from late June until September, most being recorded during the early part of their flight period (Reichert 1914, Hartigg 1929, Nixon 1935).

Some confusion still exists concerning the names of *Sphecophaga* species since the discovery that the earlier collections of *S. vesparum* were comprised of two species which Perkins (1937) called *S. sericea* Thompson and S. *thuringiaca* Schmiedeknecht. Potter (1965) believes that *S. sericea* is the original *S. vesparum* although he found a third, as yet unnamed, species or polymorph in a *P. vulgaris* colony.

Other ichneumonid species have been found parasitizing social wasps. Species of *Polistophaga* are major parasitoids of *Polistes* with up to 63 per cent of one *Polistes* species being affected and levels of parasitism per colony reaching 23 per cent (Rabb 1960). *Pachysomoides* sp., which may produce up to 12 parasitoids per host, is another common enemy of *Polistes* colonies (Nelson 1968). *Polistophaga fulva* (Cresson) has been bred artificially on *Vespula* by A. T. Gaul (Thomas 1960), although it is normally parasitic on *Polistes*.

A chalcidoid parasitoid, the pteromalid *Nasonia vitripennis* (Walker), has been confirmed as an inhabitant of vespine nests where it behaves as a parasitoid on larvae and pupae of the wasp (Gauss 1968, 1970). Gauss also recorded another pteromalid, *Dibrachys vesparum* (Ratzeburg), which was parasitic on immature wasps and hyperparasitic on *Specophaga*. Several progeny mature in a host, with a maximum of 13 *D. vesparum* recorded from one wasp pupa. A thousand parasitoids, of which the majority are females, may be produced in a single colony (Gauss 1968). A newly-described chalcidoid parasite of American *Polistes* has been discovered in Germany where the parasitised colony was found attached to an imported motor car (Gauss 1972).

The chalcid, *Melittobia*, is reputedly a parasitoid of social wasp colonies where it rapidly decimates the brood (Zabriskie 1894, A. T. Gaul in Thomas 1960), and has been reared experimentally on *Vespula* larvae (Balfour Browne 1922), although it is most frequently encountered in eumenid nests (Chapter 3).

The tiphiid, *Myrmosa melanocephala* (F.) which has apterous females, has been recorded from a *D. sylvestris* colony which was partly subterranean (Tuck 1896). Smith (1852) collected several specimens of *Chrysis ignita* from a *V. rufa* colony, although chrysids are more commonly associated with eumenid wasps (see Chapter 3).

Coleoptera. Some of the most common beetle inhabitants of wasp colonies are members of the Staphilinidae, especially *Velleius* and *Quedius* species (Table 32). Although the majority are scavengers on carrion and faecal material, the abovementioned species occasionally raid the comb area, feeding on wasp larvae and sick or dead adults (Reichert 1914). The beetle larvae are found in autumnal colonies but they leave the nest to overwinter (Biegal 1953), pupation taking place in April with adult emergence beginning in May. *V. dilatatus* (Fig. 88) is predominantly found in *V. crabro* nests and only rarely in colonies of *Vespula* species. The clerid beetle, *Corynetes caeruleus* which has been found in *V. crabro* nests (Tuck 1896), is probably predacious on the hornet brood during its larval stages.

TABLE 32
Coleoptera associated with wasp nests

SPECIES	WASP HOST	HABITS	SOURCE
CARABIDAE			
Trechus quadristriatus (Schrank)	*P. vulgaris*	detritus feeders	Tuck 1896
T. obtusus Erichson	*P. vulgaris*		Tuck 1896
Calathus fuscipes (Goeze)	*P. vulgaris*		Tuck 1896
Metabletus foveatus (Fourcroy)	*P. vulgaris*		Tuck 1896
Metabletus foveatus (Fourcroy)	*P. germanica*		Tuck 1896
Leistus rufescens (F.)	*P. vulgaris*		Newstead 1891
Pterostichus melanarius (Illiger)	*P. vulgaris*		Newstead 1891
Bradycellus verbasci (Duftschmid)	*P. vulgaris*		Newstead 1891
Notiophilus palustris (Duftschmid)	*P. vulgaris*		Tuck 1897
Dromius linearis (Olivier)	*D. sylvestris*		Tuck 1897
Bembidion lampros (Herbst)	*P. vulgaris*		Tuck 1897
HYDROPHILIDAE			
Helophorus nubilis (F.)	*P. germanica*	feed on decomposing	Tuck 1896
H. minutus (F.)	*P. germanica*	nest material	Tuck 1896
H. brevipalpis Bedel	*P. vulgaris*		Tuck 1896
LEIODIDAE (=SILPHIDAE)			
Catops fuliginosus Erichson	*P. vulgaris*	feed on carrion	Tuck 1896
C. grandicollis Erichson	*P. vulgaris*		Tuck 1896
C. nigricans (Spence)	*P. vulgaris*		Tuck 1896
C. nigricans (Spence)	*P. germanica*		Tuck 1896
C. nigrita Erichson	*P. vulgaris*		Tuck 1896
C. tristis (Panzer)	*P. vulgaris*		Tuck 1896
C. chrysomeloides (Panzer)	*P. vulgaris*		Tuck 1896
Sciodrepa watsoni (Spence)	*D. sylvestris*		Tuck 1896

continued

SPECIES	WASP HOST	HABITS	SOURCE
STAPHYLINIDAE			
Atheta (= *Dinaraea*) *angustula* (Gyllenhal)	*V. rufa*	feed on faecal material and carrion.	Tuck 1897
Sepedophilus marshami (Stephens)	—	*Quedius and Velleius* spp.	Tuck 1897
Velleius dilatatus (F.)	*V. crabro*	predatory on wasp	Tuck 1896
Velleius dilatatus (F.)	*P. germanica*	larvae (Britten 1911)	Tuck 1896
Velleius dilatatus (F.)	*P. vulgaris*		Reichert 1914
Aploderus caelatus (Gravenhorst)	*P. vulgaris*		Morley 1898
Quedius brevicornis Thompson	*P. germanica*		Tuck 1897
Q. mesomelinus (Marsham)	*P. vulgaris*		Tuck 1896
Q. picipes (Mannerheim)	*P. vulgaris*		Tuck 1896
Q. othiniensis (Johansen)	*Vespula* sp.		Britten 1911
Philonthus laminatus (Creutzer)	*P. germanica*		Tuck 1897
P. ebeninus (Gravenhorst)	*P. germanica*		Tuck 1897
P. albipes (Gravenhorst)	*P. vulgaris*		Tuck 1896
P. fimetarius (Gravenhorst)	*P. vulgaris*		Tuck 1896
P. cognatus Stephens	*P. vulgaris*		Tuck 1896
P. sordidus (Gravenhorst)	*P. vulgaris*		Tuck 1896
Aleochara moesta (Gravenhorst)	*P. vulgaris*		Tuck 1896
A. curtula (Goeze)	*P. vulgaris*		Tuck 1896
Zyras limbatus (Paykull)	*P. vulgaris*		Tuck 1896
Ocypus olens (Mueller)	*P. vulgaris*		Tuck 1896
Xantholinus fracticornis (Mueller)	*P. vulgaris*		Tuck 1896
Rugilus rufipes Germar	*P. germanica*		Tuck 1896
Stenus bimaculatus Gyllenhal	*P. vulgaris*		Tuck 1896
S. similis (Herbst)	*P. vulgaris*		Tuck 1896
Anotylus nitidulus (Gravenhorst)	*P. vulgaris*		Tuck 1896
A. rugosus (F.)	*P. vulgaris*		Tuck 1896
A. sculpturatus (Gravenhorst)	*P. vulgaris*		Tuck 1896
A. inustus (Gravenhorst)	*P. germanica*		Tuck 1897
Omalium rivulare (Paykull)	*P. vulgaris*		Tuck 1896
Proteinus ovalis Stephens	*P. vulgaris*		Tuck 1896
Megarthrus sinuatocollis (Boisduval and Lacordaire)	*P. vulgaris*		Tuck 1896
Oxypoda spectabilis Maerkel	*Vespula* sp.		Britten 1911
O. vittata Maerkel	*Vespula* sp.		Britten 1911
CLERIDAE			
Corynetes caeruleus (Degeer)	*V. crabro*	probably predacious during larval stage	Tuck 1896
DERMESTIDAE			
Trogoderma spp.	*Vespula* sp.	feed on and destroy	Linsley 1944
Attagenus spp.	*Vespula* sp.	nest fabric	Linsley 1944
Anthrenus museorum (L.)	*Vespula* sp.		Linsley 1944

SPECIES	WASP HOST	HABITS	SOURCE
NITIDULIDAE			
Epuraea unicolor (Olivier)	*P. vulgaris*	feed on fungi and	Tuck 1896
Epuraea unicolor (Olivier)	*P. germanica*	decomposing materials of animal and vegetable origin	Newstead 1891
CUCUJIDAE			
Cryptolestes ferrugineus (Stephens)	*Vespula* sp.	possible predacious	Linsley 1944
RHIZOPHAGIDAE			
Rhizophagus ferrugineus (Paykull)	*Vespula* sp.	feed on decaying vegetable material	Morley 1898
CRYPTOPHAGIDAE			
Cryptophagus scanicus (L.)	*V. crabro*	feed on moulds and	Tuck 1897
Cryptophagus scanicus (L.)	*P. vulgaris*	fungi in nests	Tuck 1896
C. badius Sturm	*V. crabro*		Tuck 1897
C. pubescens Sturm	*P. germanica*		Newstead 1891
C. pubescens Sturm	*P. vulgaris*		Newstead 1891
C. setulosus Sturm	*P. vulgaris*		Newstead 1891
C. setulosus Sturm	*P. germanica*		Tuck 1896
C. micaceus Rey	*V. crabro*		Donisthorpe 1927
Atomaria ruficornis (Marsham)	*P. vulgaris*		Tuck 1896
PHALACRIDAE			
Stilbus testaceus (Panzer)	*P. germanica*	probably feed on decaying nest material	Tuck 1896
LATHRIDIIDAE			
Lathridius minutus (L.)	*Vespula* sp.	fungus feeders	Morley 1898
Aridius nodifer (Westwood)	*P. vulgaris*		Tuck 1896
MYCETOPHAGIDAE			
Mycetophagus quadriguttatus Mueller	*P. vulgaris*	fungus feeder	Tuck 1896
ANOBIIDAE			
Stegobium paniceum (L.)	*Vespula* spp.	feeds on carton of nest	Packard 1878
PTINIDAE			
Ptinus fur (L.)	*V. crabro*	feed on faecal	Butler 1896
Ptinus fur (L.)	*P. germanica*	material in old nests	Tuck 1896
Niptus hololeucus (Faldermann)	*D. sylvestris*		Tuck 1897
RHIPIPHORIDAE			
Metoecus paradoxus (L.)	*P. vulgaris*	parasitic on	Newstead 1891
Metoecus paradoxus (L.)	*P. germanica*	immature stages of	Rouget 1873
Metoecus paradoxus (L.)	*D. sylvestris*	wasps	Hoffer 1883
Metoecus paradoxus (L.)	*V. rufa*		Reichert 1914
CHRYSOMELIDAE			
Phyllotreta vittula Redtenbacher	*P. vulgaris*	vegetable feeder	Tuck 1896
CURCULIONIDAE			
Apion dichroum (=*flavipes*) Bedel	*P. vulgaris*	probably feed on nest fabric	Tuck 1896
A. assimile Kirby	*P. germanica*		Tuck 1897
Otiorrhynchus rugosostriatus (=*scabrosus*) (Goeze)	*P. vulgaris*		Tuck 1896

Metoecus paradoxus, the rhipiphorid beetle, is frequently found in small numbers in subterranean nests of *Vespula*, *Dolichovespula* and *Paravespula* species. This beetle is of special interest because of the phoretic nature of the first-instar larva which is transported to the wasp colony by clinging to the body of a returning forager. The life history was determined by Chapman (1870) and Murray (1870) published figures of the mature larva. The adult beetles (Fig. 86d, e) leave the wasp's nest shortly after emergence and the females lay their eggs in cracks within wood and bark (Chapman 1897) by extruding the long 'telescopic' ovipositor into the cavity (Crawshay 1905). It is not clear whether the eggs overwinter or whether the females hibernate and oviposit in the spring. At any rate, by early summer, the first-instar *M. paradoxus* larvae are found on wooden posts and the boles of trees which wasps visit to collect woodpulp. The first-instar triungulin larva (Fig. 86a), which is about 0·5 mm long, is well adapted for gripping on to a wasp should one approach near enough, for it has long prehensile legs with large suckers at the end of the tibiae, and a large double sucker on the terminal segment of the abdomen. Chapman (1870) has observed the larva, standing up on the terminal suckers, 'pawing the air with its feet, as if in search of some object to lay hold of'. The larva is black, due to the heavily sclerotized exo-skeleton. After arriving in the colony, the larva loosens its grip, falls to the comb and searches for a wasp larva which it enters by biting through the cuticle in the second or third thoracic segment. The site of entry can be seen by the formation of a black patch of scar tissue on the host's cuticle. The larva remains within the host, feeding in the haemocoele, until the wasp spins its cocoon. By this stage the parasitoid has increased in length ten-fold and in diameter six-fold, attaining an overall length of about 4·5 mm. Because there is no moult with the increase in bulk, the sclerites of the phoretic stage are now widely separated by intersegmental membrane (Fig. 86b). With the completion of cocoon spinning, the beetle emerges from the host, generally in the region of the third thoracic segment, casting the first-instar larval skin on the way out. This cast skin may help block the hole in the host's body for no oozing of haemolymph occurs following the exit of the beetle larva. The second-instar larva moves up the wasp's body and lies like a collar beneath its head (Fig. 87a) where it feeds by sucking at the host's tissues. When it grows to about 6 mm, the beetle moults into the final, third-instar, and continues feeding until the wasp is totally consumed (Fig. 87b). The beetle then pupates in the cell and about two days after wasps emerge from neighbouring cells, the adult beetle chews its way through the pupal capping. Parasitism may be readily deduced because the thoracic segments of the beetle larva press against the wasp's pupal capping, giving it a typical ivory-white appearance,

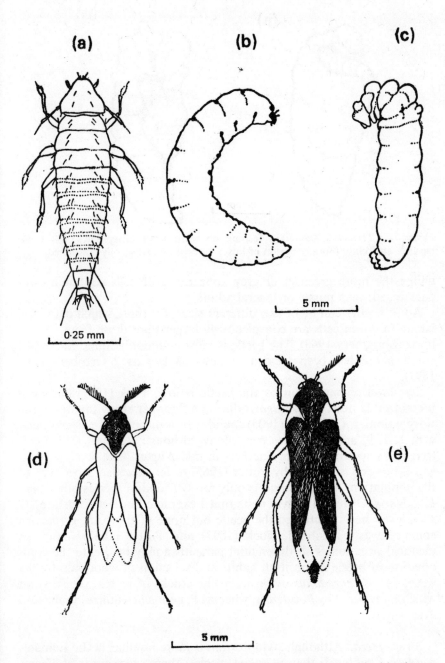

Figure 86. *Metoecus paradoxus* (after Reichert 1914 and specimens): (a) triangulinid larva; (b) second-instar endoparasitic larva; (c) ectoparasitic larval stage; (d) male adult; (e) female adult.

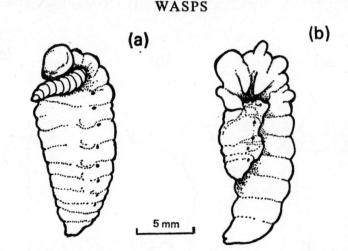

(a)   **(b)**

5 mm

Figure 87. Metoecus paradoxus feeding on wasp larva (after Tuck 1897): (a) parasite encircling thoracic region of host; (b) host almost wholly consumed.

unlike the more greenish or grey appearance of cells containing un-parasitized wasp pupae or teneral adults.

Adult beetles can be of two different sizes, for those which parasitize larvae in queen cells are conspicuously larger than those from worker hosts (Spradbery 1963). The beetle is most commonly found in August colonies but has been located in nests as late as 2 October (Tuck 1897).

The level of parasitism by the beetle is low, Tuck (1897) finding it present in 22 nests of *P. vulgaris* during a five-year study involving 106 wasp colonies. Crawshay (1905) found it in 4 out of 5 *P. vulgaris* nests with 1, 1, 9, and 24 beetles per colony, although Reichert (1914) collected 118 specimens from one nest in mid-August. The level of parasitism in nests examined by Potter (1965) never exceeded 3 per cent of the population. *M. paradoxus* is only rarely found in species other than *P. vulgaris*. Of the 115 wasp nests that I examined in Hertfordshire, 77 *P. vulgaris* nests contained the beetle but none of the 40 *P. germanica* colonies was parasitized. Tuck (1897) and Potter (1965) found an identical situation. This differential parasitism may be due to the combination of beetle oviposition habits and selection of woodpulp by the wasp, for *M. paradoxus* oviposits in the cracks of rotten, moist wood which is favoured by *P. vulgaris*, whereas *P. germanica* utilizes sound and drier wood.

Strepsiptera. Although stylopization is more familiar in the Eumenidae (see Chapter 3) than in social species, there are records of *Vespa*, *Polistes*, and several Polybiini being parasitized (Bohart 1941). Salt and Bequaert (1929) listed 15 species of Polybiini, including

Belonogaster, and 11 Vespinae including a *P. vulgaris* queen from Germany, and a *V. crabro* queen from Japan, the latter being parasitized by *Vespaxenos crabronis* Pierce. In their review of stylopization in the Vespidae, the social species only accounted for 0·9 per cent of all records. Jurine (1816) has described and figured *Xenos vesparum* Rossi, which was found infesting a *Polistes gallicus* L. female. The morphological effects on vespine hosts are slight (Salt 1931), although Strambi (1965, 1966) noted that parasitized queens have reduced ovariole development and an apparent reduction in corpus allatum activity. The corpora allata, found on either side of the oesophagus near the brain, are endocrine organs which control the deposition of yolk in the egg through the agency of the juvenile hormone. Thus, parasitism by a strepsipteran may cause ovariole castration through changes induced in the neurosecretory cells of the corpus allatum. Matsuura (1967a) has observed that stylopized *Vespa* workers remain on the nest and do not forage, and after about two weeks they leave but do not return.

Acarina – The Mites. A few species of mites have been found in wasp colonies one of the earliest records (Stone 1865) describing how an *Acarus* in a *D. sylvestris* colony had attacked the wasp larvae, sucking their haemoloymph through the punctured cuticle until they became emaciated. Vitzthum (1927) found a deutonymph (a phoretic stage) of *Parasitus vesparum* Oudemans in a wasp colony. This mite is only found in wasp nests to which they are transported in the deutonymph stage by adult fly or beetle inhabitants of colonies. Deutonymphs have been found on the fly, *Fannia* sp., in a wasp nest (Biegal 1953). Oviposition and development up to the deutonymph stage takes place in autumnal colonies, hiberation occurring in the nest together with *Fannia* pupae. When the flies emerge from their puparia, the deutonymphs climb on to them and are transferred to new colonies during July and August (Biegal 1953). Biegal considers that there are 6 to 8 generations of mite in the wasp nest, the mites living on the combs, in cells, on the wasp larvae and refuse. More than 500 mites were found in one nest.

Many mites which occur in nests are saprophagous or mycetophagous, feeding on the decaying remains of wasps, their excrement, and nest fabric, and also the moulds which grow on such organic matter. They include the ubiquitous cheese mite, *Tyroglyphus* sp. and another tyroglyphid, *Glyciphagus* sp. (Newstead 1891).

Nematoda – parasitic Worms. Nematodes, unsegmented worms with parasitic and free-living habits, have occasionally been found as parasites within adult wasps. The earliest record was by Baird in

1853 who found a long thread-like nematode in a *P. vulgaris* adult. It was incorrectly named *Gordius vespae vulgaris* by Baird and was later called *Mermis pachysoma* by Linstow (1905). The current identity of this mermithid nematode is *Agamomermis pachysoma* (Welch 1958), the genus containing a group of nematodes known only from immature stages. This nematode has been recorded from male (Kristof 1879 in Janet 1895c) and queen (Waterson and Baylis 1930). *P. vulgaris*, and also from *P. germanica*, and *D. sylvestris* (Blackith and Stevenson 1958).

The larval nematode moves freely among the wasps and fly larvae in a colony according to Kristof (in Janet 1895c) although the mode of entry and the stage at which the host is attacked are unknown. It is likely that the mature mermithid either lays its eggs in the soil or climbs plants during wet weather and oviposits on vegetation. The infection route to the wasp is possibly via caterpillar prey which had previously ingested the eggs. It is likely that the egg hatches in the alimentary canal of the host and the larval nematode bores its way through the gut wall and into the haemocoele where it develops very rapidly. The nematode grows to some considerable length, Beck (1937) finding one 9 cm long, and of fifteen specimens examined by Welch (1958), the mean length of the larval nematode was 4·6 cm (range, 2·2-7·7 cm) with a width of 0·92 mm (range, 0·63-1·01 mm). Parasitized wasps have distended abdomens with the mature larval nematode occupying most of the abdominal region, displacing or even obliterating much of the tracheal and digestive systems (Beck 1937, Gauss 1970). In an histological examination of parasitized *P. germanica* workers, Kloft (1951) noted that the nematode causes histolysis of the flight musculature in the thorax, reduction of fat body, and a degeneration of the ovaries and the connective tissue surrounding the thoracic ganglia. The nematode probably leaves its host at or shortly after the death of the wasp and enters the soil before becoming sexually mature.

Levels of parasitism are generally low, especially in workers and males, although Blackith and Stevenson (1958) found up to 34·6 per cent

TABLE 33
Parasitism by *Agamomermis pachysoma* (after Blackith and Stevenson 1958)

SPECIES		NUMBER SAMPLED	PARASITIZED NUMBER	PER CENT
P. germanica	queens	188	65	34·6
	males	393	1	0·3
	workers	67	3	4·5
P. vulgaris	queens	710	65	9·2
	males	226	0	0
	workers	218	0	0
D. sylvestris	queens	30	5	1·7

parasitism of *P. germanica* queens (Table 33). Fox-Wilson (1946) quotes O. H. Latter finding 100 per cent parasitism in several hundred male wasps, the nematode apparently causing castration of the host.

The tylenchid nematode *Sphaerularia*, which commonly parasitizes bumble bees, can also infect social wasps (G. O. Poinar, personal communication). Infection probably occurs during hibernation of the queens, the infective-stage female nematode entering the host while it is immobile, although the hibernaculae would have to be in moist situations, for locomotion in these nematodes can only take place when the humidity is 100 per cent. Parasitized bumble bees tend to be markedly inactive in the spring for they contain large sacs filled with nematode eggs and larvae which later escape through the gut wall to become free-living.

Poinar and Ennik (1972) have infected *Vespula* workers with the neoplectanid nematode, *Neoplectana carpocapsae*, which interbreeds with the commercially cultured DD-136 strain. Both strains carry the bacterium, *Achromobacter nematophilus*, which causes septicaemia in the host insect. The nematode was introduced by feeding adult wasps on a fruit extract containing infective stage nematodes. These were ingested by the wasps and, through the release of bacteria, killed the hosts. Under conditions of high humidity, the nematode was found breeding in the bodies of dead wasps. Because honeybees are not infected in the same way due to their different feeding habits (sucking rather than lapping-up fluids), the use of *N. carpocapsae* offers an interesting and more highly specific method of wasp control, although nematode locomotion demands a film of water and the humidity in wasp nests is generally less than 100 per cent (85 to 95 per cent relative humidity according to Potter (1965)).

PREDATORS

The major predators of wasps are various species of birds, a few mammals, spiders, and a number of predatory insects. While most predators pick off individual foragers, large mammals such as the badger may destroy entire colonies to obtain brood-filled comb.

Invertebrate Predators

Several species of Odonata (dragonflies) have been recorded with *Vespula* prey, namely *Aeshna cyanea* (Mueller) *A. grandis* (L.) and *Cordulegaster boltonii* (Donovan) (Hobby 1932). O. W. Richards (personal communication) has seen *A. grandis* attack a wasp in Bagley Wood, and bite off the abdomen of its prey.

The Asilidae (robber flies) will also take wasps and those species recorded with vespid prey include *Asilus crabroniformis* L. with queens and workers of *P. germanica*, and *Laphria* spp. attacking *V. rufa* (Séguy 1927).

Hornets frequently prey on wasps and in England, *V. crabro* has been recorded taking *Vespula* spp. (Tooner 1883, Walker 1901). In Japan *Vespa tropica* depends exclusively on *Polistes* and *Parapolybia* adults and brood for feeding its larvae (Matsuura 1968b) while the largest Japanese hornet, *V. mandarinia* Smith, is frequently predatory on other hornets such as *V. xanthoptera* and *V. crabro*, using the brood rather than adults as sources of larval food (Matsuura 1968c) (see Frontispiece).

Occasionally spiders will kill wasps or their webs trap foragers, and queens seeking hibernation quarters are frequently caught (Fox-Wilson 1946). Scott (1930) records how a spider, *Tegenaria atrica*, killed a *P. germanica* worker but was stung by the wasp, both combatants dying as a result of the struggle. Embryo nests are sometimes attacked by foraging centipedes (Chilopoda) whose carnivorous habits may lead to destruction of the colony or result in desertion by the founding queen (Stone 1865).

Vertebrate Predators

Hesse (1916) lists twenty-four bird species as predators on wasps. They include the Shrike, Blackbird, Great Tit, Green Woodpecker, Magpie, Jay, Buzzard, Hobby, Starling, and Hooded Crow. Stachanoff (1928) has seen *V. crabro*, *V. rufa*, and *Paravespula* species taken by Jays, and Newstead (1908) records that the Spotted Flycatcher will feed on *P. vulgaris* and *P. germanica* adults in Britain. Marie (1923) found remains of *P. germanica* queens in the gizzards of young Rooks in France. The Red-backed Shrike occasionally hunts wasps, pinning them to thorns in its 'larder' (Owen 1948).

Of the mammals in the British Isles, the badger is probably the chief predator, but stoats, weasels, and field mice probably disrupt colonies during the incipient stage especially when nests are built in the burrows of small mammals. Latter (1935) has noted badgers digging out wasp colonies, and I have seen the aftermath of badger predation on a *P. vulgaris* colony in Wales (see Fig. 40). A proportion of colonies are destroyed annually at Wisley (Fox-Wilson 1946), and Blackith (1958) found that 7 of 9 colonies at Silwood Park in Berkshire were destroyed by badgers during one year. Blackith considered that it was mainly smaller colonies (less than 500 workers) which were attacked.

In Brazil, quite large colonies of polybiine species, including *Polybia* and *Mischocyttarus* spp., are attacked at night by bats (*Phylloderma stenops*) which consume the brood with apparent impunity from the several hundred adult wasps (Jeanne 1970a). Skunks in North America are also predatory on wasp colonies, in much the same way as the badger in Europe.

COMMENSALS

The majority of organisms found associated with wasp colonies are co-inhabitants, feeding on dead material, faecal products, and other commensals, and probably perform a sanitary function in the colony. Others may be accidental introductions or soil invertebrates which happen to be active in the vicinity of wasp nests.

There are numerous species of fly which are commensal (Table 30), many feeding on the decomposing remains of wasps in the midden at the base of the nest, or mycetophagous, living off the saprophytic fungi which abound on the nest carton, faecal pellets in cells and other organic materials. The mycetophilid and phorid flies are typical of those species which feed on decaying or fungus-ridden vegetable matter, especially at the end of the season when the nest fabric begins to disintegrate. The Sphaeroceridae include a number of species which feed on decomposing animal and vegetable remains, while the Muscidae include several economically important species. For example, the 'European latrine fly' *Fannia scalaris*, and *F. canicularis*, which can cause myiasis in man and other vertebrates, are both found in large numbers in wasp colonies. These flies enter nests during July and August to oviposit, their larvae feeding on the detritus at the bottom of the nest or on the faeces in the cells. They pupate during early November in the earth below nests and overwinter as pupae (Biegal 1953). The muscid, *Acanthiptera inanis*, is a common associate in wasp colonies, the adults emerging during April to June, females ovipositing on the envelope of the nest and the resulting larvae finding their way to the detritus at the base of the nest. These muscids are similar to the syrphids, *Volucella* spp., and may become predatory on wasp larvae or weakened adults, particularly towards the end of the season. They are also predatory at times on beetle larvae, such as *Velleius* spp. (Reichert 1914).

More than 80 species of Coleoptera have been recorded from the colonies of British wasp nests of which only one, *M. paradoxus*, is an obligatory parasitoid on wasps (Table 32). The remainder are mainly saprophagous, although the larvae of some staphylinid beetles may be predatory on wasps. Dermestid beetles destroy the carton of disused nests, while at least one wood-feeding anobiid beetle, *Stegobium paniceum* (L.), has been recorded feeding on the carton (Packard 1878). Wood-boring beetles can do serious damage to nests in reference collections and exhibits. The ptinid beetles are a specialized group which feed exclusively on the hard, dried faecal pellets at the base of cells, producing a fine black powder as they bore in and out of the base of the cells (Butler 1896). *Cryptophagus* species (Fig. 88) normally feed saprophagously but Tuck (1897) remarks that they will occasionally mutilate the antennae of emerging adult wasps.

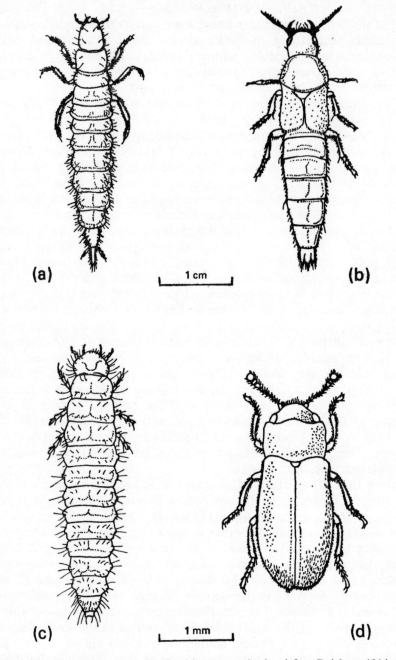

(a)

1 cm

(b)

(c)

1 mm

(d)

Figure 88. Coleoptera associated with wasp colonies (after Reichert 1914 and from specimens): (a), (b) larva and adult of *Velleius dilatatus*; (c), (d) larva and adult of *Cryptophagus pubescens.*

A number of miscellaneous arthropods have also been recorded from wasp colonies, including the thysanuran, *Lepisma saccharina* L., from a *V. crabro* colony (Tuck 1896), and the woodlice, *Porcellio scaber* (Newstead 1891), and *Philoscia muscorum* (Tuck 1896).

CHAPTER 12

THE IMPACT OF WASPS ON MAN

To most people wasps are merely a nuisance and their value in the ecosystem is rarely considered. Yet wasps prey on insect pests of economic importance although this role is probably underrated due to ignorance of their predatory habits. In many countries, the honey stored by some species of wasp forms a useful and tasty addition to man's diet. Immature and adult wasps are eaten in various parts of the world, although the prejudice of western man to an entomological menu would daunt the most enthusiastic entomo-advertising executive.

The use of hornets as test subjects in the study of drugs has shown that their responses are of pharmacological significance (Floru, Ishay and Gitter 1969, Gitter and others 1971). By administering various psychotropic drugs, including LSD 25 (lysergic acid diethylamide), and amphetamines, it was shown that, amongst other reactions, aggressiveness towards members of the same colony was sometimes elicited, distorting the normal behaviour to one with an anti-social pattern.

In this chapter, aspects of sting action and pharmacology, the pest status and beneficial effects of wasps, and methods for their control will be discussed.

THE STING

Perhaps the most outstanding biological feature of the wasp from a layman's viewpoint is its ability to cause pain and sometimes death by stinging. However, the stings they inflict are most often invited by the careless entomologist or in response to the threatening sweep of the rolled-up newspaper. The sting, which is a modification of the original ovipositor, is used almost exclusively in defence of the colony and unprovoked attack by wasps is comparatively rare, although some South American and Asian species have gained notoriety as being particularly aggressive. During the war in South-east Asia, the use of the wasp, *Polybioides*, in booby traps was one of the more barbaric aspects of the hostilities (Evans and Eberhard 1970).

Colony Defence

The range of defensive mechanisms among wasps is wide, some South American species of *Polybia* and *Apoica* have regiments of workers arranged around the outside of the nest, while other species rely on fiercely aggressive neighbouring ant colonies in the same tree (Richards and Richards 1951), and some exhibit visual and auditory warning signals by their movements which vibrate the nest to produce a drumming sound.

In the Brazilian wasp, *Mischocyttarus drewseni*, which builds nests like *Polistes* but with a long, thin supporting pillar, the females rub a repellent on to the stem which inhibits predation by foraging ants (Jeanne 1970b). The secretion is apparently produced by glands located at the terminal sternite.

Wasps and hornets seldom attempt to sting people when they are foraging or otherwise away from the nest, and then only when trapped or severely disturbed. The defence flight of wasps is generally a response to a disturbance of the nest structure and not of individual wasps at the nest entrance, although in looking down the tunnel, the observer may obstruct the flight path and elicit stinging. Returning foragers rarely engage in nest defence and do not apparently communicate impending danger to the other inhabitants, but are in turn stimulated to aggressive behaviour by the activities within the nest (Gaul 1953). Small colonies of *Dolichovespula* and immature colonies of *Paravespula* species tend to be less aggressive than larger colonies.

The number of wasps responding to a stimulus is roughly proportional to the extent of the disturbance, although a colony may become conditioned to a repeated disturbance such as an aerial nest striking the branches of a tree during windy weather. The gentle shaking of an aerial nest or tapping of a subterranean one will arouse a few defenders but a sharp blow will excite the entire colony (Gaul 1948).

When a colony is disturbed, the wasps which rush out on defence flights, operate on an individual level, each one seeking the cause of the disturbance. It is the moving target which attracts most attention, even at some distance from the nest, and it is safer to stand still near a nest than run panic stricken from a disturbed colony. Gaul (1953) determined that a defence flight lasts for between 90 seconds and 5 minutes, the duration depending primarily on weather conditions, high temperatures tending to prolong the flight.

Defending wasps will fly within a radius of about 7 metres of their nest, although if wasps land on or sting a fleeing target, they may be carried a considerable distance before they detach themselves.

T

One of the features of colony defence is an ability by the inmates to recognize their own inhabitants and distinguish intruders. This subject has been mentioned earlier in Chapter 8 where it was shown that colonies probably have a specific odour and that adults and even larvae can be recognized. The intrusion of strange wasps into colonies elicits intensely aggressive behaviour – the inmates forming a circle around the intruder, while one or more leap upon it, attempting to chew off the wings while trying to sting it. Other defenders dart towards the intruder, nipping its legs, antennae, and wings until a worker succeeds in thrusting her sting between abdominal sclerites and into the body of the victim. Even after hostilities, when the intruder is dead, it is frequently the source of aggressive behaviour before it is finally ejected from the nest (Gaul 1941).

In wasp colonies, there are invariably guard wasps positioned at the tunnel entrance, their abundance being determined by the number of adults and time of day. In populous, mature colonies there are always guards present, but in smaller ones, the guards generally occur in the early morning, evening, during bad weather, and at night (Potter 1965). At night it is common to see the entire entrance ringed with the heads of guards wasps (Plate XVIe) which require little provocation to fly up the beam of a torch and attack the observer. When a guard is disturbed it raises itself on the tips of its tarsi, arching the body with the head lowered and abdomen turned down. In this position it vibrates its wings at a particular frequency which apparently stimulates workers within the nest to emerge and run into the entrance tunnel (Potter 1965).

Sting Action

When a wasp stings, it thrusts the first and second valvulae (lancets and sting shaft respectively) into the skin or integument of the victim, and injects venom along a groove in the sting and out through its tip. Details of the mechanism of sting action have been studied in the honeybee (Snodgrass 1956), and these essential features are applicable for most stinging Aculeate Hymenoptera.

When the wasp is about to sting, the oblong plate and sting palps are swung upwards to expose the sting (tips of sheath and lancets) (Plate IIIa), which is then pushed into the victim by a downwards thrust of the abdomen. After the initial contact with the epidermis of the victim penetration is effected by the alternating movements of the lancets on the stylet. Muscles which run from the oblong plate to the quadrate plate contract and relax alternately, causing the quadrate plate to move in a fore and aft motion. This action in turn rocks the triangular plate on its articulation with the base of the oblong plate (Fig. 89), thereby pushing the lancet along the sheath.

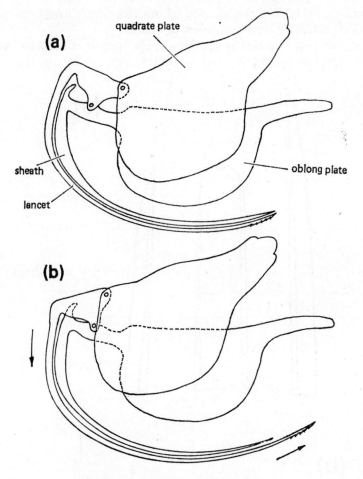

Figure 89. Mechanics of sting action.

The lancets on either side are pushed out along the sheath in alternate thrusts (Fig. 90) and, with the penetration of the barbed lancet tip, they tend to be held in the wound by the barbs (Plate Ib). Although the barbs on the wasp's lancets are small compared to the honeybee, they probably contribute towards deeper penetration in much the same way. To assist penetration the wasp grips tightly to its victim with the legs and, occasionally, the mandibles. After one lancet enters the victim and is locked to the tissue by means of the barbs, the second lancet penetrates further, subsequent alternating thrusts driving the sting more and more deeply into the body.

The movements of the lancets help to force venom from the reservoir (poison sac) down the sting shaft and out through the end of the shaft

(Hermann 1971). The contraction of muscles which invest the poison sac also contribute to the emission of venom.

When venom injection is completed, the sting is withdrawn, mainly by an upward pulling by the abdomen, and partly by the above-

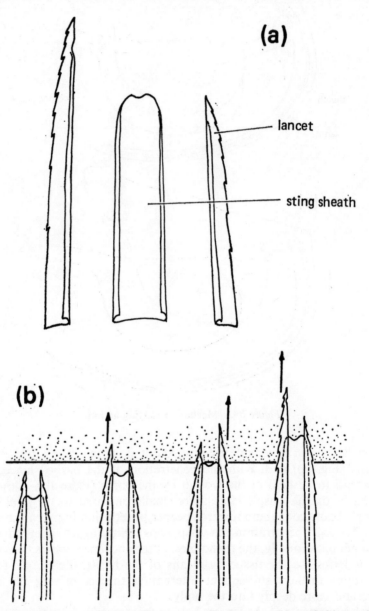

Figure 90. Vespula sting: (a) components of sting tip; (b) probable mode of penetration.

described sawing movements of the lancets. Normally there is no sting autotomy in Vespinae, the barbs not being sufficiently large to lodge into the victim's tissues with resulting self-amputation of the sting apparatus.

The venom from the poison glands is stored in a large reservoir (Fig. 13) which discharges into the bulb formed by the fused second valvulae (Plate IIIb), and from here the venom is passed along the trough formed by the second valvulae (sheath) and the first valvulae (lancets). Venom is produced by the 'acid glands' while an accessory gland, the 'alkaline gland', probably produces a lubricant to assist sting action.

Pharmacology

'The deputy coroner for the Reading division of Berkshire has held an inquest at Mortimer, a village near Reading, touching the death, under extraordinary circumstances, of Mrs. Sarah Marrett, a labourer's wife. Deceased was standing in the road near her house, when a hornet stung her on the right side of her neck. She went indoors, and a neighbour bathed her neck with water and vinegar. However, she fainted almost immediately, and expired in a few minutes, before a medical man could reach the house. The surgeon stated at the inquest that he believed the immediate cause of her death was syncope, the result of nervous shock caused by the sting. The jury returned a verdict in accordance with that opinion.' So reads an 1874 account of death by stinging in a contemporary newspaper. A similar incident occurred in North Wales when the mayor of a provincial town died of a heart attack following a wasp sting (Walker 1901).

These dramatic deaths as a result of wasp stings are fortunately few, but everyone who is stung is made very much aware that the sting causes local pain, occasional swelling, and perhaps even more alarming symptoms. All people react to insect stings and bites, although the symptoms vary much from person to person and some people may become allergic to bee, wasp, and hornet stings (Frankland 1968). Severe allergic responses causing anaphylaxis and death can result from stings, and an account of the biochemical components of venom, its pathological effects, and studies of the clinical alleviation of sensitivity are of considerable medical importance.

Apart from the danger to allergic people, the sting may also affect animals. For example, in Israel it is reported that when a farmer struck a hornet's nest while ploughing, he fled from the field, leaving his mule in harness. The animal reputedly died as a result of the stings incurred (E. Rivnay, personal communication).

For a detailed modern synthesis of insect allergies the reader is referred to the book by C. A. Frazier (1969).

The allergic reaction. An allergic response is a reaction between the injected substance, the allergic substance or allergen, and a specific antibody produced by the subject as a result of the allergen which, together, result in the local formation of histamine and other substances which have a histamine-like effect. In mammalian tissue there are considerable quantities of histamine which may be liberated following an allergic reaction. Histamine, when introduced into the epithelium via a pin prick in the skin, causes an itchy weal with a red flare developing, reaching its maximum effect after fifteen minutes. If, as a result of a sting, there is a more generalized release of histamine, the whole body may itch with urticaria ('nettle rash'), the mucous membranes swell causing sneezing, laryngeal oedema with difficulty in breathing and a feeling of suffocation and, if the bronchial tubes are affected, an asthmatic attack may follow (Frankland 1968).

When a person is stung or bitten by insects from time to time, the individual will develop a sensitivity reaction, the symptom being a local urticaria appearing after a day or so. This papular urticaria irritates and with scratching becomes infected. Further bites or stings may produce no further response at which stage the person has become *desensitized*. But, in some cases, the person may become more and more allergic with successive stings until a stage is reached when the individual has become so allergic to the insect – the anaphylactic stage – that a single sting could cause death. Anaphylaxis is the dramatic situation when a previous sting or stings renders a person dangerously hypersensitive such that a further sting (the 'shocking dose') may lead to death within half an hour or even in a few minutes of being stung. When the allergic stage is reached, each successive sting may cause more severe symptoms, unconsciousness occurring perhaps 20 minutes after stinging, followed by a decrease in this time until the person loses consciousness within 5 minutes. People who have reached this stage of hypersensitization are liable to die if stung again (Frankland 1968).

Sensitization of people can result from being stung by various types of insects such as bees, wasps and hornets, although some people only react to one species or closely allied group of insects. Foubert and Stier (1958) consider that of all wasp and hornet genera, *Vespula* venom is the most potent in producing anaphylaxis.

The quantity of venom (each stinging injects between 0·05 and 0·3 ml) does not appear too critical, for one sting in an acutely allergic person can cause death. Perlman (1955) and Frazier (1969) in reviews of several case histories noted that one adult died after 1,200 stings while another survived 2,243 and a baby suffered only partial shock and anuria from 477 stings. Symptoms following stinging in the human subject include local pain and swelling. When a patient becomes allergic, beside local swelling there is usually a centralized bronchoconstriction, abdominal cramp, diarrhoea, nausea, vomiting, fever, vertigo, laryngeal stridor, shock and uncontrolled bowel and bladder action in more susceptible cases. The pathological results of post-mortem examination of people who have died following stinging may include pulmonary emphysema, cerebral edema, dilation of heart, and epicardial haemorrhage. However, when a patient dies in under five minutes of being stung, no abnormal changes can be seen macroscopically in any organ.

TABLE 34
Deaths from wasp stings in England and Wales 1949-1969*

YEAR	MALES	FEMALES	TOTAL	YEAR	MALES	FEMALES	TOTAL
1949	1	7	8	1960	1	1	2
1950	0	0	0	1961	2	3	5
1951	1	3	4	1962	2	0	2
1952	1	2	3	1963	4	2	6
1953	1	1	2	1964	1	0	1
1954	1	2	3	1965	2	1	3
1955	3	1	4	1966	2	2	4
1956	0	1	1	1967	1	5	6
1957	1	3	4	1968	0	0	0
1958	3	3	6	1969	2	2	4
1959	2	0	2		—	—	—
				TOTAL	31	39	70

* Records kindly made available by the Registrar General of England and Wales.

In England and Wales, the number of people who die as a direct result of wasp stings is given in Table 34, there being 30 cases in two decades. During the period 1949-55, 24 people died as a result of wasp stings and only 9 people were killed by bee stings. In America, there were 101 recorded deaths from wasp stings during 1950-9 (Frazier 1969). According to the Director of the Allergy Clinic at St. Mary's Hospital London, Dr. A. W. Frankland (personal communication), it is likely that these published mortality figures are misleading because many allergic people who die after being stung are misdiagnosed as having died of a coronary, especially if the patient is over the age of 50 years.

Chemical Nature of Venom. The principal component of venom is the protein which produces allergy reactions in people. Several different proteins have been demonstrated in wasp venom, the total number and relative proportions varying among the different genera. Other components of venom include an acetylcholine-like substance, histamine, serotonin, and kinin (Edery and Ishay 1970). Kinins are peptides which cause slow contractions of isolated smooth muscle, lower arterial blood pressure, increase capillary permeability, and produce pain if put on exposed blisters on human skin (Shulman 1967). Wasp kinins can be inactivated by trypsin although the kinin from *V. crabro* venom can not (Bhoola, Calle, and Schachter 1961). Enzymes, including esterases have been demonstrated in *Polistes* venom (Said 1960). Habermann (1972) has reviewed the biochemistry and pharmacology of the peptides and enzymes in wasp and hornet venom.

Treatment. Recommended first-aid treatment for a person who has been stung is remove the sting, if necessary by scraping it off, washing in soap or antiseptic to prevent secondary infection and to rest the affected part and apply ice-cold water to the region. Anti-histamine creams may be rubbed in but they are of doubtful value and a better course of action would be to swallow an anti-histamine tablet which should reduce local or general irritation following a sting. For very sensitive people treatment includes rapid absorption under the tongue of a Neo-epinine tablet or the use of adrenaline in pressurized packs (Frankland 1968). Patients suffering from anaphylaxis are generally given injections of adrenalin, an anti-histamine and, if necessary, hydrocortisone.

Desensitization of sting-susceptible patients has been carried out with some degree of success in many parts of the world. Proprietary preparations are available for desensitizing people who have become allergic to wasp stings. Depending on the method of preparation the course of injections are given intracutaneously or subcutaneously using either whole-insect or pure venom extracts. In America Prince and Secrest (1939) caused a marked reduction in the reactions of patients to stinging by injecting small doses of bee venom, the antigens so produced conferring a degree of protection against bees, wasps and, even ants. Because wasp and hornet venom contain several antigenic fractions with only a few of them common to all species, desensitization to one species does not necessarily confer immunity to the other species (Foubert and Stier 1958) although, generally speaking, immunization confers a fairly broad-spectrum protection against many species of stinging insect (Prince and others 1939).

Edery and Ishay (1970) and Ishay, Gitter and Fischl (1971) have studied the effects of *V. orientalis* venom on laboratory animals and report attempts to produce an antiserum.

Pest Status

Several references in the Old Testament underline the fear of hornets by the inhabitants of the Middle East, the biblical writings accentuating the severity of vengeance for the enemies of the children of Israel by employing the hornet as one of the tools of punishment: 'Moreover, the Lord thy God will send the hornet among them until they that are left and hide themselves from thee will be destroyed,' Deuteronomy vii:20. Even today, the hornet in the Middle East is a pest to be feared, their ravages of fruit crops and honeybee colonies making horticulture and agriculture at times difficult, at other times virtually impossible. In a letter from Dr E. Rivnay of Israel, it was pointed out that hornets are a limiting factor in beekeeping and a serious pest of fruit crops, and much effort and money is expended on protecting agricultural interests from them.

The rate of *V. orientalis* predation of the honeybee has been estimated at 33 bees per hornet per day and at this rate, hives may soon be depleted of adults and become unprotected from the predations of the hornet on honey stores and immature stages (Ishay and others 1967). Similar economic findings have been recorded by Rivnay and Bytinsky-Salz (1949). In Japan, the large hornet, *V. mandarinia* is a scourge of bee colonies for ten workers can destroy a colony within an hour, killing as many as 5,000-7,000 bees by crushing them with their mandibles (Matsuura and Sakagami 1973).* When bee colonies are at their most vulnerable during the winter months, the workers from overwintering colonies of *P. germanica* in New Zealand frequently wipe out entire hives (Thomas 1960). The wasps tend to select a hive (not necessarily the weakest) and by persistent attacks, succeed in overcoming the inhabitants and robbing the honey or sugar stores. One hive lost 7 kg (15 lb) of honey within a week. After a hive has been ravaged in this way, the wasps then turn their attention to another.

Hornets and wasps are frequently found feeding on fruit, and the accidental introduction of *P. vulgaris* into Victoria, Australia has caused some alarm (Anon 1962a). The economic losses to fruit crops have sometimes been exaggerated (Kemper and Döhring 1967) and, in New Zealand, Thomas (1960) points out that the damage to fruit crops for which wasps could be primarily responsible is virtually negligible, especially in well-managed orchards. The official figure for crop losses due to wasps was estimated at less than 1 per cent.

Wasps do not normally feed on sound fruit, their attentions being devoted to over-ripe or bruised fruit, and the sites of previous damage by birds or other agencies. This is particularly true of pears which are damaged by starlings. An exception to this general rule applies to soft fruits such as grapes, peaches, and apricots which may incur primary damage from wasp attack.

Nevertheless, losses attributable to wasps during agricultural operations has been estimated as high as $US200,000 in California during a single year (Hawthorne in Poinar and Ennik 1972), and some private Californian resorts estimate losses of up to $US5,000 annually. In

*In one case, 2,500 bees were killed within three hours by 30 hornets, a rate of one bee per hornet every 14 seconds.

the citrus groves of Arizona, *Polistes* caused up to 20 per cent losses of marketable produce because the local workers refused to collect fruit in the infested orchards (Hopkins 1955).

With the exception of the Middle East and Oriental region, wasps are generally considered pests of secondary importance, their major claim to infamy being their extreme nuisance value, particularly to households, factories making sweetstuffs (chocolate, jam etc.), and people camping or on picnics. In some North American national parks, their nuisance value and potential health hazard by stinging is emphasized by their attraction to trash cans where the wasps scavenge for discarded foodstuffs and prey on the flies which breed in such habitats (Wagner 1961). A further potential source of trouble for which wasps may be responsible, is that their nests may act as natural reservoirs for a range of insect pests of stored food products. Linsley (1944) records several economically important stored-products pests as associates in wasp nests, including the rust-red grain beetle, *Cryptolestes ferrugineus* (Steph.), and the grain moth, *Ephestia kuehniella* Zell.

Wasps as Biotic Agents in Pest Control

Nearly sixty years ago, *Polistes* wasps were encouraged to nest on the perimeter of cottonfields in the West Indian islands of St Vincent and St Kitts to encourage control of the cotton leafworm, *Anomis argillaceae* (Hbn.) (Ballou 1913). Isely (1913) gives a list of Eumenidae which have been recorded preying on insects of economic importance. The list includes such pests as cutworms (*Agrotis* spp., noctuid moths of paramount importance in the U.S.A.); the geometrid moth larvae, *Paleacrita* spp. – canker-worms which are serious pests of American fruit frees; the tinaeid moth, *Depressaria pastinacella* (Duponchel), the parsnip web-worm of Europe and America; the larch sawfly, *Pristiphora erichsonii* (Hartig); and *Margaritia stricticalis* (L.) the beet web-worm.

In the Philippines the polistine wasp, *Ropalidia gregaria* (Saussure) is a useful control agent of a leafhopper pest of sugar cane (Evans and Eberhard 1970).

The manipulation of *Polistes*, either by grafting young (founding queen only) nests or encouraging natural nesting by providing suitable shelters in appropriate situations, has been practised on a few occasions (Kirkton 1970). Morimoto (1960a, 1960b) has studied the effect of placing different numbers of *Polistes* colonies around cabbage fields and noting the decrease in populations of the cabbage butterfly, *Pieris rapae*, introduced at various densities. Founding females took an average of 1·3-8 caterpillar larvae per day, with a gross collection of 152 prey per queen before worker emergence. With the appearance of workers, the rate of predation was about 2,000 caterpillars per colony. The proportion of prey taken varied between 14·0 and 88·2 per cent in a ten-hour foraging period, and was 81·2 per cent after 5 days foraging. Morimoto points out that *Polistes*, because of the relative ease of their manipulation and their predatory habits, could be a very useful bio-control agent against agricultural and perhaps forest pests.

A serious pest of trees, *Hyphantria cunea* — the Fall Web-worm, is heavily predated upon by *Vespula* species in Canada (Morris 1972) and *Polistes* in Japan (Itô and Miyashita 1968), the wasps playing one of the major roles in the natural control of the caterpillars.

Several species of *Polistes* have been utilized in the effective control of tobacco hornworms (*Protoparce sexta* (Johan) and *P. quinquemaculata* (Haw.)) in the southern United States (Lawson and others 1961). Artificial shelters were provided around tobacco fields to encourage nesting, and the wasps thus established were responsible for between 50 and 98 per cent predation of the moth larvae. On average, the horn-worm populations were reduced by 60 per cent and the damage they caused was reduced by 74 per cent. It must be pointed out, however, that *Polistes* were not so effective under conditions of heavy horn-worm infestation when the use of low dose insecticides were employed in a successful campaign of integrated pest control. Similar manipulation of *Polistes* in Arkansas has been attempted by Kirkton (1970).

Some of the South American wasps may be responsible for reducing the number of pest insects for Richards (1971a) records that *Polybia ruficeps* Schrottky kills and stores within the nest, thousands of the winged, sexual forms of termites. In four nests the numbers of stored termites were 12,700 to 22,900 per colony, with an average 'kill' of 10-90 termites per worker per nest. Iwata (1964) reports that the social Vespidae in Thailand are considered the major group of insects exerting biotic control of injurious pests, although data are lacking to support the claim.

WASPS AND THEIR PRODUCTS AS FOOD SOURCES

There are several species of polybiine wasps which are well-known honey storers, most belonging to the genus *Brachygastra* (=*Nectarina*). One Texas species is used by the local Mexican population as a useful source of honey, the nests being located when immature and either moved to a suitable site or kept under surveillance until they are mature. The nest is then destroyed to obtain the honey which is stored within the cells (Barber 1905), and in Mexico itself it is reported that after nest removal these wasps rebuild and the honey may be repeatedly harvested (Evans and Eberhard 1970). In Mexico, *Polybia occidentalis*

(Olivier) is a useful source of edible honey although a local species of *Brachygastra* occasionally produces a poisonous honey due to the collection of nectar from certain toxic flowers, and it is advised that visiting honey tasters obtain supplies from reputable vespiculturists (Evans and Eberhard 1970).

Although consuming wasp honey would not inhibit the appetite of many people, feeding on wasp adults or their immature stages is, perhaps, quite a different matter. In his little classic of 1885, *Why Not Eat Insects?*, Vincent Holt describes the fisherman who uses wasp larvae for bait deriving a 'delicious savoury' from the grubs:

'What disciple of old Izaak Walton, when he has been all the morning enticing the wily trout with luscious wasp grubs baked to a turn, has not suspected a new and appetizing taste imparted to his midday meal of bread and cheese or sandwich? It will, sometimes, so happen to every fisherman to get the taste and smell of cooked wasp grubs with his meal, and I have never noticed that it in any way spoilt his appetite. Attracted by the said taste and smell, and having no prejudices against insect food, I have myself spread the baked grubs upon my bread, and found their excellent flavour quite sufficient to account for the fondness of the trout for this particular bait.'

The consumption of wasps in certain parts of the world is far from being rare, however, and in Guatemala, the Chuh Indians collect nests of *Polistes* in order to feed on the pupae. These Indians believe that the black-pigmented eyes of the pupae will impart certain procreative powers enabling them to produce children with large eyes (Evans and Eberhard 1970).

While visiting Japan, I frequently saw the tins of processed *Polistes* larvae and pupae which are a popular, if expensive, delicacy for the Japanese. The wasps thus preserved are relatively hard, with excellent flavour not unlike soya beans – a tasty savoury with a glass of saki. In some parts of Japan, barbecued adult wasps are often eaten, the cooking process burning off wings and legs to leave a slightly charred and very crunchy morsel.

If any readers are tempted to brighten up their dinner table with a comb of fried wasp grubs, may I suggest, for the benefit of potentially unenthusiastic guests, that the menu be written in French, *Larves de Guêpes frites au Rayon* – at least it sounds like a gourmet's dish!

THE CONTROL OF WASPS AND THEIR COLONIES

On balance, it seems probable that wasps exert a greater beneficial effect, through their predatory activities, than a deleterious one, but there are inevitably several situations when wasps must be controlled. These include food-processing factories, food stores, orchards and vineyards, apiaries, picnic areas, and domestic buildings. Wasps may be controlled at various stages in the seasonal cycle, although the methods variously employed and the timing of control measures have rarely resulted in anything but a slight amelioration of local wasp infestations.

Destruction of Queen Wasps. Under the normal climatic conditions of temperate Europe, Asia and North America, vespine wasps are represented during the winter months solely by hibernating queens. However, the mass destruction of these potential colony founders seems to have virtually no effect on subsequent wasp populations in the succeeding summer months. For example, in an attempt to control the introduced *P. germanica* in New Zealand, a 3d bounty offered for each hibernating queen wasp resulted in a total bill of nearly £1,500 for the 118,000 queens discovered in a three-month hunt (Thomas 1960). The effects on subsequent wasp populations were negligible. A similar eradication programme in Cyprus one winter cost the government dearly in bounty dues, but was followed by one of the worst 'wasp years' on record. It is evident from the study of wasp populations that, with a mortality of 99·9 per cent of potential queens and incipient colonies being necessary to maintain the same annual number of colonies, the destruction of winter queens is likely to have little or no effect on wasp populations. Indeed, a culling of winter queens may even cause an increase in the number of wasp nests by reducing the competition for suitable nest sites in the spring.

The most vulnerable stage in the annual cycle is the period of nest establishment by single queens in the spring and early summer. Incipient colony mortality is frequently very high (Brian and Brian 1952) and every queen destroyed at this time is a potentially populous colony less, at a stage when the numbers of queens are relatively low. The spraying of insecticides on foraging sites such as sources of honey-dew or nectar may be partially successful in reducing queen numbers at this time but, as will be emphasized throughout this section, the use of insecticides in this way must always take account of the potential hazards to other organisms, especially foraging honeybees, and the fact that the diversity of foraging activities does not lend itself to these forms of control.

Colony Destruction

The killing of entire colonies is usually effective in reducing local infestations but often the whereabouts of nests are unknown and various methods have been employed in attempts to locate them. A series of letters to *The Times* newspaper underlines the problems involved:

'Sir, Many years ago I recall being shown a certain method of finding wasps' nests by the late General Prescott-Decie. The General caught a wasp on the window pane, covered it with flour and released it out of doors, saying that it would immediately return to its nest. This it did, zooming in a straight line to the local river bank, with myself and a friend running underneath the flour-coated insect.
'Today, 40 years later, I tried the same method. The wasp flew some 30 yards and disappeared into its nest. Possibly some of your country readers, plagued by wasps, may care to try this. It's a certainty!'

'Sir, I caught one just now, devouring an expensive peach. I covered it, and myself, with large quantities of flour. I descended from a great height to street level and released the insect. It did not return directly to its nest. It rose vertically and vanished towards the sun. I returned to my flat. That same white wasp was once again lunching on that same peach. How can one destroy a creature with a sense of humour?'

'Sir, I caught my wasp and coated it with flour. Then I ran down the garden beneath the whitened creature. Unfortunately it soared over a ten-foot-wall. I was not so agile. When my bruises are healed I shall try again, but this time will use self-raising flour, on myself as well as the wasp.'

The use of lengths of cotton attached to wasps which would slow their flight speed and make them easier to follow by eye has inherent flaws – frequently the wasp refuses to embark on a journey home, or becomes entangled with the thread. Given time and patience, nests may be located by following the returning foragers from a food source, the 'wasp-line' giving a reasonably good bearing on the nest. (See Appendix III for more details.)

Where wasps prove particularly annoying, local factories or councils may offer bounties to people locating nests which can later be destroyed. One example known to me is that of a large chocolate factory in Tasmania which has successfully alleviated its wasp infestation problems in this way.

A variety of materials has been employed in the destruction (or attempted destruction) of wasp colonies, from pouring boiling water, petrol, or kerosene down the entrance tunnel, to the more sophisticated but no more effective use of insecticides or more general poisons such as cyanide. The safest time to kill off a nest is after dark, when foraging activities cease, although a careful approach armed with a teaspoonful of insecticide may be safely undertaken during daylight hours. To eliminate a colony, the United States Department of Agriculture (Anon 1954) recommend the injection or blowing-in of 2 per cent chlordane in oil emulsion, or 5-6 per cent chlordane dust. Carbon tetrachloride may also be poured down the entrance tunnel which is then plugged with cotton wool. To destroy aerial nests the U.S.D.A. suggest plugging the entrance hole with cotton wool, cutting the nest down and then soaking with carbon tetrachloride.

The British Ministry of Agriculture (Anon 1968) advise the use of powders containing 25 per cent BHC, or derris powder as 2 per cent rotenone, at a rate of one tablespoon per nest inside the entrance tunnel. BHC can also be introduced, using the type of smoke bomb utilized in the control of glasshouse pests. Carbon tetrachloride is recommended for killing all stages at once, the fluid being poured or syringed down the entrance tunnel at a rate of 140-280 ml ($\frac{1}{4}$-$\frac{1}{2}$ pint) per nest. The use of insecticide dusts are particularly useful when nests are in inaccessible situations such as cavity walls or under roofing tiles. In these cases, the dust may be flicked into or around the entrance area, returning foragers carrying it into the nest on their bodies. Because wasps suffering from the toxic effects of insecticides are erratic in their behaviour it is advisable to keep clear of treated nests for a day or so, until all adults have died.

Some testing of materials which could be used to kill off colonies was carried out by Thomas (1960) in New Zealand. In trials, the following were found successful:

10, 25, and 50 per cent DDT dust or wettable powder, 25 per cent DDD wettable powder, 50 per cent 'Methoxychlor' wettable powder, 40 per cent toxaphene dust, 'Gammexane', calcium cyanide, carbon disulphide, 'Chloropicrin', and 15 per cent parathion.

Boric acid powder and lead arsenate failed to reduce the activities of colonies.

There are several proprietary wasp killers available, most of which use relatively low concentrations of insecticide (e.g. carbaryl) in powder form which can be spooned down the tunnel leading to the nest. Various insecticides for spraying on *Polistes* nests have been tested by Hopkins (1955), and Johansen and Davis (1972) have compared the toxicity of various insecticides by topical application to adult *Vespula*. The latter authors discovered that young queens were forty times more tolerant of the most toxic insecticide (methomyl) than were the workers, after allowing for difference in their weights.

In my experience, the easiest, cheapest, and safest method of killing subterranean colonies is to pour a gallon of kerosene or petrol down the entrance after dark and plugging the hole with soil. Lighting the fuel after application is useless, for the effectiveness of the method relies on the heavy vapour permeating the nest. I destroyed a six-foot long subterranean nest of *P. germanica* in this way, covering the nest area with plastic sheeting to aid penetration of the vapour. Colonies may also be killed with chloroform by pouring it down the tunnel and blocking the entrance. Similarly, colonies may be anaesthetized by using ether if the wasps are to be used for biological study — chloroform generally kills wasps after only a short exposure.

Destruction of Workers

Some of the oldest methods of wasp control involve the trapping of adult wasps in suitable containers in which an attractive substance is placed, or the destruction of foragers at a foraging site by mechanical or chemical means. One of the earliest accounts of a technique for controlling the depredation of wasps appeared in the *Gentlemen's Magazine* in 1765 (Anon 1765):

'In the very dry, hot summer, 1762, wasps were so numerous and alert, that it looked as if no fruit could have hung till it was fit for the table. They began on the grapes before they were half ripe; and getting into the melon frames, scooped out all the pulp of the fruit, leaving only the empty shells. I tried phials, as usual, filled with sugared beer, etc. This destroyed some, but did not at all seem to lessen the swarms. At last I bethought myself to buy some bird-lime, with which I tipp'd several taper hazle rods of different lengths, and so began catching them by hand, applying the top of the rod as they settled on the fruit. This appeared at first to be a tedious method; but after a little practice it soon had the desired effect; for a handy person or two would, in a few hours, entangle four or five hundred; and it soon appeared that they were not so numberless as we imagined; and taking the workers starved the grubs, which are supported by them, and prevented a succession. By this simple method (ineffectual as it may appear) I saved my fruit entire, which hung till it was ripened to great perfection. Hornets, as they are a larger mark, and more sluggish, are easily taken. This method of touching them is a sort of angling, and not a bad amusement for half an hour. As fast as they are caught, they must be squeezed to death with a flat piece of a lath, and the tip of the rod refreshed with bird-lime now and then.'

To protect an individual tree if one has ample leisure time and requires 'amusement', this method may have appeal.

The use of tins or jars containing an attractive substance is widely practised, the attractants ranging from a bouillon of honey and pollen (Nesterovodsky 1947) to meat or molasses in blowfly traps (Thomas 1960) and jam or fermenting beer (Anon 1956). The problem with trapping is competition from naturally occurring food sources, and the method is not really a feasible control technique except perhaps in or around buildings. The attractive fluid should have a wetting agent such as liquid soap added in order to reduce the surface tension and cause trapped insects to sink to the bottom of the container.

The application of poisons to foraging sites was recommended as long ago as the end of the last century when Heim (1893) suggested spraying mercuric chloride and honey on to lilac branches where hornets were collecting bark or feeding at the sap flow. Heim stated that this method was successful in killing off entire colonies with the introduction of poisoned food or pulp by the returning foragers.

Palmer-Jones and Devine (1948) sprayed natural honey-dew areas with a DDT solution but, because of the problems of killing visiting honeybees, Palmer-Jones and others (1949) evolved an 'artificial honey-dew' of glucose and sucrose containing DDT with the addition of dextrin to make it less attractive to foraging honeybees. To control the wasps visiting trash cans in National Parks in America, Wagner (1961) recommended spraying the inner surfaces of emptied cans with 0·75 per cent DDVP emulsified spray which proved effective for about six days, and achieved a 99 per cent control in the picnic areas. Spraying cans in the early season proved the most effective means of control, possibly causing premature colony failure.

Wasp Baits

If wasps can be encouraged to collect food which contains an insecticide, there is the possibility that the returning foragers will distribute the poison to the inmates of the colony, bringing about its demise. The two major problems besetting this manner of control are firstly to find a bait which is highly attractive to foraging wasps so that it will compete successfully with naturally occurring food sources, and secondly that the poisoned bait is specific enough to prevent possible ill effects on other organisms, especially honeybees. A further factor which detracts from this method is the lack of communication between returning foragers and the other inhabitants of the colony, thus preventing a mass exploitation of poisoned food sources.

Thomas (1960) achieved a limited effect on wasp populations by using poisoned baits composed of 2 per cent sodium arsenate in a molasses solution, although Rivnay and Bytinski-Salz (1949) obtained satisfactory results with meat baits in which thalium sulphate, lead arsenate, or BHC had been incorporated.

A commercially prepared bait ('Waspex') was evolved in Britain (Jefkins 1961) which was enthusiastically claimed as a major break-

U

through in wasp control. The bait consisted of a sugar-candy base, highly attractive to wasps, containing a balanced concentration of a chlorinated hydrocarbon insecticide (probably dieldrin). It was designed to produce delayed action mortality, following the return of foragers and distribution of the bait material within the colony. During trials in the vicinity of food factories, bakeries, and orchards, up to 90 per cent control was achieved. An inherent defect in the use of 'Waspex' or similar baits is the fact that the sugars with which they are made are hygroscopic and may become attractive to bees which can feed on the poisonous liquid, although normally they would not feed on the solid form. Communication of such a bait source to the remainder of the colony would lead to its rapid extinction. Several such cases of the accidential poisoning of honeybees were recorded following the wide-spread use of Waspex bait and the spraying of field crops with insecticides (Needham and Stevenson 1966, Needham, Solly, and Stevenson 1966).

Nevertheless, the development of highly specific poison baits remains one of the more profitable areas of investigation for the localized control of wasps.

Biological Control

The range of predatory and parasitic organisms which are found associated with wasp colonies offers some hope that biological methods of control may be achieved. The manipulation of biotic factors to control wasps is fraught with considerable problems, however, one of the most daunting being the aggregations of wasps in well-protected colonies, and the rapid population growth during the short period of colony development. To wipe out colonies using pathogens requires organisms capable of locating colonies or being introduced by returning foragers. Once within the colony, a high degree of multiplication would be necessary to achieve effective control. Destruction of potential queens should be the aim of control, either by killing off colonies before queen production begins, or the introduction of organisms which attack immature and adult queens, possibly by establishing sufficient numbers on worker hosts prior to queen rearing.

As seen earlier (Chapter 11) parasitoid density in colonies is invariably very low and natural infestations appear to exert little if any population control. One of the more recent approaches to possible biotic control is the use of neoplectanid nematodes which are taken from fruit concentrates by visiting wasps. The release of bacteria by the infective stage kills the wasp and under humid conditions (which would occur in subterranean nesting species), the nematode can establish breeding colonies in the host's cadaver (Poinar and Ennik 1972). Fluid baits containing the infective stage nematode may prove a more attractive proposition for wasp control than poison baits for it has been established that the nematode causes no ill-effects when offered to honeybees (Niklas, *in* Poinar and Ennik 1972). Nevertheless the nematode requires a film of water or a relative humidity of 100 per cent for locomotion and this factor may well be a severely limiting one in the use of nematodes for wasp control.

CHAPTER 13

VARIOUS VESPIDAE

This chapter, which is mainly concerned with non-British wasps, has been included to give a background to the range of social organization found in the Vespidae, provide the basis for a discussion of the evolution of social life in wasps, and act as a source of reference to the more common genera in the family. Their distribution, range of nest structures, and degree of sociality will be outlined. There are only seven species of social wasp in the British Isles of a total estimated number of about 800 subsocial and social species (see Table 35,) and it is therefore unwise to be too insular about the British fauna. However, *Polistes* has been found in Britain occasionally although it has never become established (Nurse 1913, Morice 1916). Much of our knowledge of vespid wasps has been derived from studies on a few species of *Vespula* and *Polistes* occurring in temperate and mediterranean Europe, species which are recognized as being highly evolved and certainly not representative of all wasps. Aspects of polistine-wasp biology have already appeared in previous chapters, particularly studies of *Polistes* which is the most cosmopolitan genus. Recent expeditions to South America – in particular, Brazil – and South-east Asia have resulted in a resurgence of interest and proliferation of knowledge on the vespid faunas of these regions where wasps originated and diversified.

STENOGASTRINAE

The most primitive wasps in the family Vespidae are represented by some forty to sixty species of *Stenogaster* and *Parischnogaster* which occur in South-east Asia (Fig. 92). These species are somewhat intermediate between eumenid wasps and the truly social vespids.

The Stenogastrinae do not fold their wings longitudinally when in repose like other Vespids (Williams 1919, Yoshikawa and others 1969). They inhabit the shady parts of tropical rain forests, generally constructing delicate nests near streams or waterfalls. These wasps vary in size from 12-25 mm in length and their colours range from black to yellow, with or without additional 'wasp-like' markings (Iwata 1967).

Their nests are architecturally diverse, built from masticated vegetable fibres and/or particles of soil, hanging from roots and ferns or plastered on stones, leaves, and the bark of trees (Fig. 91d). The simplest nests are composed of a series of downward-facing cylindrical or bell-like cells attached to a root, either in single file or in three lines, twisting round each other like a woven rope (Plate XXVIe). Up to 20 cells may be found in a single nest (Williams 1919). Other species build roughly hexagonal cells of carton in small combs of up to 23 cells with an envelope extending from the outer walls of the peripheral cells to enclose the comb (Plate XXVIf). A similar style of nest, reminiscent of a *Vespula* embryo nest with the envelope extending from the pedicel rather than the cells, has been described by Sakagami and Yoshikawa (1968). The third type of nest is constructed from sandy mud and decayed wood particles, and is composed of one or more rows of downward-facing cells plastered to the substrate. Up to 39 cells per nest have been recorded (Iwata 1967). Some species have 'ant guards' strategically placed around the rootlets supporting the nest which are similar to the rat guards on ships' hawsers.

Williams (1919), who considered the Stenogastrinae to have both solitary and social members, found nests with more than one female present, but there was apparently no co-operative building, each female constructing its own cells. It is likely that newly emerged adults may remain on the nest for a while before their final departure. Although there is probably no collaboration between adults, contact between the female and the developing larvae is pronounced. The young larvae are fed on a jelly-like paste which contains no recognizable insect remains and Iwata (1967) suggests that it may be glandular in origin, produced by the tending female like the honeybee's royal jelly. Maturing larvae are fed on a finely masticated paste of arthropod origin, dominantly chironomid midges and occasionally spiders. The midges are frequently taken from spider's webs which abound in the gloomy forest habitat of the Stenogastrinae (Williams 1928).

Some species oviposit in the newly constructed cell bases, extending the cell walls as the larvae grow (Iwata 1967), a habit similar to the extension of the cell wall in *Polistes*. The larvae do not spin silken cocoons and in some species at least, the female seals the cell when the larva is mature (Iwata 1967). The progressive provisioning of the larvae defines the group as being at least subsocial but the contact between parent and adult offspring is often ephemeral and true sociality has not evolved very far. However, Yoshikawa and others (1969) found a number of multiple-female nests, although the adults could not be distinguished from each other morphologically and all the mature ones were inseminated. Sometimes males were found in these associations. In one nest of *Parischnogaster* sp. with 6 females, a definite dominance

TABLE 35

Taxonomy and distribution of wasps, family Vespidae (modified from Richards 1971a)

SUBFAMILY AND TRIBE	PRINCIPAL GENERA	ESTIMATED NUMBER OF SPECIES	DISTRIBUTION
STENOGASTRINAE	*Stenogaster*	25(1)	New Guinea, Indonesia, India to Vietnam
POLISTINAE			
Ropalidiini	*Ropalidia*	112	Africa, Iran, S.E. Asia, New Guinea, Hong Kong, Taiwan, Australia
Polybiini	*Belonogaster*	35	Tropical Africa, Arabia
	Polybioides	5	West and Central Africa, Indonesia
	Parapolybia	5	Iran to Japan, Korea, Indonesia
	Apoica	5	Tropical Central and Southern America
	Mischocyttarus	200	British Columbia, Bahamas to Argentina
	Brachygastra (=*Nectarina*)	7	Southern U.S., South America
	Chartergus	2	South America
	Clypearia	4	Brazil
	Synoeca	3	Northern South America, Trinidad, Panama
	Polybia	51	Mexico to Argentina
	Protonectarina	1	S.E. South America
	Protopolybia	20	Tropical Central and South America
	Parachartergus	13	Mexico to Argentina
	Pseudopolybia	4	Tropical Central and South America
	Angiopolybia	4	Tropical South America
	Stelopolybia	17	Mexico to Argentina
Polistini	*Polistes*	150	Whole world except New Zealand to limits of temperate regions (2)
	Sulcopolistes	4	Palearctic
VESPINAE	*Vespa*	19	Europe to South China, Mediterranean to Ethiopia, Malaysia (3)
	Vespula	33	Holarctic (4)
	Provespa	3	Indo-Malaya

NOTES (1) Schulthess (1927) lists 40 species.
(2) One Australian species introduced into New Zealand.
(3) *Vespa crabro* introduced into the eastern United States of America between 1840 and 1860 (Cory 1931, Van der Vecht 1957).
(4) *Paravespula germanica* established in New Zealand by 1945 and Tasmania, Australia by 1959;
P. vulgaris established in Victoria, Australia by 1960.

order was noted, similar to that occurring in *Polistes* when several founding queens initiate a colony. Two of the females had well-developed ovaries and one of them exhibited a high level of dominance behaviour towards the others and never showed subordinate responses. The dominant female never left the nest to forage, most of the extra-colonial activities being performed by the two lowest-ranking females which, it was discovered later, were not inseminated. In other species drifting of females from one nest to another was observed.

POLISTINAE

The polistinae are conveniently divided into three tribes, the Ropalidiini, Polybiini, and Polistini. The subfamily is dominantly tropical in its distribution, although *Polistes* has spread throughout much of the warmer temperate regions of the world (Fig. 92).

Ropalidiini

There are more than one hundred species of *Ropalidia* distributed in Africa, South-east Asia, the Indian sub-continent, and Australia. Despite their wide range, remarkably few biological data are known, the more recent observations resulting from expeditions to Thailand by the Japanese entomologists, Professor K. Iwata and Dr. K. Yoshikawa. The Ropalidiini are a primitively social tribe and colonies are initiated by a single female or a group of females.

The simple nests are made in strands, each cylindrical cell built below and suspended from the rim of the cell above with up to 22 cells in a row (Fig. 91a) (Iwata 1969a), although in other species there is a double row of cells or hexagonal-shaped cells forming *Polistes*-like combs (Van der Vecht 1962). Some species build an envelope around the comb in much the same way as *Vespula* while others construct two or more vertical combs within hollow bamboo stems (Yoshikawa 1964). One Javanese species builds several pairs of horizontal combs of 200-400 cells each, back to back within a carton envelope (Fig. 91c) (Van der Vecht 1940).

Despite a great similarity in morphological detail among the species of *Ropalidia*, there is an enormous range of nesting behaviour, underlining the diverse evolutionary avenues explored by this group in its tropical environment.

Polybiini

There are about 20 genera of Polybiini, the majority occurring in South and Central America with *Belonogaster*, *Polybioides*, and *Parapolybia* representing the tribe in Africa and South-east Asia. The polybiine wasps exhibit a wide variety of social behaviour, from relatively simple associations of females founding nests, to multi-queened colonies which emit swarms from large parental nests. Nest architecture is extremely varied, ranging from simple exposed comb-structures of a few dozen cells to enormous nests of up to a cubic metre in volume. Some colonies have a life expectancy of a few months whilst others survive for many years.

Belonogaster. About 35 species of this genus occur in tropical Africa, extending northwards as far as Arabia. Some of the earliest studies of Polybiini were made on *Belonogaster* in the Congo by the French entomologist, Roubaud (1910, 1916). Nests were found with one to four associated females which were indistinguishable from each other morphologically, although in one colony a markedly smaller female joined the foundress after its emergence. Although this female behaved rather like a worker, when dissected it was found to be inseminated. Richards and Richards (1951) noted that 'workers' from a *Belonogaster* colony taken in Natal, were smaller and had fewer hamuli than the 'queens' but these differences were not statistically significant. However, in a later study of *Belonogaster* in Ghana, Richards (1969) found statistically significant differences in the number of hamuli between queens, intermediates, and workers, and differences in wing length between queens and workers. Richards defined the mature females as follows: queens had developed ovaries with eggs ready for laying, intermediates had slightly developed ovaries with eggs much smaller than those of the queens, and workers had thread-like ovarioles. Thus it appears that a rudimentary caste differentiation occurs in this relatively primitive social wasp. The nests are superficially similar to those of *Polistes*, with a single pedicel or pillar from which the comb is suspended. The shape of the comb is sub-spherical or saucer-like with hexagonal cells constructed on the outside (Fig. 91f). In large nests, which have up to 450 cells (Iwata 1966), a second pedicel may be built to support the comb. The carton is predominantly of plant fibres although Iwata (1968) noted that in an Ethiopian nest some wood had been incorporated into the structure. The size of cells tends to increase with the age of the nest, although the smaller ones are generally broken down during its development and the carton used to build other cells. They are not apparently used for rearing a second generation of brood (Evans and Eberhard 1970). Colonies are founded by single females which may soon be joined by others, or initiated by several females from the outset (Iwata 1966). One colony from Natal had a 65-cell nest with 16 'queens', 7 'workers', and 4 males present (Richards and Richards 1951).*

*Belonogaster has recently been the subject of intensive study by an Italian research group (Pardi and Piccioli 1970, Piccioli and Pardi 1970).

Polybioides. This genus occurs in South-east Asia and central Africa where it constructs nests varying in structure from spirally produced combs (Van der Vecht 1966) to vertical combs surrounded by an envelope (Richards and Richards 1951, Richards 1969). *Polybioides* colonies may attain a large size with several thousand wasps, and it is wasps of this genus which have been used in booby traps during the Vietnam hostilities. In common with most *Ropalidia*, *Belonogaster*, and *Parapolybia*, the wasps remove faecal pellets from the cells by chewing out the base often sealing the hole with a salivary secretion which dries to form a mica-like window (Evans and Eberhard 1970). Richards (1969) found some slight morphological differences between queens and workers of *P. tabidus* (F.) in Ghana.

Parapolybia. This genus is distributed in the Old World tropics (Fig. 92) where some species build nests similar to *Polistes* with up to 1,800 cells and more than 100 females present (Iwata 1969b). Small colonies (from 13-54 cell nests) have only one female or a queen and a few, possibly newly emerged, workers. It appears that colonies are founded by one female (Iwata 1969b). Van der Vecht (1966) illustrates some nests which were found in Sumatra.

Angiopolybia. This genus occurs in the South American tropics where colonies are founded by swarming. The nest of one species is composed of a number of horizontal combs suspended by fine pillars and surrounded by a globular envelope extended downwards to form a spout-like entrance (Richards and Richards 1951).

Apoica. These nocturnal wasps are found from southern Mexico to Paraguay where they build sessile nests, the comb being broadly cone-shaped and without an envelope. The nest material consists of plant hairs which are stuck together, and the number of cells may approach 500 in mature colonies (Richards and Richards 1951). *Apoica* founds colonies by swarming. During the day, the wasps form a tight ring around the nest, their bodies so aligned that their heads form a circle around the periphery of the comb – a formidable sight for any approaching predator.

Mischocyttarus. This, the largest genus of Polybiini with more than 200 species, builds relatively small nests, similar to *Polistes* with a long, thin pedicel and no envelope (Fig. 91g), although some nests may have up to 400 cells. There is no evidence of swarming in this genus, the founding of colonies being carried out by a queen or a queen with a few workers (Richards and Richards 1951). The carton is fabricated from old wood and bark but mica-like windows formed from the wasp's saliva frequently occur in the carton (Williams 1928). *Mischocyttarus drewseni* Saussure protects its nest from the predation of ants by smearing on to the pedicel a repellent produced by a gland on the terminal abdominal sternite (Fig. 91g) (Jeanne 1970b). The taxonomy of *Mischocyttarus* species has been revised by Richards (1945), and details of colony development and social behaviour of *M. drewseni* have been studied by Jeanne (1972).

Brachygastra (=*Nectarina*). The famous honey-producing wasps are included in this group, some species being maintained in a semi-domesticated state by the Mexican Indians. The nests, which are built by swarms, are basically similar to *Chartergus* nests (Plate XXVIa) but usually less symmetrical, there being several horizontal combs with the cells facing downwards, surrounded by an envelope which is in contact with the edge of the combs. Colonies may continue for many years with nests composed of several thousand cells, swarms being emitted from time to time. Several thousand adult wasps may be found in a colony of which up to 17 per cent may be queens (du Buysson 1905) with many intermediates (females with partially developed ovaries).

Chartergus. Species of *Chartergus* build cylindrical or bell-like nests with a particularly tough envelope to which combs are attached, each having a central hole to allow passage between the horizontal combs (Plate XXVIa). In common with some other South American wasps, the nests of *Chartergus* are frequently found hanging from trees in which tree-nesting ants have established their colonies, the wasps gaining a measure of protection from marauders due to the aggressive behaviour of their neighbours.

Clypearia. Species of *Clypearia* are apparently restricted to Brazil where they found colonies by swarming, the resulting nests consisting of a comb or combs fixed directly to the substrate, frequently the branch of a tree. There is an envelope fixed around the edge of the comb, not unlike the nest of the *Ropalidia* sp. in Figure 91b but covering it more completely.

Synoeca. This genus is distributed in northern South America and Central America, where it builds single-comb nests attached directly to tree branches with a domed envelope which covers the cells. The nests are founded by swarms from perennial colonies, one such colony being reputedly sixteen years old (Evans and Eberhard 1970). In one species, several combs are fixed to the inside walls of the envelope and the branch (Fig. 91k).

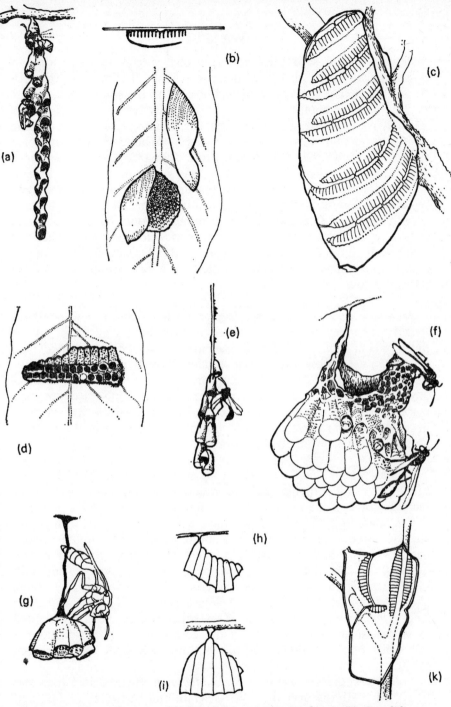

Figure 91. Nest structures: (a) *Ropalidia variegata jacobsoni*; (b) *Ropalidia* sp.;
(c) *Ropalidia flavopicta* (Smith); (d) *Stenogaster nitidipennis* Saussure; (e) *Parischnogaster* sp.; (f) *Belonogaster junceus* F.; (g) *Mischocyttarus drewseni* Saussure; (h)
Polistes pacificus liliaciosus Saussure; (i) *Polistes tepidus malayanus* Cameron;
(k) *Synoeca virginea* (F.). (a and b, after Yoshikawa 1964; c, after Van der Vecht
1940; d and e, after Iwata 1967; f, after Roubaud 1916; g, after Jeanne 1970b;
h, i, k, after Van der Vecht 1967).

Polybia. With more than 50 recorded species from Mexico to Argentina, this genus is one of the most widely distributed in the neo-tropical area. The nests are attached directly to the substrate without a pedicel, and the combs are placed horizontally below each other with a protective envelope, ovoid in shape, surrounding them. Although the majority use materials of vegetable origin to build their nests, some species use mud (Plate XXVIc, d). More than 18 combs per nest have been found and thousands of adults may occur in a colony. Several species store honey in the cells, particularly those from the more arid regions. Colony-founding is by swarming, some swarms containing several thousand females of which a number would be queens. These swarms build nests within a few days, oviposition beginning when the nest is well established. Some morphological differences between queens and workers have been demonstrated in a few species of *Polybia* (Richards and Richards 1951).

Protopolybia. This wide-ranging group from central and southern America attaches its combs to leaves or branches by means of one or more pillars, each comb having a separate envelope like *Ropalidia* sp. (Fig. 91b) with successive combs attached directly to the undersurface of the preceding envelope. In some species the workers are morphologic-ally distinct from queens while in others, queens, intermediates, and workers are indistinguishable except by examination for ovariole development and presence or absence of spermatozoa in the sperma-theca. Colonies are founded by swarms.

Stelopolybia. This South American genus is, morphologically, very similar to Angiopolybia and, to a lesser extent, *Parapolybia*, and includes some of the most commonly found – and aggressive – species of the continent. Although many have queens and workers which are alike in external features, W. D. Hamilton (personal communication) has found that in *S. flavipennis*, workers are structurally distinct and markedly smaller than queens. Two major nest types occur, one built in cavities such as hollow trees where combs are suspended by pillars like a *Vespula* nest, but without envelopes. The second type is suspended from a leaf or twig and consists of several combs as above surrounded by a carton envelope, free from the combs and with or without a spout-like entrance funnel at the bottom (Richards and Richards 1951).

One extraordinary nest of a *Stelopolybia* sp. (figured in Evans and Eberhard 1970) discovered by W. D. Hamilton was underground and composed of a series of concentric vertical cylinders with the cells opening laterally around the outward-facing side of the combs. This genus founds new colonies by swarming.

Polistini

The Polistini are composed of two genera, *Polistes* with some 150 species, and four socially parasitic species of *Sulcopolistes*. The biology of the temperate species is well known through the studies of Pardi in Italy, Yoshikawa in Japan, Deleurance and Gervet in France, and Rau in North America, and much of their findings have appeared in preceding chapters. The brief survey of *Polistes* offered here will attempt to emphasize the similarities and differences between the temperate and tropical members of the genus.

Nests are constructed from a carton of vegetable origin, generally dead, sound wood similar to Vespinae, with a similar variety of textural differences. The range of nest forms is considerable with some species (e.g. *P. goeldii* Ducke of South America) constructing a series of cells one below the other in much the same way as *Stenogaster* (Fig. 91a), some have almost vertical combs (e.g. *P. canadensis* (L.)), semi-horizontal (Fig. 91h), and the more familiar horizontal combs (Fig. 91i). One feature common to all *Polistes* nests however is the pedicel, a mainstay pillar which supports the comb of cells and probably affords some protection because the pillar can more easily be defended from marauding ants than a comb attached directly to the substrate. Some species which build large combs have accessory pillars for additional support. No envelopes are constructed by *Polistes*.

The wide range of climatic areas occupied by the various species has given rise to some interesting differences between temperate and tropical forms. Recent detailed studies on temperate species by Soichi Yamane (1969, 1971) in Japan, and on tropical species by Mary Jane Eberhard (1969) in Colombia, underline the modifications in behaviour imposed by widely different climatic régimes. It may be assumed that *Polistes*, in company with other vespid genera, originated in the tropics and their colonization of a non-tropical environment has been achieved by a high degree of specialization during their evolution into the present-day fauna.

In the tropics there is little if any synchrony between colony development and the rainy and wet seasons, colonies in all stages of development being found at all times. The foundation of colonies is similar throughout their geographical range, one or a group of 2-10 associated founding females initiate a nest and, through the action of dominance hierarchies, differential egg-eating and foraging activities, one female becomes the queen, the remainder either acting as foragers or leaving the embryo colony. A type of swarming (really, nest replacement) may take place if the nest is destroyed or the brood taken by raiding ants, and swarms composed of a queen and a few workers may occur in the tropics (Richards and Richards 1951). There is no hibernation among tropical *Polistes*, new colonies being founded by females soon after leaving a declining or disrupted parental nest. In one instance, eight new colonies were initiated within two metres of the parental nest.

Because of the marked fluctuations in temperature associated with the temperate climate, *Polistes* queens must hibernate during the winter months and, depending on the location, the dormant period may last from 4 to 6 months or more. This adaptation to a cold temperate climate is emphasized by Yamane's work on *P. snelleni* Saussure in the northernmost island of Japan, Sapporo, compared to similar studies on *P. jadwigae* in central Honshu near Osaka City by Yoshikawa. In the north, the queens hibernate from early October to late April but in the south, the period is from mid-November to mid-March. With a shorter active season available to the northern species, the pattern of colony development is such that very few workers (5-15) are produced, male emergence begins only a week after the emergence of the first workers, and queens shortly afterwards. Indeed, the founding queen is responsible for rearing many of the reproductives herself. The ratio of workers to males to queens was 2 : 3 : 8 in *P. snelleni* and 8 : 1 : 1 in *P. jadwigae*.

Colony development in *Polistes* is typically cyclic, being from 4-5 months in temperate species where the weather imposes a seasonal programme of development, to 6-7 months in tropical species where the cycles are independent of climatic variations. A further interesting difference between temperate and tropical *Polistes* is that the period for development of egg to adult is 35-50 days in the former and about 65 days in the tropical *P. canadensis*. Yamane (personal communication) has found that nests of *P. biglumis* (L.) from the cold areas of Japan have a peripheral ring of deep, vacant cells which could act as a 'functional envelope', affording some measure of insulation to the brood in the centre of the comb.

VESPINAE

The Vespinae are represented by three major genera of highly evolved wasps, *Vespa*, *Vespula*, and *Provespa*. Their world distribution (Fig. 92) illustrates the south-east Asiatic origins of the subfamily, the genera radiating out from the common origin in Indomalaysia (Van der Vecht 1957). All build nests of paper carton, although the incorporation of quantities of inorganic material such as grains of sand and small stones is frequently recorded in *Vespa* nests. They are composed of a series of round combs attached horizontally below each other by pillars or ribbon-like supports, the combs generally surrounded by a multi-layered envelope with considerable insulation qualities. Species of *Vespa* and *Vespula* build their nests both above and below ground, while *V. crabro* shows a preference for hollow trees.

Colonies are initiated by a single queen without help from workers, swarming being quite unknown in the subfamily, although if a *Vespa* nest is destroyed, the adults may rebuild some distance from the original site (Matsuura, personal communication). Large colonies are a feature of many *Vespula* species although some (e.g. *V. rufa*, *D. norwegica*) are small, and *Vespa* species, though large in size of adult, have less populous societies compared to some *Vespula* species. The differences between queens and workers is generally marked, the queens being larger and often differently coloured, and these caste differences are reinforced by behavioural characteristics. However, there are two species of *Vespa* in which queens and workers cannot be reliably separated on morphological characters (Van der Vecht 1957). The Vespinae are the only wasps which build special queen-rearing cells.

The three known species of *Provespa* occur in Malaysia, Sumatra and Borneo (Van der Vecht 1936, 1957) and are of some considerable interest for they are nocturnal wasps like *Apoica*. Van der Vecht (1959) has also described a species of *Vespa* (subgenus *Nyctovespa*) which has nocturnal habits.

In this survey of the principal members of the Vespidae, ranges of social organization, caste differences and nest structures have been described which single out the wasps as one of the most ethologically fascinating groups of insects. From an evolutionary point of view they represent a rich field for experimental, taxonomic, and deductive studies.

CHAPTER 14

THE EVOLUTION OF SOCIAL WASPS

'Although the wasps have attracted fewer investigators than the ants and bees, they are of even greater interest to the student who is tracing the evolution of specialized instincts and social habits.' So wrote W. M. Wheeler (1922) in his series of classic lectures on social life in insects. In entomological terms, a truly social species is one in which the offspring co-operate with the parent or parents in the rearing of siblings. Subsocial behaviour is indicated by a degree of contact between parent and developing offspring such as occurs during feeding, but no collaboration with the parent takes place after emergence of the adults. Using the word 'wasp' in its broad sense, there are many families in which more than 10,000 species are found of which only 800 or so are social or subsocial. These wasps belong to two main groups, the distantly related Sphecoidea and Vespoidea and among them are species which exhibit a range of behaviour from the wholly solitary to the social. Many of them may be justifiably regarded as present-day examples of the different levels of social organization attained during the evolution of social life over the past fifty or sixty million years. Evolution is a continuing process, however, and it is therefore unlikely that the contemporary fauna exactly duplicates the sequence of events which has led to the advanced social organization of the higher wasps, for the ancestral forms which gave rise to subsocial and social groups have disappeared long ago. What is so exciting and revealing about vespid evolution is the diversity of behavioural avenues explored by wasps as exemplified by today's fauna.

The raw materials for deductive studies on wasp evolution are the morphological, anatomical, genetic, and behavioural characteristics of present-day wasps, their geographical distribution, and a consideration of the likely dispersal routes of ancestral wasps during geological time.

Social organization is found in several groups of Hymenoptera having separate ancestries, demonstrating that sociality arose many times in this order while among all other insects, only one, the Isoptera (termites), has achieved a similarly high level of social organization. Contemporary estimates suggest that sociality has been achieved independently at least ten times in the Hymenoptera (Wilson 1966). To have evolved social life so often the Hymenoptera must be undoubtedly predisposed for sociality and a consideration of some of these pre-adaptations are highly relevant to this discussion. For social life to evolve there must be some definite advantages for the species such as communal defence and protection of the reproductives, the control of the physical environment within a colony, and a capacity to rear a large quantity of brood in the small protected enclave of a nest yet exploit widely dispersed food supplies in the surrounding area.

One of the basic pre-adaptations for the evolution of the complex behaviour which makes possible social organization is the possession of efficient and adaptive sensory equipment. The Hymenoptera are notable for their high degree of nervous organization, the well-developed visual and olfactory powers of the parasitic Hymenoptera being well known. The ability to locate food sources and detect hosts and prey all underline the potential for orientation and locality learning which is so crucial to the development of nesting habits. Studies on the structure of the insect brain have shown that there is an increase in size and complexity of the calyces from the primitive Hymenoptera such as sawflies and woodwasps through the parasitoid ichneumons to the social wasps (Howes 1970), an anatomical development which helps make possible the complex behaviour necessary for sociality. Allied to the development of a highly organized nervous system is the capacity for wasps to manipulate and transport food and nesting materials, a development which reaches some remarkable levels in many sphecid wasps. The construction of a nest or even a primitive food niche for rearing the young plus an ability to orientate to the nest provide the foundations for the development of social organization. The establishment of a rearing site (cell or nest) to which the female repeatedly returns with food for its offspring, may lead to the development of a more advanced situation in which several cells are prepared, one after the other, so that offspring of different ages occur together in the cell cluster. With the emergence of adults, a situation arises in which the young adult has the option of leaving the nest site or helping to rear brood, or at least contribute to nest defence by simply being present when the parent is away foraging. The development of this situation presupposes increased longevity of the parent so that she may overlap her offspring and provide the opportunity for true social behaviour.

Another significant pre-adaptation for the development of social life in the Hymenoptera is the haplo-diploid method of sex determina-

x

tion which is so characteristic of the order. Males are invariably haploid, developing from unfertilized eggs and therefore having only one complement of (maternal) genes, while female eggs are diploid, carrying also the paternal set of genes. This makes for close relatedness of female offspring for all the paternal genes will be the same. The significance of this state of affairs will be discussed more fully at a later stage in this chapter.

PHYLOGENETIC CONSIDERATIONS

Using contemporary examples, several authors (notably Wheeler 1922, Evans 1958, and Malyshev 1968) have traced the likely stages encountered during the evolution of social organization, and the present account makes no claims to originality. A discussion of the phylogenetic origins of social wasps may be conveniently divided into two parts, first the increasing complexity of brood care and nesting in the Scolioidea, Pompiloidea, and Sphecoidea and, secondly, the developments which probably took place within the Vespoidea.

It is generally agreed that the Aculeata were derived from parasitoid ancestors (see Fig. 1) and many primitive aculeates hardly differ from present-day parasitoids. Typically, the Parasitica (or Terebrantia) deposit their egg or eggs in or on a host insect (generally an immature stage) which may or may not be paralysed by stinging. Normally the host, after detection and oviposition, is left *in situ*, there being no physical attempt to hide or protect the host from superparasitism by the same species of parasitoid, or from multiparasitism and predation by other species.

There are a few exceptions, notably among the Bethyloidea which are a group of rather wasp-like parasitoids which, on morphological grounds, qualify for a place in the Aculeata. Several bethyloid species have been recorded dragging their prey to hiding places (W. D. Hamilton, personal communication). The ovipositor in the Parasitica is used for injection of paralysing venom and egg emplacement, while in the Aculeata, the ovipositor is no longer used for egg laying but is reserved solely for stinging prey, or for the defence of the colony, although there are some exceptions to this general rule.

The Scolioidea are the most primitive aculeates, the majority behaving like typical parasitoids, paralysing their beetle prey and ovipositing on them before departure, although some species practise a primitive nesting behaviour by moving the prey to a more suitable location or even preparing a rudimentary cell in which the prey is concealed. Among the Scolioidea are the only aculeate species which lay more than one egg on a single prey, a common practice among the Parasitica.

The Pompiloidea or 'Spider-Wasps' have certain characteristics which label them as being intermediate between the Scolioidea and Sphecoidea with a range of behaviour intermediate between the two superfamilies. The most primitive members simply oviposit on their hosts wherever they are located, while others practise various degrees of nesting behaviour. The least specialized of the latter category merely drag the paralysed spider to a suitable hole or cavity whereupon the egg is laid on the prey and the hole covered with surrounding debris. The majority of pompilids, however, prepare simple cells by digging a cavity in the soil into which the prey is placed, while a few make well-constructed cells from mud. Some of the more advanced species have undergone an important change in behaviour, for the sequence of prey–egg–cell has been re-arranged and a cell is prepared *before* the location of suitable prey. This represents a significant advance towards the attainment of sociality, especially in those cases where several cells are prepared at the same site and the word 'nest' can be properly used for the first time. The preparation of a cell before prey capture indicates that among some pompilids at least, considerable powers of orientation have been evolved. It must be emphasized, however, that in no instances have the pompilids achieved even subsocial behaviour for there is no contact with their offspring, even during larval development, a feature which is emphasized by the practice of supplying only one prey-spider per cell.

The Sphecoidea are of special interest for it is from primitive sphecids that the bees were probably derived. The nesting and subsocial behaviour exhibited by the sphecoid wasps spans an enormously diverse range, from typically primitive behaviour to a degree of subsocial behaviour characteristic of many vespid species. The least specialized sphecids (family, Ampulicidae) drag their single prey to a suitable hole or cavity, sealing the niche after oviposition, while others dig a nest after prey capture. The majority of sphecids, however, prepare a nest before hunting for prey and oviposition takes place after the prey is placed in a niche or cell. A modification to this sequence of events is practised by many species of *Ammophila* and *Sphex*, namely, the provisioning of several more prey after oviposition on the first. The adding of more prey to a cell already containing an immature stage affords the opportunity for contact between a developing larva and the tending female, especially if prey proves difficult to locate for reasons of weather or prey scarcity and the provisioning period is protracted. Although some species of *Ammophila* and all *Sphex* species practise multiple-prey provisioning, they generally complete storing paralysed caterpillars or crickets before the egg hatches. However, in at least two species, additional prey are not added to the cell until the egg hatches (on the first prey), thereafter the feeding of the developing larvae being on a day-to-day basis. The studies of Baerends

(1941) on *Ammophila campestris* Latreille have revealed how this species provisions several cells simultaneously although in each the developing larva is at a different stage of growth and consequently requires different sizes or numbers of caterpillar prey. The female, during an early morning reconnaissance of the cells, determines each larva's requirements and feeds them accordingly. Thus, a stage is reached in which the parent female maintains several cells in a nest complex, rearing offspring of different ages, and having daily 'contact' with them when she determines their trophic requirements. At least two biological features are lacking for true wasp-like sociality; the female does not live long enough to be joined by her emerging offspring, and the paralysed prey is stored in the cells intact, there being no or little previous maceration of larval food which is so characteristic of the social wasps. Also, there is no reciprocal exchange of food or secretions, trophallaxis appearing to be wholly distinctive of advanced social communities.

A remarkable exception to this typical sphecoid behaviour has recently been described by Matthews (1968). In Costa Rica, the sphecoid, *Microstigmus comes* Krombein, builds bag-like nests suspended by long, thin pedicels from the leaves of trees. In half the nests studied two or more females and the occasional male were in attendance, the maximum being 18 adults. Although no morphological differences between females could be found, dissections showed that only one female in a nest exhibited ovariole development – a reproductive division of labour. The females co-operate in provisioning the cells with Collembola prey and, if disturbed, they will all assist in the defence of the colony. The collaboration between parental female and her offspring and the reproductive distinctions which occur are major qualifications which distinguish *Microstigmus comes* as a fully social wasp. A more tenuous social existence occurs in another sphecid, *Trigonopsis cameronii* Kohl, in which up to four females construct and provision their cells in a group nest (Eberhard 1972). Although they concentrate their efforts on their own cells, some females add mud to the cells of others and, despite opportunities to 'steal' a nestmate's prey, the practice is rare and generally only takes place during times of need. Because nestmates are likely to be closely related, maintaining a provisioning programme by stealing the occasional prey from a neighbouring cell would be of benefit to the group as a whole, while failure to steal regularly was described by Eberhard as evidence of altruistic behaviour.

Among the contemporary members of the Vespoidea are species which echo the levels of pre-social behaviour found in the higher sphecids. This is particularly true of the majority of Eumenidae and certainly all the British eumenid species. Here the cell – often an elaborate and beautifully constructed affair – is built by the female and oviposition takes place in it before mass provisioning with several paralysed prey after which the cell is finally sealed. Even some of the sphecoids, for example members of the tribe Bembicini, deposit an egg in a previously constructed cell prior to provisioning.

Among some of the African species of eumenid wasps there exists a series of examples which illustrate the possible steps taken by wasps on their road to sociality (Table 36). In Roubaud's (1911, 1916) studies of *Synagris*, a number of species were found which practised mass provisioning in previously constructed mud cells, some fed their larvae on a day-to-day basis, while one species malaxated the food before offering it to the developing larva. At the lowest end of the social scale, *Synagris sicheliana* Saussure and many other species of eumenid wasps, provision their cells with numerous paralysed caterpillars immediately after oviposition, sealing the cell before the egg hatches. *Synagris calida* L. practices mass provisioning during the season when caterpillars are abundant but, when prey is scarce during the rainy season, this species frequently practises progressive provisioning. An even more adaptable species is *Synagris spiniventris* which varies its provisioning regime on a day-to-day basis, mass provisioning when prey is readily obtainable, but bringing in caterpillars during larval development if, for one reason or another, the prey is not easily found. In both these species, the cells are generally sealed before the larva is fully grown. *Synagris cornuta* L. not only practises progressive provisioning but offers the larva a chewed-up paste of caterpillars in much the same way as the social Vespinae.

Among other families of Vespoidea are species which exhibit certain elements characteristic of the social wasps, yet others such as the Masaridae, have reverted to a vegetable diet, storing honey and pollen in mud cells or subterranean cavities. The Zethinae, a eumenid subfamily which occurs in South America and the Philippines, are of interest because many of them construct small groups of cells made from chewed-up fragments of leaves (Williams 1919). The female rests inside the cell after it is built, even during the early stages of larval development, practising progressive provisioning with partly malaxated caterpillars before she closes the cells.

The remaining subfamilies of the Vespidae (Stenogastrinae, Polistinae, and Vespinae) are all either subsocial or fully social, with a wide range of habits indicative of the kinds of societies through which the evolution of social life may well have passed. The most primitive group, the Stenogastrinae of South-east Asia, build a variety of nests from vegetable material and/or mud, ranging in architecture from bell-like cells to combs with hexagonal cells surrounded by a carton envelope. Socially, they exhibit several different levels of behaviour from the primitive condition previously described for *Synagris cornuta*, to an advanced form of organization redolent of *Polistes* species (Table 36). In *Stenogaster depressigaster* Rohwer, one or more females establish rope-like nests (see Plate XXVIe) and emerging offspring remain with the nest and aid in its enlargement (Williams 1919). The larvae are fed on a gelatinous paste of well-masticated flies like the Vespinae, although there is no evidence of trophallactic exchange. In another species, *Stenogaster varipictus* Rohwer, rows of cells are fixed to leaves or the bark of trees and two or more females are found in attendance, but Williams was not able to determine if each female was tending

TABLE 36

Relative levels of sociality among the Vespoidae

LEVEL OF SOCIAL ORGANIZATION	EXAMPLES			
	EUMENIDAE	STENO-GASTRINAE	POLISTINAE	VESPINAE
8. Worker caste well differentiated, few intermediates present			some *Polybia* spp. *Stelopolybia flavipennis*	*Vespula* spp. *Vespa* spp.
7. Differential larval feeding, workers present, intermediates common			*Protopolybia* spp. *Stelopolybia* spp.	
6. Original foundress females are queens, work distribution based on social hierarchial system		*Parischnogaster* sp.	*Polistes* spp.	
5. Division of labour, trophallaxis, weak caste differences			*Belonogaster* spp. *Polybioides tabidus*	
4. Female longevity prolonged, offspring remain on nest		*Stenogaster depressigaster*	*Ropalidia* spp.	
3. Prey macerated and fed directly to larvae	*Synagris cornuta*	*Stenogaster micans*		
2. Cell built, egg laid, followed by progressive provisioning	*Synagris calida*			
————————————*Synagris spiniventris*————————————				
1. Cell built, egg laid, followed by mass provisioning	*Synagris* spp. *Eumenes* spp. (all British Eumenidae)			

its own group of cells or whether true co-operative nesting was taking place. *Stenogaster micans* (Saussure), which builds small combs of hexagonal cells with a protective envelope (Plate XXVIf), was definitely subsocial and Williams (1919) records that a partly finished nest was taken over by another female which continued building the structure. The *Parischnogaster* sp. studied by Yoshikawa and others (1969) which exhibited typical dominance behaviour (see Chapter 13) shows a remarkable level of social organization with all the basic elements of a pleometrotic *Polistes* society.

Turning to the Polistinae we find the greatest diversity of nest structures and societies of all the Vespidae. It is this subfamily which diversified considerably after extending its range over much of Central and South America and Africa from its south-east Asiatic origins. The most primitive members are the little studied Ropalidiini of Africa, South-east Asia, and Australia. The nests of *Ropalidia* species are small and simple like those of *Polistes*, or complex structures similar to those of the more advanced Polybiini (see Fig. 91c) and their social organization is apparently similar to some *Stenogaster* species with several females co-operating in nest building and possibly also in nest foundation. Of all vespid wasps, the Ropalidiini are deserving of the most immediate study for it appears that a whole spectrum of variously organized societies await description, and, as primitive members nearer to ancestral vespoid stocks, knowledge of their biology should undoubtedly help in the understanding of social evolution.

Among species of *Belonogaster* and in many other Polybiini the first signs of primitive caste differentiation appear (Richards and Richards 1951, Richards 1969). Their colonies vary in size from a few individuals to thousands of adults, the larger populations indicating a high level of social integration and likely division of labour. The small morphological differences between egg-laying females and the others are a significant step in the direction of the high-level social organizations which are characteristic of some *Polybia* and most vespine species. With the appearance of morphologically and physiologically distinct castes, there remains only the refinements to the basic plan: greater discrimination of the queens and workers with elimination of intermediate females as in *Vespula*, and a system of social organization based on a chemical regime (i.e. pheromones) rather than the time and energy consuming hierarchial system of *Polistes*.

The incidence of trophallaxis and its possible role in the development of social organization loomed large in the discussions of Roubaud (1916) and Wheeler (1922). In species which practise mass provisioning with entire, paralysed prey, there is no contact between parent and offspring, for the food supplied is sufficient and suitable for larval development. Yet, when progressive provisioning with partially or wholly malaxated prey takes place, some of the prey's juices may be extracted by the adult and the resulting paste or pâte offered to the growing larva during mouth to mouth contacts. Under these circumstances Roubaud suggested that the larva may well produce a saliva to aid ingestion of the food bolus, a saliva that is secreted at the time food is offered. There now exists a situation in which a tending female comes into contact with a secretion produced by its offspring and, if the saliva is attractive, the wasp may actively provoke its production and, as Roubaud postulated, there follows a tendency to increase the number of larvae to be reared simultaneously in order at the same time to satisfy the urgency of oviposition and to profit by the greater abundance of the secretions of the larvae. This is obviously an oversimplification of a situation which may well have evolved during the development of social life in wasps, and it appears somewhat naïve to suggest that the rearing of several brood under colonial conditions is a direct response to the demand for larval saliva. Nevertheless, the importance of trophallaxis among present-day wasps is undisputed for, in *Vespa orientalis*, Ishay and his co-workers have demonstrated that without the saliva queens die and workers desert their colonies. (See Chapter 8 for a more detailed account of trophallaxis.)

Roubaud developed this idea to include caste differentiation due to over-exploitation of larval saliva resulting in under-nourished, smaller adults with undeveloped ovaries. This 'alimentary castration' as it was called by Roubaud could be reinforced by the demands of a foraging existence during adult life so that sterility would be maintained. Marchal (1897) had previously suggested the term 'nutricial castration' to describe the effects of foraging and brood care on the reproductive system of worker wasps. As is apparent from current ideas on caste determination however (Chapter 9), over-exploitation of larval saliva is quite unlikely to be anything but a very minor contribution.

THE GENETIC BASIS OF SOCIAL EVOLUTION

The increased longevity of female wasps, such that emerging offspring have the opportunity to co-operate with the parent in enlarging a colony and tending the siblings, provides the biological basis for the development of social organization. In ancestral societies, the offspring may well have undergone an age polyethism – the young adults collaborating with the parent by contributing to nest defence or even helping to build new cells and forage for materials with which to feed developing larvae. With approaching maturation, the offspring would have the option of remaining with the parental colony as potential reproductives, or leaving to found new nests. A situation very similar to this state of affairs was recorded for *Belonogaster* by Roubaud (1916) who detected few if any differences among the females of a colony except those based on behaviour which were in turn determined by the age of the wasp. The big breakthrough in the development of social life was the appearance of a caste system such that a non-perpetuating, sterile worker class was evolved. The sacrifice of personal fecundity so that the success or fitness of the group or family may be enhanced is an extraordinary step for an animal to take and even troubled Charles Darwin when he developed his theory of natural selection.

The basic genetic problem involved in the evolution of self-sacrificing altruistic behaviour is an intriguing one which has recently occupied the attention of geneticists.

During the evolution of social behaviour in wasps, two major steps may be distinguished, first the early developments when social life began, and second the subsequent diversification of the embryonic societies in response to ecological demands (Richards 1971a). The first problem is primarily a genetic one, namely, how natural selection can favour genotypes that cause sacrifice of reproductive ability. At first sight, it seems that more fertile genotypes are bound to propagate themselves more effectively than less fertile ones so that the latter, if they occurred at all, would always be decreasing in frequency.

It is obviously essential that there be advantages gained by relatives to compensate in some way, for the sacrifices made by an altruist. Parental care or defence of a community by post-reproductive individuals may be claimed as altruistic traits which benefit offspring or other members of the group and the selection of these traits is not difficult to understand. In the case of wasps however, certain members – the workers – have gone to the far extreme of sacrificing virtually all their reproductive potential for the benefit of the colony.

The key lies in the fact that all members of a colony are related and therefore genetically similar to one another. In full diploid animals, both parents contribute equally to the genotype of their offspring and daughters possess one-half of their genes alike. Fractions of this kind can be worked out for other pairs of relatives and are known as co-efficients of relatedness b. They measure how similar two relatives are expected to be genetically. As regards altruism, it can be shown that if k is the ratio of gain by beneficiary to loss by altruist, resulting from some altruistic act, then for genes causing the act to receive positive selection, k must fulfill the condition $k>1/b$. For sisters b is one half; for half sisters it is one quarter, and for first cousins it is one eigth. Thus, if sisters are involved, their reproductive rate must be doubled, half-sisters quadrupled, etc, if complete sacrifice of reproduction in the form of a mutant 'altruist' (i.e. a worker) is to be selected for. In

Hamilton's (1964a, b, 1971) examination of the genetics of social evolution it is pointed out that, due to the haplo-diploid method of sex determination in the Hymenoptera, the coefficient of relatedness between mother and daughter remains one-half, but – because the paternal genes are identical (assuming a single insemination) – the relationship between sisters is three-fourths. Therefore, daughters may increase their 'fitness' – in the sense of propagating their genes through the reproduction of their relatives – by aiding their mother in helping to rear sisters (which are three-fourths related) rather than producing their own daughters (which would only be one-half related). Thus, when the opportunity arises through increased parent longevity, assistance by offspring in rearing sisters would benefit the group more than an equivalent effort in rearing their own brood.

Hamilton has emphasized that the closer the relationship the more likely it is that altruistic behaviour will be evolved. For example, in an out-breeding population which practises multiple mating, a sacrifice in fecundity must be matched by four times the social advantages to the group, while with single mating, the rate drops to one and one-third times, and with an inbreeding population practising single mating the ratio drops even further. To sum up, a group with haplo-diploidy has more chance of evolving a sterile worker caste than a group practising normal reproduction, and the factors of monogamous mating and inbreeding, which serve to tighten further the relatedness of potential worker and queen, may increase the chance still more. Some alternative explanations for the evolution of social behaviour have recently been discussed by Lin and Michener (1972).

From a genetic point of view, selection should favour the haplo-metrotic society in which the offspring of a single egg-laying female are all closely related. Yet in many species of wasps, the societies are pleometrotic with several queens so that many workers will be tending nieces, even if we assume that the queens are all sisters. In the swarming species of Polybiinae which practise pleometrosis, the queens are probably closely related. This makes the genetic justification for altruism less formidable, but when colonies are founded by an association of potential queens as in many *Polistes* species, the relationships are rather different. M. J. West and V. M. Rodrigues (personal communication) have shown by marking experiments that associates are normally derived from a single parent colony. When all but the one, dominant egg-laying female relinquish their potential fecundity during the establishment of the social hierarchy, there must presumably be some comparisons made between the relative fecundities of the females such that one eventually becomes the dominant (queen) and the others either support her as functional workers or leave the nest. Generally, the successful queen in such an association is the one with better-developed ovaries and therefore the subordinate females, which undoubtedly augment the reproductive capacity of the dominant egg-layer, probably also fulfill the criterion that what she gains is more than one and one third times what they sacrifice (by not fighting harder for dominance or trying to nest alone) (see West 1967). Associations of potential queens during nest founding may have an additional advantage for should the dominant female perish, one of the auxiliary females can assume the role of queen and colony life will be maintained.

Other factors have contributed to the diversification and evolution of social organization in wasps.

In pleometrotic societies of Polybiini, the fecundity of individual queens is considerably less than that of the single queen in a haplometrotic colony (Richards and Richards 1951). This differential fecundity illustrates the diversity of social organization among wasps, the differences underlining the ways in which wasps have become adapted for survival. Two principal classes of society are found in wasps, the single and multiple queened communities and in each the colonies may be either small or large. Where colonies are small, oviposition rate is low and the queen or queens retain their mobility so that in the event of attack by raiding ants or vertebrate predators, the adult population, complete with its queen(s), may evacuate the nest and rebuild rapidly elsewhere. Nest evacuation may also be successfully conducted by large pleometrotic colonies in which the several queens retain their mobility.

In the large haplometrotic colonies characterized by *Vespula* species, the single queen loses her mobility through the enormous increase in size and weight of the ovaries and wearing away of the wings. In these cases, the defence of the colony depends on the large numbers of workers attacking potential predators. It is interesting that *Vespula* colonies are found in temperate regions where invertebrate predators such as the Driver Ants (*Eciton* spp.) are absent and the principal predators are large mammals which would be discouraged by the numerous stings inflicted on them by a disturbed worker force. Some Polybiini enter into loose symbiotic relationships with tree-nesting ants (e.g. *Azteca* spp.) from which they gain a measure of protection from marauders (Richards and Richards 1951). Richards (1971a) emphasizes that, in the tropics, predation is probably one of the more important ecological factors influencing the diversification of wasps in the region.

The development of a comb pedicel which may be more easily guarded, and the further developments in nest structure which have given rise to hard, protective envelopes with one or more easily defended entrance holes, further illustrate the adaptations made by wasps in response to predator pressure during their evolution.

Where wasps have penetrated temperate regions, the climatic extremes encountered in these areas have imposed certain modifications on the behaviour and biology of wasp societies. Swarming is no longer the principal means of dispersal for the harsh conditions of winter place a limit on the duration of the active season and, unless stores of food are available, colonies would be unable to survive the winter months. With the exception of honeybees and ants, all other social insect societies of temperate areas break up in the autumn, and only the newly produced queens survive by hibernating, colony foundation taking place in the following spring by individual females or associations of potential queens.

The various societies and their methods of dissemination, defence, and nesting outlined in this and the previous chapter indicate how the vespid wasps have responded to the demands of the environment, by ensuring optimum fecundity within the unit while providing for the defence of the community.

GEOGRAPHICAL ASPECTS OF WASP EVOLUTION

Behavioural characteristics and paper nest structures do not lend themselves to fossilization and, as a result, the palaentological evidence for the evolution of social Vespidae is sparse. Bequaert and Carpenter (1941) have reviewed the fossil evidence accumulated so far which shows that the Hymenoptera were prevalent during the Jurassic (130-180 million years ago) although none of the social families are represented in strata older than the Baltic amber of the Eocene (40-60 million years). The vespids found in the Baltic amber are not differentiated into the solitary and social forms that we know today and there is no evidence of any morphological differentiation of castes which would in any case be a later development following the establishment of social life. Termites had apparently evolved by the Oligocene (less than 40 million years ago) and typical *Eumenes* cells have been found in the Upper Oligocene strata by Handlirsch (1910). Despite the inadequate fossil records, it may be assumed that the Vespoidea diversified during the Cretaceous (70 to 130 million years) and that social life first appeared during the Eocene (Richards 1971a).

The present-day distribution of wasps (Fig. 92) underlines the southeast Asiatic origins of the Vespidae for it is the only area where all the subfamilies are represented and where *Polistes* is structurally most diverse (Richards 1971a). The Stenogastrinae occur exclusively in the Oriental and Papuan regions, their restricted distribution in these areas being due no doubt to their specialized adaptations to the tropical rain forest (Van der Vecht 1965). The Polistinae and Vespinae probably evolved separately from a common social ancestor for the Vespinae

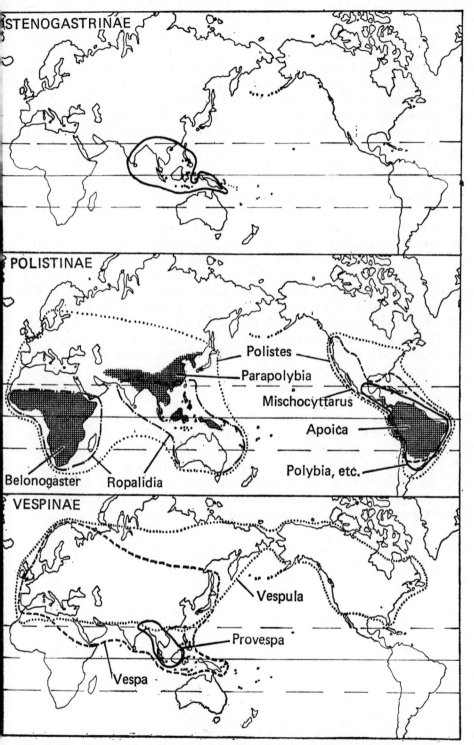

STENOGASTRINAE

POLISTINAE

Polistes
Parapolybia
Mischocyttarus
Apoica
Polybia, etc.
Belonogaster   Ropalidia

VESPINAE

Vespula
Provespa
Vespa

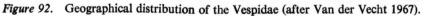

Figure 92. Geographical distribution of the Vespidae (after Van der Vecht 1967).

are structurally more similar to the Eumenidae than the Polistinae (Richards 1971a).

During the Eocene, when the major land masses of the present-day Americas, Africa, and Asia were beginning to separate as a result of continental drift, the subfamilies of Vespidae were well established and Polistinae and Vespinae in particular were beginning to diversify in the favourable environment provided by the tropical Old World. In common with the dispersal of most other animals, the dominant groups which evolved in the Indo-Malayan tropics began to spread into the less favourable areas of temperate South Africa, Australasia, temperate Eurasia, and North America and thence to tropical Central and South America (Darlington 1957). The dispersal routes taken by the Vespinae and Polistinae were almost certainly north-west across Eurasia, one group reaching Africa, the other crossing the Behring Straits into North America. The absence of Vespinae and Polybiini in Australia strongly suggests that the movement of vespid wasps did not take place across any antarctic land bridge. With the encroaching ice age, those vespid species which had reached America would be forced to retreat until only Central and South America were occupied. In this tropical environment, the diversification of the Polybiini has taken place. There is evidence that the first wasps to colonize South America were the *Stelopolybia* group for succeeding Polistinae, especially *Polistes* species, have mimicked the colour patterns of *Stelopolybia* species.

While our knowledge of the genetics, behaviour, and distribution of wasps is still inadequate, the past few years have seen enormous progress in our understanding of how social life in the Vespidae could have evolved. With the general pattern of evolution now reasonably well established, we can look forward to a period when many of the innumerable gaps in our knowledge will be filled by the contributions of wasp-orientated entomologists throughout the world.

APPENDICES

I

Taxonomy of British Wasps

With a taxonomically 'difficult' group it is often impossible to reconcile the viewpoints of all specialists when preparing a key and where possible the serious student of taxonomy must judge the usefulness of a key by comparison with others which are available. Keys to species of British Vespoidae include Felton's (1967) key to *Odynerus* and *Symmorphus* species, and Guichard's (1972) key to *Symmorphus* species, the latter including a discussion of the complexities of synonomies in the genus.

In a group which depends to some extent on colour and colour pattern differences to distinguish species, there are certain dangers due to the inherent variability of biological material. Generally, no one character can safely be used to separate a species and the taxonomist must assess the validity of a determination by reference to all the characters available in a key. Geographical varieties of wasp species undoubtedly occur, often reflected in colour differences such as the markedly white-banded form of *Ancistrocerus oviventris* from Ireland, the Outer Hebrides and the Isle of Man (K. M. Guichard, personal communication). Differences in the number of yellow gastral bands in Eumenidae may be an expression of varietal differences, although the number of available specimens of many species is often too few for detailed analysis of such phenomena.

While the Vespidae present few taxonomic problems, except perhaps when examining worker adults in some instances, the Eumenidae have undergone several changes in nomenclature during recent years (see Blüthgen, 1961, for example), and can prove difficult to key down to species. I hope the liberal use of figures and plates will ease some of the problems involved in their determination. The keys for eumenid taxonomy are based entirely on the works of Felton (1954, 1966, and

1967) and Blüthgen (1961) with additions and corrections made by Dr I. H. H. Yarrow.

The principal characters which distinguish the Vespoidea from other superfamilies of British Hymenoptera are: (1) the forewings are folded longtitudinally when at rest; (2) forewing cell M+(Rs+M) is very elongate and longer than cell M (Plate II); (3) the antennae are distinctly elbowed; (4) the glossa and paraglossae of the labium end distally in sclerotized pads (Fig. 3); (5) eyes generally emarginate. For a detailed key to families of British Hymenoptera the reader is referred to the *Introduction and Keys to Families of Hymenoptera* by O. W. Richards (1956). Details of the taxonomy and distribution of North American species of Vespinae have been published by C. D. F. Miller (1961) and descriptions and keys to continental European Vespoidea are given by P. Blüthgen (1961).

There is only one British species of *Eumenes*, *Gymnomerus*, *Pseudepipona*, *Euodynerus*, and *Microdynerus* and they will therefore be separated in the key to genera of Eumenidae.

Key to Families of British Wasps

1. Tibia of mesothoracic legs with a single spur, tarsal claws with an inner tooth (Fig. 8d), mandibles grooved (sulcate) (Fig. 4b), hindwing with anal lobe (Plate IIb)..................EUMENIDAE.
— Tibia of mesothoracic legs with 2 spurs (Fig. 8a), tarsal claws without teeth (Fig. 8c), mandibles not grooved (Fig. 2b), hindwing without anal lobe (Plate IIa).............................VESPIDAE.

Key to the British Genera of Eumenidae

1. 1st gastral segment petiolate, constricted apically, and about half as wide as 2nd gastral segment (Fig. 93a)......*Eumenes coarctatus* (L.).
— 1st gastral segment sub-petiolate, not, or only slightly, constricted apically, far more than half as wide as 2nd.............................2.

2. Tegula entire (Fig. 93c); coxa III evenly rounded, not tuberculate, on its inner margin where there is a small, raised, longitudinal carina (Fig. 93h); labrum entire (Fig. 93f); propodeum evenly rounded (Fig. 93j), ventral shelf flat at right angles to the posterior face and continued laterally into a ventral coxal shield (Plate XXVIIa); male antennae rolled (Fig. 93n)............................3.
— Tegula emarginate on inner side posteriorly (Fig. 93d, e); coxa III tuberculate on its inner margin (Fig. 93i), if a longitudinal carina is present it is usually markedly wider at the apex of the tubercle; labrum sinuate (Fig. 93g); propodeum with at least a ventro-lateral

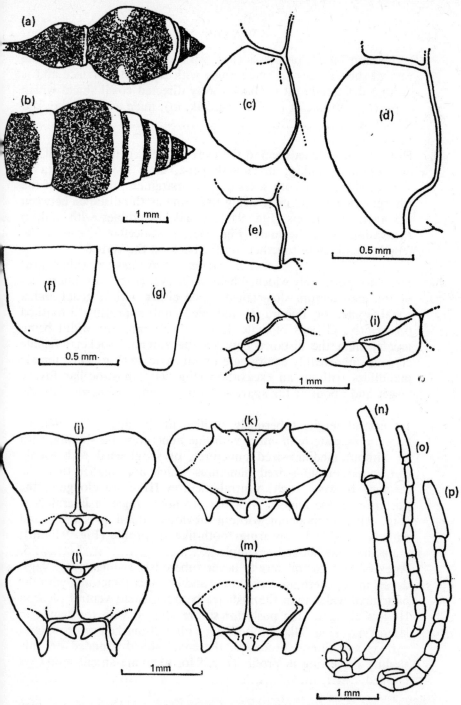

Figure 93. Taxonomy of Eumenidae (after Felton 1954): (a) *E. coarctatus* dorsal view of male gaster; (b) *A. parietum* dorsal view of male gaster; (c) *O. spinipes* dorsal view of left tegula; (d) *A. parietum* left tegula; (e) *M. exilis* left tegula; (f) *O. spinipes* labrum; (g) *E. quadrifasciatus* labrum; (h) *O. spinipes* dorso-lateral view of right hind coxa; (i) *A. parietum* hind coxa; (j) *O. melanocephalus* posterior view of propodeum; (k) *E. quadrifasciatus* propodeum; (l) *S. gracilis* propodeum; (m) *P. herrichii* propodeum; (n) *O. spinipes* anterior view of left antenna of male; (o) *S. gracilis* male antenna; (p) *E. quadrifasciatus* male antenna.

Y

carina and lateral processes (Fig. 93k), or if these are absent the ventral shelf makes an acute angle with the posterior face and is produced laterally into a backwardly directed coxal shield which appears tooth-like in profile (Fig. 94k, m); male antennae hooked or simple..4.

3. Head much widened behind the eyes (Fig. 94a); interstices of the mesoscutum shining; male with gena, coxa II and femora II simple; clypeus of both sexes deeply emarginate, the width of the emargination in the male being the same as the distance between the antennal sockets (Fig. 94c); female mandibles with a deep excavation as in the male (Fig. 94e); post-ocellar foveae of the female small, close together, set far back on the vertex..............
....*Gymnomerus laevipes* (Shuckard)
— Head not noticeably widened behind the eyes (Fig. 94b); interstices of the mesoscutum shagreened; male either with a genal and a coxal spine, or femora II modified and appearing 3-toothed posteriorly; clypeus of male deeply emarginate, the width being greater than the distance between the antennal sockets; female clypeus only weakly emarginate or subtruncate (Fig. 94d); female mandibles without an excavation (Fig. 94f); post-ocellar foveae larger and about as far apart as lateral ocelli...*Odynerus* Latreille

4. 1st gastral tergite tuberously swollen at the apex (Fig. 94i, j); dorsal mesepisternum either with fine punctures and shining, with or without medium-sized punctures, or shagreened with evenly distributed medium-sized punctures which are smaller than the distance between each; ventral pleuron III more elongate, the posterior suture aligned with the pro-notal angle in lateral view (Fig. 94l); propodeum without obvious lateral processes, and with coxal shield appearing tooth-like in profile (Fig. 94l, m); male antennae hooked or simple...5.
— Apex of first gastral tergite never tuberously swollen (Fig. 94g); dorsal mesepisternum very closely and coarsely punctured with the punctures wider than the distance between each; ventral pleuron III less elongate, the posterior suture aligned with the tegula in lateral view (Fig. 94k); propodeum with well-marked ventro-lateral carinas and lateral processes, the coxal shield rounded or only slightly projecting in profile (Fig. 94o, n); male antennae always hooked ....6.

5. 1st gastral tergite with the anterior surface evenly rounded into the dorsal surface (Fig. 94j); only a slight indication of a longitudinal furrow along the mid-line of the tergite; 2nd gastral

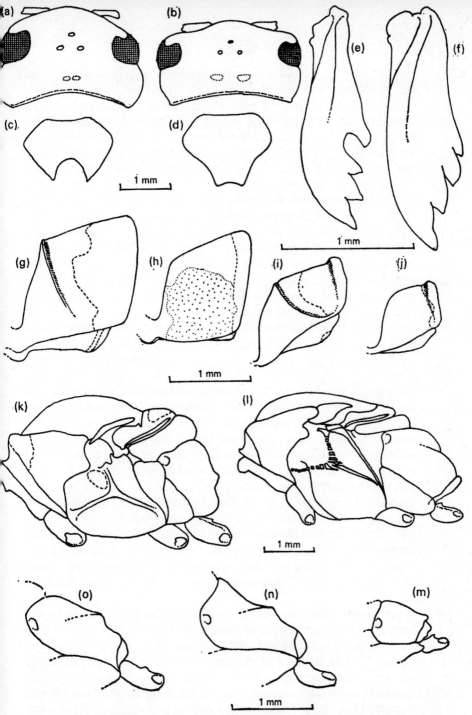

Figure 94. Taxonomy of Eumenidae (after Felton 1954): (a) *G. laevipes* dorsal view of head of female; (b) *O. spinipes* female head; (c) *G. laevipes* anterior view of clypeus of female; (d) *O. spinipes* female clypeus; (e) *G. laevipes* anterior view of right mandible of female; (f) *O. spinipes* mandible of female; (g) *A. parietum* lateral view of first segment of gaster; (h) *P. herrichii* first segment of gaster; (i) *S. gracilis* first segment of gaster; (j) *M. exilis* first segment of gaster; (k) *A. parietum* lateral view of thorax; (l) *S. gracilis* thorax; (m) *M. exilis* lateral view of propodeum; (n) *E. quadrifasciatus* lateral view of propodeum; (o) *P. herrichii* lateral view of propodeum.

tergite with an apical white, transverse seam; propodeum with the posterior and lateral faces evenly rounded, and punctured alike; parapsidal furrows very weakly developed; male with the antennae hooked (cf. Fig. 94p); female without post-ocellar fovea..........................*Microdynerus exilis* (Herrich-Schaeffer).

— 1st gastral tergite with a distinct transverse ridge at the junction of the anterior and dorsal surfaces, this ridge continuing along the lateral margin of the tergite to the apical swelling (Fig. 94i); a marked longitudinal furrow present along the mid-line of the tergite; 2nd gastral tergite without a terminal seam; propodeum with the lateral and dorsal faces very coarsely punctured, the posterior face smooth or weakly rugose, dorso-lateral and ventro-lateral carinae are simulated by the abrupt change of sculturing (Plate XXVIIb); a smooth, oval depression present between the propodeum and notum III in the mid-line (Fig. 93l); parapsidal furrows well developed at least posteriorly; male antennae simple (Fig. 93o); female post-ocellar foveae deep, a little larger than a lateral ocellus, and as far apart as the lateral ocelli.....................
....*Symmorphus* Wesmael

6. 1st gastral tergite with the anterior surface evenly rounded into the dorsal surface (Fig. 94h); propodeum with ventro-lateral carinae and lateral processes, with or without an erect tooth-like lamina dorso-laterally, under the lateral margin of notum III, no obvious dorso-lateral carina present; anterior face of the ventral mesepisternum smooth and clearly marked off by a ridge from the rest of the episternum..7.

— 1st gastral tergite with an obvious transverse ridge separating the anterior and dorsal surfaces (Fig. 94g); propodeum with a shield-like dorsal lamina continuous laterally with the lateral process, completely enclosing the posterior face; anterior face of the episternum smooth and rounded into the rest of the episternum, with at most a very slight, incomplete ridge......*Ancistrocerus* Wesmael

7. Propodeum with an erect, tooth-like lamina dorso-laterally beneath the lateral margin of notum III (Fig. 93k) (Plate XXVIIc), hind angle of coxal shield slightly angulate in profile (Fig. 94n); notum III with dorsal and posterior faces at right angles or nearly so, the posterior edge of the dorsal surface being irregularly toothed; male antennal segment 13 reaching to the base of segment 10 (Fig. 93p); female with a pair of post-ocellar foveae, each as large as the ocellar area, set close together, covered with dense brown pubescence and with a small area of black setae on each side of the mid-line..................*Euodynerus quadrifasciatus* (F.).

— Propodeum without such an erect lamina, but with a very faint
    indication of a transverse carina at about two-thirds the height
    of the median carina (Plate XXVIId) (Fig. 93m); coxal shield not
    at all angulate in profile (Fig. 94o); notum III evenly rounded
    posteriorly; male antennal segment 13 reaching to base of segment
    11 only (cf. Fig. 96j); female with a single median post-ocellar
    fovea, smaller than the ocellar area, and divided longitudinally by
    a narrow keel.......................*Pseudepipona herrichii* (Saussure).

Key to Species of *Odynerus* Latreille, 1802

Males

1. Femur III flattened with 2 emarginations posteriorly so that it
    appears 3-toothed; tibia II expanded distally (Fig. 95a, b); coxa II
    unmodified ....2.
—   Femur and tibia II simple; coxa II with ventrally directed spines
    (Fig. 95c)...3.

2. Gaster with 6 apical yellow bands on tergites 1 to 6, 1 interrupted
    apical band on sternite 2; pubescence of head long and black;
    femur II with central process truncate apically (Fig. 95b)............
    ....*spinipes* (L.).
—   Gaster with 6 apical yellowish-white bands, apical 3 shortened
    laterally; only lateral spots on sternite 2; pubescence of head
    shorter and white; femur II with central process rounded apically
    (Fig. 95a) ....*melanocephalus* (Gmelin).

3. Gaster with 6 apical yellow bands, apical 1 shortened laterally
    metanotum with a yellow spot; propodeum with 2 small lateral
    spots ....*reniformis* (Gmelin).
—   Gaster with 5 apical yellowish-white bands, apical 1 shortened
    laterally; metanotum with a spot, but propodeum unmarked
    ....*simillimus* Morawitz.

Females

1. Clypeus and metanotum without yellow markings...................2.
—   Clypeus either with a basal yellow band or a pair of lateral yellow
    spots; metanotum with a yellow spot.....................................3.

2. Gaster with 5 yellow apical bands, apical 1 and 3-5 shortened
    laterally; sternite 2 with an interrupted apical band; clypeus
    slightly but angularly emarginate (Fig. 94d); scape and pedicel
    of antennae black beneath, tarsi darkened basally and externally
    ....*spinipes* (L.).

—   Gaster with 5 apical yellowish-white bands, apical 1, 4 and 5 shortened laterally; sternite 2 with only lateral spots; clypeus very slightly but regularly emarginate; scape and pedicel reddish-brown beneath; tarsi reddish-brown......*melanocephalus* (Gmelin).

3.   Clypeus with a basal yellow band (Fig. 95d); propodeum with large spots; tergal bands yellow and expanded laterally (Fig. 95f) ....*reniformis* (Gmelin).

—   Clypeus with 2 basal spots (Fig. 95e); propodeum unmarked; tergal bands yellowish-white and linear.........*simillimus* Morawitz.

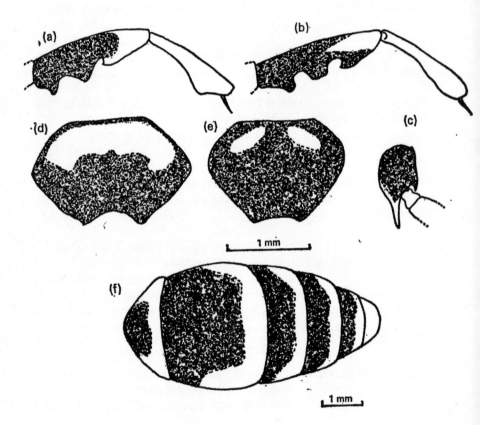

Figure 95. Taxonomy of *Odynerus* species (after Felton 1954): (a) *O. melanocephalus* posterior view of right femur and tibia of mesothoracic leg of male; (b) *O. spinipes* femur and tibia of mesothoracic leg of male; (c) *O. simillimus* postero-lateral view of second coxa of male; (d) *O. reniformis* anterior view of clypeus of female (e) *O. simillimus* clypeus of female; (f) *O. reniformis* dorsal view of gaster of female.

Key to species of *Ancistrocerus* **Wesmael, 1836**

Males

1. Gastral sternite 2 with intercostal spaces of basal transverse
    sulcature less than one and a half times as long as broad, sternite 2
    impressed posterior to the sulcature (Fig. 96s); 4-6 gastral tergal
    bands ....2.

—   Intercarinal spaces of basal sulcature twice as long as broad or
    longer; sternite at least not impressed posterior to the sulcature
    (Fig. 96t-w); if the sternite appears slightly impressed (*trifasciatus*)
    only 3 tergal bands are present, with sometimes an incomplete 4th
    ....4.

2. Posterior face of propodeum very finely diagonally striate, scarcely
    shining; transverse carina of first gastral tergite clearly indentate
    in the mid-line; puncturation of 2nd gastral tergite close and fine;
    pronotal angles not sharply pointed, the yellow collar narrow;
    costae of 2nd gastral sternite very short, rather shorter at mid-
    disc than at its sides; scutellum rarely with, postscutellum always
    without, yellow spots; gaster with 5 complete yellow tergal bands,
    with or without an incomplete 6th; black cutting band of 1st
    gastral tergite more or less angularly in the mid-line (Fig. 96a)
    ....*parietum* (L.).

—   Posterior face of propodeum rather coarsely diagonally striate;
    transverse carina of 1st gastral tergite not indentate on mid-line
    though its line may be broken by punctures; postscutellum fre-
    quently yellow spotted; black cutting band of 1st gastral tergite
    rectangularly (Fig. 96b)...3.

3. Pronotal angles sharp, thornlike, the yellow collar narrow;
    puncturation of 2nd gastral tergite coarser and deeper and wider
    apart; costae of 2nd gastral sternite short and of even length
    across disc; hypoepimeral area (=upper part of mesepisternum)
    rugo-punctate, the punctures close and the interspaces raised;
    gaster with 4 complete yellow bands, with or without a complete 5th
    .... *gazella* (Panzer).

—   Pronotal angles not thornlike, the yellow collar broad; punctura-
    tion of 2nd gastral tergite finer and closer (intermediate between
    parietum and *gazella*); costae of 2nd gastral sternite longer at
    mid-disc than at its sides; hypoepimeral area punctate, the punc-
    tures large and the interspaces for the most part flat; gaster with 5
    complete yellow bands and an incomplete 6th ...*quadratus* (Panzer).

4. 2nd gastral sternite abruptly raised distal to the sulcature (Fig.

96u, v); 5 or 6 tergal bands..5.
— 2nd gastral sternite evenly convex distal to the sulcature (Fig. 96t, w); if it appears abruptly raised (*scoticus*) then there are only 3 complete tergal bands..6.

5. Clypeus deeply, more than semicircularly, excised (Fig. 96f); posterior face of propodeum finely diagonally striate and dull ventrally; yellow band of 1st gastral tergite linear; 2nd gastral sternite as Fig. 96u................................*oviventris* (Wesmael).
— Clypeus little excised (Fig. 96g); posterior face of propodeum diagonally striate and shining ventrally; yellow band of 1st gastral tergite rectangularly emarginate; 2nd gastral sternite as Fig. 96v .... *nigricornis* (Curtis).

6. Lateral and posterior faces of propodeum with large smooth and shining areas; 13th antennal segment very short, not nearly reaching apical border of the 10th segment (Fig. 96h); yellow band on 1st gastral tergite often as Fig. 96c......*antilope* (Panzer).
— Posterior and lateral faces of propodeum striate and/or coarsely punctured, dull or only slightly shining; 13th antennal segment at least attaining apical border of 10th segment (Fig. 96i-k)............7.

7. Excised part of clypeus as broad or broader than distance between the antennal sockets; 1st gastral tergite between transverse carina and apical border more than twice as broad as long; 13th antennal segment as Fig. 96i; 5-6 gastral tergal bands; band on 1st gastral tergite rectangularly excised, rarely linear............*parietinus* (L.).
— Excised part of clypeus slightly narrower than distance between the antennal sockets; 1st gastral tergite twice as broad as long or less; 3 complete and sometimes 1 incomplete tergal bands; band on 1st gastral tergite linear..8.

8. 13th antennal segment thin, reaching apex of 10th segment, rarely beyond (Fig. 96j); 2nd gastral sternite very slightly convex, level, or very slightly impressed posterior to the sulcature (Fig. 96w); hind tibiae yellow with black internal markings, and sometimes reddish-brown apically, rarely entirely yellow (Fig. 96d)............
....*trifasciatus* (Müller).
— 13th antennal segment stout, reaching beyond the apex of the 10th segment (Fig. 96k); 2nd gastral sternite markedly raised posterior to the sulcature (Fig. 96t); hind tibiae, reddish yellow or yellow externally, reddish-brown internally and apically, sometimes with a small black mark internally (Fig. 96e).....................
.... *scoticus* (Curtis).

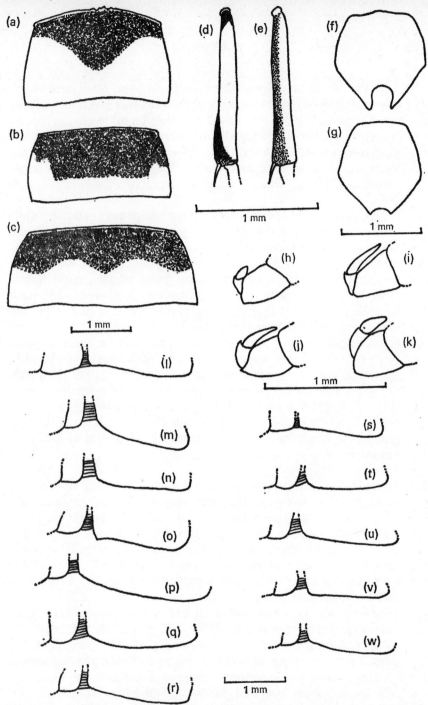

Figure 96. Taxonomy of *Ancistrocerus* species (after Felton 1954): (a) *A. parietum* dorsal view of first gastral tergite; (b) *A. gazella* first gastral tergite; (c) *A. antilope* first gastral tergite; (d) *A. trifasciatus* posterior view of right hind tibia of male; (e) *A. scoticus* hind tibia of male; (f) *A. oviventris* anterior view of clypeus of male; (g) *A. nigricornis* clypeus of male; (h) *A. antilope* terminal segments of antenna of male; (i) *A. parietinus* male antenna; (j) *A. trifasciatus* male antenna; (k) *A. scoticus* male antenna; (l-r) lateral view of second gastral sternite of females; (s-w) lateral view of second gastral sternite of males; (l) *A. parietum*; (m) *A. scoticus*; (n) *A. oviventris*; (o) *A. nigricornis*; (p) *A. antilope*; (q) *A. parietinus*; (r) *A. trifasciatus*; (s) *A. parietum*; (t) *A. scoticus*; (u) *A. oviventris*; (v) *A. nigricornis*; (w) *A. trifasciatus*.

Females

1. 2nd gastral sternite impressed posterior to basal transverse sulca-
    ture (Fig. 96l); intercostal spaces of the sulcature less than one and
    a half times as long as broad; 4-5 complete tergal bands............2.
—   2nd gastral sternite at least slightly convex posterior to the sulca-
    ture, often markedly raised (Fig. 96m-r); intercostal spaces of the
    sulcature twice as long as broad or longer; 3-5 complete tergal
    bands.. 4.

2. Posterior face of propodeum finely diagonally striate, dull;
    transverse carina of 1st gastral tergite broadly indentate in the
    mid-line; puncturation of 2nd gastral tergite close and fine;
    gaster usually with 5 complete tergal bands, with or without an
    incomplete 6th; black cutting yellow band of 1st gastral tergite
    more or less angularly (Fig. 96a); forewing with brownish mark
    from base to apex of anterior margin; costae of 2nd gastral sternite
    very short, rather shorter at mid-disc than at its sides; hypoepimeral
    area densely rugo-punctate, interspaces almost non-existent;
    pronotal angles not sharply pointed; scutellum usually with,
    postscutellum always without, yellow spots.........*parietum* (L.).
—   Posterior face of propodeum rather coarsely diagonally striate,
    shining; transverse carina of 1st gastral tergite not or only very
    slightly indentate on mid-line, though its line may be broken by
    punctures; black cutting yellow band of 1st gastral tergite rect-
    angularly..3.

3. Forewing with brownish mark from base to apex of anterior
    margin; pronotal angles frequently sharply pointed; puncturation
    of 2nd gastral tergite coarser, deeper and wider apart; costae of
    2nd gastral sternite short, of even length across disc; hypo-
    epimeral area rugo-punctate, the narrow interspaces sharply
    raised; scutellum and postscutellum frequently with two yellow
    spots each; gaster usually with complete bands on first 4 segments,
    and sometimes an incomplete band on the 5th...*gazella* (Panzer).
—   Forewing almost clear along apical margin; pronotal angles
    almost rounded; puncturation of 2nd gastral tergite finer and
    closer (intermediate between *parietum* and *gazella*); costae of 2nd
    gastral sternite longer at mid-disc than at its sides; hypoepimeral
    area punctate, the punctures, large and isolated by wide, flat
    interspaces; scutellum and postscutellum always (?) with two
    yellow spots each; gaster with 5 complete yellow bands and a spot
    on the apical tergite....................................*quadratus* (Panzer).

4. 1st gastral tergite between transverse carina and apical border

twice or less as broad as long; never more than 3 complete tergal bands, though sometimes an incomplete 4th is present; clypeus usually without yellow markings...5.

— 1st gastral tergite twice or more as broad as long; always with at least 4 complete tergal bands; clypeus with or without yellow markings...6.

5. 2nd gastral sternite fairly abruptly raised posterior to the sulcature (Fig. 96m); hind tibiae and tarsi reddish-brown; mesoscutum as broad as long or broader...........................*scoticus* (Curtis).
— 2nd gastral sternite slightly and evenly convex posterior to costa (Fig. 96r); hind tibiae yellow, marked with black or reddish-brown basally and apically; tarsi dark reddish-brown; mesoscutum longer than broad...*trifasciatus* (Müller).

6. 2nd gastral sternite evenly convex posterior to costa (Fig. 96p, q); hind tarsi black, sometimes marked with dark reddish-brown......7.
— 2nd gastral sternite abruptly raised posterior to the sulcature (Fig. 96n, o); hind tarsi light reddish-brown............................8.

7. Posterior and lateral faces of propodeum with large smooth and shining areas; post-ocellar area without a hair patch; gaster with 4 complete tergal bands, and yellow dots on tergites 5 and 6; 1st tergal band often as Fig. 96c....................*antilope* (Panzer).
— Posterior face of propodeum finely diagonally striate, only slightly shining, lateral face finely longitudinally striate; post-ocellar fovea often with a brown patch of short, fine hairs; gaster with 5 complete tergal bands, and a yellow spot on tergite 6............*parietinus* (L.).

8. 2nd gastral sternite raised perpendicularly from the sulcature (Fig. 96o); clypeus with yellow marks, and with very coarse punctures forming marked striations; hind tibiae yellow with black or brown internal markings.................*nigricornis* (Curtis).
— 2nd gastral sternite very slightly receding posterior to the sulcature (Fig. 96n); clypeus usually without yellow markings, and the punctures not forming marked striations; hind tibiae reddish-brown...*oviventris* (Wesmael).

Key to species of *Symmorphus* Wesmael, 1836

Males

1. Scape of antenna yellow anteriorly; tibia III yellow with or without black internally and apically; 4 or 5 complete tergal bands.........2.

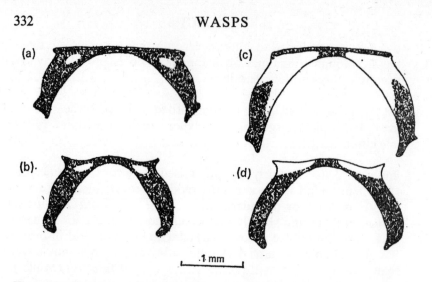

Figure 97. Taxonomy of *Symmorphus* species (after Felton 1954): (a) *S. crassicornis* dorsal view of pronotum of male; (b) *S. gracilis* pronotum of male; (c) *S. crassicornis* pronotum of female; (d) *S. gracilis* pronotum of female.

—   Scape black anteriorly; tibia III black, only ringed with yellow basally; 3 complete tergal bands on tergites 1, 2 and 4...............3.

2.   Pronotal angles not produced, slightly receding (Fig. 97a); tibia III entirely yellow; tarsus III with basal 3 segments yellow, segments 4 and 5 darkened; 4 complete tergal bands...*crassicornis* (Panzer).
—   Pronotal angles produced (Fig. 97b); tibia III yellow externally, black internally and apically; tarsus III with 1st and 2nd segments yellowish-red, segments 3-5 darkened; 5 complete tergal bands
....*gracilis* (Brullé).

3.   Dorsal mesepisternum with series of punctures, becoming very coarsely punctured posteriorly (Plate XXVIIIa); tarsus III with basal segment yellowish-red.....................*sinuatissimus* Richards.
—   Dorsal mesepisternum smooth, with only a few scattered punctures (Plate XXVIIIb); tarsus III with the basal segment black, similar to the other segments.....................................*connexus* (Curtis).

Females

1.   Pronotal angles either rounded or markedly produced (Fig. 97c, d); tibia III either reddish-brown or yellow with black internally and apically; 4 or 5 complete tergal bands............................2.
—   Pronotal angles transverse; tibia III black, ringed with yellow apically; 3 complete tergal bands on tergites 1, 2 and 4...........3.

2. Pronotal angles rounded (Fig. 97c); tibia III reddish; scape black anteriorly; mesoscutum with pale hairs; 4 complete tergal bands .... *crassicornis* (Panzer).
— Pronotal angles produced (Fig. 97d); tibia III yellow with black internally and apically; scape yellow anteriorly; mesoscutum with dark hairs; 5 complete tergal bands.................*gracilis* (Brullé).

3. Dorsal mesepisternum shining with series of punctures (Plate XXVIIIa); mesepimeron with large close punctures wider than the interstitial spaces; tarsus III with 1st segment reddish-yellow...... ....*sinuatissimus* Richards.
— Dorsal mesepisternum smooth and shining with very few medium-sized punctures (Plate XXVIIIb); mesepimeron smooth with a few scattered punctures; tarsus III with 1st segment darkened......... ....*connexus* (Curtis).

Key to species of Vespidae

1. Antennae relatively short, 12 segments; gaster with 6 visible tergites; sting present......(females)..2.
— Antennae relatively long, 13 segments; gaster with 7 visible tergites; sting absent......(males)...8.

Females (queens and workers)

2. Vertex and genae enlarged above and behind compound eyes; distance between lateral ocellus and occipital carina 3-4 times greater than the distance between the lateral ocelli (Fig. 98a); body dominantly yellow and brown; large size, length 18-35 mm ....genus *Vespa* L.

One British species, *Vespa crabro* L.

— Vertex and genae not or only slightly enlarged behind compound eyes; distance between lateral ocellus and occipital carina about the same as the distance between the lateral ocelli (Fig. 98b); body dominantly black with yellow markings; smaller size, length generally less than 20 mm......genus *Vespula* Thompson.........3.

3. Malar space less than the distance between the antennal sockets; pronotum without a vertical carina (Fig. 98c)......(Sub-genera *Vespula* Thompson and *Paravespula* Blüthgen)........................4.
— Malar space about as long as the distance between the antennal sockets (Fig. 99c, d); pronotum with a vertical carina (Fig. 98d) ......(Sub-genus *Dolichovespula* Rohwer)...............................7.

4. Ventral surface of antennal scape yellow (Fig. 90f); outer surface of middle and hind tibiae with long, black hairs; gaster with orange-brown areas, especially on gastral tergites 1 and 2 (Fig. 99l); parasitic species without workers....................................
....*Vespula austriaca* (Panzer).

— Antennae wholly black; outer surface of middle and hind tibiae without long, black hairs...5.

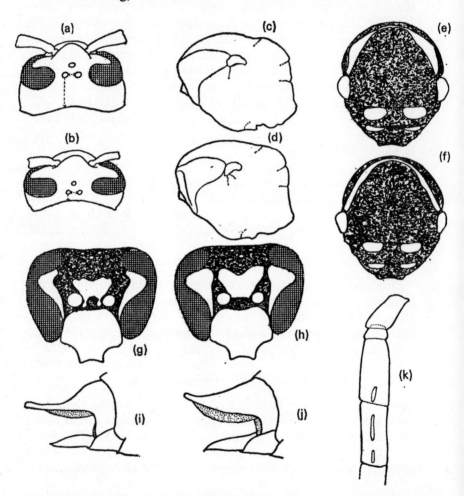

Figure 98. Taxonomy of Vespidae: (a) *V. crabro* dorsal view of head; (b) *Vespula* dorsal view of head; (c) sub-genus *Vespula* lateral view of thorax, vertical carina lacking; (d) sub-genus *Dolichovespula* thorax with vertical carina on pronotum; (e) *P. germanica* dorsal view of thorax; (f) *P. vulgaris* thorax; (g) *P. vulgaris* frontal view of head; (h) *P. germanica* frontal view of head; (i) *P. vulgaris* distal end of gaster of male; (j) *P. germanica* distal end of gaster of male; (k) tyloids on antenna of male *Vespa crabro* ((i) and (j) from Yarrow 1955).

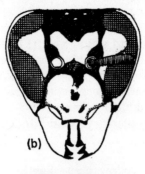

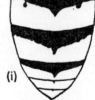

Figure 99. Taxonomy of Vespidae: (a)-(f) frontal view of head of queens; (a) *P. vulgaris*; (b) *P. germanica*; (c) *D. sylvestris*; (d) *D. norwegica*; (e) *V. rufa*; (f) *V. austriaca*; (g)-(l) dorsal view of gaster of queens; (g) *P. vulgaris*; (h) *P. germanica*; (i) *D. sylvestris*; (j) *D. norwegica*; (k) *V. rufa*; (l) *V. austriaca.*

5. Ocular sinus with broad yellow area (Fig. 99a, b); tergites without coarse punctures; no red markings on gaster............................6.
— Ocular sinus with narrow yellow band on lower margin only (Fig. 99e); gaster with deep, coarse punctures; gastral tergites 1 and 2 with variable reddish areas; clypeus with wide black margin and broad, black, vertical band in the middle (Fig. 99e) .... *Vespula rufa* (L.).

6. Ocular sinus with yellow area slightly emarginate along inside border and nearly parallel with margin of eye (Fig. 99a); yellow area of gena and subgena interrupted; clypeus typically with anchor-shaped black marking; inner (third) tooth of mandible not projecting; yellow band on pronotum with parallel sides (Fig. 98f); 1st gastral tergite with black band pointed in middle (Fig. 99g) though in many workers diamond shaped as in *P. germanica*...... ....*Paravespula vulgaris* (L.).
— Ocular sinus with yellow area almost filling sinus; yellow area on gena and subgena complete; clypeus typically with three black spots; middle one often bar-shaped (Fig. 99b); inner tooth of mandible projecting and margin behind it slightly concave; yellow band on pronotum not parallel-sided, extending antero-laterally (in queens) (Fig. 98e); 1st gastral tergite with black, diamond-shaped mark in middle (Fig. 99h)............................. ....*Paravespula germanica* (F.).

7. Clypeus with broad, black band extending from upper to lower margins, and fine punctures between the coarse ones; gaster usually with lateral red markings on tergites 1 and 2 (Fig. 99j)...... .... *Dolichovespula norwegica* (F.).
— Clypeus all yellow or with small black spot centrally (Fig. 99c), and fine punctures evenly distributed between medium punctures; gaster without red markings......*Dolichovespula sylvestris* (Scopoli)

Males

8. Gena and subgena enlarged behind compound eyes; distance between lateral ocellus and occipital carina 2-3 times greater than the distance between the ocelli; antennae with distinct tyloids (Fig. 98k); body yellow and brown; large size, length 21-28 mm ....*Vespa crabro* L.
— Gena and subgena not enlarged behind compound eyes; distance between ocellus and occipital carina about the same as the distance between the lateral ocelli; antennae with or without tyloids; body with black and yellow markings; smaller size, length less than 20 mm ....9.

9. Malar space less than the distance between the antennal sockets; pronotum without a vertical carina; antennae without tyloids; aedeagus fused distally (Plate XXIIIa, b, e, f) (Fig. l00h, i, l. m). (Sub-genera *Vespula* Thompson and *Paravespula* Blüthgen)......10.

— Malar space about as long as the distance between the antennal sockets; pronotum with a vertical carina; antennae with or without tyloids; aedeagus not fused distally (Plate XXIIIc, d) (Fig. l00j, k) (Sub-genus *Dolichovespula*)...13.

10. Outer surface of middle and hind tibiae without, or with very few long, black hairs...11.

— Outer surface of middle and hind tibiae with long, black hairs; aedeagus saddle-shaped (Fig. 100m) (Plate XXIIIf)...................
....*Vespula austriaca* (Panzer).

11. Ocular sinus with broad yellow band; tergites without coarse punctures; no red markings on gaster; aedeagus spoon-shaped distally ....12.

— Ocular sinus with narrow yellow band on lower margin only; gaster with deep, coarse punctures; gastral tergites 1 and 2 with red markings, often pronounced; gastral tergite 7 without emarginate posterior margin (Fig. 100e); aedeagus saddle-shaped (Fig. 100l) (Plate XXIIIe) ....*Vespula rufa* (L.).

12. Yellow area of frons (=coronna) continued ventrally to form a lobe or an isolated yellow spot below the antennal socket (Fig. 98g); 'scale' of 7th gastral sternite forming a small, semi-transparent area on the lateral margin of sclerite (Fig. 89i); aedeagus with large, barb-like processes, and distal end entire (Fig. 100h) (Plate XXIIIa)..................................... *Paravespula vulgaris* (L.).

— Yellow area of frons not extended beneath antennal sockets (Fig. 98h); 'scale' of 7th gastral sternite forming a broad, semi-transparent area on the lateral margin of sclerite (Fig. 98j); aedeagus with small, rounded processes, and with distal end emarginate (Fig. 100i) (Plate XXIIIb) ...*Paravespula germanica* (F.).

13. Clypeus with fine punctures between the coarse ones; 2nd gastral sternite with red markings laterally (Fig. 100d); antennae with a single tyloid on each of the last 5 or 6 segments; aedeagus enlarged distally (Fig. 100k) (Plate XXIIId)...*Dolichovespula norwegica* (F.).

— Clypeus with evenly distributed, medium punctures; gastral sternites without red markings; antennae without tyloids; aedeagus tapering to a point distally (Fig. 100j) (Plate XXIIIc) ....
....*Dolichovespula sylvestris* (Scopoli).

z

WASPS

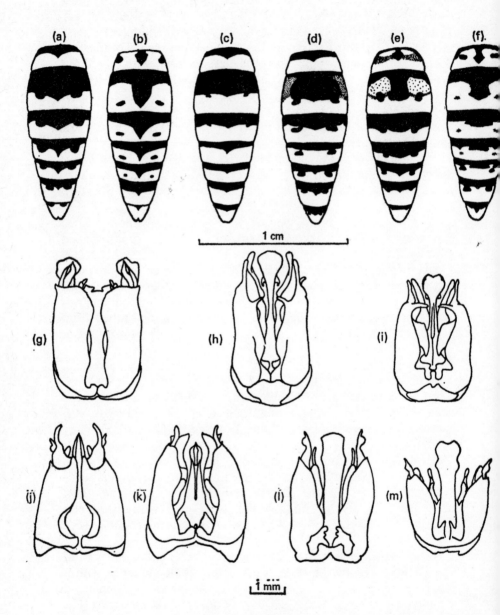

Figure 100. Taxonomy of Vespidae: (a)-(f) dorsal view of gaster of males;
(a) *P. vulgaris*; (b) *P. germanica*; (c) *D. sylvestris*; (d) *D. norwegica*; (e) *V. rufa*;
(f) *V. austriaca*; (g)-(m) male genitalia; (g) *V. crabro*; (h) *P. vulgaris*; (i) *P. germanica*;
(j) *D. sylvestris*; (k) *D. norwegica*; (l) *V. rufa*; (m) *V. austriaca*.

CHECK LIST OF BRITISH VESPOIDEA

Family Vespidae

Vespa crabro Linnaeus, 1758 (British sub-species, *V. crabro gribodoi* Bequaert, 1932)
Vespula austriaca (Panzer, 1799)
   [=*Vespa borealis* Smith; *Vespa arborea*, Smith]
Vespula rufa (Linnaeus, 1758)
Paravespula vulgaris (Linnaeus, 1758)
Paravespula germanica (Fabricius, 1793)
Dolichovespula norwegica (Fabricius, 1781)
   [=*Vespa britannica* Leach; *Vespa borealis* Zetterstedt]
Dolichovespula sylvestris (Scopoli, 1763)
   [=*Vespa holsatica* Fabricius]

Family Eumenidae

Eumenes coarctatus (Linnaeus, 1758)
   [=*Eumenes atricornis* Fabricius]
Odynerus spinipes (Linnaeus, 1758)
Odynerus melanocephalus (Gmelin, 1790)
   [=*Pterocheilus dentipes* Herrich-Schaeffer]
Odynerus reniformis (Gmelin, 1790)
Odynerus simillimus (F. Morawitz, 1867)
Gymnomerus laevipes (Shuckard, 1837)
   [=*Odynerus rubicola* Dufour]
Pseudepipona herrichii (Saussure, 1856)
Euodynerus quadrifasciatus (Fabricius, 1793)
   [=*Odynerus tomentosus* Thompson, *Pseudepipona quadrifasciata* (Fabricius)]
Ancistrocerus parietum (Linnaeus, 1758)
Ancistrocerus quadratus (Panzer, 1799)
   [=*Ancistrocerus claripennis* Thompson]
Ancistrocerus gazella (Panzer, 1789)
   [=*Ancistrocerus pictipes* Thompson]
Ancistrocerus trifasciatus (Müller, 1776)
   [=*Odynerus trimarginatus* Zetterstedt]
Ancistrocerus parietinus (Linnaeus, 1761)
   [=*Odynerus parietinus* (Linnaeus)]
Ancistrocerus antilope (Panzer, 1789)
   [=*Odynerus pictus* Curtis]
Ancistrocerus nigricornis (Curtis, 1826)
   [=*Ancistrocerus callosus* (Thompson), *Odynerus callosus* Thompson]

Ancistrocerus oviventris (Wesmael, 1836)
  [=*Odynerus oviventris* Wesmael, *Odynerus pictus* auctt. Brit. nec
  Curtis]
Ancistrocerus scoticus (Curtis, 1826)
  [=*Odynerus albotricinctus* Zetterstedt, *Odynerus trimarginatus*
  auctt. nec Zetterstedt]
Symmorphus crassicornis (Panzer, 1796)
  [=*Odynerus crassicornis* (Panzer)]
Symmorphus gracilis (Brullé, 1833)
  [=*Odynerus elegans* Wesmael]
Symmorphus sinuatissimus Richards, 1935
  [=*Odynerus sinuatus* (Fabricius)]
Symmorphus connexus (Curtis, 1826)
  [=*Odynerus bifasciatus* auctt. nec Linnaeus]
Microdynerus exilis (Herrich-Schaeffer, 1839)
  [=*Odynerus exilis* Herrich-Schaeffer]

II

CLASSIFICATION OF WASP NESTS

Technically speaking, British wasp nests are described as being calyptodomous stelocyttarous – having a surrounding envelope with combs attached by a system of pillars or stalks. Although they all conform to the same basic plan, there are several differences in their architecture and carton fabric which permit their identification. The basic characters used in nest identification are the colour and texture of the carton, the form of envelope design and the method of suspending combs. Size can be a useful criterion but the time of collection will determine whether the nest is immature and small or otherwise, while overwintered colonies may attain a prodigious size in their second season.

When presented with an unidentified nest there is always the possibility that a number of dead adult wasps may be found between combs or in cavities within the envelope. Their identification would be a most useful adjunct in determining which species of wasp built the nest.

The following key is intended to be used in conjunction with the description of nests in Chapter 5.

Key to the Nests of British Wasps

1. Carton of nest yellow or brown and brittle............................2.
— Carton of nest grey and supple...3.

2. Envelope where present composed of tunnel-like, elongated shells; carton composed of coarse wood particles (Plate XIVa); worker cells large (at least 6 mm wide)..........................*Vespa crabro.*
— Envelope composed of small shells (Plate Xc); carton composed of finer wood fragments (Plate XIVb); worker cells small (less than 5 mm wide)......................................*Paravespula vulgaris*

3. Envelope composed of shells, or loosely overlapping sheets without straight edges and attached to underlying sheets at various points to form occasional shell-like pockets..........................4.
— Envelope composed of flat sheets of overlapping carton with straight or flounced edges...5.

4. Mature nest large; envelope composed of flat shells; carton closely woven (Plate XIVc); pillars column-like (Plate IXb).........
....*Paravespula germanica*
— Mature nest small; envelope composed of sheets; carton loosely woven (Plate XIVd); comb supports ribbon-like (Fig. 48a).........
....*Vespula rufa*

5. Envelope sheets close together with straight edges (Plate Xb); carton compact with few holes (Plate XIVf)............................
....*Dolichovespula sylvestris*
— Envelope sheets loosely overlapping with flounced edges (Plate Xa); carton less compact with holes or gaps present (Plate XIVe)
....*Dolichovespula norwegica*

III

COLLECTION, PRESERVATION, AND STUDY OF WASPS

Collecting

A knowledge of the most suitable places and times to collect wasps is more useful than a host of sophisticated techniques for trapping them. The maps in Appendix IV show the distribution of the different species in the British Isles, and Figures 16 and 26 illustrate the times of the year when they are likely to be found. However, the maps and figures were compiled from data on specimens in museum collections and literature records and allowance should be made for recent urbanization and modern farming practice (e.g. elimination of hedges and small copses) restricting some nesting habitats and for the possibility of 'early' or 'late' seasons.

Collecting Adult Wasps. Most solitary wasps are likely to be found in sheltered lanes, sun-baked banks or, in the case of tube-nesting species, around fences and posts with insect emergence holes, areas of old bramble, and the eaves of thatched roofs. *Symmorphus* species prefer damper situations near streams and ditches where the adults form definite flight paths along areas of foliage exposed to full sunlight (Guichard 1972). The most attractive trees seem to be poplar, aspen, and elder. Sandpits may provide a plentiful source of certain species such as *Odynerus spinipes* and *Ancistrocerus parietum* while the Potter Wasp, *Eumenes coarctatus*, is reasonably abundant on heaths in southern England (Boyd 1943). Some species are extremely local in their distribution, the notable example being *Pseudepipona herrichii* which is restricted to one or two heathland areas in S.E. Dorset (Spooner 1934).

In warm sunny weather, food sources provide good locations for finding wasps. These include flowers with exposed nectaries e.g. Umbelliferae and Rosaceae, and aphid and coccid honey-dew. Chapters 3 and 6 list some of the plants which wasps visit in their search for nectar.

There is little problem in finding adult workers of the most common species of social wasps from mid- to late-summer, and queens in the early autumn when they are searching for hibernation quarters or during the spring when seeking nest sites. Hornets may be sought in deciduous woodlands, such as the New Forest, where they frequently feed at the sap oozing from oak trees. The tree- or bush-nesting species (*Dolichovespula sylvestris* and *D. norwegica*) are rarely located in an urban environment although *D. sylvestris* is still to be found in some London suburbs such as Blackheath and Hampstead.

When wasps are discovered feeding at flowers, sap, or on honey-dew covered leaves, they can be picked up by their wings and dropped into a collecting bottle or tube. Even the social wasps may be handled with safety by this method although a small entomological net could be employed by the wary. A venturi-operated aspirator or pooter (Fig. 101a) will be helpful, especially with the smaller species of wasp, this particular model relying on blowing rather than sucking to collect specimens.* Captured wasps can be temporarily stored in glass or plastic vials or in a cyanide killing-bottle.

Trapping Wasps. The use of traps or baits can eliminate a lot of wasted time spent in searching for wasps or their nests in natural habitats. Some of the simplest methods of trapping wasps are to attract them to food sources. Social wasps seem to be especially partial to fermenting liquor. A jar containing a little beer or diluted jam with a drop or two of liquid soap to lower the surface tension of the fluid will invariably be successful. Wasps are also attracted to decomposing meat, fish, and carrion (see Plate XVd).

A method of collecting both solitary and social wasps is with suction traps (see Chapter 7) and the reader is referred to the papers by L. R. Taylor (1951, 1963) in which the trap is described and the interpretation of results is discussed. The suction trap is probably the most suitable type of trap for large, strong-flying insects such as wasps. This is particularly so if the purpose of the collection is to study the natural population in relation to time or a component of the physical environment such as temperature. Because the trap catch is proportional to the total available population × the proportion in flight (equivalent to activity) it gives a quantitative measure of their aerial density.

A trap for recovering the prey from foragers returning to the nest has been designed by Broekhuizen and Hordijk (1968). Their ingenious apparatus is made from Perspex and can be fitted to the entrance

*For details of the aspirator and many other methods and techniques which will be found immensely useful to the collector I recommend to the reader the handbook, *The Collection and Preservation of Insects* (1966) by K. R. Norris published by The Australian Entomological Society.

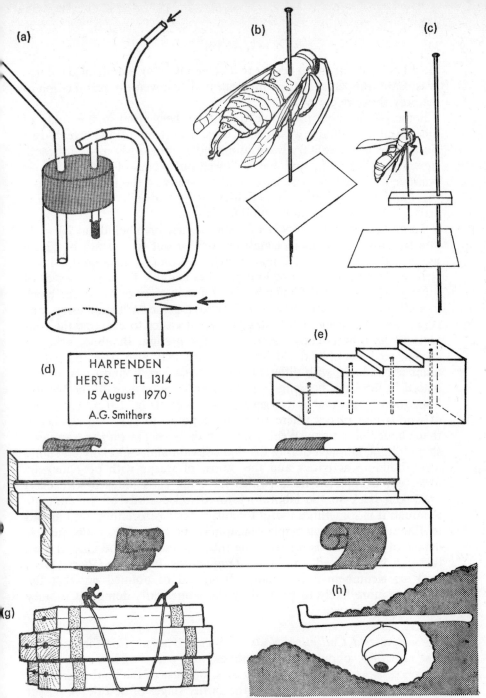

(d)

HARPENDEN
HERTS.   TL 1314
15 August 1970
A.G. Smithers

Figure 101. Techniques for collecting, preserving and trapping wasps: (a) venturi-operated aspirator, detail of venturi fitting inset, arrows indicate direction of blowing; (b) large specimen pinned through right side of mesothorax, note extruded genitalia; (c) small specimen set on micropin and mounted on polyporus strip; (d) specimen label with minimum required information; (e) height-gauge block in Perspex, different heights for label (12 mm), polyporus strips (20 mm and 22 mm) and cards or triangles (24 mm); (f) soft-wood block drilled and split before taping together, for trapping tube-nesting wasps; (g) group of traps under field conditions; (h) artificial nest site for subterranean-nesting queen wasps. (a) and (e) after **Norris** 1966, (g) after **Krombein** 1967.

tunnel of a subterranean nest or to a box containing a domiciled colony. Wasps are trapped at regular intervals and removed for examination of the prey they are carrying.

Some of the most profitable traps have been used in the study of tube-dwelling solitary wasps and bees. Fourteen of the twenty-two British species of solitary wasp utilize holes previously made in wood, stones or brickwork, and the hollowed-out stems of plants such as bramble and reed. It is easier to make a study of the populations and the building and foraging activities of tube-dwellers by providing artificial nesting material in suitable sites.

To make trap nests, blocks of wood (spruce or pine) about 20 × 30 mm square and 15 cm in length are drilled out to a depth of 12 cm using metal drill bits of 3·2 mm ($\frac{1}{8}$ inch), 4·8 mm ($\frac{3}{16}$ inch) and 6·4 mm ($\frac{1}{4}$ inch) to give a variety of hollow tubes suitable for wasp species of different sizes. After drilling a hole down each piece of wood, the block is split along the drill hole and bound together with adhesive tape (Fig. 101f). Splitting at this stage makes it easier to examine the contents if the tube is subsequently used for nesting. Bamboo, drinking straws, reed stems, and old bramble stems may also be employed. A number of blocks with different-sized borings are bound together and placed in the field, hanging from trees or fence posts with the borings horizontal to prevent water getting into them (Fig. 101g). The edges of woods and places where traps are exposed to sunshine are better than shaded situations. Weekly or even daily checks on the trap nests should be maintained during the flight season and, especially on sunny days, building activities and the return of wasps with prey may be observed. Completed nests (which have the ends plugged with clay) are taken back to the laboratory for detailed study of the contents although it is sometimes useful to collect nests before they are finished to obtain details of egg emplacement and numbers of prey. For further details of the methods for trapping tube dwellers and the kind of data that can be obtained, the book, *Trap-nesting Wasps and Bees* (1967) by Karl Krombein is invaluable. It should be pointed out that the traps are more likely to be used by the numerically dominant solitary bees than by wasps.

Locating and Collecting Nests of Social Wasps. For the study of nest structure, populations, inquilines, and parasites of social wasps it is necessary to obtain entire colonies. Because of the unobtrusiveness of embryo and juvenile colonies, the earlier stages of nest development are rarely found, although maturing colonies of the commoner species are more easily located as their adult populations increase and the flow of foragers at the entrance tunnel advertises the presence of a nest.

Embryo nests of the ground-dwelling species of wasp may be

encouraged by digging small cavities in the soil of flower or lawn borders and hedgerows and placing a tile or piece of slate over the cavity so that a small entrance hole results (Fig. 101h). As Potter (1965) has noted, queen wasps searching for nest sites in the spring are attracted to any dark hole or depression in the ground and some success in attracting queens may be expected by this method. I can give little advice on locating nests of the rarer species other than that of earning a local reputation as a waspologist and maintaining contact with regional beekeepers or pest-infestation officers who may be approached by people discovering wasp nests. Advertisements for nests in newspapers invariably stimulate a degree of interest but the majority are likely to be of the common *Paravespula* species. Because of the comparative rarity of *Dolichovespula* species and the hornet, I would not recommend taking their nests until after they had matured and produced young queens, a practice which would also be scientifically more useful because of the greater information accruing from an expended nest (see Chapters 5 and 7).

Apart from attempting to locate nests by following the 'wasp-line' of returning foragers, by walking slowly alongside hedgerows or in rough scrubland and concentrating one's attention some yards ahead, it is often possible to see a number of wasps flying to and fro across the line of vision which would indicate the proximity of a nest. As in most biological quests, familiarity with the organism being sought quickly results in the acquisition of an extra 'sense' which only experience can earn.

The only really suitable time to collect a wasp colony is during the hours of darkness when the majority of foragers are inside the nest although embryo nests with the founding queen or small juvenile colonies may be taken safely enough during daylight. Armed with torch, ether, cotton wool, a spade, and box or stout polythene bags the nocturnal capture of a subterranean wasp nest is a comparatively easy exercise. After locating the entrance some ether (200 ml would be adequate for a mature colony with a short entrance tunnel) is poured down the tunnel which is then blocked with a cotton-wool plug. If the nest is situated at the end of a short tunnel, the violent buzzing of the inmates can be readily heard, but often in two or three minutes there is complete silence as the anaesthetic takes effect. The exact position of the nest is best located by following the entrance tunnel while excavating. After exposing the entire nest by carefully removing soil and stones from around the envelope, it is gently lifted out and put into a suitable box or polythene bag. Large numbers of wasps will be found in the bottom of the nest cavity and it is important that these are all collected for the founding queen may be among them. If desired, the midden at the base of the nest may be scraped into a jar or tin for the subsequent examination of inquilines and other refuse-inhabiting organisms. If the excavation of the nest is not too prolonged, the wasps will remain anaesthetized for the journey home, otherwise a few drops of ether may be poured over the nest envelope before sealing the container.

Unless the colony is to be re-established *in toto* at a more convenient site for general observations or stored entire in a deep freeze, the nest should be removed from the box or bag and taken apart as soon as possible otherwise heavy mortality of adults and brood will occur within a few hours followed by rapid decomposition of the corpses. After ensuring that the wasps are still anaesthetized, the envelope is removed and the combs separated by inserting a spatula or trowel between them to break the pillars. Adults on the envelope and combs, including those which have burrowed into the cavities of the envelope or into cells, should be removed. If the colony is to be used for experimental studies, some or all of the combs are placed in an incubator or temperature-controlled box with an appropriate number of adults. The exact procedures for housing and maintaining live material will be determined by the nature of the experiment.

Captured wasps should always be examined for signs of mites, strepsiptera or the phoretic stages of other arthropods such as beetle parasites (e.g. *Metoecus paradoxus*). A special examination of immature stages and adults should be standard practice to determine the incidence and extent of parasitism. Chapters 3 and 11 should help in determining what to look for.

Experimental Colonies

Wasp colonies which have been excavated can generally be re-established in laboratory or garden where it is often more convenient to study their foraging activities and general behaviour. There are several ways of maintaining colonies, the method depending on the size of nest and the purpose of the investigation. The simplest procedure is to suspend the nest from the roof of a box by passing wire through the upper envelope and between the first two tiers of combs. If the box has a front which can later be removed, the wasps can be prevented from foraging for a day following their capture. This policy overcomes the problem of wasps leaving the nest and being unable to navigate back to the new site. After a day of imprisonment, wasps leaving the nest invariably perform orientation flights and the colony will continue to develop satisfactorily.

The siting of colonies is a matter of personal choice. Nests can be placed in the open, preferably with some overhead cover to protect them against heavy rain, or maintained in a shed or vespiary. Jacob Ishay (Ishay and others 1967) housed twelve colonies of Oriental

Hornet in each of his vespiaries, using wooden boxes with glass roofs for individual nests. Although considerable information on foraging and building activities may be obtained in this way, the envelope will prevent detailed observations of the activities within the nest.

It was pointed out in Chapter 5 that envelope building is made in response to low temperature and the incidence of light – with sub-optimal temperatures stimulating the building of a thick insulating envelope, and light stimulating the production of a thin veneer of carton to cut out the light entering the nest. Nests maintained at 28-30°C in an incubator can be kept for several weeks without the wasps building an envelope, especially if observation periods when the nest is illuminated are not too protracted. Individual combs with attendant wasps can be kept under direct observation for several days before their activities are screened from view with layers of carton. Envelope can, however, be removed from time to time after lightly anaesthetizing the wasps with ether, carbon dioxide or nitrous oxide. Experimental colonies will thrive if allowed to forage outdoors although food can be provided in a 'foraging arena' if more controlled conditions are required.

Preservation

A most useful method of temporary storage for specimens and even entire wasp colonies is deep freezing. When I was collecting colonies during the Hertfordshire census (see Chapter 7), many were kept in cold store until more time was available to carry out detailed counts of the immature stages and adults. Adult wasps stored in this way may be mounted on pins during periods when experimental studies or field work make fewer demands on time.

When mounting wasps on pins, it should be stressed that the insect be prepared for the microscope rather than the eye of the layman, except when specimens are required for demonstration purposes or museum exhibitions in which case they can be artistically arranged in the manner of pinned butterflies. Important features which should be emphasized are the mouthparts and male genitalia. After pinning through the right side of the mesothorax, the mandibles should be opened – closed forceps inserted between the mandibles and allowed to open will usually be successful in displaying the mandibles clearly. Because of the taxonomic importance of the male genitalia, these should be pulled out slightly with forceps or a hooked needle. The venation of the wings is relatively unimportant in wasp taxonomy and there is usually no need to set wings, simply ensuring that they do not cover the thorax in such a way as to obscure the lateral and propodeal views (Fig. 101b). Specimens of the smaller solitary wasps can be set on micropins and, when dry, staged on a small length of polyporus strip (Fig. 101c).

The basic information accompanying a pinned specimen is the

locality and date of capture including, if possible, the grid number which may be conveniently obtained from the Ordnance Survey Gazetteer of Great Britain. The name of the collector may also be added to this label (Fig. 101d). Pinned specimens without locality data are frustrating for the specialist who is attempting to study distribution patterns. When labelling large numbers of specimens and also to maintain uniformity in the collection, the use of a 'height gauge' is recommended. This simple item of equipment can be made from wood or Perspex and consists of a series of steps with holes drilled through at the different heights for labels, polyporus strips, and card triangles (Fig. 101e).

The distributions of plants and animals in the British Isles is being systematically mapped by the Biological Records Centre at Monk's Wood, Huntingdonshire. Computer techniques are used for plotting distribution data and standard data cards are supplied to the recorders who contribute locality records. The serious collector is urged to take advantage of this system and thereby help in the plotting of distribution maps on a national scale. It may be pointed out here that distribution records of the most abundant wasp species are often ignored by collectors and during the preparation of the distribution data in Appendix IV, more distribution records were obtained from museums and the literature for some of the less common species than for *Paravespula vulgaris* and *P. germanica*.

The immature stages of wasps, larval parasites, inquilines, and prey should be fixed in solutions such as K.A.A.D. (1 part kerosene, 10 parts of 95 per cent ethanol, 2 parts glacial acetic acid, 1 part dioxane; the quantity of kerosene may be reduced for very fragile specimens such as early-stage larvae). Several well-established methods are available for fixing material which may be required for histological work. Fixed specimens are stored in 80 per cent ethanol, with a few drops of glycerol making sure that the containers have adequate caps to prevent evaporation of the alcohol.

When preserving specimens, be they pinned adults or larvae in fixative, it is good policy to ensure that adequate numbers are prepared, for a series of wasps is usually more helpful than a single specimen. This is particularly true if a taxonomist wishes to check a particular character, or if specimens are to be sent to specialists for examination and exchanged with other collections. For specific projects such as morphometric studies, greater numbers are required and in these cases the nature of the study will determine the quantity of material required for preservation.

Photographic Techniques
In view of the considerable amount of photographic work that has

been undertaken in the preparation of the plates for this book, the experience that has been gained may help others to overcome some of the technical problems involved in insect photography. It would be unrealistic to pretend that good quality close-up photographs of insects can be easily taken with cheap box cameras, although techniques are available for the impecunious experimentalist (O'Farrell 1943). Nevertheless, by careful choice of equipment, macro and microphotography for naturalist and research scientists need not be too financially intimidating.

The basic requirement is a 35 mm single lens reflex camera body capable of accepting a range of lenses and other accessories. It is important that the body incorporates a socket for an electronic flash unit. A 135 mm telephoto lens is considered the basic requirement with a standard 50 mm lens or 28 mm wide-angle lens adding considerably to the system. It is most important that the telephoto lens should have an automatic diaphragn or be capable of being pre-set. A micro-lens with a 1 : 2 magnification will be found a most versatile if expensive extra. Accessories should include an electronic flash – preferably of the ring type, a bellows, tripod, and cable release. A light meter is essential although many modern cameras have a 'through-the-lens' measuring system.

To obtain 'action shots' of wasps, the use of a telephoto lens and bellows attachment was found to be the most practical, the lens permitting the photographer to keep his distance, especially when taking photographs at the nest entrance. The bellows are preferable to other methods of extending the lens from the film (to achieve greater magnification) because of the ease of adjusting bellows to accommodate the subject. When using a magnification greater than 1 : 1, it is advisable to reverse the telephoto lens by using a reversal ring to minimize distortion of the subject. The use of an electronic flash in conjunction with the bellows set-up is necessary because, at the higher magnifications, the depth of field is small and the amount of light reaching the film is thereby reduced. A powerful light source must be used to ensure that the smallest aperture – and hence greatest depth of field – can be used. Furthermore, movements by fast-moving insects do not permit the use of low camera speeds, while camera tremor would produce a blurred picture. The speed of the electronic flash – usually 1/1000 second – is fast enough to compensate for normal movements of the camera or subject. The ring flash eliminates shadows to a large extent but is a costly item and we have found that an ordinary flash mounted on a bracket at the end of the bellows just above the lens gives very good results. As the bellows is extended, the flash is moved nearer to the subject and thereby compensates for the reduction in light.

Camera speed depends on the type of camera but synchronization with an electronic flash will generally be from 1/60 to 1/125 second. However, with small apertures (f=8, 11, or 16) incidental light plays but a small part in picture-making, the flash contributing almost all the light when the bellows is extended. As with all photographic equipment, expenditure of a few test films using a variety of speed and aperture settings will be found most useful in determining the performance of the equipment. Fine-grain films (low ASA rating, e.g. ASA 32 or 64) will give best results while specific film for use with photoflood lamps is essential when using colour.

Insects do not usually pose for photographs and certain photographic techniques and an appreciation of the animal's behaviour are required for successful photography in the field. Once a subject has been located, it is usually good policy to set the camera, flash, and bellows so that the particular activity fills the frame and, by moving the camera to the subject rather than attempting to focus the lens mechanically, photographs are more readily obtained. If the activity occupies a specific place, such as the entrance to a wasp nest, the camera can be pre-set and fitted to a tripod. By using a cable release and knowing the field of view occupied by the camera, the insects can be observed without peering through the camera lens.

Many activities can be observed and photographed under controlled conditions in the laboratory. This is particularly true of feeding and trophallaxis and a piece of brood-filled comb with a few adults can be maintained on the laboratory bench for this purpose. The use of a bell-jar cover or glass desiccator lid will contribute to the safety of the photographer – the cover being lifted whenever a particular action is to be photographed.

To photograph relatively inactive or immobile subjects such as nests and immature stages in cells, the use of photoflood lamps gives the photographer complete control over the lighting situation, enabling shadows and reflections to be reduced (by using a pair of lamps) and allowing emphasis of particular aspects of the subject. As with all photography, attention to background and a graphic designer's appreciation of framing will contribute greatly to the production of worthwhile pictures.

To take photographs of set specimens, the use of a thin sheet of Perspex mounted about 15 cm (6 inches) above white card will eliminate all background shadow with the appropriate lighting. Small holes are drilled in the Perspex, the arrangement depending on the number of specimens. The pins to which the insects are attached are passed through the holes and made secure with small pieces of Plasticine. Lighting is provided by two photoflood lamps directed at an angle from either side of the camera. Care must be taken to avoid reflections from the Perspex sheet and unwanted highlights from the specimens, and the use of ground-glass sheets in front of the lamps helps to scatter the light more evenly and reduce highlights. It is important that the camera is mounted firmly on a heavy-duty tripod or copying stand to prevent camera shake, while the use of a cable release will further reduce vibration. With important subjects it is advisable to take at least one picture on either side of the estimated setting and to use a reasonable range of speed and shutter settings after checking with a light meter.

For very small subjects such as the male genitalia illustrated in Plate XXIII a simple photo-microscope was developed. By reversing a 28 mm wide-angle lens on the bellows extended fully to 190 mm, a magnification of $\times 7$ was achieved. This system requires considerable light and the camera and subject must be mounted very rigidly to prevent blurring due to vibration. If the object to be photographed is translucent or lightly stained the electronic flash can be mounted beneath the subject. To obtain an even spread of light, one or two opal glass plates should be placed between the flash and the subject. Density of staining and degree of magnification will dictate the aperture setting but for a good depth of field, a maximum opening of f.8 is essential.

IV

DISTRIBUTION OF BRITISH WASP SPECIES

The distribution of wasps in the British Isles (Figs. 102-130) has been mapped by the Biological Records Centre, using a punched card system which plots the presence of a species in each 10 km square of the Ordnance Survey National Grid. Distribution data were obtained from museum collections, private collections, personal communications, the scientific literature, and in response to advertisements placed in the national press for wasp specimens. More than two hundred references not listed in the bibliography provided many of the distribution records. This is the first occasion that maps for wasp distribution in Britain have been published and obvious inadequacies will be found. The paucity of data relating to the common species, *P. vulgaris* and *P. germanica*, highlights the attitude of many collectors who tend to ignore the abundant species and restrict their collecting and publication to the rarer ones. Despite their shortcomings, it is hoped that these maps will provide a useful first step in a national survey of vespoid distribution. In the future there are plans to publish maps by date classes (e.g. pre-1940, 1940-60 and post-1960) which should indicate changes in distribution brought about by environmental factors such as climate and urbanization and thus monitor differences in distribution which might require remedial action by conservationists.

The absence of records for particular 10 km squares does not necessarily indicate an actual absence of a species but may be due to incomplete data. The situation map (Fig. 131) shows from which squares records have been obtained and a comparison with species distribution maps may explain some of the anomalies in the data. It is clear that the populated area around London with its parks and gardens is well recorded and also the popular summer resorts along the coasts, especially the south west of England. Where human populations are sparse, this feature is reflected in the small number of distribution records.

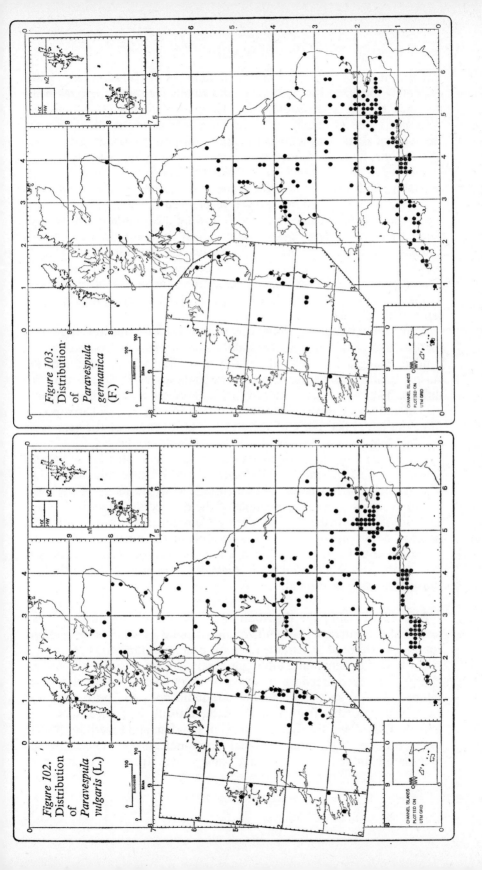

Figure 102.
Distribution
of
Paravespula
vulgaris (L.)

Figure 103.
Distribution
of
Paravespula
germanica
(F.)

The first major impression after scanning the distribution maps is the extremely localized distribution of the Eumenidae, most species being confined to England south of the Thames. Richards (1964) has discussed this paucity of entomological fauna and restricted distribution in the light of Britain's geological history and present-day climate. Some 18,000 years ago, the British Isles were covered in ice as far south as a line between the Bristol Channel and the Thames. During the post-glacial period which followed, some re-invasion by the continental fauna was accomplished but this was severely curtailed about 6,000 years ago when Britain became an island following the inundation of Dogger Land by the sea. The re-population which followed the most recent glaciation period was probably slow because the amelioration in climate would have been achieved only shortly before Britain became separated from the continent of Europe. As indicated in the introductory chapter, of the 100 Eumenidae listed in Europe, only 22 are recognized inhabitants of the British Isles.

Although extremes of climate in Britain are rare and the rainfall is reasonably well distributed, the climate is notoriously unpredictable with sudden changes in temperature and a severe lack of sunshine, yet wasps favour sunny situations and are most active in dry, warm conditions. The mild, wet winters which characterize the British climate also create major problems for hibernating insects. As Richards points out, 'the unpredictability of the weather at all times of the year is as troublesome to most insects as it is to field entomologists.'

The presence of man, extended urbanization and reduction of natural vegetation must also influence the distribution and abundance of insects. This is particularly true of southern England where many of the most localized wasps occur. An example of the destruction of suitable wasp habitats is the virtual loss of Parley Common to Hurn airport and housing development. It was in a sandpit at the northern end of the Common that Boyd (1943) found an abundance of *Odynerus spinipes* and *Ancistrocerus parietum* while *Eumenes coarctatus* was plentiful on the surrounding heathland.

Before discussing the distribution of the indigenous British Wasp fauna, the occurrence of *Polistes* in England is deserving of some comment. Although *Polistes* is the most cosmopolitan genus of wasp, it is not native to our fauna although specimens are occasionally found. *Polistes* may even breed for a season or two under exceptional circumstances. Several species (including one indigenous to South America) have been recorded from Co. Durham, Cardiff, Penzance, Cheshire, Suffolk, Chandler's Ford, Southampton, London, and Liverpool (Nurse 1913, Morice 1916, and personal communications). Queen wasps hibernating in materials awaiting consignment from ports are most

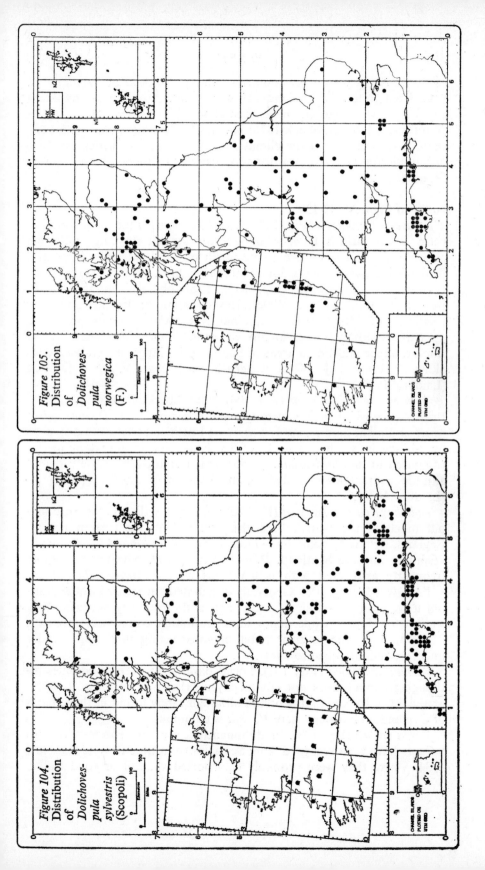

Figure 105.
Distribution
of *Dolichoves-
pula
norwegica*
(F.)

Figure 104.
Distribution
of *Dolichoves-
pula
sylvestris* (Scopoli)

easily transported to other countries although workers of *P. gallicus* L. have been found in England (Morice 1916). Attempts to maintain colonies in their gardens have been reported by some entomologists (Westwood, 1845, Lubbock 1876) but their efforts have met with little success. It is clear that the climatic conditions in the British Isles are unsuitable for *Polistes*, even for those species or races which occur in Scandinavia.

Notes to Figures 102-130

Paravespula vulgaris (Fig. 102). With *P. germanica* the most common wasp in the British Isles. Abundant throughout its range although possibly absent from the extreme north of Scotland while in central Scotland it ceases to be the dominant species as *D. norwegica* takes over.

Paravespula germanica (Fig. 103). Probably as abundant as *P. vulgaris* in England and Wales, less common in Ireland and very localized in Scotland. It is predominantly a lowland species, preferring drier areas although occasionally common in sheltered valleys of the Border, Clyde and Forth areas of Scotland. Its range probably extends along the low valleys of the eastern Scottish coast as far as Deeside (Laidlaw 1934).

Dolichovespula sylvestris (Fig. 104). Probably occurs throughout the British Isles where it is generally more common than *D. norwegica*. More abundant than *D. norwegica* in the Forth and Clyde but displaced by this species in the far north of Scotland. Not an abundant species compared to the *Paravespula* species. It is found over a wide range of altitude with males recorded at an elevation of 2,000 feet (625 m) (Laidlaw 1934).

Dolichovespula norwegica (Fig. 105). Generally distributed throughout much of the British Isles although rare in the eastern half of England. Relatively common in Dorset and Dartmoor and the dominant vespid in northern Scotland. *D. norwegica* and *D. sylvestris* are not so frequently associated with urban areas as the *Paravespula* species.

Vespula rufa (Fig. 106). Generally distributed but rather local and unobtrusive. Seems to prefer coastal areas and apparently flourishes in a warm, dry climate while damp summers inhibit colony development. This could be due to their habit of constructing nests superficially underground, attached to roots.

Vespula austriaca (Fig. 107). Social parasite in *V. rufa* colonies although its range does not completely overlap that of its host. Most abundant in Ireland and Scotland although rarely found in those parts of England and Wales where *V. rufa* is common.

Vespa crabro (Fig. 108). Predominantly a southern species although hornets have been recorded from Scotland from time to time (Laidlaw 1934) where they were probably transported via rail or road traffic.

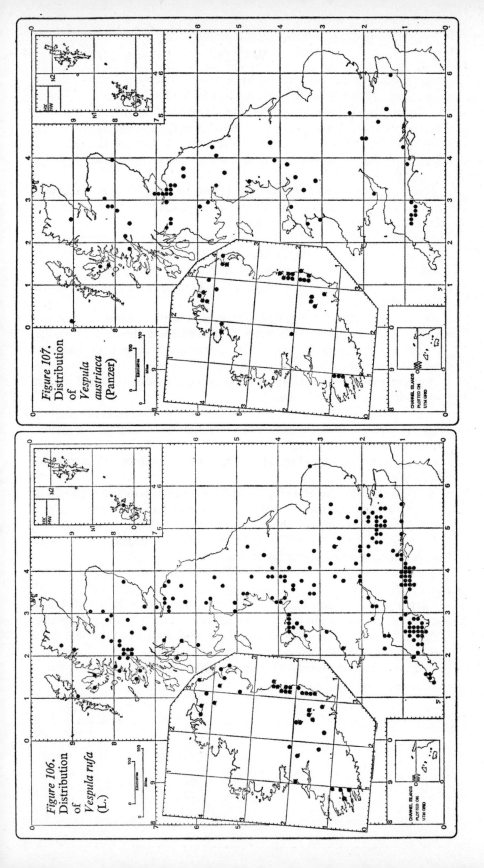

Figure 107.
Distribution
of *Vespula
austriaca*
(Panzer)

Figure 106.
Distribution
of *Vespula rufa*
(L.)

There is no evidence that the hornet can successfully establish colonies in Scotland. The hornet is not found in Ireland. The imposing size of the hornet has probably led to the numerous records in southern England. Although no longer a common species, during the unusually warm period, 1931-50, hornets were relatively abundant (Lloyd 1942, Lloyd and Benson 1945) but their numbers have apparently receded (Richards 1964).

Eumenes coarctatus (Fig. 109). Restricted to heathlands of southwest England and around London. Very local in distribution but frequently recorded from Chobham Common.

Odynerus spinipes (Fig. 110). Fairly abundant in sandy lanes during June and July, especially in the southwest of England. Where site conditions are favourable, nest densities may be high.

Odynerus melanocephalus (Fig. 111). Locally frequent in Devon, Dorset, and Kent.

Odynerus reniformis (Fig. 112). Very local species, rare. An obvious example of a 'continental' species at the extreme limit of its range.

Gymnomerus laevipes (Fig. 114). Generally frequent in southern England where it constructs nests in bramble stems.

Pseudepipona herrichii (Fig. 115). Very local species confined mainly to the Purbeck area of Dorset.

Ancistrocerus parietum (Fig. 117). Generally abundant throughout England, Wales, and Ireland. Probably the most common eumenid species in the British Isles.

Ancistrocerus gazella (Fig. 119). Frequent in southern England and South Wales.

Ancistrocerus trifasciatus (Fig. 120). Generally distributed throughout the British Isles but more common in Ireland and southern England where it frequently nests in holes of fences and palings.

Ancistrocerus parietinus (Fig. 121). Abundant throughout the British Isles, utilizing hollow stems for its nests.

Ancistrocerus antilope (Fig. 122). Widely distributed species but not abundant.

Ancistrocerus oviventris (Fig. 124). One of the most widely distributed species of eumenid although more abundant in southern England.

Microdynerus exilis (Fig. 130). Rare and localized species. Like *Vespa crabro*, this species enjoyed an increase in numbers during the period of warm summers between 1920-50 but has since decreased (Richards 1964).

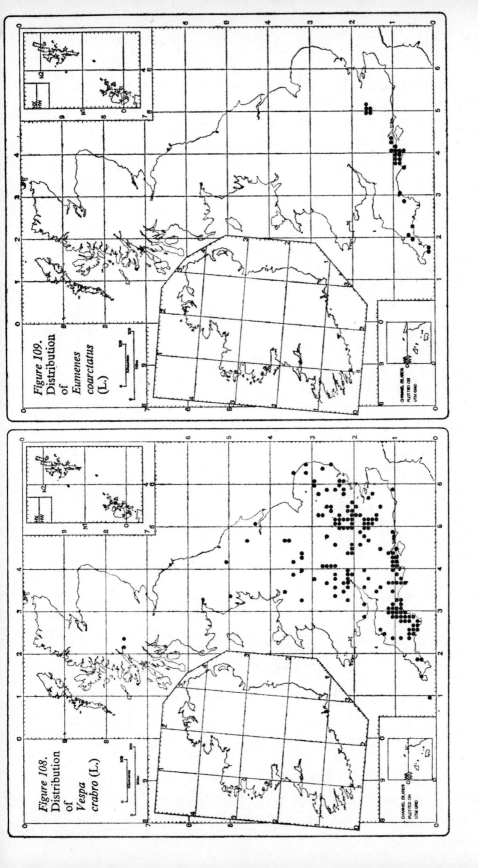

Figure 108.
Distribution
of
*Vespa
crabro* (L.)

Figure 109.
Distribution
of
*Eumenes
coarctatus*
(L.)

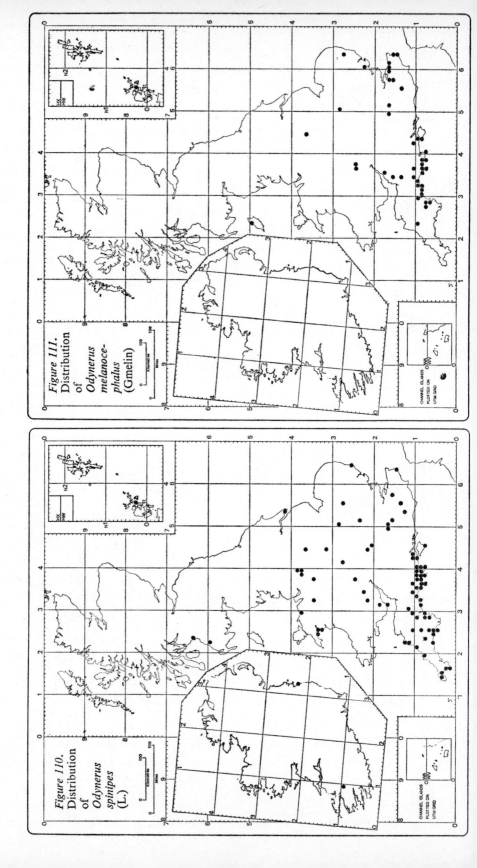

Figure 111.
Distribution
of
*Odynerus
melanoce-
phalus*
(Gmelin)

Figure 110.
Distribution
of
*Odynerus
spinipes*
(L.)

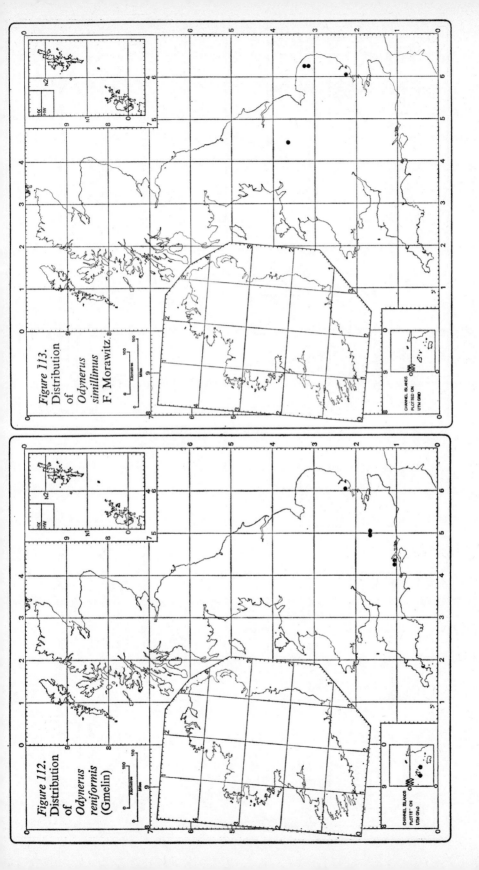

Figure 113.
Distribution
of
Odynerus
simillimus
F. Morawitz.

Figure 112.
Distribution
of
Odynerus
reniformis
(Gmelin)

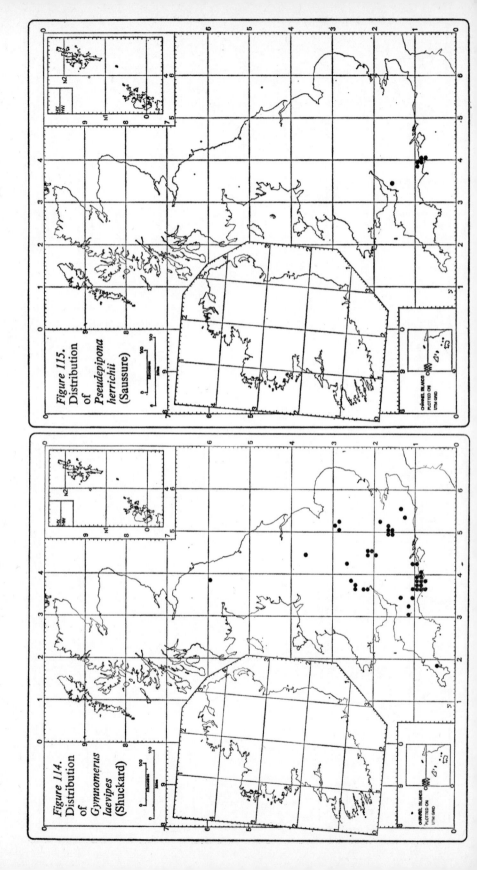

Figure 115.
Distribution
of
*Pseudepipona
herrichii* (Saussure)

Figure 114.
Distribution
of
*Gymnomerus
laevipes* (Shuckard)

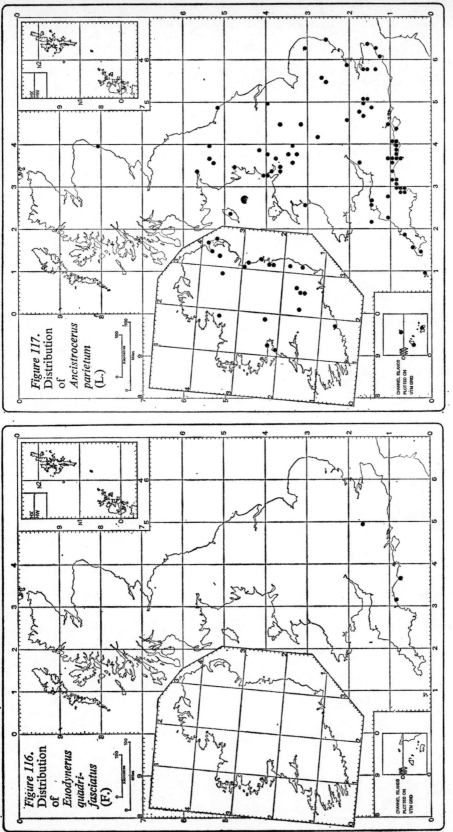

Figure 116.
Distribution
of
*Euodynerus
quadri-
fasciatus*
(F.)

Figure 117.
Distribution
of
*Ancistrocerus
parietum*
(L.)

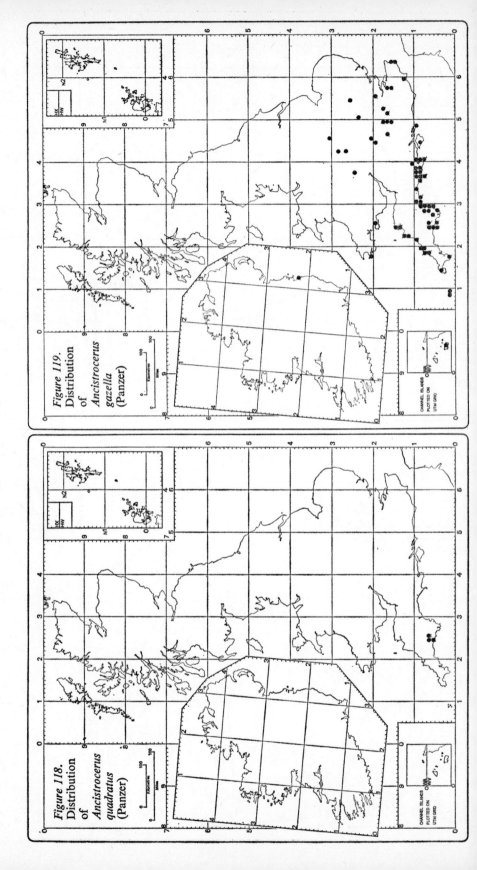

Figure 119.
Distribution
of
*Ancistrocerus
gazella* (Panzer)

CHANNEL ISLANDS
PLOTTED ON
UTM GRID

Figure 118.
Distribution
of
*Ancistrocerus
quadratus* (Panzer)

CHANNEL ISLANDS
PLOTTED ON
UTM GRID

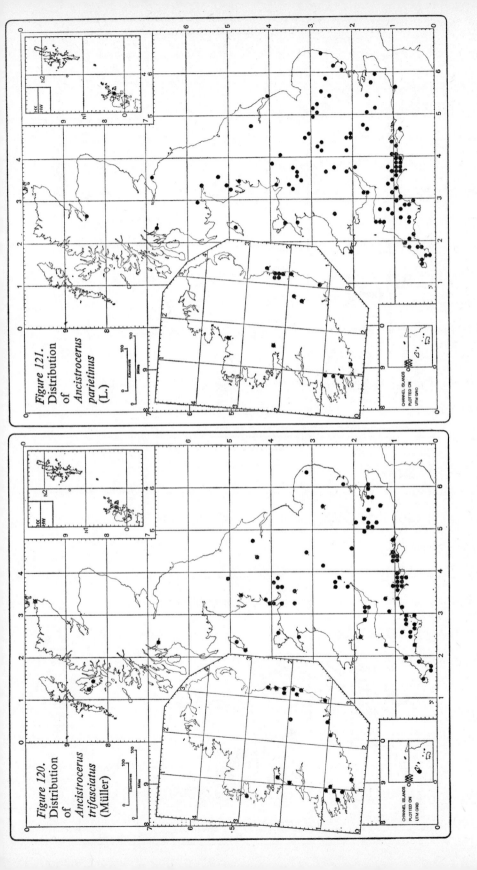

Figure 121.
Distribution
of
*Ancistrocerus
parietinus*
(L.)

CHANNEL ISLANDS
PLOTTED ON
UTM GRID

Figure 120.
Distribution
of
*Ancistrocerus
trifasciatus*
(Müller)

CHANNEL ISLANDS
PLOTTED ON
UTM GRID

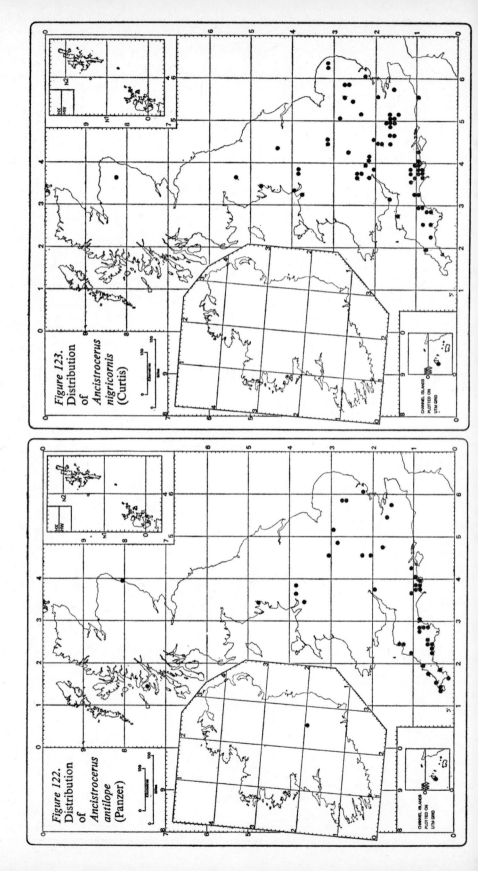

Figure 123.
Distribution
of
*Ancistrocerus
nigricornis* (Curtis)

CHANNEL ISLANDS
PLOTTED ON
UTM GRID

Figure 122.
Distribution
of
*Ancistrocerus
antilope* (Panzer)

CHANNEL ISLANDS
PLOTTED ON
UTM GRID

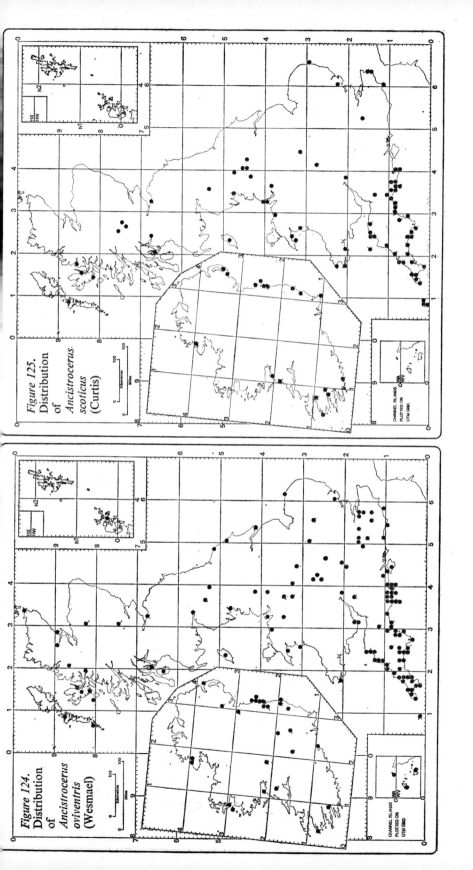

Figure 125.
Distribution
of
Ancistrocerus scoticus (Curtis)

Figure 124.
Distribution
of
Ancistrocerus oviventris (Wesmael)

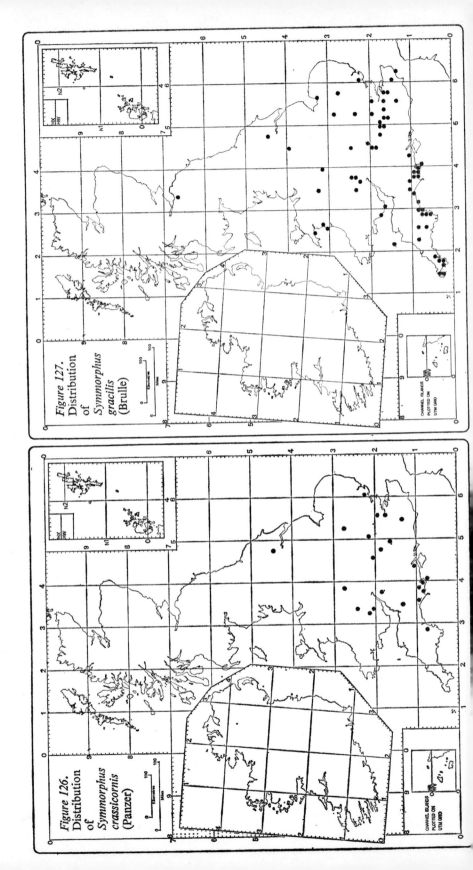

Figure 127.
Distribution
of
*Symmorphus
gracilis* (Brulle)

Figure 126.
Distribution
of
*Symmorphus
crassicornis* (Panzer)

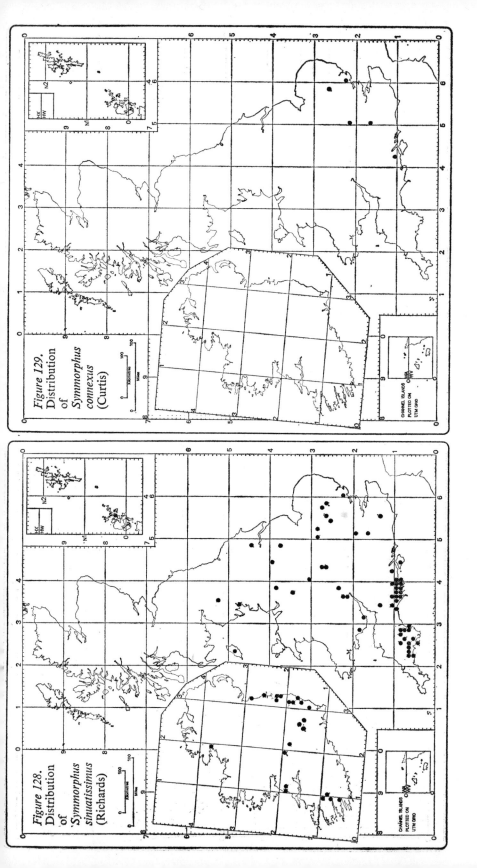

Figure 129.
Distribution
of
*Symmorphus
connexus*
(Curtis)

Figure 128.
Distribution
of
*Symmorphus
sinuatissimus*
(Richards)

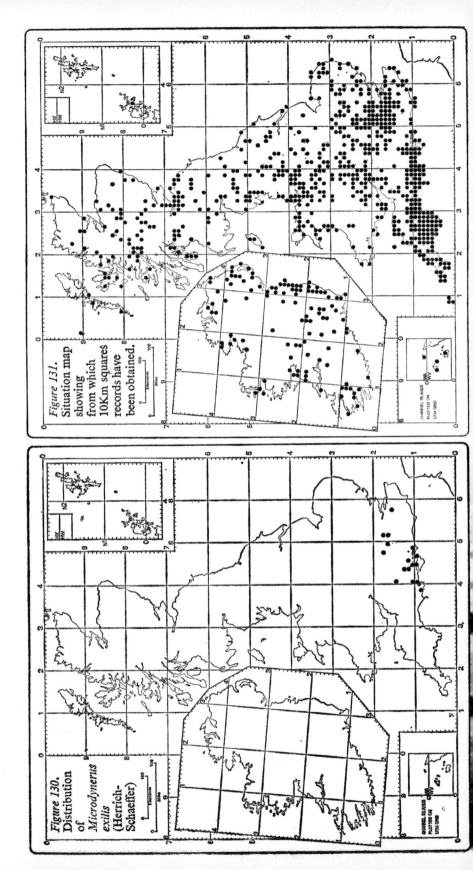

Figure 131.
Situation map
showing
from which
10Km squares
records have
been obtained.

Figure 130.
Distribution
of
*Microdynerus
exilis*
(Herrich-
Schaeffer)

BIBLIOGRAPHY

ACOLAT, L. (1953). 'Les matériaux des nids de guêpes.' *Bull. Soc. hist. nat. Doubs*. **55**, 39-43.

ADLERZ, G. (1907). 'Iakttagelser över solitära getinger.' *Ark Zool.* **3**, 1-64.

ALDOVRANDI, U. (1638). '*De animalibus insectis libri septem*' Bologna. *De Vespis* Cap. VI, 198-225.

ALFKEN, J. D. (1915). 'Verzeichnis der Faltenwespen (Vespiden) Nordwestdeutschlands.' *Abh. nat. Ver. Bremen*. **23**, 296-304.

ALFORD, D. V. (1968). 'The biology and immature stages of *Syntretus splendidus* (Marshall) (Hymenoptera : Braconidae, Euphorinae), a parasite of adult bumblebees.' *Trans. R. ent. Soc. Lond.* **120**, 375-93.

ALTEN, H. (1910). *Zur Phylogenie des Hymenopterengehirns*. Fischer, Jena.

ANDREWS, R. T. (1882). '*Vespa crabro* L. preying on honeybees in England.' *Sci. Gossip*. **18**, 282.

ANON. (1765). 'A method of destroying wasps and hornets.' *Gentlemen's Magazine*. **35**, 328.

ANON. (1954). 'Wasps and how to control them.' *U.S.D.A.* Leaflet 365.

ANON. (1968). 'Wasps.' *Min. Agric. Fish. Fd.* Leaflet 451.

ANON. (1962a). 'Common English fruit wasp, *Vespula vulgaris*.' *Victoria Agric. Dept. Biol. Branch Rpt.* **2**, 44.

ANON. (1962). 'European Wasp.' *Tasmanian J. Agric.* (1962), 341-2.

ARCHER, M. E. (1968). 'Studies of the seasonal development of *Paravespula vulgaris* (Linn.) and *Paravespula germanica* (Fab.) with special reference to worker size and queen production.' *Unpublished M.Sc. thesis*, University of Hull.

ARCHER, M. E. (1972a). 'The significance of worker size in the seasonal development of the wasps *Vespula vulgaris* (L.) and *Vespula germanica* (F.).' *J. Ent.* (A). **46**, 175-83.

ARCHER, M. E. (1972b). 'Studies of the seasonal development of *Vespula vulgaris* (L.) (Hymenoptera : Vespidae) with special reference to queen production.' *J. Ent.* (A). **47**, 45-59.

ARNOLD, T. S. (1966). 'Biology of social wasps : comparative ecology of the British species of social wasps belonging to the family Vespidae.' *Unpublished M.Sc. thesis*, University of London.

BAERENDS, G. P. (1941). 'Fortpflanzungsverhalten und Orientierung der Grabwespe, *Ammophila campestris* Jur.' *Tijdschr. Ent.* **84**, 68-275.

BAILEY, L. (1954). 'The filtration of particles by the proventriculi of various aculeate Hymenoptera.' *Proc. R. ent. Soc. Lond.* **29**, 119-23.

BAIRD, W. (1853). *Catalogue of the Species of Entozoa, or Intestinal Worms, Contained in the Collection of the British Museum*. London, British Museum.

BALFOUR BROWNE, F. (1922). 'On the life-history of *Melittobia acasta*, Walker: a chalcid parasite of Bees and Wasps.' *Parasitology*. **14**, 349-71.

BALLOU, H. A. (1913). 'Report on the prevalence of some pests and diseases in the West Indies during 1912.' *Barbados, West Indies, Bull.* **13**, 333-57.

BALLOU, H. A. (1934). 'Notes on some insect pests in the Lesser Antilles.' *Trop. Agric. Trin.* **11**, 210-2.

BARBER, (1905). (Exhibit, no title). *Proc. ent. Soc. Washington.* **7**, 25.

BARLOW, H. B. (1952). 'The size of ommatidia in apposition eyes.' *J. Exp. Biol.* **29**, 667-74.

BARRINGTON, R. M. (1900). 'Late wasp's nests.' *Irish Nat.* **9**, 108.

BARRINGTON, R. M. and MOFFATT, C. B. (1901). 'Wasps in county Wicklow.' *Irish Nat.* **10**, 197.

BECK, R. (1937), 'Mermis thread worm (Nematode) in wasp (*Vespa vulgaris*).' *Entomologist's Rec. J. Var.* **49**, 65.

BECKER, E. (1937). 'Die Rotbraune Zeichnung der Wespennestmütter, eine durch mechanischen reiz ausgelöste pigmentablagerung in Liesegangschen ringen.' *Z. vergl. Physiol.* **24**, 305-18.

BEIRNE, B. P. (1944), 'The causes of the occasional abundance and scarcity of wasps (*Vespula* spp.) (Hym., Vespidae).' *Entomologist's mon. Mag.* **80**, 121-4.

BENSON, R. B. (1946). 'A nest of the common wasp constructed partly from woolen garments.' *Trans. Herts. nat. hist. Soc.* **22**, 163.

BEQUAERT, J. (1930). 'On the generic and subgeneric divisions of Vespinae.' *Bull. Brooklyn ent. Soc.* **25**, 55-70.

BEQUAERT, J. and CARPENTER, F. M. (1941). 'The antiquity of social insects.' *Psyche.* **48**, 50-5.

BERLAND, L. (1931). 'Les nids de guêpes aeriens en France.' 64e *Congr. Soc. Savantes,* 545-8.

BEUTENMULLER, W. (1898). 'Note on a nest of *Vespa crabro*.' *Jl N.Y. ent. Soc.* **6**, 199.

BHOOLA, K. D., CALLE, J. and SCHACHTER, M. (1961). 'Identification of acetylcholine, 5-hydroxytryptamine, histamine and a new kinin in hornet venom (*Vespa crabro*).' *J. Physiol., Lond.* **159**, 167-82.

BIEGAL, W. (1953). 'Zur Biologie und Ökologie sozialer Wespen.' *S.B. Soc. Erlangen,* **76**, 115-53.

BIGNELL, G. C. (1881). '*Odynerus pictus;* contribution towards its life-history.' *Entomologist.* **14**, 188-9.

BIGNELL, G. C. (1882). *Odynerus pictus,* Curt. *Entomologist* **15**, 164.

BIGNELL, G. C. (1901). 'The Ichneumonidae (parasite flies) of South Devon. Part II. Braconidae.' *Trans. Devon. Ass. Adv. Sci.* **33**, 657-92.

BILLUPS, T. R. (1882). 'An early appearance of *Vespa germanica*, Fab.' *Entomologist's mon. Mag.* **18**, 234.

BILLUPS, T. R. (1884). '*Odynerus reniformis*, Gmel., at Chertsey.' *Entomologist's mon. Mag.* **21**, 68-9.

BISCHOFF, H. (1927). *Biologie der Tiere Deutschlands: Vol. 42.* Gebrüder Borntraeger. Berlin.

BLACK-HAWKINS, M. (1911). 'Some observations on *Vespa germanica*.' *Zoologist.* **15**, 457-63.

BLACKITH, R. E. (1957). 'Social facilitation at the nest entrance of Hymenoptera.' *Physiol. comp. Oecol.* **4**, 388-402.

BLACKITH, R. E. (1958a). 'Visual sensitivity and foraging in social wasps.' *Insectes soc.* **5**, 159-69.

BLACKITH, R. E. (1958b). 'An analysis of polymorphism in social wasps.' *Insectes soc.* **5**, 263-72.

BLACKITH, R. E. and STEVENSON, J. H. (1958). 'Autumnal populations of wasps nests.' *Insectes soc.* **5**, 347-52.

BLÜTHGEN, P. (1943). Taxonomische und biologische Notizen über paläarktische Faltenwespen. *Stettin. ent. Ztg.* **104**, 149-58.

BLÜTHGEN, P. (1961). 'Die Faltenwespen Mitteleuropas (Hymenoptera, Diploptera).' *Abh. Dt.Akad. Wiss. Berlin.* Nr. 2., 1-251.

BODENHEIMER, F. S. (1937). 'Population problems of social insects.' *Biol. Rev.* **12**, 393-430.

BOHART, R. M. (1941). 'A revision of the Strepsiptera with special reference to the species of North America.' *Univ. Calif. Pubs. ent.* **7**, 91-159.

BOISTEL, J., LECOMPTE, J., and CORABOEUF, E. (1956). 'Quelques aspects de l'étude électro-physiologique des recepteurs sensoriels des antennes d'Hyménopteres.' *Insectes soc.* **3,** 25-31.

BORDAS, L. (1917). 'Frelons chassant des Grillons pour en faire leur nourriture.' *Bull. soc. ent. Fr.* **22,** 84-5.

BORDAS, L. (1931). 'Anatomie comparée des ovaires de quelques Hyménoptères.' *C.r. Acad. Sci., Paris.* **192,** 1750-3.

BOYD, D. O. (1943). 'Hymenoptera Aculeata in East Dorset.' *J. Soc. Br. Ent.* **2,** 160-4.

BRIAN, A. D. (1951). 'Brood development in *Bombus agrorum*.' *Entomologist's mon. Mag.* **87,** 207-12.

BRIAN, M. V. (1965). *Social Insect Populations.* Academic Press, London.

BRIAN, M. V. and BRIAN, A. D. (1948). 'Nest construction by queens of *Vespula sylvestris* Scop. (Hym., Vespidae).' *Entomologist's mon. Mag.* **84,** 193-8.

BRIAN, M. V. and BRIAN, A. D. (1952). 'The wasp *Vespula sylvestris* Scopoli : feeding, foraging and colony development.' *Trans. R. ent. Soc. Lond.* **103,** 1-26.

BRISTOWE, W. S. (1931). 'Notes on the biology of spiders. VII. Flies that triumph over spiders.' *Ann. Mag. nat. hist.* **8,** 471-4.

BRISTOWE, W. S. (1948). 'Notes on the habits and prey of twenty species of British hunting wasp.' *Proc. Linn. Soc. Lond.* **160,** 12-37.

BRITTEN, H. (1911). 'Coleoptera from underground wasp nests.' *Entomologist's mon. Mag.* **47,** 89-90.

BROEKHUIZEN, S. and HORDIJK, C. (1968). 'Untersuchungen über die Beute von *Paravespula vulgaris* L. (Hym., Vespidae) und ihre Abhangigkeit von der Beutetierdichte.' *Z. angew. Zool.* **62,** 68-77.

BROMLEY, S. W. (1931). 'Hornet habits.' *Jl N.Y. ent. Soc.* **39,** 123-9.

BROWN, J. M. (1925). 'Wasps at Figwort.' *Naturalist, London,* **50,** 345-6.

BRUCH, C. (1936). 'Notas sobre el "Camuati" y las avispas que lo construyen.' *Physis, Buenos Aires.* **12,** 125-35.

BUCKLE, J. W. (1929). '*Ancistrocerus capra* and the larvae of *Epargyreus tityrus*.' *Can. Ent.* **61,** 265-6.

BURY, H. (1920). 'Diptera in south Shropshire 1913-20.' *Entomologist's mon. Mag.* **56,** 249-56.

BUTLER, C. G., FLETCHER, D. J. C., and WATLER, D. (1969). 'Nest-entrance marking with pheromones by the honeybees *Apis mellifera* L., and by a wasp, *Vespula vulgaris* L.' *Anim Behav.* **17,** 142-7.

BUTLER, E. A. (1896). 'Ptini in a hornets' nest.' *Entomologist's mon. Mag.* **32,** 109.

DU BUYSSON, R. (1903). 'Monographie des guêpes au *Vespa*.' *Ann. soc. ent. Fr.* **72,** 260-88.

DU BUYSSON, R. (1905). 'Monographie des Vespides du genre *Nectarina*.' *Ann. Soc. ent. Fr.* **74,** 537-66.

CALLAHAN, P. S. (1970). 'Insects and the radiation environment.' *Proc. Tall Timbers Conf.* No. 2, 247-58.

CARPENTER, G. H. and PACK-BERESFORD, D. R. (1903). 'The relationship of *Vespa austriaca* to *Vespa rufa*.' *Irish Nat.* **12,** 221-38.

CHAPMAN, J. A. (1963). 'Predation by *Vespula* wasps on hilltop swarms of winged ants.' *Ecology.* **44,** 766-7.

CHAPMAN, T. A. (1869). 'On the economy of the chrysids parasitic on *Odynerus spinipes*.' *Entomologist's mon. Mag.* **6,** 153-8.

CHAPMAN, T. A. (1870). 'Some facts towards a life-history of *Rhipiphorus paradoxus*.' *Ann Mag. nat. hist.* **6,** 314-26.

CHAPMAN, T. A. (1897). 'Sketch of the life-history of *Metoecus (Rhipiphorus) paradoxus*.' *Ent. Record.* **9,** 321-2.

CHARNEY, J. and TOMARELLI, R. M. (1948). 'A colorimetric method for the determination of the proteolytic activity of duodenal juice.' *J. Biol. Chem.* **171,** 501-5.

CHEVALIER, L. (1922). 'L'Eumène, hyménoptère ravisseur de chenilles.' *Bull. Soc. Sci. Seine et Oise.* **3,** 66-72.

CHEVALIER, L. (1924). 'Observations sur les guêpes.' *Bull. Soc. Sci. Seine et Oise.* **5,** 56-8.

CHEVALIER, L. (1931). '*Chrysis ignita* L. mangeur de chenilles de microlepidoptères.' *Bull. Soc. Sci. Seine et Oise.* **12,** 10-24.

COLLART, A. (1933). 'Diptères élevées des nids de guêpes.' *Bull. Mus. R. Hist. nat. Belg.* **9**, 1-8.

COLLART, A. (1936). 'Diptères élevées des nids de guêpes.' 2 note. *Bull. Mus. R. Hist. nat. Belg.* **12**, 1-12.

COOPER, K. W. (1953). 'Biology of eumenine wasps. I. The ecology, predation, nesting and competition of *Ancistrocerus antilope* (Panzer).' *Trans. Am. ent. Soc.* **79**, 13-35.

COOPER, K. W. (1955). 'Biology of eumenine wasps. II. Venereal transmission of mites by wasps, and some evolutionary problems arising from the remarkable association of *Ensliniella trisetosa* with the wasp *Ancistrocerus antilope*.' *Trans. Am. ent. Soc.* **80**, 119-74.

COOPER, K. W. (1957). 'Biology of eumenine wasps. V. Digital communication in wasps.' *J. Exp. Zool.* **134**, 469-514.

CORY, E. N. (1931). 'Notes on the European Hornet.' *J. econ. Ent.* **24**, 50-2.

CRAWSHAY, G. A. (1905). 'A large community of *Vespa vulgaris*.' *Entomolgist's mon. Mag.* **41**, 8-10.

CUMBER, R. A. (1949). 'The biology of bumblebees with special reference to production of the worker caste.' *Trans. R. ent. Soc. Lond.* **100**, 1-45.

CUTHBERT, H. G. (1914). 'Wasps preying on sawfly caterpillars.' *Irish Nat.* **23**, 238.

DAECKE, E. (1905). (No title). *Ent. News.* **16**, 95.

DANKS, H. V. (1968). 'Bionomics of some stem-nesting aculeate Hymenoptera.' *Unpublished Ph. D. thesis.* University of London.

DANKS, H. V. (1971a). 'Biology of some stem-nesting aculeate Hymenoptera.' *Trans. R. ent. Soc. Lond.* **122**, 323-99.

DANKS, H. V. (1971b). 'Nest mortality factors in stem-nesting aculeate Hymenoptera.' *J. Anim. Ecol.* **40**, 79-82.

DARCHEN, R. (1964). 'Biologie de *Vespa orientalis*. Les premiers stades de développement.' *Insectes soc.* **11**, 141-57.

DARLINGTON, P. J. (1957). *Zoogeography : The Geographical Distribution of Animals.* Wiley, New York.

DAVIS, A. H. (1833). 'Observations on *Vespa vulgaris*.' *Entomologist's mon. Mag.* **1**, 90.

DELEURANCE, E. P. (1947). 'Le cycle évolutif du nid de *Polistes* (Hyménoptères Vespidae).' *C.r. Acad. Sci., Paris.* **224**, 228-30.

DELEURANCE, E. P. (1948). 'Le comportement reproducteur est indépendant de la presence des ovaires chez *Polistes* (Hyménoptères Véspides).' *C.r. Acad. Sci., Paris.* **227**, 866-7.

DELEURANCE, E. P. (1949). 'Sur le déterminisme de l'apparition des ouvrières et des fondratrices-filles chez les *Polistes* (Hyménoptères Véspides).' *C.r. Acad. Sci., Paris.* **229**, 303-4.

DELEURANCE, E. P. (1950). 'Sur la nature et le déterminisme du couvain abortif chez le Polistes (Hyménopteres Véspides).' *C.r. Acad. Sci., Paris.* **231**, 1565-4.

DELEURANCE, E. P. (1955a). 'Contribution a l'étude biologique des *Polistes* (Hyménoptères Véspides). II. Le cycle evolutif du couvain.' *Insectes soc.* **2**, 285-302.

DELEURANCE, E. P. (1955b). 'L'influence des ovaires sur l'activité de construction chez les *Polistes* (Hyménopteres Véspides).' *C.r. Acad. Sci. Paris.*, **241**, 1073-5.

DELEURANCE, E. P. (1957). 'Contribution a l'étude biologique, des *Polistes* (Hyménopteres Véspides). I. L'activité de construction.' *Behaviour.* **11**, 67-84.

DESEY, A. (1922). 'Observation sur le rétour au nid des Hyménoptères.' *Bull. Soc. ent. Belg.* **4**, 93-99, 104-111.

DÖHRING, E. (1960). 'Zur Häufigkeit, hygienischen Bedeutung und zum Fang sozialer Faltenwespen in einer Grosstadt.' *Z. angew Ent.* **47**, 69-79.

DONISTHORPE, H. (1917). 'Attitudes of wasps and psocids in copulation.' *Entomologist's Rec. J. Var.* **29**, 231-2.

DONISTHORPE, H. (1927). '*Cryptophagus løvendali* Ganglb. a dweller in *Vespa* nests in trees.' *Entomologist's mon. Mag.* **63**, 111.

DONISTHORPE, H. (1929). 'Hornets and rare beetles from Windsor Forest.' *Proc. R. ent. Soc. Lond.* **4**, 69.

DUNCAN, C. D. (1939). *A Contribution to the Biology of North American Vespine Wasps.* Stanford University Press.

EALES WHITE, J. C. (1911). 'On the killing of flies, bees, etc. by wasps.' *Entomologist's mon. Mag.* **47**, 260.

EBERHARD, M. J. W. (1969). 'The social biology of polistine wasps.' *Misc. Pubs. Mus. Zool. Univ. Michigan.* No. 140, 1-101.

EBERHARD, W. J. (1972). 'Altuistic behaviour in a sphecoid wasp: support for kin-selection theory.' *Science* **175**, 1390-1.

EDERY, H. and ISHAY, J. (1970). 'Pharmacological actions of *Vespa orientalis* venom.' *Toticon.* **8**, 130.

EDGEWORTH, R. L. (1864). 'Notes on Irish Vespidae.' *Ann. Mag. nat. hist.* **13**, 466-74.

EDWARDS, R. (1968). 'Some experiment on the rhythmic behaviour of the wasp, *Paravespula rufa* (Linn.) (Hymenoptera : Vespidae).' *Unpublished M.Sc. thesis.* University of London.

ENSLIN, E. (1921). 'Beiträge zur Kenntnis der Hymenopteren II. 3. Biologie von *Symmorphus sinuatus* F., 4. Biologie von *Ancistrocerus trifasciatus* F.' *Dt. ent. Z.* **4**, 279-85.

EVANS, H. E. (1958). 'The evolution of social life in wasps.' *Proc. 10th int. Congr. Ent.* **2**, 449-57.

EVANS, H. E. (1966). 'The behaviour patterns of solitary wasps.' *Ann. Rev. Ent.* **11**, 123-54.

EVANS, H. E. and EBERHARD, M. J. W. (1970). *The Wasps.* University of Michigan Press.

EVENIUS, C. (1933). 'Über die Entwicklung der Rektaldrüsen von *Vespa vulgaris.*' *Zool. Jb. (Anat.).* **56**, 349-72.

FAHRINGER, J. (1922). 'Hymenopterologische Ergebnisse einer wissenschaftlichen Studienriese nach der Türkei und Kleinasien (mit Ausschlusz des Amanusgebinges).' *Arch. Naturgesch.* **88**, 149-222.

FELTON, J. C. (1954). 'The external morphology of *Ancistrocerus parietum* (Lin.) and the taxonomy of the British species of Eumeninae.' *Unpublished B.Sc. thesis.* University of London.

FELTON, J. C. (1966). 'The Hymenoptera Aculeata.' *Bull. amat. ent. Soc.* **25**, 114-6.

FELTON, J. C. (1967). 'The Hymenoptera Aculeata.' *Bull. amat. ent. Soc.* **26**, 107-9.

FIGUIER, L. (1868). *The Insect World.* Appleton & Company, New York.

FISCHL, J. and ISHAY, J. (1971). 'The glucose levels and carbohydrate autolysis in *Vespa orientalis* haemolymph.' *Insectes soc.* **18**, 203-14.

FITCH, E. A. (1879). 'Hymenoptera bred from *Cynips kollari* galls.' *Entomologist.* **12**, 113-9.

FLANDERS, S. E. (1953). 'Caste determination in the social Hymenoptera.' *Sci. Mon.* **76**, 142-8.

FLANDERS, S. E. (1957). 'Regulation of caste in social Hymenoptera.' *Jl N.Y. ent. Soc.* **65**, 97-105.

FLANDERS, S. E. (1962). 'Physiological prerequisites of social reproduction in the Hymenoptera.' *Insectes soc.* **9**, 375-88.

FLORU, L., ISHAY, J. and GITTER, S. (1969). 'The influence of psychotropic substances on hornet behaviour in colonies of *Vespa orientalis* F. (Hymenoptera).' *Psychopharmacologia (Berlin).* **14**, 323-41.

FOREL, A. (1895). 'Quelques observations biologiques sur les guêpes.' *Bull Soc. Vaud. Sci. nat.* **31**, 312.

FOUBERT, E. L. and STIER, R. A. (1958). 'Antigenic relationships between honeybees, wasps, yellow hornets, black hornets, and yellowjackets.' *J. Allergy.* **29**, 13-23.

FOX-WILSON, G. (1946). 'Factors affecting populations of social wasps, *Vespula* species, in England.' *Proc. R. ent.Soc. Lond.* **21**, 17-27.

FRANKLAND, A. W. (1968). 'Allergy and the Bee-Keeper.' *Rept. Cent. Ass. Br. Beekeep. Ass.*, 1-8.

FRASER, F. C. (1946a). '*Volucella* (Dipt., Syrphidae) larvae sp., breeding in a nest of *Vespula vulgaris* L. (Hym., Vespidae).' *Entomologist's mon. Mag.* **82**, 55-7.

FRASER, F. C. (1946b). 'A final report on the breeding of *Volucella* (Dipt., Syrphidae) larvae in a nest of *Vespa vulgaris* L. (Hym., Vespidae).' *Entomologist's mon. Mag.* **82**, 158.

FRAZIER, C. A. (1969). *Insect Allergy. Allergic and Toxic Reactions to Insects and other Arthropods.* Warren H. Green, Missouri.

FREE, J. B. (1955). 'The division of labour within bumblebee colonies.' *Insectes soc.* **2**, 195-212.

FREE, J. B. (1961). 'The social organisation of the bumble-bee colony.' *Rep. Cent. Ass. Br. Beekeep. Ass.*, 1-11.

378 WASPS

FREE, J. B. (1970). 'The behaviour of wasps (*Vespula germanica* L. and *V. vulgaris* L.) when foraging.' *Insectes soc.* **17**, 11-20.

FROHAWK, F. W. (1935). 'Martins and wasps nesting together.' *Proc. R. ent. Soc. Lond.* **10**, 77-8.

FREE, J. B. and BUTLER, C. G. (1959). *Bumblebees.* Collins, London.

FYE, R. E. (1972). 'The effect of forest disturbances on populations of wasps and bees in northwestern Ontario (Hymenoptera: Aculeata).' *Can. Ent.* **104**, 1623-33.

GAUL, A. T. (1941). 'Experiments in housing vespine colonies, with notes on the homing and toleration instincts of certain species.' *Psyche.* **48**, 16-9.

GAUL, A. T. (1947). 'Additions to vespine biology. II. Caste phases.' *Bull. Brooklyn ent. Soc.* **42**, 58-62.

GAUL, A. T. (1948). 'Additions to vespine biology. V. The distribution of labour in the colonies of hornets and yellowjackets.' *Bull. Brooklyn ent. Soc.* **43**, 73-9.

GAUL, A. T. (1951). 'Additions to vespine biology. VII. Orientation flight.' *Bull. Brooklyn ent. Soc.* **46**, 54-6.

GAUL, A. T. (1952a). 'The awakening and diurnal flight activities of vespine wasps.' *Proc. R. ent. Soc. Lond.* **27**, 33-5.

GAUL, A. T. (1952b). 'The flight of vespine wasps in relation to stormy weather.' *Jl N.Y. ent. Soc.* **60**, 17-20.

GAUL, A. T. (1952c). 'Metabolic cycles and flight in wasps.' *Jl N.Y. ent. Soc.* **60**, 21-4.

GAUL, A. T. (1952d). 'Additions to vespine biology. IX. Temperature regulation in the colony.' *Bull. Brooklyn ent. Soc.* **47**, 79-82.

GAUL, A. T. (1952e). 'Additions to vespine biology. X. Foraging and chemotaxis.' *Bull Brooklyn. ent. Soc.* **47**, 138-40.

GAUL, A. T. (1953). 'Additions to vespine biology. XI. Defense flight.' *Bull. Brooklyn ent. Soc.* **48**, 35-7.

GAUSS, R. (1959). 'Zum Parasitismus der Fächerfluger.' *Lands. Nat. Naturs.* **7**, 331-47.

GAUSS, R. (1968). 'Über Parasiten bei sozialen Wespen (Vespidae).' *Z. angrew. Ent.* **61**, 453-4.

GAUSS, R. (1970). 'Beitrag zur Kenntnis von Parasitoiden bei Aculeaten Hymenopteren.' *Z. angew. Ent.* **65**, 239-44.

GAUSS, R. (1972). 'Amerikanische *Polistes* – Art mit ihrem bislang noch unbekannten Parasiten nach Deutschland verschleppt (Hym., Vespoidea u. Chalcidoidea).'

GEORGE, C. F. (1906). 'Notes on a solitary wasp (*Odynerus parietum* Linn.)' *Naturalist, London.* **31**, 27-8.

GERVET, J. (1956). 'L'action des températures différentielles sur la monogynie fonctionelle chez les *Polistes* (Hyménoptères Véspides).' *Insectes soc.* **3**, 159-76.

GERVET, J. (1957a). 'Variations de la fécondité chez *Polistes gallicus* L. (Hyménoptères Véspides).' *C.r. Acad. Sci., Paris.* **244**, 130-3.

GERVET, J. (1957b). 'Sur la corrélation taille-fécondité chez *Polistes gallicus* L. (Hyménoptères Véspides).' *C.r. Acad. Sci., Paris.* **245**, 108-110.

GERVET, J. (1962). 'Étude de l'éffet de groupe sur la ponte dans la société polygyne de *Polistes gallicus* L. (Hyménoptères Véspides).' *Insectes soc.* **9**, 231-63.

GERVET, J. (1964a). 'Essai d'analyse élémentaire du comportement de ponte chez la guêpe Poliste *P. gallicus* (Hymén. Vesp.).' *Insectes soc.* **11**, 21-40.

GERVET, J. (1964b). 'Le comportement d'oophagie différentielle chez *Polistes gallicus* L. (Hymén. Vésp.)' *Insectes soc.* **11**, 343-82.

GIRAUD, J. (1869). 'Note biologique sur la *Melittobia audouni*.' *Annls. Soc. ent. Fr.* **9**, 151-6.

GITTER, S., ISHAY, J., MANOACH, M., FLORU, L., and FRIEDMAN-NEIGER, J. (1971). 'Studies on the behaviour of *Vespa orientalis* and the influence of drugs.' *Toxins of Plant & Animal Origin.* **1**, 47-56.

GOODALL, J. M. (1924). 'Late wasps' nests.' *Proc. I.O.W. nat. hist. Soc.* **5**, 311.

GRANDI, G. (1934). 'La constituzione morfologia delle larve di alcuni Vespidi ed Apidi sociali; Suoi rapporti con le modolita di assunzione del cibo e con altri comportamenti etologici.' *R. Acad. Sci. Bologna.* **1**, 73-9.

GRANT, J. (1959). 'Hummingbirds attacked by wasps.' *Canad. Fld. Nat.* **73**, 174.

GREEN, T. L. (1931). 'The anatomy and histology of the alimentary canal in the common wasp, *Vespa vulgaris*.' *Proc. zool. Soc. Lond.* **108**, 1041-66.

GREEN, T. L. (1933). 'Some aspects of the metamorphosis of the alimentary system in the wasp, *Vespa vulgaris* (Hymenoptera).' *Proc. zool. Soc. Lond.* **110**, 629-44.

GUICHARD, K. M. (1972). '*Symmorphus crassicornis* (Panzer) (Hym., Vespoidea) in Britain, with a key to the British species of *Symmorphus* Wesmael.' *Ent. Gaz.* **23**, 169-73.

GUIGLIA, D. (1948). 'Le Vespa d'Italia.' *Soc. ent. Ital. Mem. Suppl.* **27**, 1-84.

GUIGLIA, D. (1971). 'A concise history of Vespidae systematics in the Old World (Hymenoptera).' *Entomological Essays to Commemorate the Retirement of Professor K. Yasumatsu*, 113-7.

HABERMANN, E. (1972). 'Bee and wasp venoms.' *Science* **177**, 314-22.

HAGENMAIER, H. E. (1971). 'Purification and characterization of a trypsin-like proteinase from the midgut of the larva of the hornet, *Vespa orientalis*.' *J. Insect. Physiol.* **17**, 1995-2004.

HAMILTON, W. D. (1964a). 'The genetical evolution of social behaviour. I.' *J. Theoret. Biol.* **7**, 1-16.

HAMILTON, W. D. (1964b). 'The genetical evolution of social behaviour. II.' *J. Theoret. Biol.* **7**, 17-52.

HAMILTON, W. D. (1972). 'Altruism and related phenomena, mainly in social insects.' *A. Rev. Ecol.* **3**, 193-232.

HANDLIRSCH, A. (1910). 'Fossile Wespennester.' *Nat. Mus. Ges. Frankfurt A.M.* **41**, 265-6.

HANSON, S. W. F. and OLLEY, J. (1963). 'Application of the Bligh and Dyer method of lipid extraction to tissue homogenates.' *Biochem. J.* **89**, 101-2.

HARDY, J. (1876). 'Miscellanea. Habits of wasps.' *History Berwick. Nat. Club.* **7**, 127 (1873-1875).

HARRISON, J. W. H. (1915). '*Vespa austriaca*.' *Vasculum.* **1**, 113-5.

HARTMAN, C. G. (1944). 'How *Odynerus* suspends the egg.' *Psyche*, **51**, 1-4.

HARTTIG, G. (1929). '*Sphecophaga vesparum* Rtzb. in einem Nesten von *Vespa germanica* F.' *Z. Insbiol.* **24**, 22.

HAWORTH-BOOTH, B. B. (1896). 'Plague of wasps near Hull in 1893'. *Naturalist, Hull.* **21**, 34.

HEIM, F. (1893). 'Un procédé de déstruction des Frelons.' *Bull. Soc. ent. Fr.* **72**, 106-9.

HELDMANN, G. (1936). 'Ueber die Entwicklung der polygynen Wabe von *Polistes gallica* L.' *Arb. physiol. Ent.* **3**, 257-9.

HENSLOW, J. S. (1849). 'Parasitic larvae observed in the nests of Hornets, Wasps, and Humble Bees.' *Zoologist.* **7**, 2584-6.

HERMANN, H. R. (1971). 'Sting autotomy, a defensive mechanism in certain social Hymenoptera.' *Insectes soc.* **18**, 111-20.

HEROLD, W. (1952). 'Beobachtungen über die Arbeitsleistung einiger Arbeiter von *Vespa germanica* F. – *Dolichovespula germanica* (F.).' *Biol. Zbl.* **71**, 461-9.

HESELHAUS, F. (1922). 'Die Hautdrüsen de Apiden und verwandter Formen.' *Zool. Jb.* (*Anat.*) **43**, 369-464 (plus 11 plates.)

HESSE, E. (1916). 'Wespenfiende unter den Vögeln. *Ornith. Monatsb.* **24**, 3-4.

HEY, W. C. (1909). 'Wasps at West Ayton, Yorkshire.' *Naturalist, London.* 53-4.

HIMMER, A. (1927). 'Ein Beitrag zur Kenntnis des Wärmehaushaltes im Nestbau sozialer Hautflügler.' *Z. vergl. Physiol.* **5**, 375-89.

HIMMER, A. (1931). 'Uber die Wärme im Hornissennest (*Vespa crabro* L.).' *Z. vergl. Physiol.* **13**, 748-61.

HIMMER, A. (1932). 'Die Temperaturverhaltnisse bei den sozialen Hymenopteren.' *Biol. Rev.* **7**, 224-53.

HOBBY, B. M. (1932). 'The prey of British Dragonflies.' *Trans. ent. Soc. S. England.* **8**, 65-76.

HOBBY, B. M. (1938). '*Ancistrocerus parientinus* L. (Hym., Vespidae) and *Chrysis ignita* L. (Hym., Chrysididae) bred from cells constructed between books and bookcase.' *Proc. R. ent. Soc. Lond.* **13**, 100.

HOBBY, B. M. and KILLINGTON, F. J. (1932). 'Defensive display by *Pyrameis atalanta* L. (Lep.), against attack of Hornet, *Vespa crabro* L. (Hym.).' *J. ent. Soc. S. England.* **1**, 7.

HOFFER, E. (1883). 'Über die Lebenweise des *Metoecus paradoxus* L.' *Ent. Nachr.* **9**, 45-9.

HOLT, V. (1885). *Why Not Eat Insects.* Classey, Rickmansworth (reprinted 1967).

HOPKINS, L. (1955). 'Biology and control of *Polistes exclamans* Viereck in Arizona citrus groves.' *J. econ. Ent.* **48**, 161-3.

HOWARD, L. O. (1915). 'An unusual colour in a Hornet's nest.' *Proc. ent. Soc. Washington.* **17**, 148.

HOWSE, P. E. (1970). *Termites: A Study in Social Behaviour.* Hutchinson, London.

HOWSE, P. E. and WILLIAMS, J. L. D. (1969). 'The brains of social insects in relation to behaviour.' *Proc. VI. Congr. I.U.S.S.I. Bern.* 59-64.

HOWSE, P. E. (1972). 'The insect brain in relation to behaviour.' *Proc. R. ent. Soc. Lond.* **36**, 41.

HOUSIAUX, A. (1922). 'Les Chrysididae de Belgique.' *Bull. Soc. ent. Belg.* **4**, 19-38.

HÜSING, J. O. (1954). 'Über die Larvennahrung einiger Vespiden (Insecta, Hymenoptera).' *Wiss. Z. Univ. Halle, Math. Nat.* **4**, 231-6.

HÜSING, J. O. (1956). 'Weitere Beobachtungen über die Nahrung von Vespiden Larven.' *Insectes soc.* **3**, 41-8.

IHERING, H. (1903). 'Biologie der stachellosen honigbienen Brasiliens.' *Zool. Jb. (Syst.).* **19**, 179-287.

IKAN, R. and ISHAY, J. (1966). 'Larval wasp secretions and honeydew of the Aphids, *Chaitophorus populi* feeding on *Populus euphratica* as sources of sugars in the diet of the Oriental Hornet, *Vespa orientalis*, F.' *Israel J. Zool.* **15**, 64-8.

IKAN, R., GOTTLIEB, R. and BERGMANN, E. D. (1969). 'The pheromone of the queen of the Oriental Hornet, *Vespa orientalis*.' *J. Insect. Physiol.* **15**, 1709-12.

IKAN, R., BERGMANN, E. D., ISHAY, J., and GITTER, S. (1968). 'Proteolytic enzyme activity in the various colony members of the Oriental Hornet, *Vespa orientalis* F.' *Life Sciences.* **7**, 929-34.

IMMS, A. D. (1957). *A General Textbook of Entomology.* Methuen, London.

ISELY, D. (1913). 'The biology of some Kansas Eumenidae.' *Kansas Univ. Sci. Bull.* **8**, 233-309.

ISHAY, J. (1964). 'Observations sur la biologie de la Guêpe Orientale, *Vespa orientalis* F.' *Insectes soc.* **11**, 193-206.

ISHAY, J. (1972). 'Thermoregulatory pheromones in wasps.' *Experientia* **28**, 1185-7.

ISHAY, J. and IKAN, R. (1968a). 'Food exchange between adults and larvae in *Vespa orientalis* F.' *Anim. Behav.* **16**, 298-303.

ISHAY, J. and IKAN, R. (1968b). 'Gluconeogenesis in the Oriental Hornet, *Vespa orientalis* F.' *Ecology.* **49**, 1.

ISHAY, J. and LANDAU, E. M. (1972). '*Vespa* larvae send out rhythmic hunger signals.' *Nature.* **237**, 286-7.

ISHAY, J. and RUTTNER, F. (1971). 'Thermoregulation im Hornissennest.' *Z. verg. Physiol.* **72**, 423-34.

ISHAY, J. and SCHWARZ, J. (1965). 'On the nature of the sounds produced within the nest of the Oriental Hornet, *Vespa orientalis*, F.' *Insectes soc.* **12**, 383-7.

ISHAY, J. and SCHWARTZ, A. (1971). 'Acoustical communication between the members of the colony of the Oriental Hornet (*Vespa orientalis*, Hymenoptera).' *7th Int. Congr. Acoustics, Budapest.*

ISHAY, J., BYTINSKI-SALZ, H. and SHULOV, A. (1967). 'Contributions to the bionomics of the Oriental Hornet (*Vespa orientalis* Fab.).' *Israel J. Ent.* **2**, 45-106.

ISHAY, J., GITTER, S. and FISCHL, J. (1971). 'The production and effectivity of rabbit antiserum against *Vespa orientalis* venom.' *Acta Allergologica.* **26**, 286-90.

ISHAY, J., IKAN, R. and BERGMANN, E. D. (1965). 'The presence of pheromones in the Oriental Hornet, *Vespa orientalis*.' *J. Insect Physiol.* **11**, 1307-9.

ISHAY, J., GITTER, S., SCHAUDINISCHKY, L. and SCHWARTZ, A. (1970). 'Cybernetic processes between adults and the larvae of the Oriental Hornet *Vespa orientalis*.' *Int. Congr. Cybernetics, Namur,* 1-16.

ITÔ, Y. and MIYASHITA, K. (1968). 'Biology of *Hyphantria cunea* Drury (Lepidoptera: Arctiidae) in Japan. V. Preliminary life tables and mortality data in urban areas.' *Res. Popul. Ecol.* **10**, 177-209.

IWATA, K. (1939). 'Habits of a paper-making Potter Wasp (*Eumenes architectus* Smith) in Japan.' *Mushi.* **12**, 83-5.

IWATA, K. (1953). 'Biology of *Eumenes* in Japan (Hymenoptera: Vespidae).' *Mushi,* **25**, 25-47.

IWATA, K. (1960). 'The comparative anatomy of the ovary in Hymenoptera. Supplement on Aculeata with description of ovarian eggs of certain species.' *Acta hym. Fukuoka.* 1, 205-11.

IWATA, K. (1964). 'Report of the fundamental research on the biological control of insect pests in Thailand. I. The first report on the bionomics of Aculeate wasps.' *Nat. Life S.E. Asia, Tokyo.* 3, 317-21.

IWATA, K. (1966). 'Description of the nests of so called *Belonogaster griseus* var. *menelikii* Gribodo collected by Dr. K. Yamashita in Ethiopia, with a general consideration on the life of the genus (Hymenoptera, Vespidae).' *Mushi.* 39, 57-64.

IWATA, K. (1967). 'Report of the fundamental research on the biological control of insect pests in Thailand. II. The report on the bionomics of Aculeate wasps. Bionomics of subsocial wasps of Stenogastrinae (Hymenoptera, Vespidae).' *Nat. Life S.E. Asia, Tokyo.* 5, 259-93.

IWATA, K. (1969a). 'On the nidification of *Ropalidia* (*Anthreneida*) *taiwana koshunensis* Sonan in Formosa (Hymenoptera, Vespidae).' *Kontyû.* 37, 367-72.

IWATA, K. (1969b). 'Nidification habits of *Ropalidia* and *Parapolybia*.' *Kontyû.* 37, 437-43.

JANET, C. (1895a). 'Études sur les Fourmis, les Guêpes et les Abeilles. IXe note. Sur *Vespa crabro* L. Histoire d'un nid depuis son origine.' *Mém Soc. zool. Fr.* 8, 1-140.

JANET, C. (1895b). 'Études sur les Fourmis, les Guêpes et les Abeilles. Xe note. Sur *Vespa media, V. sylvestris* et *V. saxonica.' Mém. Soc. Acad. Oise.* 16, 28-58.

JANET, C. (1895c). *Études sur les Fourmis, les Guêpes et les Abeilles. XIe note.* Sur Vespa germanica *et* V. vulgaris. Ducourtieux, Limoges.

JANET, C. (1903). *Observations sur les Guêpes.* Naud, Paris.

JEANNE, R. L. (1970a). 'Note on a bat (*Phylloderma stenops*) preying upon the brood of a social wasp.' *J. Mammalogy.* 51, 624-5.

JEANNE, R. L. (1970b). 'Chemical defense of brood by a social wasp.' *Science N.Y.* 168, 1465-6.

JEANNE, R. L. (1972). 'Social biology of the neotropical wasp *Mischocyttarus drewseni.' Bull. Mus. comp. Zool. Harv.* 144, 63-150.

JEFKINS, F. (1961). 'Control of Wasps in Food Factories. New delayed action bait capable of destroying whole colonies.' *Food Trade Rev.* 31, 47-8, 54.

JOHANSEN, C. A. and DAVIS, H. G. (1972). 'Toxicity of nine insecticides to the Western Yellowjacket.' *J. econ. Ent.* 65, 40-2.

JONES, H. P. (1937). 'A new British "Mason Wasp".' *Entomologist's mon. Mag.* 73, 13-5.

JØRGENSEN, P. (1942). 'Biological observations on some solitary vespides.' *Ent. Meddr.* 22, 299-335.

JULLIARD, C. (1950). 'Nid de l'*Odynerus scoticus* Curtis (Hym. Vespidae).' *Bull. Soc. ent. Suisse.* 23, 369-76.

JURINE, L. (1818). 'Observations sur le *Xenos vesparum.' Mem. R. Acad. Sci. Torino* (1816), 50-63.

KAISSLING, K. E. and RENNER, M. (1968). 'Antennale Rezeptoren für Queen Substance und Sterzelduft bei der Honigbiene.' *Z. vergl. Physiol.* 59, 357-61.

KALMUS, H. (1954). 'Finding and exploitation of dishes of syrup by Bees and Wasps.' *Brit. J. Anim. Behav.* 2, 136-9.

KARL, O. (1928). 'Zweiflügler oder Diptera. III. Muscidae.' *Die Tier. Dts. Jena.* 13, 232 pages.

KARLSON, P. and BUTENANDT, A. (1959). 'Pheromones (ectohormones) in insects.' *Ann. Rev. ent.* 4, 39-58.

KEMPER, H. (1961). 'Nesterunterschiede bei den sozialen Faltenwespen Deutschlands.' *Z. angew. Zool.* 48, 31-85.

KEMPER, H. (1962). 'Nahrung und Nahrungserweb der heimischen sozialen Vespiden.' *Z. angew. Ent.* 50, 52-5.

KEMPER, H. (1963). 'Weitere Beobachtungen und Versuche über die Ernährung sozialer Faltenwespen, insbesondere über den Geschmackssinn von *Paravespula vulgaris* (L.).' *Z. angew. Zool.* 50, 49-70.

KEMPER, H. and DÖHRING, E. (1961). 'Soziale Wespen als Schädlinge des Obstbaues und des Obsthandels.' *Anz. Schädlingsk.* 34, 17-19.

KEMPER, H. and DÖHRING, E. (1962). 'Untersuchungen über die Ernährung sozialer Falten-wespen Dentschlands, insbesondere von *P. germanica* und *P. vulgaris.*' *Z. angew. Zool.* **49**, 227-280.

KEMPER, H. and DÖHRING, E. (1967). *Die sozialen Faltenwespen Mitteleuropas.* Paul Parey, Berlin.

KILLINGTON, F. J. (1932). '*Vespa vulgaris* attacking *Forficula auricularia* L.' *J. ent. Soc. S. England.* **1**, 34.

KILLINGTON, F. J. (1940). 'Birds and easps attacking Pieridae (Lep.).' *J. Soc. Br. Ent.* **2**, 85-6.

KIRKTON, R. M. (1970). 'Habitat management and its effects on populations of *Polistes* and *Iridomyrmex.*' *Proc. Tall Timbers Conf. No.* **2**, 243-6.

KLOFT, W. (1951). 'Pathologische untersuchungen an einem Wespenweibchen, infiziert durch einen Gordioiden (Nematomorpha).' *Z.f. Parasitenkunde.* **15**, 134-47.

KÖNIG, C. (1896). 'Was wussten die alten Griechen und Römer von den Wespen und Hornissen?' *Illust. W. Ento.* **1**, 261-6.

KROMBEIN, K. V. (1967). *Trap-nesting Wasps and Bees: life histories, nests and associates* Smithsonian Press, Washington.

KÜHLHORN, F. (1961). 'Uber das Verhalten sozialer Faltenwespen (Hymenoptera: Vespidae) beim Stalleinflug, innerhalb von Viehställen und beim Fliegenfang.' *Z. angew Zool.* **48**, 405-22.

LAIDLAW, W. B. R. (1930). 'Notes on some humble bees and wasps in Scotland. II. The Social Wasps.' *Scot. Nat.* **185**, 135-6.

LAIDLAW, W. B. R. (1934). *The Wasp. The genus Vespa in Scotland.* John Baxter & Son, Edinburgh.

LAIRD, M. (1949). 'Notes on the nest-building of the solitary wasp, *Eumenes latreillei petiolaris* Shulz, 1903, at Jacquinot Bay, New Britain.' *Proc. R. ent. Soc. Lond.* **24**, 26-31.

LATTER, O. H. (1895). 'Wasps and weather.' *Nat. Sci.* **6**, 178-9.

LATTER, O. H. (1898). 'Wasps.' *Nat. Sci.* **12**, 143.

LATTER, O. H. (1913). *Bees and Wasps.* Cambridge University Press, Cambridge.

LATTER, O. H. (1935). 'A reason for the order in which the queen wasp constructs the cell of the comb; a method for computing the number of cells in a comb, and an instance of the limitation of the instincts of wasps.' *Proc. R. ent. Soc. Lond.* **10**, 74-8.

LAWSON, F. R., RABB, R. L., GUTHRIE, F. E. and BOWERY, T. G. (1961). 'Studies of an integrated control system for hornworms on tobacco.' *J. econ. Ent.* **54**, 93-7.

LECLERCQ, J. (1944). 'Fluctuations du degré d'abondance récemment observées chez Hyménopteres aculéates.' *Bull. Soc. Roy. Sci. Liège.* **7**, 262-6.

LIN, N. and MICHENER, C. D. (1972). 'Evolution of sociality in insects.' *Q. Rev. Biol.* **47**, 131-59.

LINDAUER, M. (1961). *Communication among Social Bees.* Harvard University Press. Cambridge, Mass.

LINSLEY, E. G. (1944). 'Natural sources, habitats and reservoirs of insects associated with stored-food products.' *Hilgardia* **16**, 187-224.

LINSLEY, E. G. and MACSWAIN, J. W. (1957). 'Observations on the habits of *Stylops pacifica* Bohart.' *Univ. California Pubs. Ent.* **11**, 395-430.

LINSTOW, O. (1905). 'Helminthologische Beobachtungen.' *Arch. mikr. Anat.* **66**, 355-66.

LITH, J. P. (1956). 'Merkwaardige nesten van *Dolichovespula saxonica* (F.).' *Ent. Ber. Deel.* **16**, 33-5.

LLOYD, B. (1942). 'The Hornet in Hertfordshire.' *Trans. Herts. nat. hist. Soc.* **21**, 304-7.

LLOYD, B. and BENSON, R. B. (1945). 'Hornets in Hertfordshire.' *Trans. Herts. nat. hist. Soc.* **22**, 87-88.

LÖVGREN, B. (1958). 'A mathematical treatment of the development of colonies of different kinds of social wasps.' *Bull. math. Biophys.* **20**, 119-48.

LUBBOCK, J. (1876). 'Observations on bees and wasps.' *J. Linn. Soc. (Zool.).* **12**, 110-39.

LUCAS, W. J. (1905). 'Captives and field reports. Insects at Hurst Castle.' *Entomologist.* **38**, 282-3.

LUCAS, W. J. (1929). 'British predaceous insects and spiders with their insect prey.' *Proc. R. ent. Soc. Lond.* **4**, 20.

MAETA, Y. (1963a). 'Some biological notes on *Pseudoxenos iwatai* Esaki. (II) Its biology and life history.' *Kontyû.* **31**, 113-26.

BIBLIOGRAPHY 383

MAETA, Y. (1963b). 'Some biological notes on *Pseudoxenos iwatai* Esaki. (III). Its parasitic position on the body of host wasps.' *Kontyû.* **31**, 127-39.

MALYSHEV, S. I. (1911). '(The biology of *Odynerus* and its parasites – in Russian).' *Russk. ent. Obshch.* **40**, 1-58.

MALYSHEV, S. I. (1968). *Genesis of the Hymenoptera and the Phases of their Evolution.* Methuen, London.

MANEVAL, H. (1925). 'Une nidification d'*Odynerus parietum* L. *Feuille Nat.*' **46**, 170-1.

MARCHAL, P. (1894). 'Sur le réceptacle séminal de la Guêpe.' *Ann. Soc. ent. Fr.* **63**, 44-9.

MARCHAL, P. (1896). 'La réproduction et l'évolution des guêpes sociales.' *Arches. Zool. exp. gén.* **4**, 1-100.

MARCHAL, P. (1897). 'La castration nutriciale chex les Hyménoptères sociaux.' *C.r. Séan. Soc. Biol.* 49, 556-7.

MARIE, M. P. (1923). 'Liste d'un certain nombre d'insectes trouves dans les gesiers de jeunes *Corvus frugilegus* Linné *Bull. Soc. ent. Fr.*' **28**, 135-6.

MARKL, H. (1962). 'Borstenfelder an den Gelenken als Schwaresinnesorgane bei Ameisen und anderen Hymenopteren.' *Z. vergl. Physiol.* **45**, 475-569.

MASCHWITZ, U. (1965). 'Larven als Nahrungsspeicher im Wespenvolk (Ein Beitrag zum Trophallaxiersproblem).' *Dt. zool. Ges. Jena.* **50**, 530-4.

MATTHEWS, R. W. (1968). '*Microstigmus comes:* Sociality in a sphecid wasp.' *Science, N.Y.* **160**, 787-8.

MATSUURA, M. (1966). 'Notes on the hibernating habits of the genus *Vespa* in Japan (Hymenoptera, Vespidae).' *Kontyû.* **34**, 52-67.

MATSUURA, M. (1967a). 'Life of Hornets. Part 7. (Stylopized *Vespa* workers: in Japanese).' *Jap. Bee J.* **20**, 255-9.

MATSUURA, M. (1967b). 'Life of Hornets. Part 10. (Foraging activity in *Vespa crabro*: in Japanese).' *Jap. Bee J.* **20**, 385-8.

MATSUURA, M. (1968a). 'Life of Hornets. Part 11. (Royal court around queens of *Vespa* species: in Japanese).' *Jap Bee J.* **21**, 21-5.

MATSUURA, M. (1968b). 'Life of Hornets. Part 12. (*Vespa tropica* dependence on *Polistes* for food: in Japanese).' *Jap Bee J.* **21**, 49-52.

MATSUURA, M. (1968c). 'Life of Hornets. Part 13. (Predatory behaviour of *Vespa mandarinia* on other species of *Vespa*: in Japanese).' *Jap. Bee J.* **21**, 81-4.

MATSUURA, M. (1968d). 'Life of Hornets. Part 16. (Populations in colonies of *Vespa xanthoptera* and *Vespa mandarinia*: in Japanese).' *Jap. Bee J.* **21**, 223-6.

MATSUURA, M. (1969). 'Behaviour of post-hibernating female hornets *Vespa*, in the pre-nesting stage, with special reference to intra- and interspecific dominance relationships.' *Jap. J. Ecol.* **19**, 196-203.

MATSUURA, M. (1970). 'Intraspecific invasion behaviour of *Vespa crabro flavofasciata* Cameron in early stage of nesting.' *Life Study (Fukui).* **14**, 21-6.

MATSUURA, M. (1971). 'Nest foundation by the female wasps of the genus *Vespa* (Hymenoptera, Vespidae).' *Kontyû,* **39**, 99-105.

MATSUURA, M. and SAKAGAMI, S. F. (1973). 'A bionomic sketch of the giant hornet, *Vespa mandarina*, a serious pest for Japanese apiculture.' *J. Fac. Sci. Hakkaido Univ.* (in press).

MAUVEZIN, C. (1886). 'L'instinct des Hyménoptères.' *Rev. Sci.* **23**, 427-30.

MAZOKHIN-PORSHNYAKOV, G. A. (1960). (Evidence of the existence of colour vision in wasps, Vespidae: in Russian). *Zool. Zh.* **39**, 553-7.

MEDLER, J. T. and FYE, R. E. (1956). 'Biology of *Ancistrocerus antilope* (Panzer) in trap-nests in Wisconsin.' *Ann. ent. Soc. Am.* **49**, 97-102.

MICHELI, L. (1930). 'Note biologiche e morfologiche sugli imenotteri.' *Mem. Soc. ent. Ital.* **9**, 46-66.

MICHENER, C. D. (1953). 'Problems in the development of social behaviour and communication among insects.' *Trans. Kansas Acad. Sci.* **56**, 1-15.

MICHENER, C. D. (1964). 'Reproductive efficiency in relation to colony size in Hymenopterous societies.' *Insectes soc.* **11**, 317-42.

MICHENER, C. D. (1969). 'Comparative social behaviour of bees.' *A. Rev. Ent.* **14**, 299-342.

MILLER, C. D. F. (1961). 'Taxonomy and distribution of Nearctic *Vespula*.' *Can. Ent. Suppl.* **22**, 93, 1-52.

MJOBERG, E. (1909). 'Biologiska iakttagelser över *Odynerus oviventris* Wes.' *Ark. Zool. Stockholm.* **5**, 1-8.

MONTAGNER, H. (1963). 'Étude préliminaire des relations entre les adults et le couvain chez les guepes sociales du genre *Vespa*, au moyen d'un radioisotope.' *Insectes soc.* **10**, 153-66.

MONTAGNER, H. (1964a). 'Instinct et méchanismes stéréotypes chez les guêpes sociales.' *Psych. Fr.* **9**, 257-79.

MONTAGNER, H. (1964b). 'Les chaînes réactionelles qui provoquent et maintiennent les contacts trophallactiques chez les guêpes sociales.' *C.r. Acad. Sci., Paris.* **259**, 4148-51.

MONTAGNER, H. (1964c). 'Étude du comportement alimentaire et des relations trophall-actiques des mâles au sein de la société de guêpes, au moyen d'un radioisotope.' *Insectes soc.* **11**, 301-16.

MONTAGNER, H. (1966a). 'Sur le déterminisme des castes femelles chez les Guêpes du gentre *Vespa*.' *C.r. Acad. Sci., Paris.* **263**, 547-9.

MONTAGNER, H. (1966b). 'Sur l'origine des males dans les sociétées de Guêpes du genre *Vespa*.' *C.r. Acad. Sic., Paris.* **263**, 785-7.

MONTAGNER, H. (1966c). 'Sur le déterminisme du couvain abortif dans les nids de Guêpes du genre *Vespa*.' *C.r. Acad. Sci., Paris.* **263**, 826-9.

MONTAGNER, H. (1966d). 'Le méchanisme et les conséquences des comportements trophall-actiques chez les guêpes du genre *Vespa*.' *Thèse de l'Université de Nancy*.

MONTAGNER, H. (1967). 'Contribution à l'étude du déterminisme des castes chez les guêpes du genre *Vespa*.' *Thèse de l'Université de Nancy* (unpublished).

MONTAGNER, H. and COURTOIS, G. (1963). 'Données nouvelles sur le comportement alimentaire et les échanges trophallactiques chez les guêpes sociales.' *C.r. Acad. Sci., Paris.* **256**, 4092-4.

MORICE, F. D. (1916). '*Polistes gallicus*, L., taken in Britain.' *Trans. R. ent. Soc. Lond.* **64**, lxvi-lxvii.

MORIMOTO, R. (1954a). 'On the nest development of *Polistes chinensis antennalis* Pérez. 1. (Studies on the social Hymenoptera of Japan III).' *Sci. Bull. Fac. agric. Kyushu Univ.* **14**, 337-53.

MORIMOTO, R. (1954b). 'On the nest development of *Polistes chinensis antennalis* Pérez. 2. (Studies on the social Hymenoptera of Japan IV).' *Sci. Bull. Fac. agric. Kyushu Univ.* **14**, 511-22.

MORIMOTO, R. (1954c). 'On the nest development of *Polistes chinensis antennalis* Pérez. 3. Relation between the removal of eggs and larvae from the nest and the oviposition of the founding female. (Studies of the social Hymenoptera of Japan IV).' *Sci. Bull. Fac. agric. Kyushu Univ.* **14**, 523-33.

MORIMOTO R. (1960a). '*Polistes* wasps as natural enemies of agricultural and forest pests. (Studies of the social Hymenoptera of Japan X).' *Sci. Bull. Fac. agric. Kyushu Univ.* **18**, 109-16.

MORIMOTO, R. (1960b). '*Polistes* wasps as natural enemies of agricultural and forest pests. (Studies on the social Hymenoptera of Japan XI).' *Sci. Bull. Fac. agric. Kyushu Univ.* **18**, 117-32.

MORIMOTO, R. (1960c). 'Experimental study on the trophallactic behaviour in *Polistes*.' *Acta. hym., Fukuoka.* **1**, 99-103.

MORLEY, C. (1898). 'A list of the Hymenoptera-Aculeata of the Ipswich district.' *Entomologist.* **31**, 12-41.

MORLEY, C. (1935). 'A beech-tree's insects and their parasites.' *Entomologist's mon. Mag.* **71**, 90-1.

MORRIS, R. F. (1972). 'Predation by wasps, birds, and mammals on *Hyphantria cunea*.' *Can. Ent.* **104**, 1581-91.

MÜLLER, E. (1931). 'Experimentelle Untersuchungen an Bienan und Ameisen. Ueber die Funktionsweisen der Stirnocellen.' *Z. vergl. Physiol.* **14**, 348-84.

MURRAY, A. (1870). 'Note on *Rhipiphorus paradoxus*.' *Ann. nat. Hist.* **6**, 204-13.

NAUMANN, M. G. (1970). 'The nesting behaviour of *Protopolybia pumila* in Panama (Hymenoptera: Vespidae).' *Unpublished Ph.D. thesis*, University of Kansas.

NEEDHAM, P. H. and Stevenson, J. H. (1966). 'Insecticides and beekeeping in England and Wales.' *Bee World.* **47**, 65-70.

NEEDHAM, P. H., SOLLY, S. R. B. and STEVENSON, J. H. (1966). 'Damage to honey bee colonies (*Apis mellifera*) by insecticides in Great Britain, 1956-65.' *J. Sci. Fd. Agric.* **17**, 133-7.

NELSON, J. M. (1968). 'Parasites and symbionts of nests of *Polistes* wasps.' *Ann. ent. Soc. Am.* **61**, 1528-39.

NESTEROVODSKY, V. A. (1947). 'Wasp control' (in Russian). *Pchelovodstvo.* **24**, 49-51.

NEWPORT, G. (1836). 'On the precadeous habits of the common wasp, *Vespa vulgaris* L.' *Trans. ent. Soc. Lond.* **1**, 228-9.

NEWPORT, G. (1842). 'On the habits, and on the structure of the nests of gregarious Hymenoptera, particularly those of the hive bee and hornet.' *Trans. ent. Soc. Lond.* **3**, 183-90.

NEWSTEAD, R. (1891). 'Insects, etc., taken in the nests of British Vespidae.' *Entomologist's mon. Mag.* **27**, 39-41.

NEWSTEAD, R. (1908). 'The food of some British birds.' *Suppl. J. Board Agric. Lond.* **15m**, viii + 87.

NICHOLSON, C. (1917). 'Notes from the Stroud district.' *Entomologist's mon. Mag.* **53**, 116-22.

NICHOLSON, C. (1921). 'Abundance of wasps.' *Entomologist's mon. Mag.* **57**, 234.

NIELSEN, E. T. (1932). 'Sur les habitudes des Hyménoptères aculéates solitaires. II. (Vespidae, Chrysididae, Sapygidae et Mutillidae).' *Ent. Medd.* **18**, 84-174.

NIXON, G. E. J. (1934a). 'Two notes on the behaviour of *Volucella pellucens* in its association with the wasps *Vespa vulgaris* Linn. and *Vespa germanica* Fab.' *Entomologist's mon. Mag.* **70**, 17-18.

NIXON, G. E. J. (1934b). 'Notes on wasps. I. Attempts to domesticate a queen of *Vespa rufa* Linn.' *Entomologist's mon. Mag.* **70**, 37-40.

NIXON, G. E. J. (1934c). 'Notes on wasps. II. On the adoption of an orphaned brood of *Vespa vulgaris* L. by a queen of *Vespa germanica* Fab.' *Entomologist's mon. Mag.* **70**, 87-9.

NIXON, G. E. J. (1934d). 'Notes on wasps. III.' *Entomologist's mon. Mag.* **70**, 265-70.

NIXON, G. E. J. (1935). 'Notes on wasps. IV.' *Entomologist's mon. Mag.* **71**, 106-11.

NIXON, G. E. J. (1936). 'Notes on wasps. V.' *Entomologist's mon. Mag.* **72**, 6-8.

NORRIS, K. R. (1966). 'The collection and preservation of insects.' *Aust. ent. Soc. Handbook No. 1*, 1-34.

NORRIS, M. J. (1964). 'Environmental control of sexual maturation in insects.' *R. ent. Soc. Lond. Symp. No. 2*, 56-65.

NURSE, C. G. (1913). 'Two species of aculeate Hymenoptera new to Britain.' *Entomologist's mon. Mag.* **49**, 83-4.

O'BYRNE, H. (1934). '*Vespula germanica* attacks a living *Eacles imperialis* (Hymen: Vespidae; Lepid.: Citheroniidae).' *Ent. News.* **65**, 101-2.

OCHIAI, S. (1960). 'Comparative studies on embryology of the bees – *Apis, Polistes, Vespula* and *Vespa*, with special reference to the development of the silk gland.' *Bull. Fac. agric. Tamagawa Univ.* **1**, 13-45.

O'FARRELL, A. F. (1945). 'A simple apparatus for photomicrography.' In *The Hymenopterist's Handbook* published by Dept. Agric. Univ. Leeds (1945).

OLBERG, G. (1959). *Das Verhalten der Solitären Wespen Mitteleuropas (Vespidae, Pompilidae, Sphecidae)*. Deutscher Verlag der Wissenschaften, Berlin.

ORMEROD, E. L. (1868). *British Social Wasps: an introduction to their anatomy and physiology, architecture, and general natural history*. Longmans, Green, Reader and Dyer, London.

O'ROURKE, F. J. (1945). 'Methods used by wasps in killing prey.' *Ir. Nat. J.* **8**, 238-41.

OUDEMANS, J. T. (1901). 'Ein merkwürdiges nest von *Vespa vulgaris* L.' *Allg. Zts. ent.* **6**, 97-100, 119-22.

OWEN, J. H. (1948). 'The larder of the red-backed shrike.' *Br. Birds.* **41**, 200-3.

PACKARD, A. S. (1878). *Guide to the Study of Insects*. H. Holt & Co., New York.

PACK-BERESFORD, D. R. (1899). 'Wasp Notes.' *Ir. Nat.* **8**, 209.

PACK-BERESFORD, D. R. (1901). 'Males of *Vespa austriaca*.' *Ir. Nat.* **10**, 195.

PACK-BERESFORD, D. R. (1903). 'Notes on wasps.' *Ir. Nat.* **12**, 15-17.

PACK-BERESFORD, D. R. (1904). 'Another nest of *Vespa rufa-austriaca*.' *Ir. Nat.* **13**. 242-3.

PACK-BERESFORD, D. R. (1931). 'Wasps in combat.' *Ir. Nat. J.* **3**, 223-4.

PALMER, R. (1925). 'Additional records of Hertfordshire Hymenoptera Aculeata.' *Trans. Herts. nat. hist. Soc.* **18**, 121-2.

PALMER-JONES, T. and DEVINE, B. W. (1948). 'Destruction of queen wasps by spraying.' *N.Z. Jl. Agric.*, 557-8.

PALMER-JONES, T., WHITE, E. P., DEVINE, B. W. and PATTERSON, C. R. (1949). 'Developments in control of wasps.' *N.Z. Jl. Agric.*, 229-32.

PARDI, L. (1940). 'Richerche sui Polistini. 1. Poliginia vera ed apparente in *Polistes gallicus* (L.).' *P.V. Soc. tosc. Sci. nat.* **49**, 3-9.

PARDI, L. (1942a). 'Richerche sui Polistini. 4. Note critiche sulla nidificazione di *Polistes gallicus* (L.) e di *Polistula bischoffi* Weyrauch.' *P.V. Soc. tosc. Sci. nat.* **51**, 3-13.

PARDI, L. (1942b). 'Richerche sui Polistini. 5. La poliginia iniziale di *Polistes gallicus* (L.).' *Boll. Inst. ent. Univ. Bologna.* **14**, 1-106.

PARDI, L. (1946). 'Richerche sui Polistini. 7. Poliginia eccezionale in *Polistes (Leptopolistes) omissus* Weyrauch.' *P.V. Soc. tosc. Sci. nat.* **54**, 3-7.

PARDI, L. (1948). 'Dominance order in Polistes wasps.' *Physiol. Zoöl.* **21**, 1-13.

PARDI, L. (1951). 'Richerche sui Polistini. 12. Studio della attivita e della divisione di lavoro in una societa di *Polistes gallicus* (L.) dopo la comparasa delle operaie.' *Archo. zool. ital.* **36**, 363-431.

PARDI, L. and CALVACANTI, M. (1951). 'Esperienze sul mecannismo della monoginia funzionale in *Polistes gallicus* (L.) (Hymenopt. Vesp.).' *Boll. Zool.* **18**, 247-52.

PARDI, L. and PICCIOLI, M. T. M. (1970). 'Studi sulla biolologia di *Belonogaster* (Hymenoptera, Vespidae). 2. Differenziamento castale incipiente in *B. griseus* (Fab.).' *Monitore zool. Ital., N.S., Suppl.* **3**, 235-65.

PARKER, J. B. (1928). '*Vespula* rears successive broods in the same cells.' *Proc. ent. Soc. Washington.* **30**, 14.

PERKINS, J. F. (1937). 'On the British species of *Sphecophaga* (Hym. Ichneumonidae).' *Entomologist's mon. Mag.* **73**, 103-4.

PERLMAN, E. (1955). 'Near fatal allergic reactions to bee and wasp stings: a review and report of seven cases.' *Mt. Sinai Hosp. J.* **22**, 336-48.

PICCIOLI, M. T. M. and PARDI, L. (1970). 'Studi della biologia di *Belonogaster* (Hymenoptera, Vespidae). 1. Sull 'etogramma di *Belonogaster griseus* (Fab.).' *Monitore zool. Ital., N.S., Suppl.* **3**, 197-225.

PIERRE, C. (1922). 'II. Curieux cas de nidification d'*Odynerus antilope* Panzer.' *Revue Sci. Bourbonnais*, 27-8.

PLATEAU-QUÉNU, C. (1962). 'Biology of *Halictus marginatus* Brullé.' *J. Apicult. Res.* **1**, 41-51.

POINAR, G. O. and ENNIK, F. (1972). 'The use of *Neoplectana carpocapsae* Weiser (Steinernematidae: Rhabditoidea) against adult yellowjackets (*Vespula* spp., Vespidae: Hymenoptera).' *J. Invert. Path.* **19**, 331-40.

POTTER, N. B. (1965). 'Some aspects of the biology of *Vespula vulgaris* L.' *Unpublished Ph. D. thesis.* University of Bristol.

POULTON, E. B. (1934). 'Attacks of common wasps upon butterflies: wasp carrying off a spider's prey.' *Proc. R. ent. Soc. Lond.* **9**, 71-2.

PRINCE, H. E. and SECREST, P. G. (1939). 'Use of whole bee extracts in sensitization to bees, wasps, and ants.' *J. Allergy.* **10**, 379-81.

RABB, R. L. (1960). 'Biological studies of *Polistes* in North Carolina (Hymenoptera: Vespidae).' *Ann. ent. Soc. Am.* **53**, 111-21.

RATHMAYER, W. (1962). 'Die Paralysierung der Beute Bienenwolf.' *Z. vergl. Physiol.* **45**, 413-62.

RATZEBURG, J. T. C. (1844-52). *Die Ichneumonen der Forstinsecten in forstlicher und entomologischer Bezeihung; ein Anhang zur Abbildung und Beschreibung der Forstinsecten.* Volumes I, II, III. Berlin.

RAU, P. (1928). 'The reconstruction of destroyed nest by *Polistes* wasps.' *Psyche.* **35**, 151-2.

RAU, P. (1929). 'At the end of the season with *Polistes rubiginosus* (Hymenoptera: Vespidae).' *Ent. News.* **40**, 7-13.

RAU, P. (1930). 'The behaviour of hibernating *Polistes* wasps.' *Ann. ent. Soc. Am.* **23**, 461-6.

RAU, P. (1932). 'The relation of the size of the cell to the sex of the wasp in *Odynerus foraminatus* Sauss. (Hymenoptera: Vespidae).' *Ent. News.* **53**, 119-21.

RAU, P. (1934a). '*Vespa maculata:* hibernating queens.' *Bull. Brooklyn ent. Soc.* **29**, 170-1.

RAU, P. (1934b). 'The wasp, *Vespa maculata*, stalking prey.' *Bull. Brooklyn ent. Soc.* **29**, 171.

RAU, P. (1935). 'The courtship and mating of the wasp *Monobia quadridens* (Hymen.: Vespidae).' *Ent. News.* **46**, 57-8.

RAU, P. (1941). 'The swarming of *Polistes* wasps in temperate regions.' *Ann. ent. Soc. Am.* **34**, 580-4.

RAU, P. (1945). 'The carnivorous habits of the adult wasp, *Odynerus dorsalis* Fab.' *Bull. Brooklyn ent. Soc.* **40**, 29-30.

RAU, P. and RAU, N. (1918). *Wasp studies Afield*. Princeton University Press, Princeton.

RÉAUMUR, R. de (1719). 'Histoire des duêpes.' *Mém Acad. R. Sci., Paris.* **19**, 302-64.

RÉAUMUR, R. de (1740). *Mémoires pour servir al'histoire des Insectes.* Vol. 5. Paris.

REICHERT, A. (1914). 'Die Parasiten unserer heimischen Wespen.' *Illust. Zeitg. Leipzig.* No. 3682.

REID, J. A. (1942). 'On the classification of the larvae of the Vespidae.' *Trans. R. ent. Soc. Lond.* **92**, 285-331.

RICHARDS, O. W. (1932). 'Some breeding and habitat records of British Diptera.' *J. ent. Soc. S. England.* **1**, 11-14.

RICHARDS, O. W. (1937). 'The mating habits of species of *Vespa* (Hymenoptera).' *Proc. R. ent. Soc. Lond.* **12**, 27-9.

RICHARDS, O. W. (1945). 'A revision of the genus *Mischocyttarus* de Saussure.' *Trans. R. ent. Soc. Lond.* **95**, 295-462.

RICHARDS, O. W. (1949). 'The significance of the number of winghooks in bees and wasps.' *Proc. R. ent. Soc. Lond.* **24**, 75-8.

RICHARDS, O. W. (1956). 'Hymenoptera. Introduction and keys to families.' *R. ent. Soc. Lond. Handbooks for the Identification of British Insects.* **6**, (1), 1-94.

RICHARDS, O. W. (1964). 'The entomological fauna of southern England with special reference to the country round London.' *Trans. Soc. Br. Ent.* **16**, 1-48.

RICHARDS, O. W. (1969). 'The biology of some W. African social wasps (Hymenoptera: Vespidae, Polistinae).' *Mem. Soc. ent. Ital.* **48**, 79-93.

RICHARDS, O. W. (1971a). 'The biology of the social wasps (Hymenoptera, Vespidae).' *Biol. Rev.* **46**, 483-528.

RICHARDS, O. W. (1971b). 'The thoracic spiracles and some associated structures in the Hymenoptera and their significance in classification, especially of the Aculeata.' *Entomological Essays to Commemorate the Retirement of Professor K. Yasumatsu*, 1-13.

RICHARDS, O. W. and RICHARDS, M. J. (1951). 'Observations on the social wasps of South America (Hymenoptera Vespidae).' *Trans. R. ent. Soc. Lond.* **102**, 1-170.

RICHARDSON, N. M. (1920). 'Colour sense in a key-hole wasp. (*Odynerus parietinus*, Linn.).' *Proc. Dorest nat. hist. Club.* **41**, 92-4.

RITCHIE, J. (1915). 'Some observations and deductions regarding the habits and biology of the common wasp.' *Scott. Nat.* **47**, 318-31.

RIVNAY, E. and BYSTINSKI-SALZ, H. (1949). 'The Oriental Hornet (*Vespa orientalis* L.).; Its biology in Israel (in Hebrew).' *Bull. agric. Res. Stn. Rehovet, Israel.* **52**, 1-32.

ROBBINS, J. M. (1938). 'Wasp versus dragonfly.' *Ir. Nat. J.* **7**, 10-11.

ROBSON, J. E. (1898). '*Vespa austriaca*, a cuckoo-wasp.' *Sci. Gossip.* **5**, 69-73.

ROLAND, C. (1969). 'Rôle de l'involucre et du nourissement en sucre dans la régulation thermique à l'interieur d'un nid de Vespides.' *C.r. Acad. Sci. Paris.* **269**, 914-6.

ROUBAUD, E. (1910). 'Recherches sur la biologie des *Synagris*. Évolution et l'instinct chez les guêpes solitaires.' *Annls Soc. ent. Fr.* **79**, 1-21.

ROUBAUD, E. (1911). 'The natural history of the solitary wasps of the genus *Synagris*.' *Smithson. Rep.*, 507-25.

ROUBAUD, E. (1916). 'Recherches biologiques sur les guêpes solitaires et sociales d'Afrique. La genèse de la vie sociale et l'évolution de l'instinct maternel chez les vespides.' *Annls Sci. nat. (Zool.)* (sér 10). **1**, 1-160.

ROUBAUD, E. (1929). 'Caractere obligitoire de l'hibernation chez les reines de vespides annuel. Consequences biologiques.' *Bull. Soc. ent. Fr.* (1929), 83-4.

ROUGET, A. (1873). 'Sur les coléoptères parasites des véspides.' *Mém Acad. Dijon* (Sér 3) **1**, 161-288.

ROUTLEDGE, G. R. (1933). 'Cumberland aculeate Hymenoptera.' *Trans. Carlisle nat. hist. Soc.* **5**, 83-103.

RUDEBECK, G. (1965). 'On a migratory movement of wasps, mainly *Vespula rufa* (L.) at Falsterbo, Sweden.' *Proc. R. ent. Soc. Lond.* **40**, 1-8.

SAID, E. E. (1960). 'Enzymological study of the venom of *Polistes omissa* Weyr.' *Bull Soc. ent. Egypt.* **44**, 167-70.

SAKAGAMI, S. F. and FUKUSHIMA, K. (1957a). 'Some biological observations on a hornet, *Vespa tropica* var. *pulchra* (de Buysson), with special reference to its dependence on *Polistes* wasps (Hymenoptera). *Treubia.* **24**, 73-82.

SAKAGAMI, S. F. and FUKUSHIMA, K. (1957b). '*Vespa dybowskii* André. A facultative temporary social parasite.' *Insectes soc.* **4**, 1-12.

SAKAGAMI, S. F. and YOSHIKAWA, K. (1968). 'A new ethospecies of *Stenogaster* wasps from Sarawak, with a comment on the value of ethological characters in animal taxonomy.' *Ann. zoo. Soc. Japan.* **41**, 77-84.

SALT, G. (1928). 'The effects of stylopization on aculeate Hymenoptera.' *J. exp. Zool.* **48**, 223-331.

SALT, G. (1931). 'A further study of the effects of stylopization on wasps.' *J. exp. Zool.* **59**, 133-66.

SALT, G. and BEQUAERT, J. (1929). 'Stylopized Vespidae.' *Psyche.* **36**, 249-82.

SANNASI, A. (1970). 'Manisfestation of starvation on the integument and blood of the queen of the termite *Odontotermes obesus.*' *J. Invert. Path.* **16**, 165-72.

SANDEMANN, R. G. C. C. (1936). 'Notes on the habits of *Vespa vulgaris* and *V. germanica* (Hymenoptera).' *Proc. R. ent. Soc. Lond.* **11**, 88-90.

SANDEMANN, R. G. C. C. (1938). 'The swarming of the males of *Vespula sylvestris* (Scop.) around a queen.' *Proc. R. ent. Soc. Lond.* **13**, 87-8.

SAUNDERS, E. (1896). *The Hymenoptera Aculeata of the British Islands.* Lovell Reeve, London.

SAUSSURE, H. (1852). *Monographie des Guêpes Solitaires, ou de la tribu des Euméniens.* V. Masson, Paris-Genève.

SAUSSURE, H. (1853). *Monographie des guêpes sociales ou de la tribu des vespiens. Études sur la famille des vespides.* Bineteau, Paris.

SAUSSURE, H. (1855). 'Nouvelles considérations sur la nidification des Guêpes.' *Arch. Sci. phys. nat. Genève.* **28**, 89-123.

SAUSSURE, H. (1858). *Monographie des guêpes sociales, ou de la tribu des vespiens.* V. Masson, Paris-Genève.

SCHAUDINISCHKY, L. and ISHAY, J. (1968). 'On the nature of the sounds produced within the nest of the Oriental Hornet *Vespa orientalis* F. (Hymenoptera).' *J. Acoust. Soc. Am.* **44**, 1290-301.

SCHEVEN, J. (1958). 'Biologie der Schmarotzerfeldenwespen.' *Insectes Soc.* **5**, 409-35.

SCHREMMER, F. (1961). 'Bemerkenswerte Wechselbeziehungen zwischen Orchideenblüten und Insekten.' *Natur. u. Volk.* **91**, 52-61.

SCHULTESS, A. v. (1927). 'Fauna Sumatrensis (Beitung N.52) Vespidae (Hymenoptera)' *Suppl. Entom.* **16**, 81-92.

SCHULTZ-LANGNER, E. (1954). 'Beobachtungen zur copulation gefangen gehaltener Wespen.' *Zool. Anz.* **152**, 39-42.

SCOTT, H. (1917). 'A note on *Vespa sylvestris.*' *Entomologist's mon. Mag.* **53**, 17.

SCOTT, H. (1920). 'Queen wasps on the wing in winter.' *Entomologist's mon. Mag.* **56**, 65.

SCOTT, H. (1930). 'A mortal combat between a spider and a wasp.' *Entomologist's mon. Mag.* **66**, 215.

SCOTT, H. (1944). 'Notes on the season of 1943.' *Entomologist's mon. Mag.* **80**, 1-4.

SÉGUY, E. A. (1927). '*Diptères-Brachycères. Asilidae etc. Faune de France, volume 17.*' P. Lechevalier, Paris.

SHEPPARD, T. (1926). 'Mason wasp cells in lock.' *Naturalist, Hull.* **15**, 268.

SHIDA, T. (1954). 'The life of a common wasp *Vespula lewisii* (Cameron).' *Lecture, 3rd Ann. Meeting, Jap. Sect. I.U.S.S.I., Tokyo.*

SHULMAN, S. (1967). 'Allergic responses to insects.' *A. Rev. Ent.* **12**, 323-46.

SIEBOLD, C. T. E. (1871). *Beiträge zur Parthenogenesis der Arthropeden. I. Ueber die bei* Polistes *Wahrzunehmende Parthenogenesis II. Parthenogenesis bei* Vespa holsatica. Wilhelm Engelmann, Leipzig.

SIMPSON, J. (1948). 'A hornet's nest.' *Entomologist's mon. Mag.* **84**, 128-9.

SIMPSON, J. (1960). 'The functions of the salivary glands of *Apis mellifera*.' *J. Insect Physiol.* **4**, 107-21.

SLOBODKIN, L. B. (1961). *Growth and Regulation of Animal Populations.* Holt, Rinehart & Winston, New York.

SMITH, F. (1852). 'Observations on the economy of *Vespa norwegica* and *V. rufa*.' *Zoologist.* **10**, 3699-703.

SMITH, F. (1856). 'On the manner in which *Vespa rufa* builds its nests.' *Zoologist.* **14**, 5169-74.

SMITH, F. (1858). *Catalogue of British Fossorial Hymenoptera, Formicidae, and Vespidae, in the collection of the British Museum.* British Museum, London.

SMITH, F. (1867). (no title; exhibit of eumenine nest in razor case). *Trans. ent. soc. Lond.* **5**, 90.

Smythe, J. P. (1882). (Wasps and hornets attacking flies, bees and grasshoppers). *Sci. Gossip.* **18**, 237.

SNODGRASS, R. E. (1925). *Anatomy and Physiology of the Honeybee.* McGraw-Hill, New York.

SNODGRASS, R. E. (1956). *Anatomy of the Honey Bee.* Constable, London.

SONNEBORN, H-H., PFLEIDERER, G. and ISHAY, J. (1969). 'Eine Protease vom Molekulargewicht 12500 aus Larven von *Vespa orientalis* F. mit chymotryptischen Eigenschaften.' *Z. physiol. Chem.* **350**, 389-95.

SOTAVALTA, O. (1947). 'The flight-tone (wing-stroke frequency) of insects.' *Acta ent. fenn.* **4**, 1-117.

SOUTHWOOD, T. R. E. (1967). 'The interpretation of population change.' *J. Anim. Ecol.* **36**, 519-29.

SPIETH, H. T. (1948). 'Notes on a colony of *Polistes fuscatus hunteri* Beq.' *Jl N.Y. ent. Soc.* **56**, 155-69.

SPOONER, G. M. (1934). 'Observations on *Odynerus* (*Lionotus*) *herrichi* Sauss. in Dorset.' *Entomologist's mon. Mag.* **70**, 46-54.

SPOONER, G. M. (1935). 'Aculeate Hymenoptera from Northants. and Wood Walton Fen, Hunts.' *Entomologist's mon. Mag.* **71**, 138-40.

SPRADBERY, J. P. (1963). 'A study of British vespine wasps (Hymenoptera Vespidae) with reference to the problems of caste differentiation.' *Unpublished Ph.D. thesis*, University of London.

SPRADBERY, J. P. (1965). 'The social organisation of wasp communities.' *Symp. zool. Soc. Lond. No.* 14, 61-96.

SPRADBERY, J. P. (1971). 'Seasonal changes in the population structure of wasp colonies (Hymenoptera: Vespidae).' *J. Anim. Ecol.* **40**, 501-23.

SPRADBERY, J. P. (1972). 'A biometric study of seasonal variation in worker wasps (Hymenoptera: Vespidae). *J. Ent.* (A) **47**, 61-9.

STACHANOFF, V. (1928). 'Zur kenntnis der Eznährung des Eichelhäbers *Garorulus glandarius* L.' *Defénce Plantes.* **5**, 19-23.

STELFOX, A. W. (1930). 'Wasp's nests: their normal and some unusual situations.' *Ir. Nat. J.* **3**, 98-101.

STEP, E. (1932). *Bees, Wasps, Ants and Allied Insects.* Frederick Warne, London.

STONE, S. (1864a). (No title; replacement nests of *Vespa germanica*). *Proc. ent. Soc. Lond.* **3**, 33-5.

STONE, S. (1864b). 'Wasps and their parasites in 1864.' *Proc. ent. Soc. Lond.* **3**, 62-7.

STONE, S. (1865). 'Scarcity of wasps.' *Zoologist.* **23**, 9757.

STRAMBI, A. (1963). 'Action différentielle de la température sur le debit ovarien et la ponte chez la Guêpe Poliste (*Polistes gallicus* L. et *Polistes nimpha* Christ., Hyménoptères Véspides).' *C.r. Acad. Sci., Paris.* **256**, 5642-3.

STRAMBI, A. (1965). 'Influence du parasite *Xenos vesparum* Rossi (Strepsiptère) sur la neurosecretion des individus du sexe femmele de *Polistes gallicus* L. (Hyménoptère, Véspide).' *C.r. Acad. Sci., Paris.* **260**, 3768-9.

STRAMBI, A. (1966). 'Action de *Xenos vesparum* Rossi (Strepsiptère) sur la neurosecretion des fondatrices filles de *Polistes gallicus* L. (Hyménoptère, Véspide).' *C.r. Acad. Sci., Paris*, **263**, 533-5.

SUDD, J. H. (1967). *An Introduction to the Behaviour of Ants*. Edward Arnold, London.

TAKAMATSU, Y. (1949). 'On the post-embryonic development of the genitalia of *Vespula lewisii* (Cameron).' *Seibutu*. **4**, 161-6.

TAKAMATSU, Y. (1952). 'Studies on the mechanism of the sexual function in *Vespula lewisii* (Cameron).' *J. Fac. agric. Shinshu Univ*. **2**, 1-46.

TAKAMATSU, Y. (1955). 'On the relations between the histological changes of the neuro-secretory cell and the developmental states of the egg of the wasp, *Polistes fadwigae* Dalla Torre (Hymenoptera, Vespidae).' *Rep. Nagoya State Univ*. **30**, 40-4.

TAKAMATSU, Y. (1956). 'On the relations between the neurosecretion and the ripeness of the eggs of the wasps and bees.' *Rep. Nagoya State Univ*. **31**, 47-50.

TAYLOR, L. H. (1922). 'Notes on the biology of certain wasps of the genus *Ancistrocerus*.' *Psyche*. **29**, 48-65.

TAYLOR, L. H. (1939). 'Observations on social parasitism in the genus *Vespula* Thompson.' *Ann. ent. Soc. Am*. **32**, 304-15.

TAYLOR, L. R. (1951). 'An improved suction trap for insects.' *Ann. appl. Biol*. **38**, 582-91.

TAYLOR, L. R. (1963). 'Analysis of the effects of temperature on insects in flight.' *J. Anim. Ecol*. **32**, 99-117.

THOMAS, C. R. (1960). 'The European Wasp (*Vespula germanica* Fab.) in New Zealand.' *Inf. Ser. Dep. Scient. ind. Res. N.Z*. **27**, 1-73.

TOONER, J. A. (1883). '*V. crabro* preying on *Vespa* species in England.' *Sci. Gossip*. **19**, 23, 37.

TUCK, W. H. (1896). 'Inquiline and other inhabitants in nests of aculeate Hymenoptera.' *Entomologist's mon. Mag*. **32**, 153-5.

TUCK, W. H. (1897). 'Coleoptera, etc., in the nests of aculeate Hymenoptera.' *Entomologist's mon. Mag*. **33**, 58-60.

VAN DER VECHT, J. (1936). 'Some further notes on *Provespa*, Ashm. (Hym., Vespidae).' *J. Fed. Malay States Mus*. **18**, 159-66.

VAN DER VECHT, J. (1940). 'The nesting habits of *Ropalidia fiavopicta* (SM.) (Hym., Vespidae).' *Ent. Meded. Ned. - Indië*. **6**, 47-50.

VAN DER VECHT, J. (1957). 'The Vespinae of the Indo-Malayan and Papuan areas (Hymenoptera, Vespidae).' *Zool. Verh., Leiden*. **34**, 1-83.

VAN DER VECHT, J. (1959). 'Notes on Oriental Vespinae, including some species from China and Japan (Hymenoptera, Vespidae).' *Zool. Meded., Leiden*. **36**, 205-32.

VAN DER VECHT, J. (1962). 'The Indo-Australian species of the genus *Ropalidia* (*Icaria*) (Hymenoptera, Vespidae) (second part).' *Zool. Verh., Leiden*. **57**, 1-72.

VAN DER VECHT, J. (1965). 'The geographical distribution of the social wasps (Hymenoptera, Vespidae).' *Proc. 12th Int. Congr. Ent., London*. 1964, 440-1.

VAN DER VECHT, J. (1966). 'The East Asiatic and Indo-Australian species of *Polyboides* Buysson and *Parapolybia* Saussure.' *Zool. Verh., Leiden*. **82**, 1-42.

VAN DER VECHT, J. (1967). 'Bouwproblemen van sociale wespen.' *K. Ned. Akak. Wetens., Amsterdam*. **76**, 59-68.

VAN DER VECHT, J. (1968). 'The terminal gastral sternite of female and worker social wasps (Hymenoptera, Vespidae).' *Proc. K. Ned. Akad. Wetens., Amsterdam*. **71**, 411-22.

VERLAINE, L. (1932). 'La spécialisation et la division du travail chez les guêpes.' *Bull. soc. Sci., Liége*. **1**, 186-91.

VIEWIG, K. (1896). 'Wespen als Fliegenvertilger.' *Illust. Woch. ent*. **1**, 579.

VITZTHUM, H. G. (1927). 'Eine notiz über *Parasitus vesparum* Oudemans 1905 und *Fannia scalaris* (Fabricius 1794).' *Z. wiss. Insekt Biol*. **22**, 46-8.

VUILLAUME, M. and NAULLEAU, G. (1960). 'Construction dirigée chez *Dolichovespula media*.' *Insectes soc*. **7**, 175-86.

WAGNER, R. E. (1961). 'Control of the Yellowjacket, *Vespula pennsylvanica*, in public parks.' *J. econ. Ent*. **54**, 628-30.

WAILES, G. (1860). 'The hybernation of *Vespa vulgaris*.' *Proc. ent. Soc. Lond*. **5**, 109.

WALKER, A. O. (1898). 'Wasps.' *Nat. Sci*. **12**, 72.

WALKER, F. A. (1901). 'Hornets: British and foreign.' *J. Trans. Victoria Inst. Lond.* **33**, 362-92.

WALSH, G. B. (1929). 'Unusual nests of *Vespa norwegica*, Fab.' *Entomologist's mon. Mag.* **65**, 182-3.

WALTON, C. L. (1934). 'Unusual abundance of queen wasps.' *Northwestern Naturalist.* **9**, 157.

WARD, P. (1965). 'A raid on a *Stenogaster* nest by a hornet *Vespa tropica*.' *Malay. nat. J.* **19**, 152.

WATERHOUSE, G. R. (1858). (No title: discussion on construction of hexagonal cells by bees and wasps). *Proc. ent. Soc. Lond.* **5**, 17-18.

WATERHOUSE, G. R. (1864). 'On the formation of the cells of bees and wasps.' *Trans. ent. Soc. Lond.* **2**, 115-29.

WATERSON, J. and BAYLIS, H. A. (1930). 'A remarkable parasitic worm.' *Nat. hist. Mag. Lond.* **2**, 146-9.

WATSON, E. B. (1922). 'The food habits of wasps (*Vespa*).' *Bull. Chambers hort. Soc. Lond.* **1**, 26-31.

WELCH, H. E. (1958). '*Agamomermis pachysoma* (Linstow, 1905). N. comb (Mermithidae: Nematoda), a parasite of social wasps.' *Insectes soc.* **5**, 353-5.

WEST, M. J. (1967). 'Foundress associations in polistine wasps: dominance hierarchies and the evolution of social behaviour.' *Science N.Y.* **157**, 1584-5.

WESTWOOD, J. O. (1834). 'Notice of the habits of *Odynerus antilope*.' *Trans. ent. Soc. Lond.* **1**, 78-80.

WESTWOOD, J. O. (1839). 'Memoirs on various species of hymenopterous insects.' *Trans. ent. soc. Lond.* **4**, 123-41.

WEYRAUCH, W. (1935). '*Dolichovespula* und *Vespa*. Verglichende Übersicht über zwei wesentliche Lebenstypen bei sozialen Wespen.' *Biol. Zbl.* **55**, 484-524.

WEYRAUCH, W. (1936a). '*Dolichovespula* und *Vespa*. Vergleichende Übersicht uber zwei wesentliche Lebenstypen bei sozialen Wespen. Mit Bezugnahme auf die Frage nach der Fortschrittlichkeit tierischer organisation.' *Biol. Zbl.* **56**, 287-301.

WEYRAUCH, W. (1936b). 'Das Verhalten sozialer Wespen bei Nestuberhitzung.' *Z. vergl. Physiol.* **23**, 51-63.

WEYRAUCH, W. (1937a). 'Wie entsteht ein Wespennest? 5. Teil. Experimentelle Analyse des Verhaltens von *Vespa germanica* F. und *Vespa vulgaris* L. beim Bauen mit Erde.' *Zool. Jb. (Syst.).* **69**, 215-40.

WEYRAUCH, W. (1937b). 'Zur systematik und Biologie der Kuckeswespen *Pseudovespa*, *Pseudovespula* und *Pseudopolistes*.' *Zool. Jb. (Syst.).* **70**, 243-90.

WHEELER, W. M. (1918). 'A study of some ant larvae, with a consideration of the origin and meaning of the social habit among insects.' *Proc. Am. phil. Soc.* **57**, 293-343.

WHEELER, W. M. (1922). 'Social life among the insects. II. Wasps Solitary and Social.' *Scient. mon.* **15**, 67-88.

WHEELER, W. M. (1922). 'Social life among the insects. II. Part 2. Wasps solitary and social.' *Scient. mon.* **15**, 119-31.

WILD, O. H. (1927). 'Wasps destroying young birds.' *Br. Birds.* **20**, 254.

WILLIAMS, F. X. (1919). 'Philippine wasp studies. Part II. Descriptions of new species and life history studies.' *Bull. Exp. Stn. Hawaii Sugar Planter's Ass.* **14**, 19-186.

WILLIAMS, F. X. (1928). 'Studies in tropical wasps, their hosts and associates.' *Bull. Exp. Stn. Hawaii Sugar Planter's Ass.* **19**, 1-174.

WILSON, E. O. (1966). 'Behaviour of social insects.' *R. ent. Soc. Lond. Symp. No.* 3., 81-96.

WILSON, E. O. (1971). *The Insect Societies.* Harvard University Press, Cambridge, Mass.

WINCKWORTH ALLEN, C. (1938). '*Vespa norwegica* Fab. in a suburban garden.' *Ir. Nat. J.* **7**, 10.

WYNNE-EDWARDS, V. C. (1962). *Animal Dispersion in relation to Social Behaviour.* Oliver and Boyd, London.

YAMANE, S. (1969). 'Preliminary observations on the life history of two polistine wasps, *Polistes snelleni* and *P. biglumis* in Sapporo, northern Japan.' *J. Fac. sci. Hokkaido Univ. Ser. IV Zool.* **17**, 78-105.

YAMANE, S. (1971). 'Daily activities of the founding queens of two *Polistes* species, *P. snelleni* and *P. biglumis* in the solitary stage (Hymenoptera, Vespidae).' *Kontyû.* **39**, 203-17.

YAMANE, S. and KUBO, T. (1970). 'A brief note on a labour-parasitic wasp, *Vespula austriaca*, in association with *V. rufa schrencki*.' *Kontyû.* **38**, 171-5.

YARROW, I. H. H. (1945). In *The Hymenopterist's Handbook*. The University, Leeds (reprinted 1969).

YARROW, I. H. H. (1955). 'Some ways of distinguishing between the two common wasps *Vespula germanica* (Fabricius) and *Vespula vulgaris* (Linnaeus).' *Entomologist.* **88**, 5-9.

YOSHIKAWA, K. (1955). 'Ecological studies of *Polistes* wasps, 2. A polistine colony usurped by a foreign queen.' *Insectes soc.* **2**, 255-60.

YOSHIKAWA, K. (1956). 'Ecological studies of Polistes wasps. 4. Compound nest experiments in *Polistes fadwigae* Dalla Torre.' *J. Inst. Polyt. Osaka City Univ.* **7**, 229-43.

YOSHIKAWA, K. (1959). 'Ecological studies of Polistes wasps. 5. Behaviour of *Polistes* wasps in late autumn - with special reference to their mating behaviour.' *Akitu.* **8**, 50-6.

YOSHIKAWA, K. (1962). 'Introductory studies in the life economy of polistine wasps. I. Scope of problems and consideration on the solitary stage.' *Bull. Osaka Mus. nat. Hist.* **15**, 3-27.

YOSHIKAWA, K. (1964). 'Predatory hunting wasps as the natural enemies of insect pests in Thailand.' *Nat. Life. S.E. Asia, Tokyo.* **3**, 391-8.

YOSHIKAWA, K., OHGUSHI, R. and SAKAGAMI, S. F. (1969). 'Preliminary report on entomology of the Osaka City University 5th Scientific expedition to Southeast Asia 1966.' *Nat. Life S.E. Asia, Tokyo.* **6**, 153-82.

ZABRISKIE, J. L. (1894). 'Notes on some parasites of *Vespa*.' *Jl. N.Y. ent. Soc.* **2**, 81-95.

INDEX

AUTHOR INDEX

SUBJECT INDEX

The subject index is divided into two parts, the first lists all latin names of organisms, the second gives the remaining entries. Entries in heavy type denote definition or a detailed description. The common species (i.e. *Paravespula germanica* and *P. vulgaris*) are not repeated where they appear continuously in the text.

Part 1: Latin names

Part 2: Subject Index

Gregarines, 250
Grooming, 20, 26, 43
Growth curve, 187
Guard wasps, 155, 273
Guide cells, 105
Gynaecoid, 231

Haemolymph, 44, 67, 71, 157, 204
Hair-plate, 14
Hair-tuft, 14
Hamuli, 23, 296
Haploid, 218, **225**, 305
Haplometrosis, 185, 200, 313
Hawthorn, 126, 138, 140
Heather, 139
Helleborine, 139
Hemlock, 139
Hexadecalactone, 209
Hexagonal cell, 104
Hexapod larva, 67
Hibernaculum, 80
Hibernation, **79**, 161, 193, 206, 216, **232**, 233
Hindgut, 94, 158, 203
Histamine, 278
Histolysis, 266
Holly, 140
Honey, 144, 272, 281, 283, 289, 300
Honeybee, 33, 115, 119, 137, 138, 141, 143, 144, 146, 147, 156, 209, 210, **212**, 229, 234, 241, 267, 275, 280, 290, 316
Honey-dew, 43, 138, 156, 203, 289, 343
Honey-guide, 145
Honey-stomach, 29, 141, 146
Horehound, 140
Hormones, 201, 231
Hornet (see also *Vespa* species), 8, 144, 156, 160, 212, 222, 272, 280, 347
Hornworms, 283
Horse chestnut, 126
House-martin, 121, 125
Hunger call (larval), 144, **211**
Humidity, 17, 132, 136, 193, 267
Humming bird, 144
Hydrocortisone, 280
Hypognathous, 14
Hypopharyngeal gland, **16**, 18, 34, 239
Hypopharynx, 16
Hypopus, 65

Ileum, 30
Incipient colony, 90, 150
Incubation period, 91, 162, 165
Infrabuccal sac, 16, 20
Insecticides, 231, **286**
Insemination, 69, 83, 233, 246
Intercalary cell, 52
Interganglionic connective, 37

Intermediate cell, 98
Intermediate female, 296
Intromittent organ (see also Aedeagus), 233
Invertase, 34
Ivy, 138, 139, 145

Japan, 43, 55, 69, 81, 97, 108, 150, 160, 212
Jewel wasp, 73
Johnston's organ, 18
Jurassic, 316
Juvenile hormone, 231, 265

K.A.A.D., 350
Kerosene, 287, 350
Kinin, 279

Labial gland, 34, 94, 95
Labial (larval or salivary) secretion, 94, 100, 107, 152, 157, **201**, 233, 308, 312
Labium, 16, 18, 94
Labrum, 18, 94
Lacinia, 16, 19
Lactone, 209
Lancets, 27, 294
Larva: worker ratio, 195, **222**, **226**, **239**, 241
Lead arsenate, 287, 289
Leaf hoppers, 282
Leaf sawflies, 5
Lesser Knapweed, 139
Liesegang Rings, 231
Light intensity, 110, 132, **136**, 172
Ligula, 18
Lilac, 100, 139, 289
Lime, 138, 139
Lipid, 80
Longevity, 153, 167, 189, 239
LSD (lysergic acid diethylamide), 272
Lunar cycle, 129

Mainstay pillar, 98
Malar space, 15
Malphigian tubules, 31, 94, 203
Maltose, 202
Mammals, 159, 193
Mandible, **15**, 16, 18, 101, 158, 248
Mandibular glands, **16**, **28**, 34
Marjoram, 139
Mass-provisioning, 311
Mating swarms/flights, 42, 245
Maxilla, **16**, 18, 94, 101
Meadowsweet, 43
Mercuric chloride, 289
Mesepimeron, 23
Mesepisternum, 23
Mesonotum, 23
Mesopectus, 23
Mesopleuron, 23
Mesoscutellum, 23